IET PROFESSIONAL APPLICATIONS OF COMPUTING SERIES 13

Trusted Platform Modules

Other volumes in this series:

Trusted Platform Modules

Why, when and how to use them

Ariel Segall

The Institution of Engineering and Technology

Published by The Institution of Engineering and Technology, London, United Kingdom

The Institution of Engineering and Technology is registered as a Charity in England & Wales (no. 211014) and Scotland (no. SC038698).

© The Institution of Engineering and Technology 2017

First published 2016

The Institution of Engineering and Technology
Michael Faraday House
Six Hills Way, Stevenage
Herts, SG1 2AY, United Kingdom

www.theiet.org

British Library Cataloguing in Publication Data
A catalogue record for this product is available from the British Library

ISBN 978-1-84919-893-6 (hardback)
ISBN 978-1-84919-894-3 (PDF)

Typeset in India by MPS Limited
Printed in the UK by CPI Group (UK) Ltd, Croydon

Contents

Acknowledgments

This book would not have happened without the help of a vast number of people, to whom I am eternally grateful: Xeno Kovah, who first asked me whether I'd considered teaching a class on TPMs; my many wonderful former colleagues at MITRE, particularly Amy Herzog, Joshua Guttman, John Ramsdell, Paul Rowe, Justin Sheehy, and Brian Sniffen; it's amazing what you can learn in ten years of being steeped in a subject while surrounded by smart people. Then there are also the great folks from the IAD, particularly Grant Wagner, George Coker, and Pete Loscocco, who never stopped asking really challenging questions; I'd never have figured half of this stuff out without you. There are all of my test readers, in particular the exceptionally patient Kevin Riggle and John Mainzer, who waded through multiple versions and sent extensive commentary. And above all, my amazingly patient spouse, Andrew Menard, who put up with a ridiculous amount of hassle and still never stopped telling me I could do this.

Glossary and acronym expansions

AIK Attestation Identity Key. Often simply called an identity key. A key that acts as a certifiable pseudonym for a TPM.

AMD A company that manufactures CPUs and other low-level hardware.

API Application program interface. A set of function definitions for building software applications.

Attestation The presentation of verifiable evidence about a system to another party (the verifier, sometimes called the appraiser). Usually, the verifier is off-system: we call this remote attestation. The attestation target is sometimes called the attester.

Authorization value Password, although usually with many fewer constraints about the contents than the sort of passwords users generally create. In a TPM context, sometimes used to imply a value that's been pre-hashed before transmission, versus a password transmitted in its entirety to the TPM.

BIOS Basic Input/Output system, though the expansion is almost never used. BIOS refers to the firmware which initially sets up a PC's hardware during boot. Although technically, BIOS and UEFI refer to entirely different firmware approaches that perform similar functions, because they serve the same purpose they are often lumped together under the BIOS umbrella. Most mentions of BIOS in this book actually refer to either BIOS or UEFI.

Blob A TPM-produced data structure whose contents the user is not expected to make individual use of; a black box.

Boot Loader Software that loads an operating system kernel as part of the boot process.

CA Certificate Authority. A trusted party participating in a public key infrastructure who certifies that certain keys can be trusted by anyone who trusts the authority.

Chain of Trust A trusted computing concept in which every component establishes trust in the next component before handing over control, usually rooted in a Root of Trust. Often comes up when discussing how measurements of a system state are created, although other chains of trust exist.

Clear An operation that removes most of the data from the TPM. Intended for use when a machine is sold or transferred to a new owner, so that old secrets are no longer accessible.

CMK Certifiable Migration Key. A 1.2 key that can be migrated between machines with the approval of a trusted authority, and can be certified for external verifiers.

CPU Central processing unit. The core of a modern computer.

CRTM Core Root of Trust for Measurement. Same as SRTM.

CSR Certificate signing request. A request presented to a CA to ask that a particular key be certified. Normally part of a PKI.

DAA Direct anonymous attestation. A complex form of attestation that can establish trust in a system without revealing anything about the system's identity.

DNSSec Domain Name System Security Extensions. A standard for adding security to DNS, the system that resolves hostnames on networks.

DRM Digital Rights Management. An umbrella term describing technologies for limiting unauthorized access to specific proprietary resources. Usually used in a corporate or copyright context.

DRTM Dynamic Root of Trust for Measurement. A special set of CPU functions designed to allow trust in a system's software to be established after an untrusted boot.

EA Enhanced Authorization. A new, very fine-grained, and very flexible approach to access control, introduced in 2.0 TPMs.

ECC Elliptic Curve Cryptography. An approach to public key cryptography based on finite field algebra.

EK Endorsement Key. The key on which all trust in a 1.2 TPM is based. In theory, created and certified by the TPM manufacturer.

EPS Endorsement Primary Seed. The primary seed associated with the endorsement hierarchy. The cryptographic material on which most remote trust in a 2.0 TPM is based.

FAPI Feature API. Part of the TCG's 2.0 TSS. Intended to provide a small subset of TPM functionality that would be most useful to the majority of users.

FIPS Federal Information Processing Standards. US government standards for computing, prominently including security.

GRUB A boot loader, popular on Linux.

Handle An identification value that uniquely identifies an object or resource in a given context. The context might be TPM-specific, program-specific, or software stack-specific.

Hierarchy In a TPM 2.0 context, hierarchies are sets of keys and other objects rooted in a shared primary seed, and managed with a shared set of authorization values and policies. Different hierarchies are intended for different uses, although there are no constraints on what objects can be created in what hierarchies.

HMAC Hashed Message Authentication Code. A hash combining data with a symmetric key; the authenticity can be verified by anyone else with the symmetric key.

IT Information Technology. IT departments are a common description for the people who handle computing resources in companies and other large organizations.

IP Among other meanings, Internet Protocol. IP addresses are the standard way in which machines connected to a network are identified.

KDF Key Derivation Function. Mathematical function for securely deriving a key from some initial input, called a seed.

MAC Mandatory Access Control. A system where access control is always present and enforced. Compare to Discretionary Access Control, where access control is something imposed in individual instances as desired.

MAC Media Access Control, although almost no one uses the expansion. MAC addresses are used to identify individual network interface hardware devices on a network.

NV storage Non-volatile storage. Storage areas whose contents are not erased on a reboot. Sometimes called NVRAM.

NVRAM Non-volatile Random-Access Memory. Sometimes called NV Storage.

OAEP Optimal Asymmetric Encryption Padding. A padding scheme often used with TSA, to create safe input to the encryption function.

OIAP Object-Independent Authorization Protocol. An authorization session protocol used to securely transmit authorization data to the TPM.

OS Operating System.

OSAP Object-Specific Authorization Protocol. An authorization session protocol used to securely transmit authorization data to the TPM.

Owner The person who is the local authority on how the TPM should be used (or not used). Usually, the literal owner of the machine, either an individual or IT department.

PC Although this stands for Personal Computer, in this context it actually refers to the x86 family of computer architectures, including both desktops and servers.

PCA Privacy Certificate Authority. A CA that participates in the TCG-designed AIK certification protocol.

PCRs Platform Configuration Registers. A set of registers in the TPM with highly controlled behaviour, used to contain system measurements or user data. The contents can be used to constrain access to TPM resources, or certified for external verification with a quote.

PKCS One of the Public Key Cryptography Standards. Defines a programming interface for using cryptographic hardware.

PKI Public Key Infrastructure. A distributed architecture for establishing trust in public keys. Usually involves at least one CA.

PPS Platform Primary Seed. The primary seed associated with the platform hierarchy.

Primary Seed A hidden value used to generate keys in 2.0 platforms. Each hierarchy has its own primary seed. Serves the same trust role as the root keys in 1.2 TPMs.

Root Key A key that acts as a root of trust on a given platform with a 1.2 TPM.

RoT Root of Trust. A component which is inherently trusted, and which is used to establish trust in other components.

RTM Root of Trust for Measurement. The system component that is trusted to take an initial measurement of a system, allowing a chain of trust to be started.

RTR Root of Trust for Reporting. The key that all external trust in a given TPM (and therefore system) is eventually rooted in. In 1.2 TPMs, the EK; in 2.0 TPMs, manufacturer-certified primary keys based on the Endorsement Primary Seed.

RTS Root of Trust for Storage. The key that is trusted to protect secrets in a system, directly or indirectly. In 1.2 TPMs, the SRK; in 2.0 TPMs, primary keys based on the Storage Primary Seed.

RSA A widely used public key cryptosystem based on the difficulty of factoring the products of two large prime numbers.

SAPI System Level API. Part of the TCG's 2.0 TSS.

SGX Software Guard Extensions. A set of new Intel CPU extensions providing additional security functionality.

SHA-1/SHA-256 Members of the widely used Secure Hash Algorithm family of hash functions. SHA-1 is being slowly phased out of use as of the end of 2015, owing to discovered weaknesses. SHA-256 is the recommended replacement.

SPS Storage Primary Seed. The primary seed associated with the storage hierarchy.

SRK Storage Root Key. A 1.2 TPM key which serves as the Root of Trust for Storage.

SRTM Static Root of Trust for Measurement. Same thing as CRTM.

State A computing term referring to a program's or system's status and available information at a given point in time.

SVM Secure Virtual Machine. A set of CPU technologies created and sold by AMD.

Tamper Resistance Tampering, in this context, refers to physical attacks against hardware; anything from a novice with a screwdriver to expert nation-state spies with acid, liquid nitrogen, and lasers. Tamper resistance generally refers to hardware capable of resisting some amount of tampering. This is distinct from tamper proofing, which implies an actual immunity to most forms of tampering. Tamper proofing is usually found in very expensive hardware sold to governments, and often contains explosives; you will rarely encounter it in consumer or corporate contexts.

TBS Trusted Base Services. A Microsoft interface for using 1.2 TPMs.

TCG Trusted Computing Group. An industry coalition that creates most trusted computing standards, including the TPM standards.

TCPA Trusted Computing Platform Association. An industry coalition that was a precursor to the Trusted Computing Group.

TCSI TSS Core Service Interface. A mid-level layer of the 1.2 Trusted Software Stack API.

TDDL TCG Device Driver Library. A low-level layer of the 1.2 Trusted Software Stack API.

TPM Trusted Platform Module.

Trusted In a TPM context, something whose behaviour is predictable. This allows individuals to make their own determination about which behaviour can be trusted in a colloquial sense.

TSPI TSS Service Provider Interface. The layer of the 1.2 Trusted Software Stack API intended for use primarily by applications.

TSS Trusted Software Stack or TPM Software Stack. A software layer to make using the TPM easier.

TXT Trusted Execution Technology. A set of CPU technologies created and sold by Intel.

UEFI Unified Extensible Firmware Interface. A modern, standardized replacement for a BIOS.

X.509 A widely used standard that defines formats for public key certificates, certificate signing requests, and revocation lists.

Chapter 1

Introduction

1.1 About this book

One of the major problems with trusted computing adoption has been a lack of good introductory information. People wondering what this technology is, why they should care about it, or how they should get started using it have generally not had very many resources to turn to. In this book, I will begin with the most basic questions of what the technology is; talk about when this technology is most useful (and, equally important, when it's not); and then start introducing the technical details of why and how to use the technology. If you're still at the stage of wondering if this technology is relevant to you, start with the first couple of chapters; there's enough complexity here that a classic engineer's 'jump in feet first' approach is inefficient. If you're familiar with the basics of trusted computing technology already, Chapters 4 and up will provide you with useful reference material, but you may also find new ideas for how trusted computing can be applied in your environment in Chapter 2.

This book is intended for a technical audience, but not one with any particular familiarity with trusted computing, hardware, or security concepts. If you need a refresher on or introduction to the basic cryptographic vocabulary used in this book, see Appendix A.

While this book does contain example code demonstrating how to use the functionality described, it is not intended to be a comprehensive reference for programming for the Trusted Platform Module (TPM). Instead, I provide background information and examples which should allow those with some coding experience to use freely available resources (primarily in the form of relevant specifications) to implement whatever TPM-based functionality they need. Similarly, my primary goal for this book is to teach system designers what the TPM can do and what they might want to use it for, and provide all the information you'll need to look up the details for your own projects. A comprehensive book containing everything anyone could ever possibly need would rapidly turn into an unusable tome, so I'm aiming instead to provide you with everything you'll need to work independently.

1.1.1 The enterprise approach

While there are some good use cases for trusted computing at an individual level, mostly involving protection of sensitive data, many of the most powerful trusted computing use cases need a large infrastructure to be most effective. All of the use cases for machine authentication and attestation, for example, require that there be a mechanism for one machine to recognize the keys belonging to another; a large public key infrastructure (PKI) makes this feasible and scalable, but few individuals and no existing trusted third parties want to bother with the overhead required. Additionally, large enterprises – be they companies, government agencies, or other organizations – are far more likely than most individuals to need to track machine identity and state over a network. Therefore, this book has been written with a focus on enterprise use cases and support infrastructure.

Of course, this isn't to say that the book can't be useful if you're not in an enterprise Information Technology (IT) department. Whether you're a student, a hobbyist, or a professional, this book should give you a solid grounding in what TPMs are capable of, what they're good for, and what they're not. Just keep in mind while you're reading that if you're not working in an enterprise context, you may have to think a little beyond the printed use cases to see how they apply to your own scenarios.

1.1.2   User stories

Throughout this book, I will present short user stories featuring fictional characters, intended to illustrate both a variety of use cases for this technology and the sorts of decisions that might lead to choosing one approach over another. These examples will be far from comprehensive; after all, part of the goal of this book is for you to gain an understanding of how this technology might apply in your own situation. Instead, they are meant to illustrate the concepts presented in each chapter in a practical setting, and hopefully encourage you to think how your own decisions might be similar or different from those made by Alice, Bob and their colleagues at Example, Incorporated.

1.2   What is trusted computing?

'Trusted computing' is an umbrella term, with almost as many definitions as there are people talking about it. The definition we'll use in this book is a more formalized version of the way the Trusted Computing Group (TCG) (see Section 1.2.3) uses the term:

Trusted computing refers to computing systems which use hardware to provide security support to software and to create systems with more predictable behaviour.

This covers a wide range of systems. Technologies which fall under the trusted computing umbrella include:

Trusted Platform Modules: The focus of this book, TPMs are chips, usually attached to a device's motherboard, which provide assorted cryptographic functions. I'll be providing much more detail later.

Self-encrypting Drives: Fast hardware-supported cryptographic data protection, built into a hard drive.

Secure CPU Modes: These include Intel's TXT and SGX, as well as AMD's SVM, and provide functionality such as software measurement, code signature checking, and secure execution, all in a remotely verifiable fashion.

Trusted Network Connect: A suite of networking protocols capable of integrating information from platform-level trusted computing into network access decision-making, but which can also be used without any secure hardware.

Multilevel Computing: In the government world, different classification levels of information must be kept carefully segregated, often on distinct machines or networks. Multilevel computing systems combine hardware and software to create a trustworthy whole capable of securely handling information at multiple, highly separated, classification levels simultaneously.

You may notice that I've included here both hardware components and the systems which use that hardware. That's because the various definitions of 'trusted computing' vary so widely. However, it's very common to see 'trusted computing' used as an alternative term for TPMs and systems which use them.

Why do I introduce a definition that's so very hard to pin down? I do it simply to familiarize you with a term you'll encounter often in this field, used by people who may not agree with each other. You may not always know exactly what it means, but at least you'll know to dig in a little further and find out what's actually behind it in a particular instance. And if a vendor tries to sell you something that uses 'trusted computing' without providing details, that can be a warning sign that they don't understand the technology well enough to build a useful product.[1]

1.2.1 What do we mean by 'trusted'?

To a layperson, 'trusted' usually means something close to 'good'. Trusted computing terminology employs the word slightly differently. According to the TCG (more on them shortly) and researchers in this area:

A trusted component is one which is predictable.

Why do we use predictable, rather than good, as our baseline? On the face of it, this seems nonsensical. A virus can be a trusted component according to this definition, if I know what its attack pattern is and what files it will corrupt. A well-known commercial OS may not be, despite a reputable manufacturer and good coding practices, if its behaviour is so complex that I can't determine what it may do in any given situation.

The reason we take this approach is twofold. First, anything that is predictable is much easier to evaluate. Either I can predict a component's behavior in response to certain stimuli, or I can't; and if I can, I can make useful judgments about its performance. Secondly, it's universal. 'Good' means something very different on a power station control panel (where the requirement of remaining in operation no

---

[1] For example, I've seen vendors try to claim that their product should have the 'trusted' label because it contained a TPM…which had never even been turned on, and was not being used in any way.

matter what is critical) from what it does in a high-security government workstation (where it may be better that the system becomes inoperable than to have it leak secrets) and again from what it means on a home computer. Predictability, on the other hand, doesn't change, whatever the situation.

Furthermore, this predictability-based definition of 'trust' is very powerful, because it lets us build a more colloquial version of 'trust' on top of it. If I can predict that this virus will behave badly, then I can take appropriate action, such as not executing it. Different system owners can use the same trusted system information and take the actions that reflect their own needs.

That said, the levels of predictability today's systems give us is primitive. For the computer science readers, no one in the field is claiming to have solved the halting problem. Instead, we're using reasonable approximations: if we can *identify* a component, then we can evaluate it in other contexts, and decide whether it's suitable for our purposes. Most trusted computing technologies are designed, in the end, either to allow a component to be identified, or to identify other related components, or both.

1.2.2   A brief history of trusted computing

For a long time, the only entities interested in trusted computing were governments, who invested in custom-built systems and software for their high-security needs. The Orange Book is a famous set of government guidelines from the mid-1980s for evaluating trusted computer systems; it and others from the Rainbow Book series on trusted systems, published by the US Department of Defense, are now available online for the curious.

In the early 2000s, the Trusted Computing Platform Alliance (TCPA) was formed, as a joint effort by several major consumer technology companies. The TCPA's goals were diverse and sometimes contradictory, including both increasing consumer trust in home computing systems for purposes such as banking and financial applications and increasing copyright-holders' trust in consumer systems for digital rights management (DRM), as well as generally improving computer security for home and enterprise systems. It drew up the first designs for what would eventually become TPMs. The TCPA was replaced by the TCG in 2003.

1.2.3   The Trusted Computing Group

The TCG, an industry consortium featuring contributors from around the world, seeks to provide standards for trusted computing technologies and to increase the use of trusted computing. The technologies covered by the TCG are quite diverse, ranging from self-encrypting drives and networking protocols to trusted cloud architectures and speciality embedded systems. By producing common standards with contributions from manufacturers and consumers of these technologies, the TCG seeks to make adoption easy at all levels, and thus improve the security of commercial computing infrastructure. By making the standards open and vendor-neutral, the TCG hopes to both lower the barrier to entry and reduce some of the fears of vendor lock-in and anticonsumer conspiracies that dogged the early TCPA efforts.

Companies that wish to contribute to trusted computing standards or get early access to the works in progress can join the TCG. Although full membership (and a vote) costs money, they also accept some non-voting (and non-paying) contributors, who participate in standards development.

The TCG's website, with all of their publications (including released standards, draft standards out for public review and comment, and a variety of supplementary materials) as well as contact information for those who wish to get involved, is http://www.trustedcomputinggroup.org.

1.3 TPMs at a high level

Trusted Platform Modules, or *TPMs*, are small, inexpensive chips which provide a limited set of security functions. They are most commonly found as a motherboard component on laptops and desktops aimed at the corporate or government markets, but can also be found on many consumer-grade machines and servers, or can be purchased as independent components. Their role is to serve as a ***Root of Trust***—a highly trusted component from which we can bootstrap trust in other parts of our system. TPMs can be used to bootstrap trust: in secrets, particularly cryptographic keys; in a platform's identity; and, when combined with related technologies, called ***Roots of Trust for Measurement***, in a system's software state.

TPMs provide the following features, which we'll be discussing in more detail throughout this book:

- A ***Root of Trust for Reporting***
- A ***Root of Trust for Storage***
- Limited internal storage
  - ***Platform Configuration Registers (PCRs)***
  - Key storage
  - Data storage
- Random number generation (RNG)
- Highly constrained cryptographic functions

Figure 1.1 shows a high-level diagram of the TPM subcomponents which support these features, although individual implementations vary.

1.3.1 Roots of Trust

You may notice that we've now encountered the phrase 'Roots of Trust' quite a few times. So, what are they?

Roots of trust are just that: *roots*, the pieces at the very bottom of the system. These are the components on which all other trust is based, and which themselves are trusted inherently (Figure 1.1). An important aspect of a root of trust is that it is fundamentally unverifiable; after all, if I have a proposed root of trust, and another

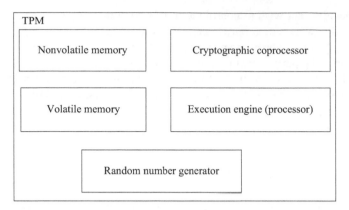

Figure 1.1   A high-level illustration of a TPM's component parts

component which I'm using to verify it, then that second component is really the root of trust, and the originally proposed root is above[2] it in the trust hierarchy.

Now, this inherent trust can (and should!) be based on out-of-band assumptions. I may not be able to verify that this chip is actually correct, but I can (hopefully) verify that it came from a reliable vendor, which I can reasonably assume means that it was built according to a standard which I can evaluate. But it's important to remember that that chain of logic is built on a set of assumptions: that the chip really came from the vendor I think it came from, that the vendor really did implement the standard, that there aren't any bugs in the implementation or weaknesses in the standard, and so forth; and to remember that if this chip we are identifying as a root of trust has a problem, we're going to have problems trusting anything built on top of it. This is one reason that enterprises with very strict security needs should pay careful attention to their supply chain when purchasing root of trust components; if your roots are good, you'll have a good chance of noticing problems above them, but if your root is compromised, the rest of the system can't be trusted.

Another important point is that trust is not generic! I trust my electrician to repair the wires in my house, but not to access my bank account; I trust my bank to keep my money secure, but not to keep my house from burning down. Similarly, I trust my TPM to keep my keys secure, but not to keep my antivirus up to date. Therefore, whenever we talk about a root of trust, we need to specify what *kind* of trust we're talking about.

In PCs, we commonly run into the following roots of trust:

- *Root of Trust for Storage (RTS)*: A component that protects secrets. Responsible for maintaining both secrecy and integrity of those secrets. Some trusted systems break this down into separate roots for confidentiality and integrity.
- *Root of Trust for Reporting (RTR)*: A component that provides accurate reporting on data stored inside it. In the PC context, this more specifically applies to accurate reporting of stored system state data. Note that the RTR is *not* responsible

---

[2]Because of the root metaphor, trust hierarchies are sometimes presented in the opposite orientation to other hierarchies, where 'below' is usually indicative of less power.

for creating the data, just for honestly informing the rest of the world about the data's content.

- **Root of Trust for Measurement (RTM)**: A component that measures other software and stores those measurements in a secure location. In the PC context, the RTM is normally part of the boot process – see Section 9.1.1 for details – which stores measurements in the TPM.

Other trusted computing systems, which I won't be discussing in this book, but which you may encounter if you're working with phones, cars, or in other non-PC scenarios, may contain different roots of trust, such as:

- **Root of Trust for Verification**: A component that verifies an integrity measurement against a policy. Normally found in systems such as some embedded or mobile devices, where the device manufacturer also defines some approved software.
- **Root of Trust for Update**: A component that verifies the legitimacy of an update, usually by checking an authorized signature. Most commonly used for firmware updates.

1.3.2   Chains of trust

Merely trusting our lowest-level components isn't sufficient for real-world use, where we often need to establish trust in a wide range of software, keys, and other data. **Chains of trust** allow us to bootstrap from the low-level root of trust to a higher-level trusted object, by using our trust in the root to establish trust in secondary objects, and then our trust in the secondary objects to establish trust in tertiary objects, and so forth.

The chains of trust that we'll be referring to most frequently in this book are **measurement chains of trust** (Figure 1.2) (sometimes called **boot chains of trust** because they're triggered most frequently during system boot), which let us bootstrap from the Root of Trust for Measurement (RTM) to measurements of higher-level software; and **storage chains of trust** (Figure 1.3), which let us bootstrap from the Root of Trust for Storage (RTS) to trust in the security of other data and keys. We'll cover measurement chains of trust in much more detail in Chapter 9, and storage chains of trust in Chapter 6.

1.3.3   The TPM threat model

The primary threat TPMs are intended to protect against is software-based attacks aimed to steal information, such as keys, or to modify the system without the user's consent. TPMs also provide some protection against simple hardware attacks; being inexpensive consumer chips, they are not designed to defend against a sophisticated attacker, but the built-in tamper resistance provides some protection against casual thieves.

TPMs also provide some protection against well-meaning but inexpert users and developers. The TPM's cryptographic functions are dramatically more constrained than would be necessary if it functioned merely as a cryptographic coprocessor, running encryption and decryption operations on command. The TPM's sometimes very

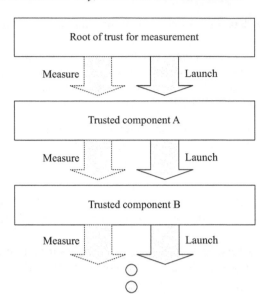

Figure 1.2   An abstract measurement chain of trust. Each component in the chain measures the next component before handing off control to it, placing those measurements into the TPM. We can trust the measurement of component A because we trust the root. If the measurement of component A corresponds to a piece of software we trust, we can then trust the measurement of component B, and so on until all trusted components have been measured and launched. The TPM provides us with a safe place to store these measurements

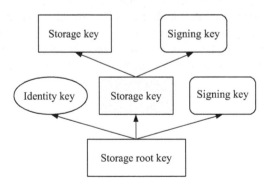

Figure 1.3   A 1.2 storage chain of trust. The Storage Root Key encrypts the secret data of several other keys, including another storage key. That storage key, in turn, can be used to encrypt the secret data of more keys. Our trust in the security of all of the keys relies, in the end, on our trust in the Storage Root Key

complex limitations on the use of keys or commands act as safeguards against potentially dangerous actions. For example, the limitations in 1.2 TPMs against the same key being used for both signing and decryption operations directly prevent an entire class of attacks which can result in unintentionally signed data, accidentally decrypted secrets, or the loss of key material. Without those constraints, it would be easy for an uninformed user or software bug to take actions with very severe unnoticed and unintended consequences. It is important to note, however, that many actions which would be limited in an ideal perfect-security world are essential for the smooth operation of real-world systems. TPMs therefore have plenty of compromises in their design; places where they will allow common (but dangerous) operations, or where they will inconveniently prevent such an operation even if that makes compatibility difficult. Some of the biggest differences in TPM versions (see Section 1.3.6) result from changing opinions about which compromises are necessary.

1.3.4   What TPMs are good for

Protecting Cryptographic Keys: The keys a TPM creates are either stored inside the TPM, in its internal protected storage, or encrypted with other protected keys for secure storage outside the TPM. These keys never exist unencrypted outside the TPM, and are thus protected from software-based theft of the key material.

Protected Cryptographic Functions: TPMs can perform both generic and specialized cryptographic functions internally, ensuring that key material is safe even during use.

Protected State Registers: TPMs can be used to track system state and other data recorded by software, in registers that are easy to add data to but very difficult to forge. In combination with TPM-aware software, these can be used to create verifiable records of software on the system.

Trustworthy Reporting: The TPM has several functions that allow a remote party to verify parts of the TPM's internal state, including keys and register contents. Used in combination with external state reporting tools, this can be used for remote attestation of the system's state.

Cheap Tamper Resistance: TPMs aren't designed for protecting high-security data against expert attackers, but they do provide hardware-level protection more than adequate for defence against casual thieves, for a very low cost.

Through the course of this book, we'll talk about how these simple advantages can be turned into powerful real-world functionality. TPMs can be used to identify machines, protect data from theft, and allow verification of a machine's software. They are very powerful building blocks for inexpensive system security today.

1.3.5   What TPMs aren't good for

Fast, frequent cryptography: Commercial TPMs are built to be inexpensive, not fast. Don't try using them for operations requiring high speed and volume, such as packet encryption.

System monitoring: While TPMs can be used to support system-monitoring software and provide reliable cryptography for reporting on the results of such
monitoring, a TPM does not perform any monitoring itself. All system measurements are provided by external components. (See Section 9.1.1.) The external
components available today are primarily useful for boot-time state verification,
rather than runtime system monitoring.

Bulk Encryption: This is particularly true for 1.2 TPMs (see Section 1.3.6), which,
in addition to being small and inexpensive chips, do not support the symmetric
encryption algorithms that are best for large-scale encryption.

System control: TPMs have no ability to control the system they're installed in;
they cannot prevent bad software from booting, shut down a system if malware
is detected, or otherwise change the state of software. They are entirely passive
devices.

1.3.6   TPM versions

There are three versions of PC TPMs that you may see references to. The version
numbers here refer to the version of the TPM specification implemented.

- 1.1 TPMs were the first on to the market. Rare even at the time, these were
  replaced by the new version in the mid-2000s; you're unlikely ever to encounter
  one unless you're using some rather unusual and now-obsolete hardware. We
  won't be covering them in this book, although many of the same principles apply.
- 1.2 TPMs are very common; as of the end of 2015, almost all commercially
  available TPMs are 1.2 TPMs. They use RSA for encryption and signatures, and
  SHA1 for hashes. Their functionality is highly constrained, to make safe usage
  of keys, data, and cryptography more likely, and because the older technology
  could not support a multitude of features at the desired cost point. Software for
  using 1.2 TPMs exists on Windows and Linux platforms. (Apple devices do not
  have TPMs as of the end of 2015.)
- 2.0 TPMs arrived on the market in late 2014, although as of the end of 2015
  they were still being sold primarily to platform manufacturers rather than consumers. 2.0 TPMs support both the older RSA and SHA1 algorithms and the
  newer elliptic curve cryptography (ECC) and SHA256 hashing; in addition, they
  now support symmetric cryptography, which was previously not included owing
  to cryptographic export regulations. 2.0 TPMs are more compliant with external
  standards such as X.509, are highly configurable, and support extremely powerful
  and flexible authentication mechanisms, but a higher level of skill is required to
  use them safely. As of the end of 2015, there is only a small amount of software
  support for 2.0 TPMs, although Application Program Interfaces (APIs) have been
  released.
- Some TPMs are 1.2/2.0 TPMs, and can be used in either a 1.2 or a 2.0 mode,
  although they may have reduced 1.2 command sets. These chips are designed
  to be compatible with today's 1.2-focused infrastructures, while providing future
  proofing against a day when the 1.2 algorithms are no longer considered secure,
  or when enough 2.0-compatible TPMs have entered the market for enterprises to

switch to the new technology. Although there are no standard interfaces allowing such chips to switch modes, at least some of the chips currently on the market require a firmware update to be performed to make the transition. Consult your manufacturer for details if you have a hybrid chip.

There are also specifications being written for TPMs outside of PCs, for scenarios including mobile devices, embedded devices, even motor vehicles. These variations are not covered in this book; however, because the core TPM functionality remains the same while the details (such as command structure, supported algorithms, and number of registers) vary, it should not be difficult to apply the techniques discussed in this book to these alternative architectures.

1.3.7   Common TPM myths

There are a number of myths and misconceptions about TPMs that you may encounter. Most of them are misunderstandings from oversimplified summaries of a very complicated technology; some of them are the result of somewhat deceptive early marketing. All of them have a core of truth behind them.

1.3.7.1   Myth: the TPM makes everything more secure

Every so often, you may encounter products which advertise that they include a TPM, and therefore claim that their system is more secure. The TPM is treated as magic pixie dust, which, when added to a system, improves security.

While I'd love this to be true, it's not. For one thing, using the TPM isn't trivial; hence the existence of this book. Secondly, the TPM is useful for solving only certain specific problems. For example, a TPM won't help at all if your primary goal is preventing viruses and keyloggers from being installed on a consumer system. Whenever you see a system that calls out a TPM as a security feature, it's worth asking how they're using it, if it's provided as a resource that the system purchaser can use, or if the mere existence of the TPM is being treated as sufficient. By the time you're even a few chapters into this book, you should have a clearer idea of the sorts of problems TPMs are actually good at solving, which will help you ask meaningful questions of vendors.

1.3.7.2   Myth: the TPM controls system boot

There's a common idea that TPMs can keep a system from booting if the right software isn't running. This comes in several variants, including one which claims that the reason TPMs are put in PCs is to ensure that only manufacturer-approved software runs, and another which claims that if a system has a TPM, it will keep bootkits, rootkits, or other malware from running. There are three primary reasons that neither of these applies, for better or worse.

First and foremost, the TPM has no definition of 'right'; it has no way to tell what software measurements mean, or what their expected values should be. There's nowhere in a TPM that such reference values are stored, and none of the internal logic looks for them. Nor does the TPM have a way to set a signing authority who could approve software. Is it possible that a TPM-like system could be built with such reference values? Yes, and some speciality systems may include them, particularly if the device manufacturers have an investment in the initial boot software. However, it's not a feature of commercial PC TPMs, and the combination of the wide variety of PC software and the ownership model of PCs makes it highly unlikely that it will appear in the future.

Secondly, the TPM has no control over system boot at all. The TPM interacts with the rest of the system purely by responding to requests; the only direct knowledge it has about the state of the system is that it's signalled during certain power events, so it can reset its volatile state on reboot or save state when the system goes to sleep. All other information in the TPM is the result of API calls by software. Even if it knew about the boot events, the TPM has no control at all over the system and couldn't possibly stop boot.

Thirdly, the TPM itself can't inspect the system software. All information about system state in the TPM is put there by the RTM.

There are two truths behind this myth. The first is that the RTM, and more usefully, software higher in the measurement chain of trust, is in a position to inspect system software. Because it's part of the boot control flow, such software does often have the ability to stop the boot process. If the software is designed to do so, it can evaluate the measurements it's making relative to some definition of correctness. For example, TrustedGRUB is a TPM-aware boot loader that can check the hashes of a set of user-provided files and stop boot if any of the hashes don't match those included in the TrustedGRUB configuration file. The second is that the TPM does store the system measurements given to it by the RTM, and can use those measurements to limit access to keys, internal storage, and other resources. Those constraints are set up on a resource-by-resource basis (see Chapter 6), so do not constrain the system as a whole, but if the system is set up to use those resources – for example, if a disk encryption solution is set up to use a TPM key with measurement constraints on it – the net effect can look a whole lot like the TPM constraining boot. It's important to keep in mind, however, that this kind of TPM-supported boot constraint can easily be bypassed by anyone who can change the initial boot software; it can be useful for protecting sensitive data, but not for keeping a unsecured kiosk running its intended image.

1.3.7.3   Myth: the TPM is tamper-proof

While the TPM is tamper-resistant, it is far from tamper-proof. Real tamper-proof systems, resistant to government-level attackers and experienced electronics hackers, cost thousands of dollars. At a cost of less than a dollar for a 1.2 TPM, and what looks like $2 or less for a 2.0 TPM, the level of protection TPMs can provide is vastly lower. A determined, targetted attacker who gets their hands on the physical system and who has electronics expertise is very likely to be able to take the secrets out of a TPM. However, TPMs do dramatically increase the amount of skill required to retrieve data from a machine, and the currently public attack methods all require the destruction of the chip. For most enterprise purposes, where the threats tend to be casual theft of a machine, the accidental sale of a deprecated machine still containing sensitive data, or 'evil maid' espionage attacks which attempt to steal data without the machine being missed, the TPM can still be a powerful tool.

If your enterprise requires true tamper-proofing, the principles described in this book can still be useful, but you're going to want to look into the highly specialized tamper-proof cryptographic coprocessor market for your physical devices. Some high-security cryptographic coprocessors can be used in a manner similar to the way TPMs are; others can execute code that gives them a TPM's full functionality and features. (On the bright side, these much more expensive devices also tend to have much more processing power than a normal TPM!)

1.3.7.4   Myth: the TPM works for [insert corporation here]

Because so many of the original sponsors of what became the Trusted Computing Group were companies known for defending their intellectual property from consumers – sometimes the same consumers who had purchased said software or content, but who wished to use it in ways the originators did not approve of – there is a strong suspicion in many parts of the Internet that all trusted computing technologies exist to give control of a computer to a corporation, rather than to the person who purchased it. If you'd like to know the full details, just look for Richard Stallman's essay on Treacherous Computing. In this view of the world, TPMs exist to keep your computer from running anything other than the manufacturer-approved operating system (OS), prevent you from running any media software that won't enforce strict DRM constraints, or even prevent you from installing any unapproved software whatsoever.

There's just enough of a grain of truth in this myth to make life uncomfortable. The mobile device market, for example, which sometimes claims that devices belong to carriers rather than consumers, is considering using TPMs as part of a 'trusted boot' sequence designed to ensure that only manufacturer-approved software can run in a high-security partition, intended for financial and banking applications. However, TPMs are really secondary to these software-limited systems; as passive devices, they cannot enforce any constraints, and merely act as a secure storage location that provides a record of the approved boot sequence or a reliable check of the manufacturer's signing key. It is the boot software that truly locks down such a system; if the boot software is replaced, there's nothing the TPM will do to prevent the system from being used. The TPM *can* be used to ensure that data created when the machine was in its original state cannot be retrieved in a non-manufacturer-approved state, but if the user is willing to replace that data, there's nothing the TPM can do to stop it.

TPM 2.0 also introduces new features that are intended to be useful for DRM, such as time-based access to keys and encrypted data. However, the TPM has no ability to control what happens to decrypted data once it has left the TPM, and no ability to perform useful non-cryptographic actions on data inside the TPM, so this feature by itself is of limited utility for distributing sensitive content. That means that this feature is only useful in combination with trusted software, which brings us to the next set of problems associated with using TPMs for consumer DRM.

First and foremost is identifying what 'safe' playback software looks like, based on the measurements in the TPM. As I'll discuss extensively in Chapter 9, measuring software is hard, and the more variable and less controlled that software is, the harder the problem gets. It may be possible to use a TPM with the sort of measurement techniques we have today to identify approved playback software in a special-purpose media device; it certainly isn't possible in a random user-maintained Windows desktop. Secondly, there's the fact that TPMs are only tamper-resistant; if you're relying on them to prevent unauthorized copying of high-value content, but giving the hardware to untrusted parties – which in the DRM use case includes consumers – the fact that someone with reasonable skill and access to a decent electronics lab can get access to the keys inside if they don't mind destroying the hardware means that dedicated pirates won't have any trouble. And all it takes is one competent pirate, and your content will be available on the Internet.

Ironically, TPMs *can* be used effectively for many of these same functions inside an enterprise environment, but that's because of a few very critical differences between enterprise and consumer scenarios:

- The enterprise is assumed to be the owner of the machine, and significant access to the hardware is usually assumed to be limited to trusted parties, except in the event of theft.
- An enterprise can maintain a limited list of trusted machines, and remove stolen machines from that list.
- An enterprise may be able to constrain the software used on its machines in ways that consumer machines can't (and shouldn't) be constrained.

The first and second differences mean that we aren't trying to defend against a hostile party with physical access at the same time that we're trying to distribute content or use the machine for its approved purposes. The third means that the state of the machine can be made more predictable, either because enterprise workers are more willing to use constrained systems or because an enterprise can deploy state-based attestation on high-value servers and other machines which should already have limited configuration variations.

In short, a TPM has some utility for DRM in special-purpose consumer devices with highly predictable software, such as gaming consoles or network-aware appliances, or in enterprise systems where software is limited and users are expected to cooperate. However, even at their best, TPMs only raise the bar against local tampering and provide a helpful local tool in protecting against malicious activity such as modified software updates; they can't maintain complete control of high-value content in the face of motivated and unhappy users.

1.4   Where to find TPMs

TPMs come included in many laptops and desktops intended for enterprise use, although they can no longer be found in most lower-end consumer-grade electronics, and are no longer included in Apple devices. They are often offered as options on servers. Ask your vendor, if you're not sure whether a TPM is included in a particular device.

It's also important to ask about both the TPM version, now that there are multiple versions on the market, and the TPM vendor. There are a steadily increasing number of TPM vendors signing up with the Trusted Computing Group, and it's not yet clear what the quality of the various new vendors may be. The four vendors who have been providing TPMs extensively for the last several years are Atmel, Infineon, Broadcom, and STMicroelectronics. Several Infineon and STMicroelectronics TPMs have gone through Common Criteria certification using a TCG-created protection profile. By the time, this book comes out, additional certified products may be available; a full list is always available at https://www.trustedcomputinggroup.org/certification/certificationtpm_certified_products_list (this web page is kept updated), and the protection profile is available at https://www.trustedcomputinggroup.org/certification/certificationtpm_certification. Of course, not everyone needs fully certified TPMs; the certification program is designed for companies willing to pay extra to demonstrate that their chips meet a high standard, but companies catering to the mass market often provide cheaper chips that meet the basic functionality requirements, without investing in an expensive certification program.

1.5 TPM software options

At the time of writing, there are very few off-the-shelf applications that use TPMs, though the number is steadily increasing. The majority of existing applications are written by hobbyists, are intended for individual rather than enterprise use, and predominantly implemented for Linux; for example, there are Mozilla add-ons that use the TPM to protect the certificate store, but have no integration with corporate certificate handling or IT infrastructure. The best-known enterprise application which uses TPMs is Bitlocker, Microsoft's built-in disk encryption software.

Because there are so few commercial applications, many enterprises or curious individuals seeking to take advantage of TPM functionality will be creating their own software, and there is plenty of room on the market for ambitious software developers. Software APIs for both 1.2 and 2.0 TPMs exist. The most prominent of these are the TCG-defined *Trusted Software Stacks (TSS)*[3] which provide standardized higher-level APIs for using TPMs and support functionality for smooth management of TPM communications. Microsoft has also released the *Trusted Base Services (TBS)* interface for Windows, which provides a very low-level interface that provides software access to 1.2 TPMs. Microsoft Research has released *TSS.Net* and *TSS.C++* for 2.0 TPMs, which provides a higher-level set of functionality that still adheres closely to the TPM functionality. *IBM's TSS 2.0* offers similar C functionality for Linux and Windows systems, providing access to the full TPM 2.0 command set while keeping the programmer from needing to worry about the details of communicating with the TPM hardware. We discuss these interfaces and where to find them in more detail in

---

[3]Sometimes expanded instead to TCG Software Stack or TPM Software Stack. The TCG versions are entirely distinct from Microsoft's TPM Software Stack for TPM 2.0 and IBM's TSS 2.0.

Chapter 11. Code examples throughout this book are implemented using either the TCG TSS 1.2 or the IBM TSS 2.0; Chapter 4 provides a detailed introduction to these two APIs.

Given the existence of (somewhat) standardized, high-level software APIs, why does this book focus on lower level hardware interfaces? There are a few reasons.

First and foremost, the capabilities of the hardware are what shapes all of the software interfaces, and understanding what the trusted hardware does (and doesn't do) is critical for designing secure systems. Most good software interfaces will parallel the hardware commands in core functionality, if not in the API.

Secondly, there are too many different software interfaces to cover them all in detail: a firmware author or someone writing minimalist code to execute in a processor's secure mode may be interacting directly with the TPM hardware or driver, while an application author may be using a TSS or the Windows TBS interface, and even the TSS may vary dramatically – the TCG 2.0 TSS, as discussed in Section 11.2, actually has two completely distinct APIs released and a third planned, one that provides a simple interface to a small subset of TPM behaviours expected to be commonly used, another which provides access to a much wider range of the TPM's functionality at the cost of more complexity, and a yet-to-be-released version that holds the middle ground. The currently available 2.0 programming interfaces follow none of the TCG specifications.

Thus, this book will cover the TPM itself in detail, since the TPM's features define what is possible, while providing enough information about software imple-mentations to allow an interested application developer to use the resources described in Chapter 11 to implement functionality that will achieve your security goals. I will not provide code examples for all commands, but will show how to use some of the most critical features at the end of each associated chapter. Background information on the libraries used in the code examples and explanations of some of the com-mon functions used can be found in Chapter 4. For those looking for more in-depth discussions of programming techniques, see the references in Chapter 11.

Chapter 2

When to use a TPM

TPMs are most useful for three kinds of tasks: remotely identifying a machine, or *machine authentication*; providing hardware protection of secrets, or *data protection*; and providing verifiable evidence about a machine's state, or *attestation*. Each of these categories covers a wide range of real-world applications, and some applications take advantage of multiple categories.

In all cases, it's important to consider whether a TPM is the best tool for the job. TPMs are ubiquitous among enterprise computers, and have zero or minimal additional purchase costs, in contrast to smart cards or high-end cryptographic coprocessors. They have a number of specialized functions which can be very powerful in enterprise environments, and which are hard to find elsewhere. However, TPMs are also slow and not suitable for rapid, bulk operation. Using them, at least today usually requires investing in specialized software, often written in-house; in some cases, they even require custom changes to an enterprise's PKI. If you have a single use case which could use the TPM and a more widely deployed technology equally well, you may consider the overhead costs of setting up and integrating TPMs a negative deciding factor. However, if your enterprise is well placed to take advantage of several TPM features in diverse applications, the net benefits from TPM integration may well justify the initial overhead costs; if TPM deployment is done well once, the cost of each additional use case will be quite small.

2.1 Machine authentication examples

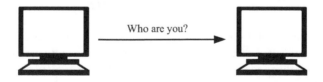

Any scenario where knowing the identity of the machine being communicated with would be useful is a potential machine authentication use case. While there are many technologies that offer a form of machine authentication, many of them – such as the commonly used IP or MAC addresses – are trivially spoofable. TPMs permit cryptographic verification of a machine's identity, and allow that identity to be associated with data travelling to or coming from the machine.

For example, TPMs can be used to:

- Ensure that only enterprise-owned machines can connect through the corporate VPN.
- Provide cryptographic proof that a given sensor uploaded data to a central repository.
- Verify that the daily patch status report from each enterprise machine was actually sent by the machine in question.
- Limit access to a database full of sensitive information to approved desktop machines in a protected location.
- Target downloads of a software update containing sensitive and proprietary information to the destination device.
  - It is important to note that targeting downloads of consumer multimedia to a specific device, and other consumer DRM use cases, are not well supported by the TPM. See Section 2.4.1 for details.
- Distribute a new shared key to a targeted group of machines.

There's a critically important caveat to machine authentication using the TPM. The TPM has no insight into activity on the machine outside of the TPM chip. There's no way for it to distinguish between information created on the machine and information sent from elsewhere. Similarly, the TPM can't distinguish between a request coming from legitimate software on the machine and a request coming from off the machine and forwarded to the TPM by malware. This means that TPM-based machine authentication isn't a guarantee that no other machines are involved in creating or sending content; it does, however, mean that any malicious activity has to involve the machine in question. This raises the amount of skill and effort required by a malicious actor who wishes to masquerade as the machine, and also gives a forensic analysis a solid starting point to work from.

2.2   Data protection examples

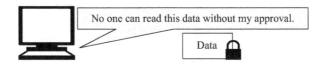

A TPM is most useful for data protection when the extra layer of hardware protection it provides. Data theft scenarios, where malicious software steals sensitive data, are particularly good targets for a TPM, since TPM-encrypted data is useless off the machine, although it is important to note that all such data is vulnerable while it's decrypted and in use on the machine.

TPMs should also provide some additional tamper resistance beyond that found in most consumer computing hardware, but since there are no precise standards for how much tamper resistance each TPM must have, it is best for enterprises which care deeply about the details to contact the manufacturer.

The TPM can also be used for data protection in the integrity sense, as well as the secrecy sense. An enterprise root CA's public key, for example, is public information, but can cause serious damage if a malicious actor manages to substitute their own version. The TPM offers some features which allow information to be stored by trusted parties but read by everyone, or otherwise defend against data substitution attacks.

Some examples of data protection using the TPM:

- Encrypt hard drive with keys protected by tamper-resistant hardware, and with no risk of a copied hard drive being decryptable with a dictionary attack on a password.
- Store the correct hash to verify the enterprise DNSSec (Domain Name System Security Extensions) root server.
- Encrypt password or certificate stores.
- Encrypt a log-in picture so that it can only be decrypted if the machine booted in a known state.
- Create a secure audit log file that is verifiably encrypted on this machine and not decryptable off of the machine.

2.3   Attestation examples

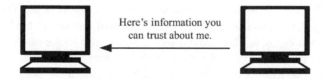

Attestation is the presentation of verifiable evidence about the state of a machine. We'll most often be talking about *remote attestation*, which involves the presentation of said evidence over a network. Local attestation is a much harder problem, since we use cryptographic signatures to prove the identity of a machine, and human beings aren't very good at doing public key cryptography in our heads. Attestation relies heavily both on the TPM's data protection capabilities and on having software designed to provide useful information to the TPM.

When considering attestation examples, it is important to note that many of the best attestation use cases are very hard to implement in practice. We'll discuss those problems in more depth in Chapter 9 but some commonly encountered use cases include:

- Send sensitive data to a remote server, knowing it can only be used if the server is in an acceptable state.
- Verify that a machine's software is up to date before allowing it on the internal network, and otherwise shunt it on to a subnetwork, allowing access only to a patch server.
- Ensure that sensitive files can be decrypted only if the machine is running the expected software.
- Centrally collect a trustworthy remote report about the most recent boot states of enterprise machines daily.

- Combine an antivirus report with evidence that the correct antivirus software is running with up-to-date definitions.
- Require authorized users to log in from enterprise machines running the current approved software configuration in order to access their networked files.
- Use a phone app to verify that a public kiosk is running a known, unmodified image before using it to log into e-mail or banking sites.

2.4   When not to use a TPM

A common misconception in organizations which have heard third-hand commentary about TPMs is that having a TPM in your computer will make it magically more secure. Not only is that not the case, but TPMs are not suited for every use case, and not every TPM is equally suited for every user.

2.4.1   When not to use: consumer DRM

One of the first use cases proposed for trusted computing, back when the Trusted Computing Platform Alliance was active and hadn't yet become the Trusted Computing Group (TCG), was DRM. In this vision, trusted computing could be used to ensure that downloads of digital media could be locked to a single machine, or even a limited number of views. High-value data, such as valuable media properties or consumer banking information, could be protected by the trusted hardware and accessed only when approved software, such as a content-owner-approved media player or the bank's official application, was running. Trusted computing might even be used to prevent piracy of OSes. However, the trusted computing we've ended up with is radically different from what this early vision foresaw.

Some of the difference is due to consumer groups' activism; after all, 'trusted computing' that met the above definition might be trusted by Hollywood and the RIAA,[1] but it would hardly be trusted by consumers. That vision could all too easily lead to a world where computers work only on the whim of the software manufacturers, and data could be held hostage. Modern technologies are still trying to walk the fine line between preventing malicious substitution of trusted software, such as bootkits that replace a trusted BIOS with a corrupted one or specialized malware which can place an entire OS within a hostile virtual machine, while allowing users to install home-brewed versions of Linux with their own custom kernel modules; the controversy over the secure boot functionality in UEFI (the technology replacing BIOSes for early boot) is a prime example of the continuing controversy. However, because of the backlash, the modern TPM has been designed to limit the power device manufacturers and software companies have over a machine's physical owner.

---

[1] Recording Industry Association of America, the primary music industry trade group that handles copyright infringement of musical works in the United States.

The unanticipated practical difficulties of identifying a consumer machine far outweigh the deliberate pro-consumer features introduced into the TPM in preventing consumer DRM.

2.4.2   When not to use: primary defence against physical threats

While TPMs are designed to provide basic physical protections against simple tampering, the TPM's security model is fundamentally focussed on software threats. Many people who work on physical threat use cases – anything from sensor networks to military equipment to servers operating in potentially hostile data centres – are very excited by TPMs, since they promise tamper resistance cheap. There are several fundamental problems with this. First, TPM tamper resistance is inexpensive, and although some brands have been established by researchers to have a rather astonishing cost-benefit ratio in terms of tamper difficulty, that doesn't necessarily hold true for all chips – the TCG requires only that there be tamper resistance, not that it meet any particular standard. Secondly, even if the TPM were perfectly tamper-proof, the connections between the TPM and other components on the motherboard aren't tamper-protected at all in most systems. Thus, an attacker with skill and convenient physical access to the system can potentially change the measurements transmitted to the TPM, the TPM's sense of the system state, and even the relationship between the system power cycle and the TPM's.

While a TPM can be a useful component of a comprehensive physical protection solution, providing remote reporting capabilities to other on-system components which protect against physical tampering, by itself it doesn't offer anything like the necessary features to protect a system against physical threats.

2.5   Complicating factors

Unfortunately, many applications where TPMs could hypothetically be very powerful are harder to deal with in the real world than they look on paper. There are a number of complicating factors for TPM adoption of which you should be aware if you're considering making use of TPMs. It is worth noting that none of these complicating factors are significant for the individual user; significant investment may, however, be required to overcome them in large-scale enterprise or consumer applications.

All of these complications are both symptoms of low application-level adoption and causes of that low adoption. As of the end of 2015, any enterprise which wishes to deploy a large-scale TPM use case is very likely to need to develop its own individualized solutions to some of these problems. However, the more enterprises invest in using their TPMs, the more infrastructure will exist, and the less any given enterprise will need to work to overcome these hurdles.

2.5.1   Identifying TPMs

If a TPM is to be used for any kind of remote application, its keys must be recognizable by servers and other systems which will be verifying the TPM's cryptographic identity. Unfortunately, although TPM manufacturers in theory should be providing TPMs with pre-provisioned keys and associated certificates, most manufacturers are not doing so today. Even if your TPM does come with a certified key, discovering the manufacturer's signing key to verify the legitimacy of the certificate is not always easy. Although some large-scale enterprises would prefer to certify their own TPMs anyway, in today's world most enterprises will be forced to do so whether they want to or not. This certification step requires some non-standard CA capabilities, as described in Section 5.6.1, and adds to the overhead costs of deployment.

This problem is doubly significant for geographically distributed enterprises. It is possible to certify a TPM's keys reasonably securely if you have the physical machine in a trusted environment, such as an IT department (see Chapter 5 for more information on how), but enterprises which ship machines around the world to data centres or non-technical end users will have a significant problem bootstrapping from a non-certified TPM to a trusted, remotely verifiable TPM.

If you're considering deploying TPMs in a geographically diverse enterprise, or otherwise want to avoid the cost of self-certifying TPMs, you may want to contact the manufacturer and see if you can purchase TPMs with keys already loaded that have been certified by the manufacturer.

The lack of centrally certified keys is one reason that TPMs are not recommended for most consumer applications. Unless you are building your own devices to sell, such as in an 'Internet of things' scenario with networked appliances, each with a unique cryptographic identity, there's no reason to expect even consumer devices which contain a TPM to have that TPM be remotely verifiable. Although convenient for consumer privacy, since it prevents any applications from creating a universal identity for a computer without the owner's permission, it does limit the market for TPM-rooted consumer applications.

2.5.2   Enterprise PKI integration

TPMs were designed with an elegant security model, in which some keys can certify other keys, allowing trust to be bootstrapped from a single root key to a wide variety of other keys, while maintaining a strong cryptographic binding between the keys and the chip. The certification mechanisms support pseudonymity without sacrificing trust, so that the claim 'This key belongs to a trusted TPM' can be supported without knowledge of which TPM a given key came from, or even whether two distinct keys came from the same TPM. TPM keys, particularly in 1.2 TPMs, are also constrained in how they can be used, automatically preventing a family of attacks that can result from the same key being used for both decryption and signing operations.

Unfortunately, all of this elegant design doesn't play well with standard enterprise PKIs. Many certification infrastructures don't have any room for certificates signed by something other than a full Certificate Authority (CA); in contrast, the certificates TPMs issue for their own keys should be trusted, but TPMs should not be trusted to act as general-purpose CAs. The usage constraints mean that many TPM keys – almost all 1.2 keys, and any non-signing 2.0 keys – can't even participate in a normal X.509 certificate request protocol, which requires that the certificate signing request (CSR) for a key be signed using that key. TPM decryption keys, and 1.2 keys, which can safely be used to sign TPM-internal data such as certificates (Section 6.11) and quotes (Section 9.3), are not capable of signing data in an X.509 format. While TPM 2.0 keys are more compatible with standard protocols such as X.509, since keys can be created to be capable of both signing and decryption and the high-security signing keys are capable of signing some user-provided data (see Section 6.2.2), keys must be created with certifiability in mind. In addition, the protocols for supporting pseudonymous certification of keys (see Section 6.11.1) – which are nearly mandatory if a 1.2 TPM's internal key certification features are to be used – make assumptions about signed certificates being secret that are dangerously undermined if a standard CA is used.

What this means is that if TPM keys are going to be integrated with an existing enterprise PKI, adjustments and accommodations will need to be made. Those accommodations can vary, ranging from custom CA modules through custom CAs to simply recertifying all TPM keys centrally and ignoring the TPM's powerful but difficult-to-use certification entirely. But until commercial CA software vendors start supporting TPM features, enterprise PKI support for TPMs will be a trade-off between features and integration overheads.

2.5.3 Universal software support

Support for TPMs in software has come a long way in the last few years. Linux and Windows OSes both come with built-in or easy-to-install TPM drivers; software for setting up the TPM is included or available for both OSes. (See Chapter 5 for more on this software.) Programming interfaces exist on both OSes. Unfortunately, what doesn't exist is a single reliable, free, standardized, and cross-platform interface. This is true even when using a single TPM version, let alone when writing software to support multiple TPM versions.

The TCG defines standard programming APIs for the TPM, called the Trusted Software Stack[2] (TSS); it is intended to keep programmers from needing to know about hardware details, and to hide some of the complexity of interfacing with the TPM. The *TrouSerS* implementation provides a reliable open-source implementation of the 1.2 TSS for Linux, but the TrouSerS port to Windows is as of the end of 2015 the product of a graduate school research lab last updated in 2011, and neither well supported nor well tested. Commercial TSS implementations for Windows and other OSes exist, most notably the NTRU TSS, but are usually delivered as integrated parts of software suites provided by vendors such as Wave, which may not meet all the needs of enterprises. Windows' built-in TPM interface, the TBS module, is almost driver-level, and difficult to work with; it has no Linux equivalent.

The TCG's 2.0 TSS has only recently been released at the time of writing, so the availability of implementations is uncertain. It comes in two distinct abstraction levels, one of which (the Feature API, FAPI) is small and aimed at providing the most commonly used subset of TPM functionality in an easy-to-use fashion, and the

---

[2]Or, in some cases, the TCG Software Stack, or the TPM Software Stack.

other one of which (the System Level API) is comprehensive and aimed at providing access to the full range of TPM features at the cost of higher complexity. Microsoft Research has released convenient programming libraries for TPM 2.0, called TSS.Net and TSS.C++, but these implementations do not follow the official TSS API, instead providing a simplified version of the TPM hardware commands. IBM has created its own 2.0 TSS variant, which uses the command parameters defined in the TPM specification but helpfully manages the finer details of communicating with the TPM, such as session management.

This means that while writing custom code for TPMs can be quite straight-forward in some circumstances – for example, when the code will run on a single OS, with a single TPM version, and a single TPM API – it can rapidly become complex in environments which use multiple OSes, let alone multiple TPM versions. The safest option for compatibility today is to use a 1.2 TPM and a 1.2 TSS, and hopefully in the near future move to 2.0 TPMs and TSSes; however, this comes at the cost of not being able to take advantage of some of TPM 2.0's powerful new features. Hybrid 1.2/2.0 TPMs are designed to bridge this gap, allowing 1.2 functionality to be used initially without requiring a hardware replacement to upgrade later. Enterprises with varied systems should be prepared for potential compatibility issues. In this book, we'll be using the 1.2 TSS and the IBM TSS 2.0 for our code examples, as discussed further in Chapter 4.

A full list of interfaces available at the time of writing and where to get them can be found in Section 11.1.

Chapter 3

TPM concepts and functionality

In this chapter, we will cover some of the core concepts and vocabulary we'll be using over and over again in this book; in some cases, the concepts will be completely new, and in others we'll be adding more detail to what we introduced back in Chapter 1. We'll also give you a basic idea of how these ideas will be used and in which chapters you'll see a lot more of them.

3.1 Ownership and authority

1.2 TPMs are designed to have an *owner*: a single party, which could be a person for a consumer TPM or an entire IT department for an enterprise machine, who is responsible for configuring the TPM appropriately. The TPM owner is not equivalent to a root or administrator account in an OS; the owner cannot read secrets belonging to other TPM users, or use the owner password to bypass other access controls. The owner does, however, have a few useful unique powers compared to other users.

2.0 TPMs have a more complex division of ownership; see Section 3.2.2 for details. The powers listed below are divided between four different *primary authorizations*: the *platform*, representing the low-level system firmware or other early boot software; the *owner*, representing the person who uses the TPM to protect data on the system; the *privacy administrator*, representing the person who approves the use of the TPM for providing information about the system to external parties; and the *lockout* authorizations, used to recover quickly from dictionary attacks and reset (*clear*) the TPM. Each of these is identified by a password (hence, authorization), or by a more complex access control policy, as described in Section 6.13.3.

- The owner (in 2.0, platform and lockout authorization) can clear the TPM of approximately all data, including almost all keys.[1]

---

[1] Unlike other owner commands, in a 1.2 TPM (and on 2.0 TPMs whose system firmware allows it), this one can also be performed by anyone with physical access to the machine. Why? Because the TPM's security model generally assumes that whoever owns the computer with the TPM attached is the owner. While this is a tremendously useful feature in some circumstances, such as when trying to use the TPM of a machine that's been out of commission for a while and whose owner password is long forgotten, or when using the TPM of a purchased used machine, it does mean that a machine which is under the physical control of an adversary can be cleared, causing the loss of any encrypted data. Backing up your data is always recommended.

- The owner (in 2.0, owner and platform authorization) can allocate regions of the TPM's internal storage for use, and set access controls on these regions.
- The owner (in 2.0, owner and platform authorization) can keep certain keys loaded into the TPM and ready to use at all times.
- The owner (in 2.0, privacy administrator) can create new cryptographic identities for the TPM. *Identity keys* (1.2) or *restricted signing keys* (2.0) are used to provide information from the TPM itself in a trustworthy fashion. This information includes things such as certificates for keys created in the TPM or signed reports on the TPM's internal state.
- In 1.2 TPMs, the owner can permanently disable the TPM.[2] In 2.0 TPMs, individual hierarchies can be disabled by the platform authority or by the authority governing that hierarchy, allowing slightly more discrete disabling of functionality.
- In 1.2 TPMs, the owner can read certain values, such as the public portion of root keys or the values of some flags, which are not strictly secret but which are controlled to prevent possible misuse.[3]
- In 1.2 TPMs, the owner can change any of the TPM's internal flags that are not locked down during the manufacturing process. In 2.0, there are no adjustable flags, but the platform authorization can be used to change a variety of TPM functions, including turning off access to certain hierarchies and changing available registers.
- In 1.2 TPMs, the owner can delegate specific other-owner capabilities to another user, identified by authorization value (password).

Owner authorizations, or the primary authorizations, can be rotated by anyone who knows the old password. If an authorization is forgotten, the only way to change it is to clear the TPM (see Section 10.2), erasing most of its data, and create a new authorization. Owner and primary authorizations are not required for most routine TPM uses.

A 1.2 TPM cannot operate usefully without an owner, since the Storage Root Key (SRK) (see the next section) is created along with the owner. 2.0 TPMs always technically have an owner and storage seed; however, the owner password is initially empty, allowing anyone to use the owner's privileges until the authorization is changed.

3.2   Root keys and primary seeds

A *root key* is a key (more precisely, an asymmetric key pair) which acts as one or more of the roots of trust for a given platform. 1.2 TPMs contain several root keys. A *primary seed* is the 2.0 TPM equivalent; instead of being keys, however, these seeds are random values which can be used to generate keys, given a template. Primary

---

[2]This feature was added due to the privacy concerns of some activists, in order to guarantee that the TPM could not be turned on and used against the computer owner by powerful software vendors.
[3]Why is the public portion of a key security-relevant? Because it can be used to uniquely identify the machine.

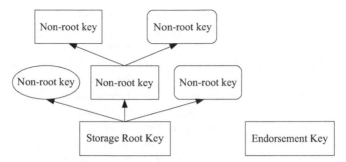

Figure 3.1 An example 1.2 key hierarchy structure. The Storage Root Key encrypts the private portions of other non-root keys, which may in turn encrypt additional non-root keys. The EK is separate, used only to establish the TPM identity and establish trust in other TPM keys, as discussed in Section 6.11

seeds allow a TPM to have multiple effective root keys, using distinct cryptographic algorithms, while minimizing on-chip storage. Root keys and primary seeds never leave the TPM.

3.2.1 TPM 1.2 root keys

Endorsement Key: The Endorsement Key, or **EK**, acts as the Root of Trust for Reporting (RTR), and is a permanent feature of the TPM throughout its life.[4] That means that whenever we trust some claim the TPM makes – a claim about the current system measurements, about the trustworthiness of a given key, about the current values of a counter – we are basing that trust, eventually, on the EK. To prevent the EK from being used to track a system or system user, the EK itself can be used only to certify *identity keys*, also called *Attestation Identity Keys* or *AIKs*, which are cryptographic pseudonyms for the EK and are used to sign most TPM-produced data. Because we can trace our trust in the identity key to our trust in the EK, the EK is our root of trust. Sections 5.2.1.3 and 6.11.1 have more information about creating an EK and certifying identities.

Storage Root Key: *SRK* acts as the Root of Trust for Storage. All secrets protected by the TPM are protected, directly or indirectly, by the SRK (Figure 3.1). Unlike the EK, the SRK can be used for a wide variety of routine TPM activities, including encrypting the secret portions of newly created keys.

3.2.2 TPM 2.0 primary seeds and hierarchies

All keys and objects in a 2.0 TPM belong to a hierarchy. Each hierarchy is rooted in a single primary seed (Figure 3.2). Seeds are long-lived; while they can be reset, they

---

[4]There is an optional feature in some TPMs allowing a non-permanent EK to be created (Section 10.2.1), but it is uncommon.

remain until explicitly cleared, and the conditions for clearing them vary. **Primary keys** and other **primary objects** are derived directly from the seed of a given hierarchy, based on a template; we'll discuss how to create these primary keys in Section 5.3.3. The process for creating a key from a given seed and template pair is predictable: the same template used with the same seed will produce the same key every time. This means that seeds are the true cryptographic root of each hierarchy, and also has the interesting property that primary keys can be created, forgotten, and recreated.[5] Other keys can be derived from or protected by the primary keys.

Each hierarchy has an **authorization value**, or password, and an **authorization policy**, which uses the 2.0 **Enhanced Authorization** scheme described in Section 6.13.3 to define any additional mechanisms through which control of the hierarchy can be acquired. Enhanced Authorization, or EA, can be used to create fine-grained access control policies; rather than having a universal hierarchy owner, an EA policy can allow a certain password to be used to authorize only specific commands, or allow a particular private key to be used to make a limited number of changes to the hierarchy. Each hierarchy also has a **proof value**, which is used in some data structures to prove that they were created by this TPM.[6]

Hierarchies can be individually enabled or disabled. When a hierarchy is disabled, neither the authorization value nor the authorization policy for that hierarchy can be used to authorize any TPM activity.

3.2.2.1   The platform hierarchy

The platform hierarchy is controlled by the earliest boot code on the system. If you're writing platform firmware, you can probably choose to use the platform hierarchy. On each boot, the policy for accessing the platform hierarchy is cleared, and the authorization value is set to a length zero password. Platform firmware can then generate a new authorization value by selecting a random value on each boot, which can either be remembered or forgotten as needed, and can define any desired authorization policies, which can be used to delegate access to specific platform hierarchy resources.

The platform hierarchy controls can be used to allocate the TPM's non-volatile storage (called *NVRAM* or *NV storage*); to configure PCRs; to enable or disable other hierarchies; to change the primary seeds of any hierarchy; to create primary objects in the platform hierarchy; and to reset the authorization values and policies of any hierarchy.

The platform hierarchy's broad power is intended primarily to allow low-level firmware to take a similar role to the one it played for 1.2 TPMs: a user can use the platform BIOS menu to turn on and off various TPM capabilities, or to reset relevant permissions and data.

---

[5]TPM manufacturers are expected to use this property to minimize the amount of data shipped with a TPM. Since templates are expected to be public and standardized, a manufacturer can create a key with a known template, certify it, and then provide only the certificate inside the TPM. The user can then recreate the key using the known template, and the certificate will work.
[6]2.0 proof values are hierarchy-specific instead of TPM-specific because the different hierarchies and their associated proof values are reset at different times and in different ways.

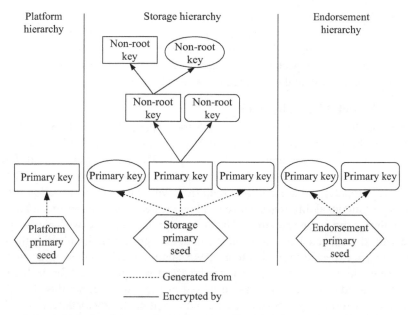

Figure 3.2   A high-level example of the three TPM 2.0 hierarchies. Each hierarchy consists of a primary seed, from which primary keys are generated; some number of primary keys; and some number of non-root keys, which are encrypted with other keys. Although only the storage hierarchy here has non-root keys, because that is the most common expected use, any hierarchy can have any kind and number of keys

3.2.2.2   The storage hierarchy

The storage hierarchy is controlled by the owner; the authorization value and policy are referred to as *ownerAuth* and *ownerPolicy*, unlike the other hierarchy authorizations which are named after the hierarchy. The owner can use the hierarchy authorizations to allocate NVRAM, to create storage hierarchy primary objects, and to control the availability of all key and object hierarchies that are part of the storage hierarchy. The owner also has a few special permissions: they can tell the TPM to keep certain loaded objects in the TPM even through reboots (Section 10.6), establish command auditing (Section 10.7), and adjust the TPM's internal clock (Section 10.10.2).

3.2.2.3   The endorsement hierarchy

The endorsement hierarchy is used to prove that keys and other objects originated with a TPM. Because many endorsement hierarchy-related activities pose a risk to privacy by linking activity to a particular machine, the person with access to the endorsement authorization and policy is called the *Privacy Administrator*. The Privacy Administrator has much more limited powers than the platform firmware or the platform owner; all the Privacy Administrator can do is enable or disable the Endorsement Hierarchy, and authorize the creation of primary objects in the hierarchy. Although these are far from the only privacy-sensitive actions on the platform, since any key in any hierarchy could be used to link various activities with a single machine, all of the others require the use of objects in the endorsement hierarchy to establish trust, and the Privacy Administrator is thus expected to take reasonable actions to only create objects and grant access according to their desired privacy policy.

3.2.2.4 Which hierarchy to use

Fundamentally, the difference between the three hierarchies has to do with who's expected to have authority over the entities (keys or other objects) in the hierarchy, and what can cause that hierarchy to be changed. There is no functional difference between the objects created in different hierarchies: if I'm setting up a 2.0 TPM for my home computer and am acting as both the owner and the privacy administrator, there is no functional difference between a key created in the endorsement hierarchy and another in the storage hierarchy. The differences between the two have everything to do with the expected use. Keys in the endorsement hierarchy identify the hardware, and are expected to be tied to a TPM manufacturer's credential; as such, the endorsement hierarchy seed is expected to be effectively permanent for the life of the TPM. (The seed can be changed, as discussed in Section 5.3.2, but this should only be done when absolutely necessary, because this will break any manufacturer created certification.) Primary keys created in the endorsement hierarchy can be recreated even after the TPM has been cleared, erasing the Storage Primary Seed (SPS) and all associated keys. This is both an advantage (it is difficult and requires special authorization to effectively erase primary keys in the endorsement hierarchy, so the TPM can maintain an identity through a wide range of operations) and a disadvantage (primary keys in the endorsement hierarchy cannot be eliminated before the machine is provided to another party without eliminating the manufacturer's guarantees about the TPM's trustworthiness, so in most cases all secondary keys must be deliberately and completely removed).

In general, the endorsement hierarchy should be used for keys which will identify this TPM to remote parties, and which are not tied to a particular use case (such as enterprise authentication). Keys with specific use cases for which a more limited lifespan is useful can be created in other hierarchies and certified using keys in the endorsement hierarchy, with no loss of trust.

Temporary objects, such as public keys loaded into the TPM for encryption or verification operations, can be loaded under the null hierarchy, so no hierarchy authorization is required.

3.3 Non-root keys

In addition to root keys, TPMs are designed to provide a wide range of other high-security keys for a variety of purposes. These keys are created by the TPM's users based on their needs. TPM keys, particularly in 1.2 TPMs, are designed with limited functionality in mind, to prevent any possible compromise that might result from the same key being used for both decryption and signing. Some TPM keys are used for encrypting data securely, others for signing TPM-produced data, and yet others for signing user data. A full discussion of the types of keys available and when they're useful can be found in Chapter 6. The use of specific keys is discussed extensively throughout the book.

Non-root keys are not stored inside the TPM unless the owner explicitly forces them to be, because the TPM has a very limited amount of internal storage. Instead, non-root keys are returned to the user on creation in a custom data structure called a *blob*,[7] which stores the private half of the key encrypted and integrity-protected. The blob is stored on disk or even off-platform. This allows the TPM to be used to create arbitrarily many keys despite its limited storage capability. When a non-root key is to be used, it is *loaded* back into the TPM, where the TPM will decrypt its private portion.

Unless explicitly created to allow it to be used outside of the TPM with the *migratable* option, TPM keys can only be used by the TPM that created them. This means that a non-migratable TPM key can be used to reliably identify a machine, if it can be tied to a particular TPM.

TPM 1.2 non-root keys can be constrained so they are only usable with a password, or in specific machine states; in TPM 2.0, a wide range of nearly arbitrary constraints can be placed on the use of a key. I discuss these briefly in Section 3.10 and in more detail in Section 6.13.

3.3.1 Root and non-root key relationships

All non-root keys are dependent in some fashion on the root keys.

In 1.2 TPMs, non-root keys depend directly on the SRK for secrecy: either their private data is encrypted directly by the SRK, or that data is encrypted by another key which is in turn protected by the SRK. They depend indirectly on the EK for their association with a trustworthy TPM; the EK is used to certify identity keys, which are effectively cryptographic pseudonyms for the TPM. Identity keys are then used to certify other TPM keys.

In 2.0 TPMs, primary keys are directly dependent on the primary seed of their hierarchy; the keys are generated directly from the seeds using predictable templates, and can even be reconstructed using the same seed and template. Primary keys never leave the TPM. Non-root keys are dependent on primary keys for their secrecy; they have their private data encrypted by primary keys' secrets, which causes them to be part of the same hierarchy. If a primary seed is changed, the primary keys become unavailable, and the non-root keys' secrets can no longer be decrypted, turning them into junk data. Note that trust established by a key rooted in a given primary seed may not immediately be eliminated, since any restricted signing key can certify any other TPM object. The expected behaviour is that all keys in any hierarchy are certified by an endorsement primary key that is itself certified by the manufacturer, and are thus

---

[7]Yes, really. Blob is a technical term when dealing with TPMs. You can think of these as black boxes: the intent is that the user should never have to know or care about the structure of a blob.

indirectly dependent on the Endorsement Primary Seed (EPS) for their association with the TPM.

3.3.2   *Externally created keys and the TPM*

All TPMs can use keys created outside the TPM in some fashion, although 2.0 TPMs do so more broadly. Externally created keys must be formatted using the appropriate TPM formats—the 1.2 TSS even has an API call to do this, TSS_ WrapKeyToPCR—but once loaded into the TPM, they are used just like other TPM keys. Externally created keys with private data (2.0 TPMs also allow public keys with no private data to be loaded, for use in encryption to external parties) are almost always encrypted to TPM storage keys, and are thus also part of the TPM's key hierarchies, although because they also exist outside of a TPM do not share the security guarantees of a TPM-created key.

TPM keys that are created to be migratable can be exported from one TPM to another. These keys provide a middle ground between the security of a key bound tightly to a single TPM, and the convenience for many use cases of a key held externally or on multiple machines. From the perspective of any individual TPM, these keys are indistinguishable from keys created externally in software; from the perspective of an enterprise, however, they are much more secure, since if the migration commands are performed correctly the keys never exist in the clear outside of a TPM.

3.4   Key certification

The TPM is designed to support trustworthy certification of TPM keys. Once one TPM key has been certified—normally the RTR, sometimes another key if an organization does not want to support the full complexity of the TPM certification architecture—it can be used to certify arbitrary other TPM keys, providing proof that each key belongs to the same TPM and has the same protections against theft or misuse as any other TPM key. TPMs also include in their certificates information about how a key can be used, and about any constraints it may be subject to. This means that TPM-created certificates not only provide evidence that a key is trustworthy, but can also be used to provide evidence about the state of the machine when a given key is used. The TPM's internal key certification approaches do not, however, correspond well to widely used PKI standards, losing in compatibility what is gained in security. Certification of TPM keys is discussed in much more detail in Section 6.11.

3.5   Roots of trust for measurement

In addition to the root keys listed previously, there are other Roots of Trust in the PC platform. These roots are not, however, in the TPM itself. The TPM is designed to work in close conjunction with roots of trust for measurement (RTMs) provided by either the BIOS (what we call the ***Static Root of Trust for Measurement***, or ***SRTM***) or by certain secure CPU modes (what we call the ***Dynamic Root of Trust for***

Measurement, or *DRTM*). In either case, the RTM is intended to provide the TPM with an initial, trustworthy assessment of the machine state. RTMs are designed to execute either extremely early in the boot process, for the SRTM, or immediately after the processor enters a protected execution mode, for the DRTM, and measure the next piece of code to run by taking a hash of that code before launching it. The launched code can then take a measurement of the next piece of code before handing off control, and so forth. This produces what we call a *chain of trust*. At the time of this writing, chains of trust usually do not extend up into the OS, and normally do not use measurements more complicated than a simple hash of a file or code segment; however, there is plenty of potential for more sophisticated measurement to be used in the near future.

3.6 Platform configuration registers

Where do measurements provided by the RTMs go? The TPM contains a number of *PCRs*, used primarily to store data about a machine's boot state. In 1.2 TPMs, these consist of a fixed number of 20-byte registers—each the length of a SHA-1 hash. In 2.0 TPMs, they are a somewhat flexible number of variable length registers, to accommodate both the backwards compatible SHA-1 and the stronger SHA-256 hash algorithm. PCRs are numbered, and referred to by index number. 2.0 PCRs are also organized in banks, named by hash algorithm. Each bank has registers of the appropriate digest length for its hash algorithms; a SHA-1 bank would have 20-byte registers, and a SHA-256 bank would have 32-byte registers. Each bank has the same number of registers, and uses the same indexes, for reasons I'll discuss later.

PCRs don't act quite like normal computing registers; there is no simple write operation. Instead, PCRs create a hash chain of every value added to them—we call this *extending*—since the machine has rebooted or the register is otherwise cleared (Figure 3.3). This somewhat odd behaviour is to support the primary use case of PCRs: reporting on the machine state as measured by the measurement chain. As we discussed briefly in Chapter 1, the Roots of Trust for Measurement and all other components in the measurement chain exist outside of the TPM, but in order for an outside verifier to trust those measurements, they have to be stored somewhere

936AA11BA2F...	44852FBD5D4...	A89FB8F88CA...			00000000000...
0	1	2		...	23

Figure 3.3   Platform Configuration Registers are a set of numbered registers – 24 of them in a 1.2 or minimal 2.0 implementation – which are used to store hashes of system measurements and other data. PCRs cannot be overwritten directly by the user; instead, they are extended, combining old and new content in hash chains. PCRs are reset, or restored to a default value, on boot; some PCRs can also be reset during normal operation

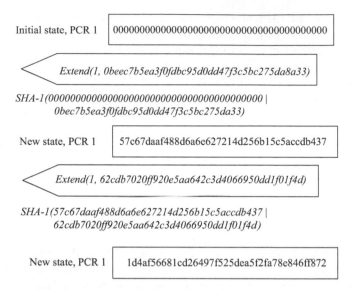

Figure 3.4   A sequence of PCR extend operations. Each time a digest is extended into PCR 1 (first the hash of 'foo', then the hash of 'bar'), the TPM concatenates the old value and the new value, takes the hash of the result, and makes that hash the new PCR value

trustworthy: the TPM. However, in order for these measurements to actually be useful, we need to be certain that the measurements came from the measurement chain, and not from any other component which might be able to rewrite the register and produce a fake good value.

The Extend command for either 1.2 or 2.0 TPMs is straightforward: it takes the current value in a PCR and the new value to be added to that PCR, hashes these two values together, and sets the PCR to the combined hash (Figure 3.4). Thus, if the original value in PCR 1 was A, and software called the *Extend* command on PCR 1 to add value B, the resulting contents of PCR 1 would be hash(A, B). This gives PCRs an interesting property: we can always add data to them, but we cannot remove data from them. And because the hash algorithms used are one-way functions, it is infeasible for an adversary to calculate the correct input required to make a bad measurement look like a good one.

PCRs are reset to known values whenever the machine reboots, so that the measurements stored in the registers correspond to the software the machine most recently booted with. We'll talk about the full details of how different measurement options work, how they use PCRs, and other ways PCRs can be used in Chapter 9.

3.7   Quotes

One of the most powerful tools the TPM provides for reporting about machine state is the *quote*. There are several Quote variants, but all of them serve the same role: to report on the current state of the TPM's PCRs. Quotes are signed data structures which combine a hash of selected PCRs' contents and a user-provided nonce; this means that challenge–response protocols can be used to provide trustworthy evidence about the current contents of the TPM. Chapter 9 talks more about quotes and how the current contents of the TPM can be used to provide evidence about the current state of the whole system.

3.8 NVRAM and key storage

In addition to PCRs, the TPM has two distinct kinds of internal storage. One is key storage: the TPM has space to hold a small number of keys, both root keys and loaded non-root keys ready for use. The other is non-volatile storage (called *NVRAM* or *NV storage*, depending on TPM version), which is used to store any credentials that the TPM manufacturer may have provided, in addition to small quantities of user data. Because TPMs today are almost all inexpensive devices, the amount of NVRAM is sufficient only for small, high-value data, such as hashes of trusted public keys. NVRAM is also write-limited; although the approximately 10,000 write limit will not be any trouble for the vast majority of applications, it does mean that the TPM's NVRAM is not suitable for rollback protection for frequently updated files or storage of other rapidly changing data.

Most of the TPM's storage functionality is discussed in more detail in Chapter 8. Key storage is discussed in Chapter 6 and Section 10.6.

3.9 Utility functions

The TPM also has a number of small-scale useful functions, which we'll discuss in much more depth in Chapter 10. These include monotonic counters, which can be particularly useful for rollback detection; audits of executed commands; tools for discovering the TPM's internal configuration and available resources; and RNG. 2.0 TPMs add a clock.

Some TPMs may support firmware upgrades to allow for bug fixes. In 2.0 TPMs, these upgrades can even add new features, such as additional cryptographic algorithms, to the TPM.

Some 1.2 TPMs also support backing up the whole TPM via the creation of a TPM archive; this is especially useful if you are concerned about the motherboard failing or the machine containing the TPM being stolen, although I'll also discuss other useful data backup mechanisms later in this book.

3.10 Access control mechanisms

The TPM provides some basic access control mechanisms for TPM keys, encrypted objects, and other resources. In 1.2, there are three mechanisms: authorization values, or passwords; PCR restrictions, in which a resource is only available if the current contents of the PCRs match the restriction; and locality restrictions, in which a resource can be made available only if the CPU is executing code in particular secure modes. (See Section 9.1.3.1 for a full introduction to locality.) Some commands are limited by *physical presence*, a mechanism for detecting whether a user is present at the machine that varies between systems.

In 2.0, a new EA model allows for a much wider range of possible constraints, including time, the state of a monotonic counter, and public key authentication, as well as PCR and locality status. The EA model also allows access control constraints to be combined in nearly arbitrary fashion, supporting complex policies. 2.0's extended authorization model supports access control policy updates as long as a given policy was designed to be updatable. This is a powerful feature which mitigates the fragility common to 1.2 TPM objects constrained with PCRs or locality, for which a choice must generally be made between their having a long usable life or being highly constrained; however, EA can make establishing trust in a key's behaviour noticeably harder, and implementation can be complex.

I'll be discussing the access control model in much more detail in Section 6.13.

3.11   Cryptographic algorithms

1.2 TPMs support a single encryption algorithm, RSA, with multiple options defined per key (see Section 6.4.2.1). No symmetric encryption algorithm is made available to the TPM's users, owing to export control regulations in place during the 1.2 TPM standard's development phase. All hashes are SHA-1. While theoretically a 1.2 TPM could support additional algorithms, in practice this is not supported.

2.0 TPMs support a larger set of cryptographic algorithms. In addition to RSA, 2.0 TPMs are guaranteed to support ECC, with multiple curves: NIST P256 and BN P256. For symmetric encryption, AES is provided, and there are commands to support bulk encryption; the TPM is still an inexpensive part which is unlikely to support high-speed operations, however, so using it for large-scale encryption is not recommended. For hashing, in addition to the backwards-compatible SHA-1, 2.0 TPMs support SHA256 and can be configured to use it for PCRs if the platform firmware supports it. 2.0 TPM commands and data structures are designed to work seamlessly with a wide range of algorithms, rather than having the fairly baked-in choices of 1.2 TPMs, and some TPMs may offer more than the minimum set of cryptographic algorithm options.

3.12   Communicating securely with the TPM

TPMs provide several communications protocols, called authorization and transport sessions, designed to ensure that user-level software and the TPM can communicate in a secure fashion, without misbehaving drivers or other intermediary software having a chance to interfere or steal passwords. These can even be run over a network connection so that TPM commands can be issued in an integrity-protected and authenticated fashion remotely.

Actually implementing these protocols, however, is tricky, and if you're using a pre-built API such as the TSS it should provide the secure communications sessions for you. Because of the combination of complexity and lack of practical need, we won't cover them in detail in this book; but if you'd like to learn more, Section 6.10 has a basic overview and Chapter 11 will explain where to find the TPM specifications which contain the comprehensive definitions and provide tips for using those specifications productively.

3.13 The TPM in action

3.13.1 Possible TPM states

TPMs have multiple states, and many of them are shipped effectively turned off, to prevent people with privacy concerns from being worried about their TPMs being used against them. TPM states are generally set in the BIOS, and we discuss how to change those states in Section 5.2.1.1.

1.2 TPMs actually have two distinct 'on/off' states: active/inactive, and enabled/disabled. Anyone wishing to use the TPM will need their TPM both active and enabled; the distinction between active/disabled and inactive/enabled has to do with which extremely limited set of functionality the TPM supports while 'off'.

2.0 TPMs do not have the same kind of 'off' state that 1.2 TPMs do, in order to support use of the TPM by platform firmware even in situations where the higher-level software or user does not want to use the TPM. Instead, individual TPM hierarchies can be disabled, shutting down the associated functionality. Keys and other resources associated with a given hierarchy become unavailable. Thus, a machine owner wishing to ensure privacy by keeping the TPM from certifying keys could disable the endorsement hierarchy.

3.13.2 Reboots, and why they matter

Understanding TPM reboot behaviour is important for using a TPM well. TPMs take certain actions reliably every time a machine is shut down, and others on startup; with these combined, a freshly rebooted TPM is in a clean state. For the purposes of this book, we won't go into the details of shutdown versus startup behaviour, because most users can treat reboots as an atomic action. If you'd like more details, see Chapter 11, which covers where to learn more about TPM-related topics.

When a machine is rebooted, the TPM takes two important actions. The first is to reset all PCRs to their default state; the register will contain either all ones or all zeroes, depending on the PCR in question. The second is to remove most loaded non-root keys, unless they have been locked into the TPM by the owner (see Section 10.6). Technically, the TPM is only required to remove any key which would have required a particular PCR or locality state to load (see Section 6.8); however, most implementations remove all loaded keys.

Note that merely putting a machine to sleep (suspending it) does *not* count as a reboot; it will not reset PCR values or unload keys. The intent of the TPM's reboot behaviour is that if the machine's software has an opportunity to change significantly, the measurement infrastructure will have an opportunity to execute and the TPM state will reflect the current machine software.

3.13.3   Clearing: erasing your TPM

Sometimes it is necessary to erase all data from the TPM. Perhaps a machine is being sold. Perhaps the machine contains highly sensitive encrypted data that you would like to delete securely en masse. Perhaps the owner password has been lost and you'd like to put the TPM back into a clean slate and reprovision it. Perhaps you're teaching yourself to use the TPM and want to run through the provisioning process repeatedly to test your scripts.

In any of these cases, you're going to be *clearing* the TPM. Most TPMs offer two ways to clear the TPM: with a command, such as 1.2's TPM_OwnerClear, or via the BIOS. The BIOS approach often requires proof of physical presence; sometimes, merely accessing the BIOS menu is sufficient, but in other systems, particular buttons must be pressed or confirmation given early in the boot sequence. Either of these clearing mechanisms can be disabled, but it is not possible for a TPM to enter a state where neither clear option will work.

Clearing the TPM will erase most non-volatile data. In 1.2 TPMs, the exceptions include the EK, which is the TPM's permanent identity, monotonic counters, and manufacturer-provided certificates. The SRK, many non-manufacturer-set NVRAM contents, any loaded user keys, and a wide range of other internal data will be erased. The TPM's configuration options will all be reset to the manufacturer defaults. In 2.0 TPMs, clearing is slightly more complicated due to the multiple hierarchy model. Clearing the TPM erases everything other than the primary seed in the Endorsement hierarchy (equivalent to the EK), clears the owner's internal storage, and replaces the old primary seed in the Storage hierarchy with a new one, rendering all data encrypted with Storage hierarchy keys unusable. In short, clearing the TPM returns it to an approximation of the state in which it was expected to come from the manufacturer.

Clearing the TPM does *not* erase the PCR contents, in order to prevent the clear operation from being used to forge a false machine state report. Clearing is discussed in more detail in Section 10.2.

Chapter 4

Programming introduction

While the specifics of programming applications that use the TPM are not the focus of this book, I will be presenting short examples of how to implement many of the TPM functions I discuss. Readers planning on programming TPM applications may find it helpful to have context on the libraries being used for these examples, so that you can try them out and gain maximum benefit.

If you're not planning on programming for the TPM immediately, you probably want to skip this chapter; the code examples for individual functions will generally be comprehensible without it, and you don't need to know anything explained here to understand how to use the TPM.

Please note that for brevity, the code examples in this book are teaching tools focussed on TPM-specific functionality. Many secure coding practices, such as input verification and proper memory management, have not been used because they would make the included text longer and make the TPM-specific code harder to follow. If you are building your own applications for anything other than learning purposes, please make sure to not treat the code samples here as canonical good practice. The complete TSS 2.0 sample code included in Appendix C.2 is written by a professional developer of security libraries, and is a useful resource for those wanting to understand more about the context in which the examples throughout this book are used.

4.1 TSS 1.2 code introduction

TSS 1.2 implementations should all follow the same C API, as defined in the TCG specification (see Section 11.1.1 on page 269), although there may be a few additions or variations. For this book, all code has been tested using the Linux TrouSerS interface. Complete code samples can be found in Appendix C.1, for those who would like to see how some of the various functions discussed here and throughout the book fit together in practice.

There are actually several different abstraction levels of interface provided in the TSS 1.2 specification: the TCG Device Driver Library (TDDL) to provide a standard API for TPM drivers; the TSS Core Service Interface (TCSI) to provide a streamlined interface to the userspace TPM service; and the TSS Service Provider Interface (TSPI), intended for use by applications. The TSPI interface is, at times, more complex than the underlying TCSI, but is designed to better support multithreaded applications and to provide a more unified object interface. Most importantly, unlike the TCSI, the TSPI is guaranteed to always be available in any TSS implementation. Thus, it's the TSPI we'll be using throughout the 1.2 TSS examples in this book. The TCSI, if you choose to use it, closely reflects the underlying TPM interface, and should be fairly intuitively accessible to someone familiar with the associated TPM commands.

TSS programs need to include a number of header files. The following set will cover all TSS functionality:

```
#include <tss/tss_error.h>
#include <tss/platform.h>
#include <tss/tss_defines.h>
#include <tss/tss_typedef.h>
#include <tss/tss_error.h>
#include <tss/tss_structs.h>
#include <tss/tss_error.h>
#include <tss/tspi.h>
```

TrouSerS programs may also want to include the following header file, which can help interpret error messages by turning the hexadecimal error codes into the corresponding error strings:

```
#include <trousers/trousers.h>
```

It is often useful, if you will be working with the contents of data structures returned by the TPM, to include also the TSS header files defining the various TPM data structures:

```
#include <tss/tpm.h>
```

These files can be found in `/usr/include` in most Linux package installations.

All programs using the 1.2 TSS share some features. A TPM and a context must be defined; the TPM variable indicates which device commands will be sent to, and the context tells the TSS supporting software to make sure the TPM state matches the program's expectations. TSS contexts allow programs running in multithreaded environments to use the single-threaded TPM easily; they also keep higher-level programs from having to deal with some of the TPM's constraints, such as how many keys can be in the TPM simultaneously, and the overhead used to maintain communications with the TPM hardware. You will also want to define a variable to hold the result values from TSS commands you run; this will contain your success or error code.

For example:

```
int main(int argc, char**argv){
    TSS_HCONTEXT    hContext;
    TSS_HTPM        hTPM;
    TSS_RESULT      result;
```

The next TSS-specific step is to create the context, connect that context to your chosen TPM, and get the handle for the TPM. When using a system's TPM hardware – which should almost always be the case, unless a simulator is in use – the system TPM is indicated with a null value in the `Tspi_Context_Connect` command.

```
/* Create the new context handle */
result = Tspi_Context_Create(&hContext);
printf(''Context creation returned %08x, %s'',
       result, (char*)Trspi_Error_String(result));
/* Connect the context to the system TPM (NULL) */
result = Tspi_Context_Connect(hContext, NULL);
printf(''Context connection returned %08x, %s'',
       result, (char*)Trspi_Error_String(result));
/* Define the TPM object which will be passed to later commands */
result = Tspi_Context_GetTpmObject(hContext, &hTPM);
printf(''Getting TPM object returned %08x, %s'',
       result, (char*)Trspi_Error_String(result));
```

The above code snippet also provides a simple example of how the result values produced by TSS functions can be used. The `Trspi_Error_String` function is from the `trousers/trousers.h` file included previously, and translates the error code into a human-readable (if not always intuitively so) form. The full list of return codes can also be found in the `tss/tss_error.h` file of your TSS, and the return codes' basic meaning can be found in the TSS specification.[1] Chapter 12 has some tips to help with debugging and pointers to useful parts of the specifications.

Once you've set up the context and TPM handles, you're ready to use the other functions described in this book. Note that in future examples, we will skip both those setup steps and the corresponding cleanup steps described next, in order to focus on

---

[1]If you aren't using TrouSerS and your TSS does not provide an equivalent translation function, you probably want to write your own translation function if you'll be doing significant amounts of TPM development work. The `tss_err.c` file in the TPM Quote Tools project (see Section 11.8.4.2) provides a useful example.

the functions being introduced. Full code samples which combine setup, cleanup, and practical functionality can be seen in Appendix C.1.

Many TSS commands allocate memory for you, and can cause problems if they are passed variables whose memory has already been assigned where they expect to allocate it themselves. Object creation, for example, allocates memories for some objects. Other functions that could return objects of different kinds will often ask for a pointer to a byte array, and allocate the memory themselves based on the assumption of the object being returned. If you want to reuse a variable that has previously had memory allocated by a TSS function, you can clear that memory using the `Tspi_Context_FreeMemory` command, which has the context handle as its first argument and the object handle as the second.

When your program has completed all of its desired TPM operations, the TSS objects and context should be cleaned up, to free up the automatically allocated memory. There are two commands relevant for this: `Tspi_Context_Close`, which deallocates the memory associated with an object pointed to by a handle, and `Tspi_Context_FreeMemory` with NULL as its second argument, which cleans up the more complex contents of the TSS context before it is closed.

```
Tspi_Context_Close(hTPM);
Tspi_Context_FreeMemory(hContext, NULL);
Tspi_Context_Close(hContext);
```

The examples in this book were compiled using the following gcc command:

```
gcc example.c -o example -ltspi
```

4.1.1   Categories of TSPI commands

Commands in the TSPI layer of TSS 1.2 tend to follow a basic naming scheme which shows the kinds of command they are. Some command names start with `Tspi_Context`; these commands operate on the software state of the TSS itself. Others start with `Tspi_TPM`; these commands are passed to the TPM to perform the corresponding hardware operation, although the software layer will process the arguments and responses. Some commands are named to indicate the kind of data that they process; `Tspi_Hash` commands operate on hash data structures, `Tspi_Key` commands on keys, and so on.

The command name is not always a perfect reflection of how the command operates. `Tspi_Hash_Sign` is actually passed behind the scenes to the hardware `TPM_Sign` operation, and there is no `Tspi_TPM_Sign` command, for example, while `Tspi_Hash_UpdateHashValue` is a purely software-based operation updating a data structure's contents. However, the command names will often indicate what object they are primarily intended to operate on; the first argument in most commands will reflect the name. `Tspi_TPM` commands will expect the handle of the TPM, while `Tspi_Context` commands expect the TSS context, and so forth. This is primarily useful to know when sanity-checking code returning bad parameter errors, but it's also worth noting for anyone using the TSS specification to look up functions, since commands aren't necessarily grouped in the way that someone thinking purely from a TPM command perspective might expect. If you don't find a command in the Context or TPM sections, think about what data structures it might apply to and check there.

4.1.2   TSS objects

TSS 1.2 is an object-oriented library. In addition to the TPM and context objects I've just introduced, TSS 1.2 uses a generic object type to represent the vast majority of TPM concepts. Keys, certificates, authorization policies, and a wide range of data structures are all represented in the TPM as objects. Commands referencing TSS objects will all use handles for the relevant object; you'll see most variable definitions begin with 'h' to clearly indicate that the variable is a handle. The objects referred to by these handles are created with the `Tspi_Context_CreateObject` command, which you'll be seeing repeatedly; it performs memory allocation for you. All objects must be associated with a TSS context, and must specify a type and relevant flags for that type of object. I'll cover the details of object types and flags as we encounter them through the book. To deallocate an object, use `Tspi_Context_CloseObject`. Remember, all objects should be deallocated before the associated context itself is deallocated.

```
Tspi_Context_CreateObject(hContext, objectType, objectFlags, &hObject);
Tspi_Context_CloseObject(hContext, hObject);
```

4.1.3   Policies: providing passwords to the TPM

Policies are objects used to manage authorization data (i.e., passwords) for commands that require authorization. The details of these commands and when you'll need authorization will be discussed in each chapter, but it's useful to be familiar with the idea. There are multiple kinds of policies, but in almost all cases you'll want general-purpose usage policies; as the name suggests, usage policies are called for whenever an object is being used, as well as in a few other generic situation. I'll discuss migration policies in Chapter 6. The third type of policy, operator policies, I won't cover in this book – they're only used when the TPM is deactivated – but they work the same way.

There are three steps you'll normally perform before using a policy in TSS 1.2: creating the policy object, assigning it a secret, and assigning the policy object to another object, such as a key. There is also a command that can be used to flush a secret from memory; this is particularly useful for long-running programs where authentication is meant to be temporary. Policies can also be configured to have secrets automatically expire after a certain number of uses or seconds using the general-purpose

`Tspi_Set_AttribUint32` command, which sets the attributes of many TSS objects; see the TSS specification for details of its many options.

```
TSS_HPOLICY hPolicy;
BYTE *pwd = ''BadPassword''

/* Setup */

Tspi_Context_CreateObject(hContext,TSS_OBJECT_TYPE_POLICY,
                          TSS_POLICY_USAGE, &hPolicy);
Tspi_Policy_SetSecret(hPolicy, TSS_SECRET_MODE_PLAIN,
  strlen(pwd), pwd);
Tspi_Policy_AssignToObject(hPolicy, hObject);

/* Commands using authorized object */

Tspi_Policy_FlushSecret(hPolicy);
```

There are five different modes that `Tspi_Policy_SetSecret` can use. In general, plain mode isn't recommended except for testing, but it does provide a handy example of what the arguments are used for.

TSS_SECRET_MODE_NONE: There is no secret associated with this policy. It will generate errors if used with any command that requires authorization. Primarily used for creating objects that shouldn't require authorization to use. The secret length and secret arguments will be ignored.

TSS_SECRET_MODE_PLAIN: The secret is expected to be in plain text; the TPM will internally produce a SHA-1 hash. A zero-length secret is valid.

TSS_SECRET_MODE_SHA1: The secret is passed in as a 20-byte SHA-1 hash of the password.

TSS_SECRET_MODE_POPUP: The TSS will provide an interactive dialog for the user to enter their password in. The secret length and secret arguments will be ignored. This is the default mode if `Tspi_Policy_SetSecret` is not called, but some TSS implementations do not provide a functional non-GUI option for command-line programming.

TSS_SECRET_MODE_CALLBACK: The application writer can use the `Tspi_SetAttribData` command to define the address of a callback function which is expected to return the password. The secret length and secret parameters are ignored. For more information, see the TSS 1.2 specification.

4.1.3.1   Providing owner authorization

In the previous example, I created a new authorization policy and assigned it to an object; however, when you're trying to authenticate as the TPM owner, you'll need to use an existing authorization policy which is already assigned to the TPM.

```
Tspi_GetPolicyObject(hTPM, TSS_POLICY_USAGE, &hOwnerPolicy);
```

We can then assign secrets to the owner policy just as we do to any other authorization policy.

4.1.3.2 Flushing authorization secrets

Sometimes, especially in long-running programs, it's important to not leave working authorization policies around for keys that shouldn't be available at all times. In these cases, it's possible to use the TSS to flush the stored secret easily:

```
Tspi_Policy_FlushSecret(hPolicy);
```

4.1.4 Object attributes

One of the abstractions that the 1.2 TSS relies upon is object attributes. Objects of all sorts, including keys, data, contexts, policies, and even TPMs, have attributes. Each kind of data has a set of attribute flags and subflags which are used to access various parts of the data structure. While this can make for a lot of table lookups, it also means that a small number of commands with a common format arc uscd for a wide range of operations, and the user interactions with some extremely complicated and multilayered data structures are minimized.

The four commands used for managing object attributes are:

```
TSS_HOBJECT hObject;
TSS_FLAG attributeFlag, subFlag;
UINT32 AttribDataSize, AttribValue;
BYTE* AttribData;

Tspi_SetAttribData(hObject, attributeFlag, subFlag,
                   AttribDataSize, AttribData);
Tspi_GetAttribData(hObject, attributeFlag, subFlag,
                   &AttribDataSize, &AttribData);
Tspi_SetAttribUint32(hObject, attributeFlag, subFlag, AttribValue);
Tspi_GetAttribUint32(hObject, attributeFlag, &AttribValue);
```

`Tspi_SetAttribUint32` and `Tspi_GetAttribUint32` are used to set and retrieve 32-bit attributes of objects; `Tspi_SetAttribData` and `Tspi_GetAttribData` set and retrieve all other attributes.

I'll be covering particularly useful attributes of various objects as related topics are introduced throughout the book, but Section 2.3.2 of the TSS 1.2 specification (see Section 11.5.1 for where to find it) has complete lists of all attribute flags and subflags for all object types.

4.2   IBM TSS 2.0 code introduction

For this book, I'll be using the IBM 2.0 TSS to create example code. All code referred to as 'TSS 2.0' for the rest of this book uses this library. This C library supports a wide range of systems, is compatible with the Microsoft TPM 2.0 simulation as well as with hardware TPMs, and closely follows the abstraction level I focus on in this book. See Section 11.2.1 on page 270 for information about where to get it. All TSS 2.0 example code in this book is adapted from Ken Goldman's sample code packaged along with the IBM 2.0 TSS library, and is included with his kind permission; see Copyright Notices for the code licence. Any errors are mine, not his.

There is only one core command in the IBM TSS API: TSE_EXECUTE. It is used to execute all TPM commands, using a straightforward if not immediately intuitive set of arguments.

```
TPM_RC TSE_Execute(
                   RESPONSE_PARAMETERS *out,
                   COMMAND_PARAMETERS *in,
                   EXTRA_PARAMETERS *extra,
                   TPM_CC commandCode,
                   ...);
```

The library includes data structures for the response and command parameters for each TPM command, which are passed in as the *out and *in arguments; for example, the TPM2_GetTime command has GetTime_In and GetTime_Out data structures pre-defined. These data structures correspond exactly to what the TPM is expecting: the GetTime_In components are TPMI_RH_ENDORSEMENT privacyAdminHandle, TPMI_DH_OBJECT signHandle, TPM2B_Data qualifyingData, and TPMT_SIG_SCHEME inScheme. (See Figure 11.4 on page 282 for an illustration of the underlying TPM2 specification command structure.) The commands are defined in the TPM 2.0 Command specification, and the data structures in the TPM 2.0 Structures specification. (See Section 11.6.2 on page 281 for where to find these and how to use them.)

The optional *extra argument is rare: a very few commands (two so far, TPM2_StartAuthSession and TPM2_PolicySigned) require one, in cases where the normal TPM command and response parameters are not sufficient.

The commandCode is the TPM command code, found just above the command parameters in the TPM specification. The command codes also follow a convenient pattern: for command TPM2_XXXX, the command code will be TPM_CC_XXXX. So, for the TPM2_GetTime command, the command code is TPM_CC_GetTime.

The least intuitive arguments are the ones described above as "...". These are used for passing in sessions. Each argument is a three-tuple of the form (TPMI_SH_AUTH_SESSION sessionHandle, const char *password, unsigned int sessionAttributes). A list of arguments is passed in the order requested by the TPM; the list is terminated with the three-tuple

(TPM_RH_NULL, NULL, 0). Up to three sessions can be used per command. The library will handle all session setup, communication, and cleanup for you.

Sessions here cover the frequently used authorization sessions, used to pass in authorization values or policies; they also include encryption, decryption, and audit sessions. The type of session is indicated by the session attributes. Session types are not necessarily mutually exclusive: a non-password authorization session can also be set to be an encryption session, for example. Using two sessions of the same type will generate errors for anything but authorization sessions.

Audit sessions are used to create an audit digest of all commands run as part of the session. In addition to the digest of all commands run, the audit session tracks whether other commands were run between commands in the session. Set using the TPMA_SESSION_AUDIT attribute.

Authorization sessions are used to provide information to authorize the use of a command or object. This can be a password or an authorization policy. (See Section 6.13.3.) 0 is a valid session attribute for authorization sessions.

Decrypt sessions are used to encrypt the first parameter[2] of command input so that only the TPM can read it. This only works if the parameter is a data type that starts with TPM2B. 'Decrypt' is used because it's the action the TPM takes. Set using the TPMA_SESSION_DECRYPT attribute.

Encrypt sessions are used to encrypt the first parameter of command output so that only the requestor can read it. Only works if the parameter is a data type that starts with TPM2B. 'Encrypt' is used because it's the action the TPM takes. Set using the TPMA_SESSION_ENCRYPT.

So an example call to the GetTime command would look like this:

```
TPM_RC rc = 0;
GetTime_In in;
GetTime_Out out;

TPMI_SH_AUTH_SESSION    sessionHandle0 = TPM_RS_PW;
unsigned intsessionAttributes0 = 0;
TPMI_SH_AUTH_SESSION    sessionHandle1 = TPM_RS_PW;
unsigned intsessionAttributes1 = 0;
TPMI_SH_AUTH_SESSION    sessionHandle2 = TPM_RH_NULL;
unsigned intsessionAttributes2 = 0;


/* handle of the privacy administrator */
in.privacyAdminHandle = TPM_RH_ENDORSEMENT;
/* Handle of key that will perform signing */
```

---

[2]Not counting size fields.

```
in.signHandle = signHandle;
in.inScheme.scheme = TPM_ALG_RSASSA;
in.inScheme.details.rsassa.hashAlg = TPM_ALG_SHA256;

...
/* Retrieve passwords from user */
...

rc = TSE_Execute((RESPONSE_PARAMETERS *)&out,
                 (COMMAND_PARAMETERS *)&in,
                 NULL,
                 TPM_CC_GetTime,
                 sessionHandle0, endorsementPassword,
                   sessionAttributes0,
                 sessionHandle1, keyPassword,
                   sessionAttributes1,
                 sessionHandle2, NULL, sessionAttributes2,
                 TPM_RH_NULL, NULL, 0);
```

The return code (rc) will be 0 when the command has executed successfully. When writing production code, you will want to check the return code from each command, but I will be leaving it out of the code examples in this book, for brevity.

While the IBM TSS 2.0 API does have a small number of other functions, they are all focussed on making sure the library is properly configured to access the machine TPM or installed simulation, and will not be covered in this book. The documentation included with the package provides complete information.

4.2.1   TPM 2.0 utilities sample code

If you plan on working through the examples in the book, you may find it useful to refer to the source files in the *utils* directory of the IBM TSS 2.0 distribution. The code here has all been taken from those files; each function is named after the corresponding TPM 2.0 command, so you can easily look up the utilities related to the section of the book you're reading. Some complete programs have been reprinted for your convenience in Appendix C.2, to provide full context and examples of good coding practice for the commands described here.

4.2.2   File handling helper functions

Included in the IBM TSS 2.0 files, although not in its official API, are some useful helper functions for combining file operations with common TPM 2.0 data structures. These functions, which interface with data structure marshalling, are in more active development, so are more likely to change than the previously described API; the tseutils.h header file has function definitions. For the most part, their naming scheme is entirely intuitive (File_ReadBinaryFile does exactly that, reading a file of binary data into a byte array), but there's one function that will come up on occasion in the example code in this book which is worth calling out.

`File_Read2B` is very similar to `File_ReadBinaryFile`, but reads TPM 2.0 TPM2B data structures. All the `TPM2B_` prefix means on a data structure is that it's provided as a size field and a data buffer with that many bytes; however, these data structures are frequently used as a way to take several pieces of data, combine them in a data structure contained in the buffer, and treat them as a single parameter. This allows the TPM to perform a single encryption or decryption operation as though all of the pieces of data were one parameter; it also allows the OS or other software to treat the data structure contents as an opaque blob.

You'll see these functions used frequently in the sample utilities, because so many TPM commands take as input the output of other TPM commands and the utilities are designed to perform a single command at a time. Data structures returned by the TPM are stored in user-chosen files, so that they can be provided later to other utilities or reused in multiple commands.

Chapter 5
Provisioning: getting the TPM ready to use

5.1 Provisioning: what it means, and why it matters

Provisioning generally has two goals: setting up the necessary initial configuration and establishing trust in the TPM.

TPMs today do not come ready to use. Every TPM, whatever the version, needs to have some initial values provisioned before the TPM can generate and use keys; without keys, none of the TPM's features work. What the initial values are varies from version to version. Provisioning can in some cases also determine who has permission to use certain TPM functionality.

5.2 Basic steps of 1.2 TPM provisioning

TPM provisioning falls into three general categories:

- Setting up the TPM
- Establishing trust in TPM keys
- (optional) Configuring the TPM

In many real-world situations, there is an additional fourth kind of activity that happens during the provisioning process, which is the setup of commonly used keys, user identities, and other TPM resources before a machine is turned over to the user. We won't discuss this in detail in this section, because it's neither necessary for provisioning nor inherently different from the activities one might perform with a TPM during its routine working life. However, it is worth noting that for enterprise use cases, if an IT department is already required to put their hands on a machine for setup, it is often worth performing other management steps at the same time, to limit the complexity users deal with. In addition, if TPMs are being used for disk encryption or key store encryption (see Chapter 8), the keys may need to be created early in the machine configuration process, such that adding the key creation steps to the provisioning routine may be a convenience.

Establishing trust in your TPM keys is by far the most critical step in the TPM provisioning process, and the one which is highly security-sensitive. There are two core ways to establish that trust: the first is by having your TPM certified by a trusted party, such as a manufacturer, whose certifying authority you can then trust, and the second is to establish trust directly in the keys of this particular piece of hardware.

Unfortunately, most TPM manufacturers today do not certify their TPMs' keys;[1] although at the time of publication there is some hope that this may change in the future, especially for 2.0 TPMs and for large enterprise customers who request the feature. Today, this option is unlikely to be feasible unless you buy your hardware with this goal specifically in mind, and even then may be difficult if you are purchasing off-the-shelf systems with other constraints.

Regardless of whether a system comes with a certificate for the TPM, the provisioning process will need to associate a cryptographic key with an enterprise machine in a trustworthy fashion. Without a manufacturer's key, the provisioning process will additionally need to establish that the key existed not only on that machine, but in that machine's TPM.

If the associations between key, TPM, and computer are not created accurately and securely, an attacker could masquerade as a trusted computer's TPM, rendering all future uses of the TPM untrustworthy in a potentially undetectable fashion.

5.2.1   Setting up a 1.2 TPM

5.2.1.1   Turning on the 1.2 TPM

Today's TPMs normally ship turned off; in some OSes, you won't even be able to determine if a machine has a TPM at all until the TPM is turned on. Whether a TPM is turned on or off is controlled in the BIOS, although some computer vendors have worked with Microsoft to create Windows utilities which can change the BIOS settings conveniently.

There are several factors making the supposedly simple act of turning the TPM on more complicated. The first is that 1.2 TPMs don't really have a single 'on' state, they have two: 'activated' and 'enabled'. The distinction between these two states is irrelevant for practical purposes, and exists only to prevent a hypothetical attack where a rogue party manages to take ownership of the TPM and use it before the legitimate owner can; an enabled but deactivated TPM cannot perform normal TPM operations, but can execute the TPM_TakeOwnership command. However, in order for a TPM to be used, it has to be both activated and enabled, and in practice, these are normally changed simultaneously.

The second complicating factor is that there are many BIOS vendors, and no standard ways that these vendors handle TPMs. It's not possible for this book to provide precise instructions for where in the BIOS to look, and exactly which options to select, because no two BIOSes are quite the same, and some are radically different. Even two machines which were purchased at the same time from the same equipment vendor may have different BIOSes with different interfaces. However, there are some common factors. In most recent BIOSes, TPM options will be under a category such as

---

[1]Infineon and ST appear to be the current exceptions to this rule; however, these vendors are not the standard choices for consumer PCs in the United States, making it difficult for the author to verify this information directly.

'Security', 'Physical Security', or 'Security Chip'. They will usually then be called out as TPM or TPM options, although you will sometimes still see the euphemism 'Security Chip' used. Within the TPM options, you will often see some kind of on/off option; it might be labeled 'On', 'Activated', 'Enabled', 'Active', or even have two 'Activated' and 'Enabled' options, both of which must be turned on. Turning the TPM on requires the machine to be rebooted after the BIOS settings are saved; in some BIOSes, most commonly on Hewlett–Packard machines, the process of turning the TPM on in the BIOS and rebooting must be done multiple times for the TPM to actually be turned on.

In short, if you are using Windows and have a convenient utility to turn the TPM on for you, such as the tpm.msc command in Windows 7 and 8, it's often worth using. (See Section 5.2.1.4 for more on how to use the Windows TPM setup utility.) Even the convenient utilities sometimes require that the TPM already be turned on in the BIOS, however, depending on the BIOS manufacturer's compatibility with the tool.

In the BIOS, you will also usually find a 'Clear' or 'Reset' option; using it will erase all non-factory data from the TPM, restore it to its default configuration, and turn the TPM back off again. (See the Clearing Section 10.2 for more information on exactly what this option does.) Note that unlike turning the TPM on, clearing the TPM takes effect immediately; don't do this unless you really want to! If you're setting up machines for enterprise use, it may be worth setting up your BIOS to require a password to change settings, to minimize the risk of users accidentally clearing the TPM; however, the same Windows tpm.msc utilities that can make turning the TPM on easy include a utility for clearing the TPM which entirely bypasses BIOS passwords, at least in some versions of Windows.

Once your TPM has been turned on, you will need to *take ownership* of the TPM. In some cases, you will need to create an EK (see Section 3.2) first, if the TPM did not come with one.

5.2.1.2   Testing to see if your 1.2 TPM is really on

How can you tell that you've succeeded in turning your TPM on and that it's working? You can often use your OS's basic device interfaces to read the contents of the TPM's PCRs. We'll discuss how to use these and what they do in Chapter 9, but they make a handy test of a functioning TPM.

On Linux OSes, somewhere in the device information there will be a virtual file containing the current contents of the TPM's PCRs. A common location is /sys/class/misc/tpm0/device/pcrs, but the exact location may vary between distributions.

Some versions of Windows, but not all, provide information about the TPM PCR contents in the device configuration settings. In later versions of Windows, you can check the TPM status using tpm.msc, regardless of whether the device configuration information includes PCR contents.

5.2.1.3   Creating an EK

Creating the EK if your TPM does not have one must be done, after the TPM has been turned on, but before anything else. An EK must exist in order for other TPM functions, such as taking ownership, to work. On Linux machines, the `tpm-tools` package (see Section 11.8.1) contains a `createek` function which will create an EK for you. On Windows machines, the `tpm.msc` utility provides this functionality; this utility provides a number of features but should be used carefully, as I'll discuss later in this chapter.

You can also implement your own EK creation utility using either the `TPM_CreateEndorsementKeyPair` or `TPM_CreateRevocableEK` commands. The basic `TPM_CreateEndorsementKeyPair` command is accepted by all TPMs, and it is what is used by the easily available utilities; it generates an RSA key pair of at least 2048 bits within the TPM and stores it permanently as the EK. The `TPM_CreateRevocableEK` command is optional, and may not be supported by any given TPM; when available, it also creates a 2048-bit or better RSA key pair and stores it as the EK, but it also takes an arbitrary user-provided value. That value is effectively a password, which can be provided to the TPM later using the `TPM_RevokeTrust` command (see Section 10.2.1) to cause the TPM to erase the EK. Note that any EK created using `TPM_CreateEndorsementKeyPair` cannot be revoked in this fashion.

5.2.1.4   Taking ownership

In a 1.2 TPM, the TPM owner is generally expected to be the owner or user of the physical machine. The owner has limited privileges: they approve the creation of identity keys, used to authenticate the TPM and sign TPM-created data; they allocate and deallocate NV storage; they can change a few, mostly minor, TPM settings; and they can clear all data from the TPM. TPM owners *cannot* access other users' secrets, change the passwords associated with keys, or otherwise access data not associated with them; they have no resemblance to an OS administrator or super user.

Taking ownership of the TPM requires the use of the `TPM_TakeOwnership` command, which does the following things:

- Confirms that the TPM does not currently have an owner.
- Establishes the owner, as identified by an owner password.
- Creates a new SRK for the TPM, with a password provided by the owner.
- Sets certain internal flags which allow most TPM commands to function.
- Creates a unique 'TPMproof' value which allows the TPM to identify certain data structures as having been created by this TPM.

The creation of the SRK is the reason that the TakeOwnership command is required to use a TPM. Without an SRK, the TPM has no secret it can use to encrypt newly created TPM keys or other secrets. The SRK and the owner are linked, since the general assumption is that ownership will change when a machine's owner changes, at which point all of the old owners' secrets should become inaccessible.

If a TPM already has an owner, you must clear the former owner before you can take ownership. See Section 10.2 for more information.

Linux:
To take ownership of the TPM on Linux, the easiest approach is to use IBM's TPM tools, available in most distributions' package management systems as `tpm-tools`

(Section 11.8.1). The `tpm_takeownership` command can be run on the command line, and by default will prompt you for two passwords, the owner and the SRK. In some cases, you will need to prove that you have physical presence on the machine in order to take ownership; you can do this on most computers by going into the BIOS menu and saving the settings, and then running `tpm_takeownership` on the same boot.

Although you can set both an owner and an SRK password, it is often most convenient (especially on a shared computer or an enterprise-owned computer) to use the null password (or, as the TPM definitions more entertainingly call it, the well-known secret) for the SRK. This is because you will need to provide the SRK password for every single operation that uses a TPM key. On anything beyond a single-user system, it's usually best to make the SRK usable by anyone and set up specific password-protected keys for more constrained uses. The `tpm_takeownership` command makes this easy by providing the `-z` command line option. (It also allows setting a null secret for the owner, but because the owner does have control over some TPM features, including the NV storage, this is not recommended.)

Windows:

Windows offers a TPM initialization wizard accessible with the `tpm.msc` utility. This can be used to turn the TPM on and off, set ownership, clear the TPM, and perform some basic troubleshooting. Some recent versions of Windows with PowerShell can also use the TPM cmdlets. These can be installed by running `dism /online /enable-feature /FeatureName:tpm-psh-cmdlets`. Documentation can be retrieved by running the `Get-Command Module TrustedPlatform Module` cmdlet.

When using the `tpm.msc` utility, you will see that it offers both 'Initialize TPM' and 'Turn TPM On' options. Selecting the 'Initialize TPM' option will both turn the TPM on and take ownership.

It is critically important when using the Windows automated programs to set the owner authorization to a value you know, whether by actually choosing the authorization yourself or by generating a random value and having the utility save it. Because the dominant use case for TPMs in Windows machines today is BitLocker, which requires no interaction between the user and the TPM, the Windows utilities make it easy to create an owner password completely unknown to the actual system owner; if you do this and want to use the TPM for any other purpose, you're likely to have to clear the TPM and start over.

It is also critically important to note that the Microsoft utilities encode passwords sent to the TPM differently from the way in which TrouSerS and other open-source libraries do. This means that even if you are careful to set the owner password to a known value in `tpm.msc`, you cannot use that value in tools created with those open-source libraries. Because of this, people planning to make extensive use of non-Microsoft tools probably want to install their library of choice and create a simple `TPM_TakeOwnership` program themselves.

The `tpm.msc` utility is also important because it can be used to determine which TPM commands are allowed to be executed from Windows. This is useful in many enterprise contexts, where only a small and well-known set of commands is used. However, the default set of allowed commands does not permit the use of several commands we will be using extensively in this book, including TPM_Quote2, TPM_Extend, and TPM_PCRReset; depending on your application, you may need to unblock a number of commands.

The default group policy in Windows 7 does not permit unblocking of TPM commands. To change this on a single machine, use gpedit.msc to open the local group policy editor. Select Computer Configuration > Administrative Templated > System > TPM Services. This will provide you with a number of options. Use the 'Edit policy setting' option to configure your local policy according to your needs. If you want to take full advantage of your TPM, you should enable 'Ignore the default list of blocked TPM commands'. The commands you wish to block, if any, can then be configured easily either at the group policy level using 'Configure the list of blocked TPM commands' or locally using tpm.msc. (Note that you may need to refresh the command management screen in tpm.msc to see any changes made.)

5.2.2   Establishing trust in a 1.2 TPM

This is the most critical, and least documented, step in TPM setup, and cannot be skipped if you will be using a TPM for any remote authentication or attestation use cases. You are establishing trust in your root of trust's cryptographic identity; in a 1.2 TPM, the EK. The EK isn't used directly, but we'll use it to bootstrap trust in other TPM keys, particularly identity keys (see Section 6.11).

Why is it poorly documented? Because the TPM designers anticipated this problem and expected two credentials to exist which would keep a user from ever needing to worry about how to establish initial trust: the Endorsement Credential, which would identify a legitimate TPM's EK; and the Platform Credential, which would certify that a particular TPM had been integrated with a particular machine according to the manufacturer. Today, however, these are rare (Endorsement Credentials) or possibly non-existent (Platform Credentials). If the manufacturer has provided you with one or more certificates, they will be stored in your TPM's internal non-volatile storage (NVRAM) at a pre-defined location (see Table 5.1). These certificates can be read out using the standard NVRAM commands described in Section 8.7.

Some manufacturers, such as Infineon, create the EK in the factory and issue a certificate (the Endorsement Credential) to attest to the fact that this key belongs to one of their TPMs. For this certificate to be verifiable, you will also need to know the public key with which the manufacturer has signed it; contact your vendor.[2] If you have a manufacturer-provided EK and manufacturer-signed certificate, and you trust the manufacturer to issue certificates for legitimate TPMs only, congratulations: you've established trust in your TPM, and can proceed to using the EK to certify other keys.

---

[2]It is unfortunately the case that many vendors' initial customer service contacts are not familiar enough with TPMs to understand this request, and it may take some work to find the details. In some cases, certificates are available on the manufacturer's website; Infineon sets a good example. A link can be found in Section 11.8.2.

Table 5.1   Expected locations in NV storage of manufacturer-created credentials. 2.0 TPMs have a range of NV handles rather than a single NV index because 2.0 manufacturers may issue multiple certificates of a given type for a TPM. For example, a 2.0 manufacturer may issue Endorsement Credentials for both an RSA and an ECC primary key

1.2 Credentials		
Credential	**Name**	**NV index**
Endorsement Credential	TPM_NV_INDEX_EKCert	0x0000F000
Platform Credential	TPM_NV_INDEX_PlatformCert	0x0000F002
2.0 Credentials		
Credential	**NV handle range**	
Endorsement Certificates	0x01C00000-0x01C07FFF	
Platform Certificates	0x01C08000-01C0FFFF	

Most manufacturers, however, do not include an EK. Some include an EK but no certificate, or do not provide any way to verify the certificate's legitimacy. And in some cases, you may trust a vendor to manufacturer a TPM correctly but not to keep their own private certifying key safe, such that the manufacturer's certificate is not trustworthy even if you're willing to trust the TPM's keys to be securely held. In these cases, you will need to bootstrap trust from the TPM yourself.

When bootstrapping trust, there is one key question to always keep in mind: 'How do we know that the keys we're establishing trust in really belong to a TPM?'

In a 1.2 TPM, all trust is designed to be traceable back to one root key, the EK. What this means is that the only trust we really need to establish is in the binding of the EK to a particular TPM. However, if we want to do so, we may use the same processes to establish trust in other keys independent of the EK. This is primarily a useful feature in cases where implementing the full 1.2 trust hierarchy is overly complicated: if your use case requires you to establish trust in a single identity key or signing key only, you don't need the entire TPM self-certification infrastructure and may not want to invest in the overhead.

You may be wondering why establishing trust in a key that you might just have created is hard. Remember that when we communicate with the TPM, we're not communicating *directly* with the chip: those communications channels pass through software, other hardware, the CPU, and in some cases even over a network connection. Once we've established a cryptographic identity for the TPM we'll be able to verify other communications with it, but for this initial question of 'how do I know this is my TPM?' we don't have an identity to rely on. Until then, we're vulnerable. If there is malware running on that machine capable of interfering with the TPM device driver, that malware could generate its own fake EK and run a virtual TPM and we would never be able to tell; we'd just have none of the security guarantees we seek from a TPM. The situation is even trickier over a network, when the question of how you identify the remote machine you think you're talking to without a TPM, and which other software is capable of interfering, is added to the mix.

Is such an attack likely? Today, on most machines, no. TPMs are not used widely enough. However, if this technology starts being widely adopted, such an attack could be extremely profitable; while somewhat tricky to accomplish, since it has to be done during the provisioning step, it compromises the security of the TPM for the life of the device, in a way that is extremely difficult to detect. An adversary could read all secrets supposedly protected by the TPM or masquerade as the TPM's machine in remote communications. Enterprises or governments with high-value data who wish to rely on TPMs should seriously consider the long-term threat landscape when choosing their approach to establishing trust in TPM keys.

5.2.2.1   Establishing trust: high- and low-security approaches

There are two general approaches to establishing initial trust in a TPM's keys. I'll talk about the extremes of each here as the 'high'- and 'low'-security approaches, although any given implementation is likely to have a mixture of elements of each.

Although the entire provisioning process can be done using the methods described in these approaches for convenience, the question of how much trust one places in one's environment is only truly relevant when associating an EK with a TPM. The worst-case failure for other provisioning steps, such as taking ownership or establishing initial keys, is a denial of service; inconvenient, but easy to detect, often easy to fix, and with no long-term consequences.

The high-security approach:
Here, we seek to aggressively minimize the number of attack surfaces available to an adversary. A human accesses the machine locally; the network interfaces may be temporarily disabled to reduce a remote attacker's ability to interfere. Instead of running the standard operating environment, the machine is booted into a minimalist OS, such as a custom Linux live CD, with no programs other than those required to provision the TPM and read the public EK. The minimalist OS is run from trusted, write-once media. The public EK is recorded on to similar trusted write-once media, which are identified with the particular machine and hand-delivered to a trusted, off-line CA which will issue the certificate for the EK; or a human verifies a fingerprint (usually a hash) of the public EK created during the provisioning process with the CA before the certificate is issued, if a less trustworthy transmission mechanism is used for convenience.

This process is designed to ensure that each step from turning on the TPM to certifying the EK is human-verifiable, and the association between the machine and the TPM key has minimal opportunities for interference. Malware interfering with this process would likely need to be in the machine's BIOS or firmware, which is a significant barrier to most adversaries. Unfortunately, this kind of approach is also expensive to scale, and not well suited for many distributed environments. Done comprehensively, it requires a human to touch every machine for long enough to reboot it, run commands, and perform verification steps. If you're administering a handful of machines that you can freely reboot, the cost is low – just burn a minimalist Linux live CD with the `tpm-tools` package (see Section 11.8.1), and you can proceed – but for most modern enterprises, the investment is significant.

The low-security approach:
This approach prioritizes ease of use and low expense over security. Here, all steps of the provisioning process are performed by a script or other small program running in the standard operating environment. The program is often launched from a central location such as an IT department. Each machine, at the completion of the script, sends the resulting public EK, along with a machine identifier, back to the central location, where it is often stored in a database and used to create a certificate for the EK.

It should be obvious that there are numerous points in this process where an adversary could interfere: in the running of the initial script, in the saving of the results, in the transmission of results back to the central location, in the storage at the central location, etc. However, this approach is also fast, extremely easy to implement, able to be rolled out for machines that are already in the field and in use with minimal disruption to users, and achievable without any kind of training of technicians. The enterprise TPM solutions that exist today largely use this approach, because it is so seamless in user experience, and because few enterprise customers have considered the threat of a TPM replacement attack.

Finding middle ground:
Many enterprises can't afford the high-security approach but may be scared off from the low-security approach. It is, however, entirely feasible to combine them. If you're willing to trust your standard operating environment but don't have a network infrastructure you trust to identify a machine, run a local program to do the provisioning, ask your users to call the help desk, and have them read the key fingerprint that the program will pop up for them. If you don't trust the standard operating environment but are willing to trust your existing infrastructure to transmit the public EK to the CA, send each user a gold image DVD which, when rebooted, will perform all provisioning steps in a secure environment, turn on the network card, then send the public key to your CA, perhaps using a client certificate on the image.

Many enterprises may find it feasible to do something approaching the high-security approach for new machines, but not old ones. Often the IT department will reinstall each new machine with a standard image to replace the factory version; in this case, you have technicians or engineers who are already rebooting the machine and who are capable of performing straightforward technical tasks, so there's minimal overhead in adding a TPM provisioning step to the machine setup process. Machines that are already deployed, however, may be extremely costly to provision in a high-security manner, such that the risk–reward trade-off just isn't worth it. In these cases, it's often a good idea to use both approaches, but sign the EK certificates with two different keys. The low-security provisioned machines have a higher risk factor, but normal machine life-cycles will eventually bring most of them out of service.

Using two different keys to certify them means you can set an expected time frame for machine replacement – often 2–3 years – and have your trust in the old, low-security provisioning expire afterwards. At that point, only a small number of high-value targets should need a high-security certification process to be rerun, minimizing the overall cost.

5.2.2.2   Trust beyond the EK: provisioning identities and other keys

Although TPMs are designed to create trustworthy key hierarchies starting from the EK, some enterprises may want to use the same trust establishment process – create a key, collect its public key in a trusted environment, take the public key to a trusted CA, have it certified as belonging to the TPM – for other keys in addition to, or even instead of, the EK.

Not certifying the EK is, generally, not recommended: the EK lasts the life of the TPM, and is the permanent identity of the TPM itself. If the EK is certified, then bootstrapping trust from the ground up can be done again in an entirely automated and remotely verifiable fashion even if the TPM is cleared (see Section 10.2). If you certify only other keys, however, then your trust is a lot more fragile, and you may need to repeat the entire process of establishing trust multiple times in the life of a single TPM. It is sometimes worth certifying other keys in addition to the EK, however.

The first reason to certify other keys is to streamline the process of getting a TPM ready to use in places where the keys to be used are highly predictable. If an enterprise is planning to use the TPM primarily for remote authentication with a signing key, they may want to create a signing key during the provisioning process so that it is immediately available, and place it in a standard location. If you're creating a key anyway, you might as well sign it using the same process you're using for the EK, since the trust level will be the same as it would be with a trust hierarchy, and there are fewer steps required to verify the certificate.

The second reason is to avoid dependency on the complex and custom TPM key hierarchy and certification infrastructure (see Sections 5.6.1 and 6.11). 1.2 TPMs were designed to be extremely trustworthy, but their certification approach is distinctly non-standard. Some enterprises may be willing to trade the increased fragility of certifying keys during provisioning for the lower cost of not having to support the TPM's certification formats. In this case, it's often wise to ensure that at least one identity key, one signing key, and one binding key (used for sending remotely encrypted data to a TPM) are certified in this stage.

5.3   2.0 TPM provisioning and hierarchies

Because 2.0 TPMs are not easily available on the market at the time of writing, I cannot provide the same sort of step-by-step instructions for configuration and provisioning that I can for 1.2 TPMs. All information in this section is derived from the specification, not from practical experience, which means it may not reflect the eventual status quo.

2.0 TPMs have a radically different take on provisioning than 1.2 TPMs, in large part because 2.0 TPMs have a radically different take on ownership and organization. While 1.2 TPMs have a single owner, a single EK used to establish trust in other keys, and a single SRK used to protect other keys, 2.0 TPMs have multiple distinct trust *hierarchies*. One hierarchy is intended for use by the platform manufacturer, and is called the *platform hierarchy*; its purpose is to let platform firmware or other system components rely on the TPM, regardless of whether the human owner is using the TPM. One is the *storage hierarchy*,[3] which parallels the 1.2 SRK and storage key hierarchy (see Figure 6.1), and is intended for the platform owner to use to protect secrets. The third is the *endorsement hierarchy*, which parallels the 1.2 EK and certification hierarchy (see Figure 6.13), and its owner is the *Privacy Administrator*. Each of these hierarchies is configured differently, and at different stages.

The certification model for TPM 2.0 is very similar to the TPM 1.2 model at a high level: the TPM manufacturer certifies the TPM RTR as belonging to a legitimate TPM, the platform manufacturer certifies that a particular TPM is attached to a specific standards-compliant machine, and the RTR is used to certify other TPM keys. The biggest difference is that the RTR in a 2.0 TPM is the secret Endorsement Primary Seed (EPS), which can't be directly used or certified. Instead, the TPM manufacturer will generate several primary endorsement hierarchy keys from the EPS using standard templates (see Section 11.6.3), certify these, and store the certificates in the TPM using one of the handles reserved for that purpose (see Table 5.1). The keys themselves will be recreated by the system user using the same standard templates.

5.3.1   Changing hierarchy authorizations

Before a 2.0 TPM has been used, or after it has been cleared (see Section 10.2), the owner authorization, endorsement authorization, and lockout authorization (used for resetting dictionary attack protections and clearing the TPM) are reset to empty passwords, and their access control policies are set to empty policies. To prevent the misuse of the owner or privacy administrator's authority, or malicious misuse of lockout authorization, it is wise to change these authorizations before making use of the TPM. (Changing access control policies is more complex and less critical, since a blank access control policy provides no access without the basic authorization.)

To change these authorizations, the TPM2_HierarchyChangeAuth command is used. This command changes whichever hierarchy authorization is provided (lockout, endorsement, owner, or platform) to a new value. Authorization values can be no more than 20-bytes long.

The TPM2_SetPrimaryPolicy command is used to establish an authorization policy for the hierarchy authorizations or lockout authorization. Section 6.13.3 describes the policy options available, and how to use them. If certain hierarchy authorization privileges should be shared, an authorization policy can be used to provide alternative ways to authenticate.

---

[3] Or hierarchies; there can be more than one storage hierarchy in a given 2.0 TPM.

5.3.2   Changing the hierarchy seeds

In 1.2 TPMs, the SRK could be changed easily using TPM_Clear and TPM_Take Ownership, but the EK, once created, was generally permanent. 2.0 TPMs are designed to be more flexible, at least potentially, and may provide the TPM2_ChangePPS and TPM2_ChangeEPS commands, which allow the Platform Primary Seed (PPS) and EPS to be reset. (These commands are optional, but needed to meet Federal Information Processing Standards (FIPS) compliance requirements, so it is expected that many TPMs will support them.) Changing these hierarchy seeds is both dangerous and powerful, because it breaks the connection between the manufacturers and the TPM. In some rare cases, particularly for government agencies and other extremely high-security enterprises, it may be desirable to replace the EPS due to lack of trust in the TPM manufacturer or to make the TPM that much harder to identify outside of an organization. However, any certificates provided by the manufacturers to identify the TPM as legitimate will no longer be usable, since the keys and other objects based on those seeds can no longer be used by the TPM, which means machines with these changed seeds cannot safely be remotely provisioned. The TPM's identity for that hierarchy is effectively changed permanently. Both seed changing commands require platform authorization, and thus will normally need to be executed by or with assistance from the system firmware. They each reset the authorization policy associated with the seed in question; TPM2_ChangeEPS also resets the endorsement hierarchy authorization value.

To change the Storage Primary Seed, clear the TPM using the TPM2_Clear command. Note that this will also remove all access to previously created keys in the hierarchy.

Note that disabling a hierarchy does not remove a seed or erase any permanent data, although transient objects (such as loaded keys) associated with a hierarchy will be removed; access to those resources will just return errors until the hierarchy is re-enabled.

5.3.3   Creating primary keys and objects

Since hierarchies have root seeds rather than root keys, we need to create an initial set of keys that we'll use for later operations. We call keys derived from the root seed *primary keys* in a hierarchy. Each hierarchy has its own primary keys, and more than one can exist in any given hierarchy. 2.0's primary keys are not necessarily persistent in the way that root keys are in 1.2 TPMs, but they can be recreated easily as long as the seed has not been changed and the template used to create the key is available.

Primary keys are created using the TPM2_CreatePrimary command. There are a few important differences between the TPM2_CreatePrimary and TPM2_Create command, discussed in Section 6.4.2.2. One is that the CreatePrimary command derives the secret key material from the seed using a *key derivation function* (see Appendix A), rather than from bits in the TPM's RNG. One is that the TPM2_Create command requires a storage key parent and associated authorization, while TPM2_CreatePrimary uses the hierarchy authorization. The biggest, however, is that TPM2_CreatePrimary does not return the complete object, with both public and protected private halves. Instead, only public data is returned by TPM2_CreatePrimary, along with the handle of the newly generated key in the TPM's transient key storage. The private portion never leaves the TPM.

Note that the 'transient' there is important. Like any other keys loaded by the TPM, these primary keys will go away when the TPM's key storage is filled or if the TPM is rebooted. There are two options for handling this. The first is to keep the template around and re-derive the key every time it is to be used. This is a fast process for ECC or AES keys, but not so fast for RSA keys. The second is to force the TPM to make the key persistent using the TPM2_EvictControl command, covered in Section 10.6. Keep in mind that the TPM has limited internal storage for keys, so it may often be worth re-deriving the key as needed for non-RSA primary keys.

The templates that feed into the TPM2_CreatePrimary command are described in Section 6.4.2.3, since they rely on concepts discussed in that chapter. The TCG TSS, if you're using one, should provide pre-created templates for standard SRK and EK-style primary keys.

5.4 Multiversion TPMs

Some TPMs, as mentioned in Chapter 1, can operate in either a 1.2 or a 2.0 mode. These chips are not yet available at the time of writing, so I cannot provide exact instructions for what to expect. However, I can make some educated guesses.

Switching between the two modes will effectively reset the TPM to factory defaults, which may require re-provisioning. This means that these TPMs will generally be treated as either 1.2 or 2.0, rather than a true hybrid; they do, however, provide a powerful tool for enterprises which would like to use their existing 1.2 TPMs or software while preparing for a future when 2.0 TPMs will be widely available and supported. The mode could be selectable in the BIOS menu, just like turning on the TPM in 1.2. Alternatively, the manufacturer could provide a firmware update to the TPM which would switch modes.

5.5 TPM provisioning user stories

Note: Because no details exist today of how real systems with 2.0 TPMs will actually ship, most of these provisioning stories are based on 1.2 TPM processes. 2.0 user stories will be more represented throughout the rest of this book, since clear specifications exist for operating the 2.0 TPMs.

5.5.1 User stories: turning the TPM on

Alice is a security architect at SecureCorp. SecureCorp is worried about industrial espionage, and is willing to pay to get the best security. She writes up step-by-step instructions for activating the TPM on each of the corporate standard computers; in some cases, they'll take advantage of the pre-installed Windows utility to activate the TPM, but most of the staff use Linux, so most of the instructions go through the BIOS. Provisioning will be primarily handled in person by trusted on-site IT staff, either when a machine is first set up for corporate use or by asking the user to stop by for ten minutes at some point during their assigned week, but a few users at remote locations will have the instructions and a CD with provisioning software sent to them.

Bob is running Example, Inc.'s IT department TPM rollout. He's not too worried about perfect security, since he thinks even an imperfect hardware security system will be orders of magnitude better than the software solutions they have now, and Example, Inc. isn't too worried about highly skilled attackers; the risk doesn't justify the cost. Because he has thousands of users all over the world to deploy to and a limited budget to do it with, he's focussed on solutions that scale well. He purchases a commercial solution which deploys a software agent on each machine. The agent uses Microsoft's built-in TPM agent or a custom script to trigger a change to BIOS settings that turns the TPM on. The user will have to approve the change the next time they reboot, but Bob can just send out instructions in a corporate e-mail and, since the software he's using has a central server tracking provisioning status, remind the stragglers by phone.

Charlie has just purchased a new TPM-enabled computer for home use, and wants to use it to protect his personal data. Since he doesn't need to worry about his procedure scaling up to large numbers of people, he simply reboots the machine and opens the BIOS menu. He finds the 'Security" menu, and selects the 'On' option next to the 'TPM chip'. He reboots again, verifies in the BIOS menu that the TPM has in fact been turned on and the machine doesn't need to be rebooted again, and proceeds.

5.5.2   User stories: establishing trust in the TPM

Alice wants to be absolutely certain that any TPM key SecureCorp trusts is legitimate and owned by the company, no matter what the cost, so she's going to take the strongest security measures she can to tie the EK to the hardware. She's checked the computers SecureCorp has issued; one brand's TPMs come with preexisting EKs and a manufacturer-issued credential, but the other two brands don't, so she's just going to have SecureCorp issue its own Endorsement Credentials. Alice decides that since SecureCorp is worried about skilled adversaries who might have already installed malicious software on SecureCorp computers, she can't trust the normal OS or software to establish trust in corporate TPMs. She has her staff create a custom, stripped-down Linux image; it contains no software that isn't necessary, and although it has network drivers, the network devices are turned off by default, so the machine will be trusted when running the image. This image is burned to a number of CDs, and distributed to the employees who will be provisioning TPMs.

Also on these CDs is a set of automated provisioning scripts. These scripts will create a new EK in any 1.2 system that doesn't already have one, using custom software and the `TPM_CreateEndorsementKeyPair` command, since her TPMs don't support revocable EKs and SecureCorp doesn't care about the machines being potentially identifiable after SecureCorp is done with them anyway. For 2.0 TPMs, the scripts will create two primary keys in the Endorsement hierarchy to serve in the EK role, one RSA and one ECC. Once the EKs have been created, the script will display a human-readable fingerprint of the key or keys on the screen, created by taking a hash of the public key; the provisioning operator will write this down for later verification. Once the public key has been written down, the script will turn on the network drivers and send the public key, along with the machine's identifying information, to a central data collection server.

Later on, the provisioning operator will get in touch with an employee at the central location who has permission to approve keys for certification. For each machine that was provisioned, the operator will read out the associated key fingerprint, providing out-of-band verification that the key the central server received is the same one created in the trusted environment of the provisioning CD, and is associated with the same machine. Once the verification has happened, the key is approved for certification, and can be taken to the off-line corporate CA to have an Endorsement Credential created. If the machine is later stolen, the CA will issue a revocation certificate so that the EK is no longer trusted.

Bob isn't particularly worried about the trustworthiness of his user's day-to-day software. He figures that a portion of them are compromised at any given time, but that the chances an adversary is going to care enough to manipulate TPM provisioning are low enough that he's not willing to invest a lot of his time or inconvenience his large user base. He writes a TSS program that will create an EK on any TPM which doesn't already have one, and then send the public EKs back to his central server, where they will be placed into a database mapping each EK to a machine. He uses his corporate software management system to ensure that all of his users have an appropriate TSS library installed, then sends out the EK creation program to run in the background the next time the user is connected to the corporate network. When deciding whether to trust a given TPM, corporate systems can just use the database front-end software to confirm that the key is legitimate. If a machine is stolen, it will just be removed from the database or marked as no longer trustworthy. If Example, Inc. decide they want to integrate TPMs into their corporate PKI later, he'll just ship the list of currently valid EKs to the CA to certify.

Charlie isn't worried about certification – he doesn't have an infrastructure to certify to, and his TPM came with an EK and associated credential already established by the manufacturer. He writes a program to retrieve the certificate from the TPM's NVRAM.

Dana is the administrator for Responsible Finance, LLC, a small office of accountants who want to use TPMs primarily to protect secrets, audit activity, and provide attribution of documents. The office has invested in the new 2.0 technology. Dana's TPMs each came with manufacturer-issued credentials for two different standard key templates, one ECC and one RSA. Dana isn't going to worry about implementing ECC in the office just yet, so they make sure that each machine is running a software library that comes with the RSA template, and issues a `TPM2_CreatePrimary` command using that template. Because creating RSA keys is slow, they also make sure that `TPM2_EvictControl` is run to keep the newly created primary key in the TPM's internal storage where it can be used to identify the machine later. They also read the RSA credential out of the TPM's internal storage, and make sure that the corporate machines recognize the TPM manufacturer's certifying key as a legitimate CA.

5.5.3   User stories: taking ownership

Alice makes sure that her provisioning CD has software that will take ownership of the TPM. She doesn't want to use the same owner password for each machine, to make sure that no adversary who finds the password has the chance to clear large numbers of TPMs, so she makes sure that each machine has a unique password derived from the machine's property number, and puts the formula for calculating the password on paper and in encrypted backup files. The provisioning operator will establish the unique owner password for each machine during setup. Alice wants her users to be able to create TPM keys as needed, since SecureCorp encourages employees to pay attention to security, so she has her provisioning scripts set the SRK password to the well-known password.

Bob wants to make the IT department's life as easy as possible, so he has his TPM software agents on each machine set the owner password to a standard value which the IT department will automatically rotate every three months. He's not too worried about the potential of a mass clear attack, but he'll take the precaution of installing software on each machine which will automatically turn off the owner's ability to clear it (see Section 10.2). Bob's users aren't ever expected to use the TPM outside the enterprise standard software, and he wants to make sure they don't do anything by accident that might result in their data being unavailable, so he sets the SRK to another value known to the IT department. This is a very low-security password, since it will be included in all of the TPM software; it's just there to minimize the risk of user error.

Charlie is more worried about forgetting rarely used passwords than about adversaries bothering to break into his local system for a denial-of-service attack, and he backs up his important data anyway. He sets both the owner password and the SRK password to the well-known password.

Dana needs to make sure that her 2.0 TPMs have meaningful authorization setup first thing, if only because getting the TPM's functionality set up and then having a user or adversary set the values to something Dana doesn't know is going to require that the TPM be cleared, potentially putting data at risk. Dana has three values to set: the owner authorization, the privacy authority authorization, and the lockout authorization. Dana would like users to be able to use the owner authorization and privacy authority authorization freely, but also wants to make sure they can recover the machine in the event that a user locks themselves out or is terminated. The initial values of the owner authorization and privacy authority authorization are set to a randomly generated password that is given to the user on a piece of paper, using `TPM2_ChangePrimaryAuth` and the original empty password, and the user is provided with instructions for using software to change the password later. Dana also creates a simple owner authorization policy and privacy authority authorization policy (see Section 6.16.4), using TPM2_PolicyAuthValue to establish a password she knows as an alternative authentication mechanism for recovery, and sets it for both the owner and privacy authority with the TPM2_SetPrimaryPolicy command. The lockout authorization, used only for emergency dictionary attack recovery and clearing the TPM, is set to a high-security randomly generated value that Dana keeps in a password vault.

5.6 Remote verification of TPM keys

Once a set of TPM root keys has been provisioned, the next question is how the authenticity of those keys will be verified. This step is critical if a TPM is to be used for machine authentication or remote attestation; in both kinds of scenario, the whole point is that a remote party can confirm that a particular key belongs to a genuine, trusted TPM. (Data protection scenarios may or may not require remote verifiability; one reason Bitlocker does not require provisioning as described here is that the protection is local to the machine. Since no remote machines need to identify the TPM, remote verification is not set up, and the steps required to make remove verification trustworthy are skipped for ease of use.)

Performing a trustworthy provisioning process is only the first step in making remote verification possible. It is also necessary to ask a question: how will a remote user or machine determine that provisioning has been successfully performed, and establish trust in the TPM? The two most common answers are – via a public key infrastructure, or via an internal database.

5.6.1 Certification: 1.2 TPM keys and PKI

The most common standard for PKI in enterprise environments today, by far, is X.509. X.509 specifies formats for public key certificates, for CSRs, and other key features of any PKI. Unfortunately, 1.2 TPMs were not designed for today's X.509 world, and to use them with a standard enterprise PKI, some adjustments must be made.

The largest problem is that TPM keys – almost all 1.2 keys, and many high-security 2.0 keys – are designed to be used for a single kind of operation. This is a very good thing for security and prevents some easy mistakes that can compromise a key; using the same key for signing and decryption opens up a number of possible attacks with widely used algorithms. Unfortunately, standard X.509 CSRs are self-signed. This does not actually add significantly to the security of the request, it just ensures that the requester actually owns the corresponding private key. However, this means that the only TPM keys suitable for use with a standard X.509 certificate-signing protocol are signing keys. Even 1.2's identity keys can't interact with X.509 properly, despite being used for signing data, since they can sign only data produced inside the TPM and the TPM does not have a 'generate signed CSR' function.[4]

---

[4]Note that this restriction is *not* true for 2.0 restricted signing keys, which can sign user-provided data as long as it does not mimic a TPM data format.

This means that there are two ways to integrate 1.2 TPM keys into most enterprise PKI environments. The first is to extend the enterprise CA software to accept human-approved RSA public keys for signing, rather than a standard self-signed CSR. This is critical for the provisioning stage, when the public key of the EK and any other keys being certified are retrieved in a trusted fashion.

The second, which is recommended even for 2.0 TPMs for enterprises that will be using many TPM keys, is to extend the enterprise CA software to recognize the credentials produced by the TPM, so that keys created after provisioning can be identified in a trustworthy fashion. Again, this is effectively a non-standard CSR format, but with the addition of signature verification against known TPM identity keys and the parsing of the TPM's rather complex certificate signing format (see Section 6.11). The advantage of this approach is that the enterprise PKI maintains the tight bindings between keys and TPM which the TPM's certification support provides.

5.6.2 Certification: the homegrown approach

For some enterprises and small-scale implementations, it's not worth the hassle to try to get TPMs to play nicely with an existing PKI, or there may not be a PKI to integrate with; but you may still want the advantages of being able to verify that a TPM's keys are legitimate. (Remember, in order to use a TPM for any of the attestation or authentication applications we describe in this book, you'll need to be able to verify the signatures.)

In these cases, it is often easier to do one of two things. One is to have your own 'CA' (often just a well-protected signing key) whose sole role is to certify TPM root keys. In this case, rather than needing an entire PKI infrastructure, you need only to be capable of verifying the single 'CA' key against an approved list. The second is to have a trusted database of known TPM keys, which can be queried whenever one wishes to confirm that a key is legitimate. Of course, without a signature from the database confirming that the results have not been tampered with, this second is strictly less secure; but for some purposes, that trade-off of ease versus security is worth making, and some of the commercial TPM products in the marketplace use this approach.

There are, of course, arbitrary variations of these homegrown solutions. For example, an enterprise wishing to certify the known TPM keys of its 20 servers for use by those same servers could produce a single reference file describing all of those keys, stored locally on the server, perhaps signed by an existing software distribution key to ensure its integrity. This is, effectively, creating a local trusted data store; radically different in construction from the database, but identical to it in role. The one key feature that any high-security homegrown solution must provide is trusted, integrity-protected verification that a given public key belongs to a trusted TPM.

Of course, once you have a homegrown solution like this for use with TPM root keys, it can be used equally well for other TPM keys. However, it is important to remember that if you've followed the provisioning processes here, you've taken steps to ensure that the public keys retrieved actually belong to a specific machine's

TPM. When adding new keys post-provisioning, you will need to either bring the computer back into a highly trusted state or implement verification of the TPM's key certification formats (see Section 6.11).

5.7 Provisioning-time key certification user stories

Alice isn't sure that her organization is going to get a full TPM-compatible key certification architecture up and running in time for the planned deployment deadline, so she decides she'd like to create a couple of generically useful keys for each of her users during provisioning. (*I'll cover certification architectures and key creation in the next chapter.*) She creates several keys that will be used to identify the TPM to the rest of SecureCorp's computers. For each key, she follows the same fingerprint and public key verification process she used to establish trust in the EK. That way, there will be several enterprise-trusted keys available for her users immediately. Because the TPM doesn't save these keys internally, she makes sure that they're stored to disk in a location that the users can easily find.

Bob doesn't care about establishing a perfect chain of trust to each TPM – after all, he already trusted the system software to not interfere with his identification of the EK. He creates the three keys (one for signing user data, one for signing TPM data, and one for encrypting user data) he expects his users to need and uploads the keys to his central data server. User software can download them as needed later on, and since they'll only be usable on the TPM that created them, he doesn't even have to worry about secrecy of distribution. The data server creates a daily signed list of trustworthy keys and distributes it to the servers which will need to recognize user machines.

Chapter 6

First steps: TPM keys

6.1 TPM keys

At the core of the TPM's functionality are its keys. All of the TPM's ability to provide authentication, attestation, and data protection services are built around its secure keys. Before you can use the TPM for the vast majority of applications, you'll need to know how to work with its keys.

In this section, I'll discuss just what we mean by 'secure' in more detail, and why TPM keys are both tremendously powerful and sometimes tremendously inconvenient. I'll also discuss the various types of key, how to create them, and how to use them. (I'll go into much more detail about which keys to use when, in later chapters, we discuss various use cases.)

You may be thinking, 'In the provisioning chapter, I just created my root/primary keys; aren't those going to be enough?' The short answer for 1.2 TPMs is: only for a very limited set of applications, mostly having to do with local data storage: the root keys are specialized in order to be maximally secure. For 2.0 TPMs, primary keys can be more flexible, but owing to the limitations of the TPM's internal space, if you're using the TPM for a variety of applications you'll almost certainly want non-primary keys as well. And regardless, you'll still need to know something about how to use TPM keys even if you just use the root or primary keys.

6.1.1 Advantages and disadvantages of TPM keys

TPM keys are designed to be very high-security. They are, with very few exceptions, which we'll be discussing later in this chapter, tightly tied to the hardware. They exist in only two possible states, either in the clear in the TPM's internal key storage, or stored outside the TPM, encrypted with a key that never leaves the TPM. Some TPM keys never leave the TPM's internal storage at all; the root keys are the most prominent examples of such keys, although you can create others. They are also constrained in their use: because vulnerabilities exist or are suspected to exist with certain cryptographic algorithms when the same key is used for both decryption and signing, TPM keys are designed to be difficult or impossible to accidentally reuse. 1.2 TPMs are particularly strict with this, and the vast majority of keys are limited not only to either decryption or signing, but to decrypting or signing specific kinds of data. 2.0 TPMs add a great deal more flexibility in key capability, but at a noticeable cost in complexity, since users design their own custom permissions for a given key rather than picking from a limited set of key types, and must take care not to accidentally introduce a security weakness when doing so.

Because TPM keys are so tightly tied to the hardware, they can be used to identify the hardware; but at the same time, they are completely vulnerable to the loss of that hardware. Data encrypted to a TPM key will become completely unavailable if the machine containing the TPM is stolen, or badly damaged, or the motherboard fails. This is normally advantageous for attestation and authentication applications, where a loss of a machine *should* result in a permanent loss of the key. But it means that data protection with the TPM requires advance preparation to ensure that data is not lost along with the TPM. It also means that certain kinds of hardware failure – failure of the TPM itself, or failure of certain parts of the motherboard – may put the machine in a state where in order for attestation or authentication to be possible the whole motherboard or even the machine must be replaced. Given that authentication and attestation are usually secondary functions intended only to support a primary function being performed more securely, this does introduce an additional, albeit uncommon, potential point of failure.

6.2   The basic types of TPM keys

1.2 TPMs support a small number of key types, but they were widely considered to be both too constrained and highly confusing, with multiple kinds of decryption keys and signing keys usable with different commands and for non-overlapping functions. 2.0 replaced this with a new unified object model, where different key capabilities are simply options selected when creating key objects. In Section 6.2.1, we'll cover the different kinds of keys used in a 1.2 TPM, and the differences between them. In Section 6.2.2, we'll cover the different options used when creating keys in a 2.0 TPM, and how they affect what the key can be used for later.

6.2.1   TPM 1.2 key types

All 1.2 TPM keys are RSA keys, unless you have a very unusual TPM. (The 1.2 standard supports additional algorithms, but does not require them.) Keys are normally 1024 or 2048 bits; the TPM standard allows but does not require support for larger keys, and smaller key sizes are only allowed on non-FIPS-compliant TPMs. Root keys and identity keys are always 2048-bit RSA keys; the size of other keys is chosen by the user when a key is created. In general, if you're concerned enough about security to be using a TPM, you should be using at least 2048-bit RSA keys.

As Table 6.1 makes clear, TPM 1.2 has a clear division not only between signing and decryption keys, but also within both signing and decryption. The signing division is easy to understand: by having a key type that is *only* capable of signing TPM-created data, a verifier can be certain that if such a key is used, the data signed can be trusted as much as the verifier trusts the TPM itself. Although key types do not affect the RSA key itself – an RSA key is an RSA key – they affect both how the TPM will

Table 6.1　The types of keys available in 1.2 TPMs, and what they can (and can't) be used for

Key type	Used for	Additional constraints
Endorsement key	Decryption (Special)	Unique. Usually permanent. Never leaves TPM. Used only to certify AIKs. (See Section 6.11.1.)
Storage	Decryption	Used to encrypt and decrypt small quantities of data for local use. Will not decrypt data not encrypted by the same TPM. The SRK is a storage key.
Binding	Decryption	Used to decrypt data encrypted outside the TPM, or on other machines.
Signing	Signing	Used to sign arbitrary data in one of three formats. (See Section 7.2.3.1.)
Identity (AIK)	Signing	Used to sign data created by the TPM, such as quotes and certifications of other TPM keys.
Legacy	Signing, Decryption	Not constrained like most TPM keys, although not all commands allow their use. FIPS-compliant TPMs cannot create or use them.

use the key and how the TPM will certify the key (see Section 6.11 for more details). This means that the key types are, at least in enterprises which support the TPM's certification mechanisms, entirely remotely verifiable. Thus, we can use signing keys when we are not signing TPM data, and use identity keys for attestation (Chapter 9), certification, and other trusted functionality, confident that the recipient can tell the difference.

The decryption division makes much less sense on the surface: why do we care where data was encrypted in order to decrypt it? We'll discuss this in more detail in Chapter 8, but the short answer is that when the TPM is encrypting data for its own future use, it includes additional information, such as a unique TPM secret identifier and the PCR contents at the time the data was encrypted. In addition, TPM storage keys require that the TPM be used not only for decryption but also for encryption, and prompt for the key's authorization for both operations. This means that if we care about the integrity or origination of data, we can use storage keys and the TPMs internal checking mechanisms to prevent many substitution attacks. Binding keys, in contrast, are intended for what we might call 'simple' decryption operations, where the data is intended to be protected in transit but no trust in the originator is expected to result from the simple decryption. (Binding keys can, of course, be used in conjunction with signing keys to produce a different kind of trustworthy encrypted data!)

Legacy keys, as their name suggests, are intended to support legacy applications which want multipurpose keys, and are not expected to provide the same security support as other TPM keys.

Table 6.2   The different key attribute combinations available in 2.0 TPMs

Sign	Decrypt	Restrict	Use	1.2 Equivalent
1	0	0	Signing user data	Signing
1	0	1	Signing TPM-created data such as quotes and certificates, or TPM-created digests of user-created data that does not mimic TPM data structures.	Identity
0	1	0	Decryption key, usable on anything that doesn't use storage keys (below).	Binding
0	1	1	Storage key, usable on certain TPM-structured objects only, such as sealed data and keys. Used as parent key for other keys.	Storage
1	1	0	General-purpose key suitable for signing and decrypting user data. Cannot be used as a parent key.	Legacy
1	1	1	Not allowed; not FIPS compliant	N/A

6.2.2   TPM 2.0 key attributes

In TPM 2.0, we replace the key typing scheme with three primary attributes: *sign*, *decrypt*, and *restrict*. Keys can have one, two, or all three attributes, in any combination (Table 6.2). Keys with the *sign* attribute can be used to sign data. Keys with the *decrypt* attribute can be used to decrypt data. The *restrict* attribute causes keys to act similarly to the Identity and Storage keys in 1.2: a key with both *restrict* and *sign* will sign only TPM-created data, or user data that can't be mistaken for TPM data, while a key with both *restrict* and *decrypt* can be used only as part of one of the TPM's data-protection hierarchies.

(Technically, these same attributes are used for other TPM objects as well; an encrypted blob, however, has none of them!)

It may be counterintuitive that both restricted and unrestricted keys can sign TPM data or be used in a data-protection hierarchy, but remember, the restrictions here are providing us with additional guarantees about the trustworthiness of the signed or encrypted data in exchange for less flexibility in the use of the key. If those guarantees aren't worth it in a particular use case, the TPM 2.0 designers aren't going to force you to use them.

Note that one of the reasons for not using the same key for both signing and decryption in TPM 1.2 was that reusing the same key for both operations could introduce a security risk. That hasn't changed for TPM 2.0, although using algorithms other than RSA might change the risk profile. For most purposes, we therefore generally recommend using keys for either signing or encryption and not both. However, if you want a single-purpose key that can be used for some special-purpose applications – such as a decryption key capable of creating a standard self-signed X.509 CSR – you may want to consider creating a dual-purpose key and taking advantage of some of the complex authorization options TPM 2.0 provides (see Section 6.13.3).

In addition to the usage attributes, there are a number of other attributes that are selected as part of creating a 2.0 key, for example, whether a key is symmetric or asymmetric and which cryptographic algorithm it uses. These attributes are discussed in detail in Section 6.4.2.3, along with information about how key attributes are set.

6.3 Authorization options for TPM keys

TPM keys, when created, can also be configured to limit their use in ways besides the key type or options described above. In 1.2 TPMs, there are two kinds of additional constraint that can be imposed on a key's use: a secret (password) can be required, or the key can require specific values in the TPM's PCRs (see Section 9.2). In 2.0, a much broader range of authorization options is available, and these options include not only PCR values and passwords but also timers, public keys, and a variety of other mechanisms. These options are set at the key's creation, although passwords can be changed using the 1.2 TPM_ChangeAuth or 2.0 TPM2_ObjectChangeAuth commands, and a 2.0 policy can be created to support signed updates from a trusted party, using the TPM2_PolicyAuthorize policy command. Of course, all of the additional power of the 2.0 authorization model also introduces significant new complexity. The authorization options are covered in detail in Section 6.13.

6.4 Creating TPM keys

6.4.1 Parent keys

TPM keys, regardless of their type, have a *parent* (Figures 6.1 and 6.2).

The parent key is a storage key which is used to encrypt the child key's private data.

The only exceptions to this structure are the SRK in 1.2 TPMs, and primary keys in 2.0 TPMs, which never leave the TPM. Parent keys are important primarily because they are the mechanism by which keys are protected when outside the TPM. The parent is used to encrypt the key's private half, as well as the TPM-specific data structures that cover what the key can be used for and whether it was created by this TPM. When creating a TPM key, you must always select a parent key. If you're not sure what the parent should be, you can always use the SRK or the primary restricted storage key equivalent.[1] Why might you want to use something besides the SRK? There are a number of reasons.

One reason to use distinct parents is to create distinct hierarchies of keys, each with a distinct 'owner'. For example, if I have a machine with multiple users, I might let each user create their own storage key with the password of their choice, and tell them to use that as their own parent key for any additional keys or other objects they wish to create. This provides user-specific security; with software support, it can be used to create a user-specific key store with a single initial login.

[1]because this primary restricted storage key serves the same role in a 2.0 TPM as the SRK did in the 1.2 TPM, we will refer to both keys as the SRK going forward.

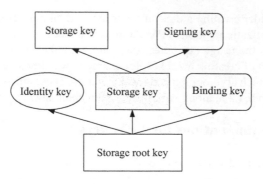

Figure 6.1   A sample hierarchy of keys in a 1.2 TPM. The arrows represent a parent–child relationship. Note that only storage keys can be parents, and identity keys can only have the SRK as a parent. Parent–child hierarchies can be arbitrarily deep

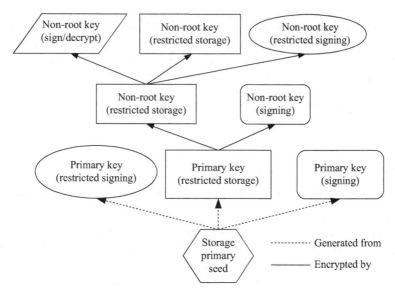

Figure 6.2   An example 2.0 storage hierarchy. The primary keys are generated directly from the protected seed and a template. Restricted storage keys can then be used as parent keys for other, non-root keys

Another is to provide temporal ordering between machine states. Because each TPM key can be set to be used only in certain conditions, having a distinct set of state requirements between a parent key and a child key means that for the child key to be used, its parent's requirements must also have been met previously. The TPM will allow keys to remain in its internal key storage over a reboot only if there were no state requirements on any parent in the hierarchy, so this ordering must have occurred since the last reboot. So if I wanted to verify that a transient trusted state has occurred in the past, I could create a parent key constrained to that transient state, and a child key constrained to the normal operating state. This is particularly useful in combination with Dynamic Roots of Trust for Measurement (DRTMs) (see Section 9.1.3). Keep in mind, however, that the normal concerns about the fragility of TPM keys due to changes in system PCR values over time are magnified when creating key hierarchies with multiple constraints, as a mismatch anywhere in the hierarchy will render the final keys unusable.

Parents are generally static for the life of a key. However, keys can be created which are allowed to change parents; these are called *migratable* keys in 1.2 TPMs and *duplicatable* keys in 2.0 TPMs. We discuss these in Section 6.6.

6.4.2 Key creation commands

6.4.2.1 TPM 1.2

The 1.2 TPM has two main commands for creating keys: TPM_CreateWrapKey and TPM_MakeIdentity.[2] The TPM_MakeIdentity command is used to create identity keys, while TPM_CreateWrapKey is used to create other kinds of keys.

TPM_CreateWrapKey is the one used most frequently, and it takes a wide range of options passed in as part of a TPM_KEY or TPM_KEY12 data structure (Figures 6.3 and 6.4):

- Key type (anything but identity)
- Parent key (a storage key, loaded into the TPM (see Section 6.8) which will be used to encrypt the private portion)
- Key length (512–2048 bits)
- Authorization value (password)
- PCR and locality constraints (limits on the machine state the key can be used in; see Section 6.13.2)
- Migratability (see Section 6.6)
- An encryption or signature scheme
  - The encryption or signature scheme defines in more detail how the TPM will perform the RSA operations. Any given key can be used with only one scheme ever, and that scheme must be specified during creation.
  - Encryption schemes define the padding that will be used to make sure messages are a consistent length before encryption. TPMs offer Public Key Cryptography Standards (PKCS) v1.5 or Optimal Asymmetric Encryption Padding (OAEP). Most TPM keys are allowed to use only OAEP, but Legacy keys (see Section 6.12) may be configured to use the weaker PKCS v1.5 to support backwards compatibility.
  - Signature schemes specify the expected structure of data to be signed: a SHA1 hash (160 bits of arbitrary data), a DER-encoded structure, or a custom TPM

---

[2]The third, TPM_CMK_CreateKey, works similarly to TPM_CreateWrapKey, but will be discussed later in this chapter when I discuss migratable keys, since it has a number of arguments that don't make sense without context.

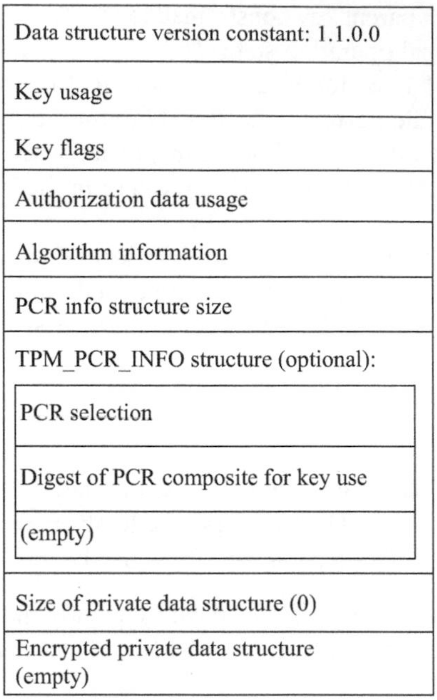

Data structure version constant: 1.1.0.0
Key usage
Key flags
Authorization data usage
Algorithm information
PCR info structure size
TPM_PCR_INFO structure (optional):
PCR selection
Digest of PCR composite for key use
(empty)
Size of private data structure (0)
Encrypted private data structure (empty)

Figure 6.3   A TPM_KEY structure, used by 1.1 and 1.2 TPMs, as passed into the
TPM_CreateWrapKey command. TPM_CreateWrapKey can
take both this structure and the more modern TPM_KEY12. The empty
fields will be filled in by the TPM during key creation. PCR information
in the form of a TPM_PCR_INFO structure should be provided if the
key will have PCR constraints on its use, and not otherwise

INFO data structure. The INFO scheme is not recommended for use. Its original intent was to allow signing keys to sign TPM internal data without allowing user data to be mistaken for TPM internal data, but the structure is flawed and allows a collision attack.[3] Whether SHA1 or DER is preferred depends on the context in which the key will be used; however, it's worth noting that SHA1 is being slowly phased out at the time of this writing, and SHA1 certificates will no longer be accepted by some major vendors starting in 2016.

TPM_CreateWrapKey outputs an RSA key in the TPM's special wrap format, called a ***key blob***. This blob is intended to be passed whole to the TPM, and not deconstructed by the user. They are, fundamentally, a way for the TPM to use the

[3]'SHA-1 Uses in TPM v1.2', Ken Goldman and Stan Potter, 2010.

Constant tag: TPM_TAG_KEY12
Constant filler byte: 0×00
Key usage
Key flags
Authorization data usage
Algorithm information
PCR info structure size
TPM_PCR_INFO_LONG structure:

Constant tag: TPM_TAG_PCR_INFO_LONG
Empty (Locality at key creation)
Locality selection for key use
PCR selection to be measured at creation
PCR selection to be measured on use
Empty (PCR values at key creation)
Digest of PCR values required on use

Encrypted data size (0)
Encrypted data (empty)

Figure 6.4   A TPM_KEY12 data structure as used to create a key. This structure is used both for the TPM_CreateWrapKey command when locality constraints are desired and for the TPM_CMK_CreateKey command. Empty fields will be filled in by the TPM during key creation. The TPM_PCR_INFO_LONG structure is optional, and provided if locality or PCR constraints should be used, or if a particular set of PCRs should be checked on key creation

much larger storage space of the computer's hard drive (or any other storage device) to augment the TPM's tiny internal storage space.

A key blob contains:

- The public portion of the key, in the clear; this can be read from the blob directly if you're willing to delve into the data structure, in addition to being read out by the TPM
- The private half of the key, encrypted with the parent key
- All of the key options described above, encrypted and integrity protected
- Internal data that the TPM uses to identify keys it created and check the key's integrity, encrypted and integrity protected.

Key blobs are *not* stored inside the TPM; if you create a key, you are responsible for making sure it's kept around. However, some TPM software libraries, including all 1.2 TSS implementations, provide an invisible-to-the-user key storage and retrieval mechanism to store the blobs internally, in addition to giving them to the user. Even if your implementation does key management for you, it's always a good idea to keep backups of your key blobs, however, to protect against hard drive failure, data corruption, or other data loss.

TPM_MakeIdentity has far fewer options, since identity keys follow a very standard structure and always use the SRK as the parent key:

- Authorization value (password)
- PCR and locality constraints (limits on the machine state the key can be used in; see Section 6.13.2)
- A label for the key; this is unconstrained and untrusted plain text, and exists solely for the user to conveniently identify the key
- A 20-byte value, intended to be the hash of the public key of the CA which will certify this identity.

Those of you who are familiar with X.509 CSRs may be confused by the CA requirement. The TPM's identity key structure was designed for use with a custom certification protocol, described in more detail in Section 6.11, and the TPM will always create a CSR to go with the new identity key. This CSR is a signed data structure containing the public portion of the identity key plus the digest. If you are not going to be using the TPM's certification protocol, the TPM will still insist on producing this data structure. You will still need to provide this hash, and some software APIs (such as the 1.2 TSS) will require you to provide a full public key of your intended CA. The public portion of any RSA key can be substituted if you are not intending to use the AIK certification protocol.

Just as with TPM_CreateWrapKey, the output of TPM_MakeIdentity is a TPM key blob; the TPM also returns the CSR structure, called an identity binding. If you are planning on ever using the TPM's certification mechanisms for that identity, you should save the identity binding to be sent to the CA; if not, it can be discarded, and the key blob used independently.

6.4.2.2   TPM 2.0: non-primary keys and objects

Primary keys, derived from the seed of a TPM 2.0 hierarchy (Section 3.2.2), are created using the TPM2_CreatePrimary command, as discussed in Section 5.3.3. Other keys and objects are created using the TPM2_Create command. Note that 2.0 does not consider keys and objects to be different: keys are just one kind of object, and the same command is used to create asymmetric keys, symmetric keys, encrypted data, and keyed hashes.

This command takes the handle of a loaded decryption key as the parent, and will require that use of the parent key be authorized. The parent will be used to protect all sensitive data for the object. The command also requires a template, describing the data structure to be created (Figure 6.5); sensitive data, whose contents will vary by what's being created; and a selection of PCRs, whose current value will be incorporated into the returned object's data structure as part of its *creation data*. The creation data is used to allow a verifier to learn about properties of the system at the time the object was created.

Size of public template structure
Public template structure:

	Algorithm
	Hash algorithm used to calculate name
	Object attribute bit array
	Authorization policy digest (optional)
	Parameters (dependent on type)
	Unique identifier (for asymmetric keys, public key)

Figure 6.5   The 2.0 object public template data structure, used with TPM2_
CreatePrimary and TPM2_Create *commands*

The TPM2_Create command returns five objects: the public and encrypted private data for the object, the creation data, a digest of the creation data, and a ticket that can be used with the TPM2_CertifyCreation command later to prove that a given object was created on this TPM.

6.4.2.3   Object templates

The templates provided to both the TPM2_CreatePrimary and TPM2_Create commands are split into public and sensitive data structures. These structures are reused for the TPM_LoadExternal command, to tell the TPM the nature of the object being provided, although not all fields are applicable. Templates include the following (non-comprehensive) information:

The type of the object: as of 2015, a symmetric key (TPM_ALG_SYMCIPHER, an asymmetric key (TPM_ALG_RSA or TPM_ALG_ECC), or an HMAC key/ encrypted data block (TPM_ALG_KeyedHash). The type will be used to determine how other parameters are interpreted, as well as what is created and returned.

The object attributes, including:
- Key use attributes, discussed in Section 6.2.2.
- For keys which can sign data, an optional signature scheme which determines the way signatures are created. Restricted keys are limited to a single scheme which must be defined here, other signing keys may choose dynamically per command.
- Duplicatability (see Section 6.6.3)
- Whether users of the object can authenticate with a policy
- Whether administrative actions (including certification of an object and authorization value changes) can be performed using an authorization value, or if an authorization policy must be used.

A selection of PCRs which will be used to produce a hash of the state of the PCR contents at the time the object was created. This hash will be included in a TPM2B_CREATION_DATA data structure returned by the creation commands.

A hash algorithm that will be used to calculate the object's **name** (see Section 6.9)

For symmetric objects (symmetric keys or keyed hashes), the user can provide the secret data, or choose to have the TPM generate it.

If an Enhanced Authorization policy (see Section 6.13.3) is to be used to authorize this object, the policy hash is included.

A full list of object attributes and how to set them can be found in sections 12 and 8 of the TPM 2.0 Structures specification and section 26 of the TPM 2.0 Architecture specification (see Section 11.6.2 for where to find these and how to use them).

There are standard template definitions for endorsement hierarchy primary keys, since manufacturers are expected to create and certify keys that users then recreate. For more information about where to find these, see Section 11.6.3. The full definition of template contents can be found in chapter 27 of the TPM 2.0 Architecture specification; see Section 11.6.2.

The TSS2 FAPI provides a limited set of key types which include precreated templates. See Section 6.16 for the full list.

6.4.2.4   Creation data

When a key or other object is created in 2.0 TPMs, a data structure is returned that describes the environment in which the object was created. This includes a hash of the PCR values, based on the selection in the template; the locality; information about the parent, or the seed if the object is a primary object; and data provided by the caller, which is intended to be used to provide locally meaningful information about the object, such as a name. This data is intended to provide a meaningful history of an object, although it is important to note that for duplicatable objects (which may move between systems with very different configurations), the creation data provides little information about the possible history of the object.

6.5   Key creation user stories

Alice is going to allow her users to create their own keys depending on the applications they use, but wants to make sure each machine has a minimum set of functionalities to interact with the corporate infrastructure. In particular, she wants to make sure that each user is capable of creating quotes so that SecureCorp can start monitoring machine state, and of certifying new keys that are created later. Since both of these require trustworthy signing of TPM-created data, Alice makes sure each 1.2 TPM has an identity key and each 2.0 TPM has a restricted signing key. She also wants to make sure that SecureCorp can securely distribute proprietary software to each user, so she issues each user a key capable of decrypting externally-created data: a binding key on the 1.2 TPMs, and a non-restricted RSA decryption key on the 2.0 TPMs. She makes sure all of these keys are stored on disk in a well-known location.

Bob needs to make sure his users have the keys required for his enterprise applications, but as with the rest of his setup, he doesn't want users to do anything that might get them (and thus his help desk) into trouble. The applications he wants to support are full-disk encryption, quotes, and data signing. For full-disk encryption, he uses a storage key for 1.2 TPMs, since the data is being used only on the system and Bob would like some of the other storage key features, and a non-restricted RSA decryption key for 2.0 TPMs, since he will be using it to protect non-TPM data in the form of the disk's bulk encryption keys. For quotes, he creates an identity key for the 1.2 TPMs, and a restricted signing key for the 2.0 TPMs. The restricted signing key will be sufficient for his data-signing use cases, since he's not trying to create anything that mimics a TPM's data structures and doesn't mind having the signing operation use the TPM to create digests of signed files, but he also needs to create a signing key on his 1.2 TPMs to support signatures of non-TPM data.

Charlie has simple needs: he wants to be able to encrypt his local browser keystore and password vault, and he'd like to experiment with using the TPM to sign e-mail. He creates a binding key, even though he could use a storage key for his local data, so he can also give the public key to his friends and have them send him data securely, and a signing key for signing e-mail.

Dana creates three keys for each of her users. One is a non-restricted decryption key, because customers will need to routinely ship the accountants sensitive financial information. Dana chooses an RSA key, because it's widely used and asymmetric, so the customers won't need to share any secrets. Dana also creates a non-restricted RSA signing key, which will be used to sign documents to prove their authenticity. Dana wants to use some of the TPM's audit features as part of the company's data tracking, which will require the ability to securely sign TPM data, so a restricted RSA signing key is also created. Dana creates all of these keys in the storage hierarchy, so that they can easily be erased later without affecting Dana's ability to identify the machine.

6.6 Migratable and duplicatable keys

Of course, sometimes we don't want our keys to be locked to a single TPM. The most common reason for this is for backup; if a machine is lost, damaged, or just getting old, most enterprises don't want to lose all of the data associated with it as well. The flip side of the power of TPM keys is that they are very vulnerable to machine loss. Migratable and duplicatable keys exist to fill the gap.

1.2 uses migratable keys, which come in two types: normal migratable keys, and certified migratable keys. 2.0 has duplicatable keys.

6.6.1 1.2 Normal migratable keys

Most kinds of 1.2 TPM key can be created with the `migratable` flag set.[4] This means that the key is migratable, and with the use of the TPM's key migration commands can be packaged into a special migration key blob: one encrypted by a key *not* inside that TPM, instead of the key's original parent. Migratable keys can be encrypted to any RSA key provided by the user; although the documentation often assumes that keys will be migrated to another TPM, the user can choose any key they like. Note

---

[4]The exceptions are the SRK, identity keys, and keys which will be used for sealing data (see Section 8.4.1).

that the key can still be loaded into the original TPM using the original key blob: the TPM does not track whether or not a key has been migrated.

This is a powerful feature in many ways, particularly for data storage. TPM-encrypted data which uses a migratable storage key can store an extra backup copy off-system, which can be decrypted by a central corporate recovery key, or by an individual user with a key stored on a USB stick in a safe. Signing keys migrated to multiple servers' TPMs can allow the group to share a cryptographic identity, while still ensuring that keys always have hardware-based protection.

However, this can also be a very dangerous feature. A migratable key cannot be used for machine authentication or attestation, because it is no longer exclusively bound to the TPM it was created in. An external party never knows for sure whether a key has been copied, and whether copies were sent to trustworthy devices or straight to an adversary.

There are a few exceptions to the blanket ban on authentication or attestation with a migratable key. One would be the aforementioned group-authentication scheme; however, in that case, the person doing the authentication is required to trust not only the TPM but the owner's key management capabilities, secure password, and good intentions. Such scenarios are often feasible for internal enterprise environments, especially on a smaller scale, but become less suitable when external entities are involved, and they do involve noticeably more risk. An untrustworthy TPM owner, or anyone who manages to gain access to the owner's password for even a short period of time, can freely export the private data for any migratable key. While that's not a trivial protection, especially since TPMs come with dictionary attack protection, it's also much weaker than the TPM's normal guarantee that the private half of a key will never exist in the clear.

Because of these weaknesses, migratable keys cannot be certified using the TPM's standard certification mechanisms (see Section 6.11), in order to prevent an external party from mistaking a migratable key for one subject to all of a TPM's protections.

6.6.1.1   How basic key migration works

The migration process begins with the TPM owner using the `TPM_Authorize MigrationKey` command to authorize a public key as a migration destination. This can happen at any point prior to migration; the command produces a migration key authorization blob that can be used and reused later.

The `TPM_CreateMigrationBlob` command is used to migrate a specific migratable key. It requires the authorization of the migratable key's parent, since that key will be used to decrypt private data, as well as the authorization for the key itself. The command also takes a migration destination key, along with the previously created authorization blob for that destination. The result is a special migration blob data structure, which contains the original key data encrypted to the destination key.

On the receiving machine, the `TPM_ConvertMigrationBlob` command is used to retrieve the key and turn it back into the private half of a standard TPM wrap key blob format for the new TPM, which is returned. The migration destination key becomes the new parent key (Figure 6.6). Note that this only migrates the private half, including all of the sensitive data, such as private key data and authorization values.

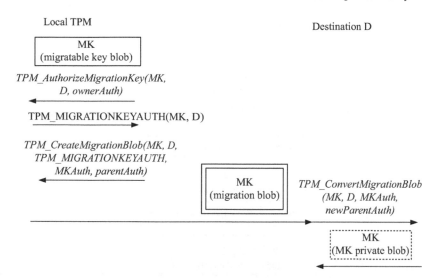

Figure 6.6   The migration process for standard migratable TPM keys. Arguments have been abstracted to make the process easier to understand; the distinction between public keys and key blobs, for example, is not being made here

The rest of the `TPM_KEY` data structure, which contains no sensitive data, must be migrated separately and reconstructed by including the newly created private data (Figure 6.7). The private data contains the TPM's integrity protection on the public data, so mistakes in the reconstruction process may result in errors but will not result in any changes to the security of the key.

6.6.1.2   Rewrapping migratable keys

Migratable keys can be rewrapped, causing their old parent key to be replaced with a new one on the same TPM. This uses the same `TPM_CreateMigrationBlob` command as any other migration, but is done locally and thus skips straight to a new wrap key blob instead of going through a migration blob and the `TPM_ConvertMigrationBlob` recovery. Because the original key blob still exists and will still be accepted, this technique allows the same child to be accessed with different parent keys (Figure 6.8). Although not a commonly desired feature, this can be used to make a resource available in multiple distinct PCR states, for example, or allow the use of multiple passwords to access the same resource, while still requiring the child key to be used only once to encrypt the resource. This is the only way a 1.2 TPM key can be made to behave at all like a 2.0 TPM key with an Enhanced Authorization policy (Section 6.13.3), although the parallel is far from perfect: there is a distinct key blob used for each access variation, rather than a single blob with multiple authorization options, and the permission checks are made on load of the child key rather than on its use. Enforcing multiple conditions on use would require

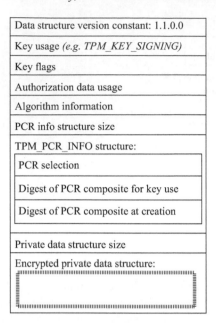

Figure 6.7   The basic structure of a TPM_KEY *data structure as returned by the TPM. The encrypted data structure highlighted at the bottom is what is returned by the* TPM_ConvertMigrationBlob *command; the remainder of the structure, which is readable from the original key blob, must be reconstructed. Note that this is exactly the same data structure as was created originally for use with the* TPM_CreateWrapKey *command, but with some additional data (such as PCR data at creation) filled in. This is only one example of a* TPM_KEY; *some use the* TPM_PCR_INFO_LONG *data structure instead of the basic* TPM_PCR_INFO *structure*

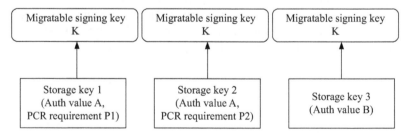

Figure 6.8   An example of a single migratable key which has been rewrapped to have multiple parents. The same key can now be loaded under three different conditions: if authorization value A is presented while the PCRs are in state P1; if authorization value A is presented while the PCRs are in state P2; or if authorization value B is presented. Note that once loaded, no authorization or PCR requirements are imposed on any signature K is used for

reliably unloading the key after each use, which may not be possible with all TPM support libraries.[5]

6.6.2   1.2 Certifiable Migration Keys

Certifiable Migration Keys (CMKs) are designed to provide much of the flexibility of migratable keys while still providing external parties with the ability to trust the key. Unsurprisingly, they are also more complicated.

CMKs are created with an extra piece of associated information: a Migration Authority's public key. When a CMK is migrated, it is never encrypted directly to an arbitrary destination key; instead, it is encrypted to the migration authority, which determines whether or not the final destination is trustworthy enough, and if so, will re-encrypt the key and send it on.[6] When the TPM certifies a CMK, the certificate includes the Migration Authority's public key, allowing a recipient to base their trust in the CMK on their trust in the Migration Authority, rather than on the original TPM's owner and TPM owner's security.

CMKs are not created with the usual TPM_CreateWrapKey command; instead, they are created with TPM_CMK_CreateKey, which works almost identically, with one major exception. A CMK is always created with a trusted Migration Authority which can approve its future migration. The Migration Authority must be owner-approved; the TPM_CMK_ApproveMA command, which requires owner authorization, is used to approve a public key or set of public keys as a Migration Authority. A CMK can be used as a normal key while on a system.

There are two distinct processes used to migrate a CMK. One is to migrate the key to the Migration Authority (MA) (Figure 6.9); the other is to have the Migration Authority approve the migration of the key to a third, destination machine (Figure 6.10). Migration, in either case, requires the approval of both the TPM owner and the key owner, as well as permission to use the parent key (since the parent is used to decrypt the CMK's private data).

To migrate a CMK directly to the MA, the TPM owner uses the TPM_AuthorizeMigrationKey command to create a TPM_MIGRATIONKEYAUTH structure which indicates the destination key. This is then handed to the key owner, who uses the TPM_CMK_CreateBlob command to create a certified migration blob. The migration blob contains the key contents, encrypted to the destination key. Blob creation will fail if the destination key is not one of the MA keys established when the CA was created. The TPM_CMK_ConvertMigration command is used to turn a certified migration blob back into a normal TPM key blob. This command also verifies that migration was approved by one of the migration authorities indicated in the CMK itself. Approval is shown by passing in two additional data structures.

---

[5]A library, such as a 1.2 TSS implementation, which does key management for you, may maintain the TPM key state in a way that is not what the user expects.

[6]Technically, it is also possible for a migration authority to preemptively issue a ticket approving the migration of a given key to a particular destination, but that's just a time-shifted version of the same decision process.

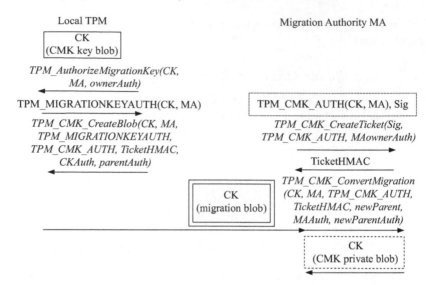

*Figure 6.9   The process of migrating a Certified Migratable Key (CMK) in the
scenario where the migration destination is also the Migration
Authority (MA). The arguments to the commands are abstracted here to
save space, but the important data is included. The TPM owner, CMK,
and CMK parent authorizations must all be used to approve the
transaction on the originating TPM. The owner, MA, and new parent
authorizations must all approve the import on the receiving end. Before
and after being migrated, the CMK can be used as a normal TPM key
blob. The MA must have been approved by the owner when the CMK
was first created, although a key can be created with multiple approved
MA options*

The first is a `TPM_CMK_AUTH` data structure, which contains digests of the MA
public key, destination public key, and CMK public key. The second is a ticket produced by the destination TPM using the `TPM_CMK_CreateTicket` command,
which verifies the `TPM_CMK_AUTH` data structure against the matching signature
from the MA.

Migrating a CMK to a third destination machine entails the same operations in
a slightly different order: the owner still uses `TPM_AuthorizeMigrationKey`
to authorize the migration and create a `TPM_MIGRATIONKEYAUTH` structure, but
before the key owner can create the blob, the migration authority must create the
`TPM_CMK_AUTH` structure which will verify the key's destination. The TPM owner
authorizes this approval structure using the `TPM_CMK_CreateTicket` command,
which verifies the MA's signature. The resulting ticket, the `TPM_CMK_AUTH`, and
the `TPM_MIGRATIONKEYAUTH` are passed to the `TPM_CMK_CreateBlob` command; together, they prove that the TPM owner has approved the key's migration, the
MA has approved a destination, and the TPM owner has confirmed the MA's signature

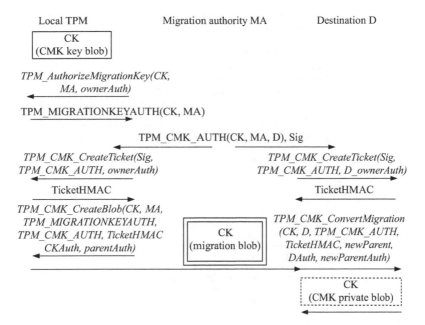

Figure 6.10   The process of migrating a Certified Migratable Key in the scenario where the destination is not the Migration Authority. Here, the Migration Authority must approve the transfer of the key to the new destination before the key blob can be created, and the owners on both the local and destination system must verify the Migration Authority's approval. The arguments are again abstracted to make the general shape of the interaction easier to follow

and choice of destination. Since the `TPM_CMK_CreateBlob` command requires the approval of the key owner, all parties involved have approved the migration process and destination. The resulting certified migration blob is sent to the destination, which performs the same `TPM_CMK_CreateTicket` approval of the MA's authorization and then runs `TPM_CMK_ConvertMigration` to turn the migration blob into a standard wrapped key blob.

It is important to note that although the instructions above, like the TPM specification, assume that the destination will be a TPM, there's no actual requirement that this be the case. Software which can mimic the TPM's decryption process can be a legitimate destination for either kind of migration operation, as long as the machine running the software and holding the key is trusted by the Migration Authority. This is particularly relevant in cases where the destination is highly trusted for other reasons, for example, if the destination is a corporate data recovery key which is kept in a safe with strict procedures imposed for its use. Because third parties which trust the Migration Authority will also trust the CMK, it is important that the migration authority not approve migration to untrusted destinations.

Constant tag: TPM_TAG_CERTIFY_INFO2		
Constant filler byte: 0×00		
Data structure version constant: 1.1.0.0		
Key usage *(e.g. TPM_KEY_SIGNING)*		
Key flags		
Authorization data usage		
Algorithm information		
Public key digest		
Nonce		
Boolean indicating if any parent keys are PCR-constrained		
PCR info structure size		
TPM_PCR_INFO_SHORT structure:		
	PCR selection	
	Locality selection for key use	
	Digest of PCR composite for key use	
Migration authority size		
Migration authority digest (if any)		

Figure 6.11   *The* TPM_CERTIFY_INFO2 *data structure contains the essential public information needed for a remote party to establish trust in a 1.2 TPM key, including any migration authorities. The nonce field can be used to prove freshness, allowing a verifier to confirm that a certifiable migratable key is present on a particular machine at the current time. Note that these structures cannot be used to certify normal migratable keys, which have no migration authority and thus no way for a verifier to establish trust in a future migration policy*

Migration does not make the original key blob unusable, although some systems may implement additional protocols in software to delete all copies of a key blob once migration has occurred if there is a need to make a key unique.

CMKs are certified using the TPM_CertifyKey2 command, which for this purpose takes a migration authority digest (the same one the owner used with the TPM_CMK_ApproveMA command, back when the CMK was created) which will be verified against the key's internal structure. The TPM_CERTIFY_INFO2 structure returned by this command will incorporate the migration authority information, allowing a remote party to verify both that this is a CMK and whether they trust the migration authority in question (Figure 6.11).

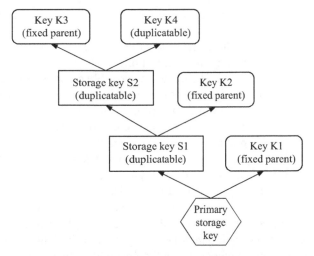

Figure 6.12   A key hierarchy with a number of duplicatable keys in it. Only key K1
and the primary storage key cannot be duplicated (migrated) to
another machine, which also means they're the only keys which have
the `fixedTPM` *flag set. If S1 is duplicated, S2, K2, K3, and K4 will*
also be loadable on the new machine. If S2 is migrated, K3 and K4
can be used on the new machine. K3 cannot be duplicated directly,
however

6.6.3   2.0 Duplicatable keys

Keys and other objects[7] in 2.0 TPMs, both primary and non-primary, can be created
to be duplicatable. Duplication works much like migration in 1.2 TPMs – duplication
is actually a more accurate term than migration, since keys remain available on the
original system even after they've been migrated – but has a different authorization
model, and entire families of keys can be effectively migrated by duplicating the
parent key (Figure 6.12).

Keys in 2.0 have two different flags related to migratability. The `fixedParent`
flag in the object template determines whether this particular object is required to have
the same parent key for its entire existence, or if the parent can be changed. If the
`fixedParent` flag is not set, then an object can be duplicated. The `fixedTPM`
flag indicates whether this object or any parent object can be duplicated; because
2.0 allows objects whose parents are loaded into a TPM to be used by that TPM
regardless of the location where the objects were created, duplicating a storage key
used as a parent will automatically let any of its children be moved to the new location.
These flags must be set in conjunction: the `fixedTPM` flag is really the result of a
calculation based on `fixedParent` and the `fixedTPM` flag of the parent of an

---

[7] For the rest of this section, I'll just refer to 'keys', but the same principles apply to keyed hashes and other
TPM data objects.

object. This means that 'non-migratable' in a 2.0 context really means a key with the `fixedTPM` flag set.

Any key that is itself duplicatable – a key that does not have the `fixedParent` flag set – is required to have a duplication policy, which is used to authorize the `TPM2_Duplicate` command. There are four possible outcomes of this command. One uses a symmetric cipher to encrypt the private portion of the object before the asymmetric parent key is used to encrypt it, producing a two-layered encryption. This approach can use either a user-created symmetric key, or one created by the TPM for this object. The second approach uses only the asymmetric parent key to encrypt the private data. The third approach uses only the symmetric key, and a null parent key. The fourth uses no symmetric key and a null parent key, and will in fact retrieve the TPM structure, including any secret data in the clear; as such, it is almost never the right choice. It is important to note that the null parent key option is not available for all keys: when a duplicatable object is created, the `encryptedDuplication` flag determines whether or not null parent keys may be used in duplicating that object, and security-minded key creators will want to ensure that the flag is set.

Because duplication can result in a key being removed from the TPM to an untrusted parent, or even in the clear, it is very important that the duplication policy for any duplicatable keys be set with care. Authorization values alone cannot be used to authorize duplication. A policy session (see Section 6.13.3) must be used, and the policy context must explicitly indicate that the duplication command is being run using the `TPM2_PolicyDuplicationSelect` policy assertion. Because child keys do not need to be explicitly duplicated, it is also important to make sure that all keys are created with a non-duplicatable parent, unless explicitly desired otherwise. However, for certain contexts (such as data backup), the ability to make all of a user's data storage descend from a single duplicatable parent, which can then be duplicated to a trusted recovery system, and then use ordinary backup methods for all of the child keys and encrypted data, is quite powerful.

Once a key has been duplicated, it can be sent to its new destination. If the destination is a TPM, the `TPM2_Import` command is used to decrypt the results and turn them into a traditional TPM encrypted object structure which can be loaded using its new parent.

There is no direct parallel to CMKs for duplicatable keys; a key is either duplicatable or not, and any duplicatable key can be certified, like any other loaded TPM object, with `TPM2_Certify`. The remotely verifiable trust that migration authorities provided for CMKs isn't entirely absent, however. Enhanced Authorization policies (see Section 6.13.3) can be used to create a similar effect using the `TPM2_PolicyDuplicationSelect` policy command, which selects a new parent to which a key can be duplicated. This can be combined with the `TPM2_PolicyAuthorize` command, which allows a trusted party's public key to authorize other policies. Together, these create an explicit migration authority effect, in which the migration authority is defined as part of the key's authorization policy but the migration destination can change. Since authorization policies must be used for duplication regardless, the additional overhead of setting up a migration authority or fixed destination is not significant.

6.6.4 When to use migratable or duplicatable keys

Use a migratable or duplicatable key when:

- Ability to back up the key or data is your top priority
- You want copies of a key, and don't care about other people trusting it
- You want to use the TPM's key generation capabilities, but want the key itself to be used by software.[8]

Use a certified migratable key or a duplication key with a verifiable destination or authority policy when:

- You need a key to be used by multiple machines while still being trusted by third parties
- You have a central authority third parties will trust to approve key migration
- You want to be able to trace every place a key has migrated to, and you trust the Migration Authority to keep a log.

Never use a migratable or duplicatable key when:

- You will be using the key to identify a single machine (see Chapters 7 and 9)
- You need an absolute guarantee that the key will always be protected by a TPM
- You or some third party need to trust the key's security and you do not have a trustworthy migration authority
- You have no infrastructure in place to identify other TPMs which would be safe targets for migration, and want hardware protection guarantees.

6.7 Migratable key user stories

Charlie wants to make sure that he can access his password vault and key storage even if the original machine is lost or damaged. He creates a migratable binding key, and migrates it to a second machine, also with a TPM. Whenever he stores his data, he will encrypt it (using the `TSS_Bind` command or an equivalent) to both his local binding key and the migratable one on his backup machine. Charlie, being the cautious type, also migrates the migratable key to a second destination; this one isn't a TPM at all, but is instead a trusted key he keeps on a USB drive in a fire safe. That migration blob, which is useless without the USB stick, is stored along with his normal backups.

Elaine is running Example, Inc.'s distributed server farm, which has been provisioned with 1.2 TPMs. While each machine has its own TPM and its own unique identity, she would like to have a shared cryptographic identity that all of the machines can use in order to hide the behind-the-scenes load-balancing process from users. She

---

[8]This is a very uncommon case, but software will be much faster than the TPM, while many software libraries have questionable sources of randomness to use when generating keys. The TPM can also be used to directly generate random bits, but it may be easier for some people to simply create and extract a migratable key, especially if using a library whose source they do not have access to.

wants to make sure that her users can trust the server key to be secure, so she creates a signing CMK with a migration authority of a trusted corporate key she controls. She uses the migration authority to authorize the migration of this CMK to each machine in the server farm, with a unique non-migratable storage key on each machine acting as the final migration destination. She then certifies the CMK, knowing that users who trust the migration authority can trust that the keys will be migrated only to new servers belonging to the corporation.

6.8   Loading TPM keys

Creating a TPM key is not sufficient to be able to use it straightaway, with the sole exception of root and primary keys. As discussed previously, when a user creates a standard TPM key, the TPM creates the key and then returns a key blob containing encrypted key material. The TPM does *not* store a copy of the key inside the TPM for later use! It has too little storage to do that. Instead, when we wish to use a TPM key we have created, or certain keys created outside of this TPM (see Sections 6.6 and 6.12) we will have to *load* the key into the TPM for use.

Loading is, at its heart, a straightforward operation: a key blob is provided to the TPM, the TPM decrypts the encrypted material, and a handle is provided back to the user so that the key can be used in later commands. However, there are a few minor complexities.

The first complexity is the parent key. Previously, we discussed how each non-root key has a parent, which is a storage key used to encrypt its private half and other TPM internal data. So in order to load a TPM key, you not only need to provide the TPM with the key blob for the key you're loading, but also the handle of the parent key, which needs to already be loaded.[9]

The second complexity, which is related to the first and is the source of most of the confusion novice users have with key loading, has to do with authentication values and key constraints. When a key is loaded, you do *not* test the key constraints – I can freely load a key whose password I don't know, for example. However, you *do* test the constraints of the *parent* key. That's because the key constraints described in Section 6.13.2 are *usage* constraints, not loading constraints; they will be tested every time the private half of the key is required for an operation.[10] When loading a key, the private key actually in use is the parent key, which is performing a decryption option. Thus, it is the parent key's constraints that need to be met, not the loaded key. This is why state dependency chains can be created using a sequence of parent and child keys. The parent key's constraints are met when the child is loaded, and later when the child is used the child key's constraints are met.

The third complexity is very straightforward: TPMs are small and have a limited amount of space for loaded keys. If the TPM runs out of space and someone attempts

---

[9]One reason to use the SRK as the parent key is for convenience; the SRK is always loaded.

[10]And in a few special cases when the public half is used but the key needs to be loaded, such as for the 1.2 Seal command; you can generally tell because the operation will require the authorization value of the key.

to load a new key, it will fail until one of the existing loaded keys has been evicted. Users of high-level software may get different behaviour, however: depending on the supporting software infrastructure, an error might be returned, the key which has been used least recently might be automatically evicted, or the software might seamlessly swap keys in and out behind the scenes.

It is possible to take a loaded key and set it to be held in the TPM's internal memory so that only the TPM or hierarchy owner can evict it; instructions for how to do this can be found in Section 10.6.

6.8.1 Additional loading features in 2.0

In 1.2 TPMs, only complete keys can be loaded into the TPM, and there are a number of constraints on those keys. In general, the TPM only expects to load keys it creates itself, or which are explicitly migrated to the TPM. In 2.0 TPMs, other objects can also be loaded using the TPM2_LoadExternal command. The most common kind of other object to be loaded is a public key. In this case, the TPM does not have a private half for the key, but loads the public key internally and provides a handle to refer to it just like any other key. This allows the 2.0 TPM to perform a variety of cryptographic operations targeting a remote key. External objects are loaded into a hierarchy, and will then be affected by any changes to that hierarchy (most notably, if a hierarchy is disabled or cleared); however, a null hierarchy (TPM_RH_NULL) can be used for transient[11] objects.

External objects that are to be loaded into a TPM must still correspond to TPM-recognizable objects, and use the same data structures as objects the TPM creates.

6.9   Handles, names, and authorization: using TPM keys in other commands

The output of the key loading operation (TPM_LoadKey2 or TPM2_Load[12]) is a *handle*: the index of a location in the TPM's memory where the key (or other resource) is stored, and which can be provided as an argument to other commands. TPM 2.0 also introduces the concept of a *name*, which is used instead of the handle when determining whether authorization has succeeded. Names are unique identifiers for an object, and are simply the hash of the object's public structure.

6.9.1   Key handles and security

It's worth noting that the key handle, most relevantly in 1.2, is not included in the TPM's session integrity protections. (See Section 6.10; this is to allow intermediary software such as drivers or the software stack to perform swapping of keys behind the scenes in order to present a seamless 'all keys are always available' interface to the user). One common question is whether this presents a security risk: after all, if

---

[11]All loaded objects in the null hierarchy are cleared on every reboot.
[12]As well as TPM2_LoadExternal, which loads just a public key rather than both public and private halves.

an adversary could change a command to use a different key, couldn't they unlock data to the user wanted protected? The short answer is 'Only in 1.2, not very often, and it's very easy to protect against'. (2.0 introduces a new feature, the object name, which is used to uniquely identify objects even when handles may change.)

First and foremost, these attacks are often fairly easy to detect; if the wrong key is being used on a signing or encryption operation, then verification or decryption should fail or produce nonsense output. Secondly, *only* the key handles are swappable; an adversary cannot cause me to decrypt different data than I was intending to decrypt, or sign data I didn't mean to sign, just to use a different key when doing it. Thirdly, even if the key handle itself is different, all of the authentication data provided along with the key is still integrity-protected; that means that this trick will only work if the keys being swapped have the same password (or lack thereof).

In short, if you're worried about this feature being misused, the only thing you have to do to keep this kind of attack from being successful is to not reuse passwords between your keys.

6.9.2   Pre-defined handles

Some handles always point to the same locations. In particular, root keys have pre-defined handles, so that users can always find them even though the handles are never returned by a command. To make the SRK the parent of a key, for example, you will use its key handle as the parent key handle. Table 6.3 presents some of the most useful handles.

Table 6.3   The pre-defined handle values for various useful TPM resources

1.2 Handles		
Resource	**Name**	**Handle**
Storage Root Key	TPM_KH_SRK	0x40000000
Public Endorsement Key[a]	TPM_KH_EK	0x40000006
TPM Owner	TPM_KH_OWNER	0x40000001
2.0 Handles		
Resource	**Name**	**Handle**
Storage Primary Seed, Owner Auth, Policy	TPM_RH_OWNER	0x40000001
Endorsement Primary Seed, Storage Auth, Policy	TPM_RH_ENDORSEMENT	0x4000000B
Platform Primary Seed, Privacy Auth, Policy	TPM_RH_PLATFORM	0x4000000C
Lockout Authorization	TPM_RH_LOCKOUT	0x4000000A
Null Hierarchy, Empty Auth, Empty Policy	TPM_RH_NULL	0x40000007

[a]While highly useful, this is only accessible using the TPM_OwnerReadInternalPub command.

6.10   Authorization sessions

For the vast majority of users, authorization sessions are something you shouldn't need to worry about. These sessions are among the first TPM functions any software library will implement to make a user's life easier, since they are used to establish secure communications with the TPM rather than to perform the kind of functions a user cares about, but require a lot of detailed calculations and session management to perform correctly. I won't be discussing them in detail here, just providing enough of a sketch to give interested users implementing low-level software context for their research. If you don't need to maintain your own authorization sessions, and aren't interested just for the sake of learning more about how the TPM works, you probably want to move straight on to the next section.

1.2 TPMs support two different authorization session types, which create nonce data that can be used to protect authorization data secrets and create session HMACs. (Authorization sessions are distinct from transport sessions, which provide integrity-protected channels between the TPM and other entities such as user software or even a remote network communications partner. They are often used in combination.) The Object-Independent Authorization Protocol, established with TPM_OIAP, allows many commands to be run from the same authorization session, using only a single setup command. OIAP allows the session to be used with many different TPM keys and other entities requiring authorization information, but requires that the authorization data be presented for each command. The Object Specific Authorization Protocol, established with TPM_OSAP, establishes a per-entity authorization session; authorization data needs to be presented only once, and can be used many times, as long as only that entity (such as a key or data blob) is being accessed. Each entity used requires a distinct authorization session. For details, refer to section 13 of the TPM 1.2 Design Principles specification and section 18 of the TPM 1.2 Commands specification (see Section 11.5.2 for where to find and how to use these). For those interested in using transport sessions, the TPM_Establish Transport, TPM_ExecuteTransport, and TPM_ReleaseTransport Signed commands are described in section 24 of the TPM 1.2 Commands specification.

2.0 TPMs integrate authorization sessions more deeply with functionality owing to the nature of Enhanced Authorization policies, where any user-created policy must begin with a default value that is tightly integrated with the TPM's authorization session architecture. The TPM2_StartAuthSession command is used to establish an authorization session, either with an HMAC or an EA policy. It creates a shared secret session key used to communicate with the TPM; an encrypted salt value (encrypted to some loaded TPM decryption key) or the authorization value of some loaded TPM object (called *bind* because this kind of session is considered bound to the object in question) or both can be provided to add entropy to the secret. (Adding entropy is always recommended, unless using the command to create a target policy that will be used to later authorize an object, as described in Section 6.13.3. Because the session key of one of these trial sessions is never used, there is no advantage to creating a secure value.) The command also takes a caller-provided nonce, the session type (`TPM_SE_POLICY` for a policy authorization session, `TPM_SE_HMAC` for an encrypted authorization value session (the default password option, used whenever we discuss authorization values), or `TPM_SE_TRIAL` for a trial session used to create a target policy for use in an object), a symmetric algorithm and key size to be used to encrypt parameters in this session, and a hash algorithm that will be used to create HMACs. The command returns the session handle, which will be used extensively in other commands, and a TPM-generated nonce which is used by the recipient to create the shared key for the authorization session. Details of key creation, HMACs, and related session topics can be found in section 19 of the TPM 2.0 Architecture specification (see Section 11.6.2).

6.11   Certifying TPM keys

One of the most powerful and underutilized features of TPMs is their ability to self-certify keys. Once you've established trust in a single TPM key, you can bootstrap to trusting other TPM keys, because the TPM itself will provide you with all of the information you need to establish that trust (Figure 6.13).

The basic principle is very simple: TPMs can recognize keys they created from part of the encrypted internal key blob data we mentioned back in Section 6.4. A TPM will issue a certificate only for a key that it created, and which is guaranteed to be

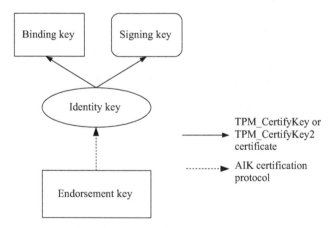

Figure 6.13   The trust hierarchy for 1.2 key certification. Identity keys are trusted because we use the AIK certification protocol to establish a pseudonymous binding between the identity key and the EK. The identity key can then be used to establish trust in other TPM keys directly using one of the key certification commands. A system can have one identity key or many; they serve as different pseudonyms for the TPM, and different use cases need different numbers

protected by the TPM at all times.[13] If you can confirm that a certificate came from a TPM that you trust, you can therefore also trust that the certificate describes a key created by and protected by that TPM.

TPM certificates are also useful in that they provide additional information about how the TPM is guaranteed to use the key. For 1.2, this is the key type, such as signing or binding, as well as the PCR and locality constraints (Section 6.13.2); for 2.0, this covers extended authorization as well as the key attributes. This means that a verifier can know not only that a key belongs to a given TPM and thus a given machine, but also, say, that it can be used only if the machine is in a specific PCR configuration, or when a particular CPU mode is active.

Of course, this scheme works only if you can confirm that a certificate was not only signed by a TPM key, but also generated by the TPM itself. This is the primary reason that 1.2's identity keys and 2.0's *restrict* attribute exist: these keys will sign data that originates in the TPM, but can never be used to sign user data that could be mistaken for a TPM structure. A TPM will never generate a certificate for a key that doesn't pass all of its internal checks, nor can any of the TPM's other internal data structures be mistaken for a certificate, so if a certificate is signed by an identity key or restricted key, we know that the certificate represents that TPM's guarantees about a given key.

The downside of the TPM's lovely self-certification architecture is that it was created in a vacuum, and does not necessarily fit well with how the rest of the world expects certificates to be generated. In most of the world's PKIs, there are CAs who are trusted when they sign any certificate, and there are clients, who can sign anything except certificates. TPMs fall into a funny middle ground: they can sign certificates for their own keys, but they're not general-purpose CAs. At the same time, they are issuing certificates, and those certificates should be trustworthy. And because CAs are highly trusted, they're normally extremely limited in number and highly restricted; no one would want to give every single laptop in a giant enterprise general-purpose certification authority, no matter how much you trust the hardware holding the key! This means that even if you can arrange for the TPM's custom certificate formats to be accepted, you're still going to have trouble integrating TPM certificates into an enterprise PKI.

There are three primary approaches to integrating TPM certificates into an enterprise:

- Ignore them entirely; certify TPM keys during provisioning, or just trust that if you created the key yourself on a given machine it's very likely to be legitimate and can be certified.[14]

---

[13]A non-migratable/non-duplicatable key or certified migration key, that is; for the rest of this section, you'll find it helpful to ignore the fact that migration exists. CMKs are certified just like any other TPM key, except for the fact that you're required to use the TPM_CertifyKey2 command instead of its just being recommended.

[14]Do I recommend this approach? In the abstract, of course not: I'm a security architect, and my natural instincts are to point out all of the holes an adversary could take advantage of in such a situation. However, in the real world, we have to balance the risks and the costs, and for many enterprises, the small risk of an adversary interfering in the key creation or TPM certification process is less of an issue than the cost of building a high-trust and potentially customized certification infrastructure, especially for machines

- Create a CA which can verify TPM-issued certificates. Have it use the TPM-issued certificates as CSRs, and issue a new, widely-trusted certificate for each TPM key with a legitimate TPM-issued certificate. These CA-issued certificates should include any information derived from the TPM certificate that the enterprise might find useful, such as the key type, key constraints, or machine identifier associated with this particular TPM.
- Update any software doing remote TPM verification operations (such as machine authentication or attestation) to be able to verify TPM-issued certificates and certificate chains, and to only require a central CA's approval for the first certificate in the chain.

6.11.1   TPM 1.2: certifying identity keys

Identity key certification is by far the most complicated and least intuitive TPM certification operation; it's worth noting that identity keys can also be certified using the vastly simpler process described in Section 6.11.2. However, the identity key certification process was designed to solve one critical and fundamental problem which otherwise cannot easily be circumvented: how does one go from a root key (the EK) which is strongly associated with a piece of hardware to a set of cryptographic identities which cannot be correlated with each other or with the original hardware, while still maintaining trust that those identities are associated with the trustworthy hardware? The answer, at least for TPM 1.2, was the AIK certification protocol.

I've mentioned previously that identity keys are sometimes called AIKs (Attestation Identity Keys), but it's worth noting here that the original meaning of the acronym was 'Anonymous Identity Key'. TPM identities, even when certified under ideal circumstances, aren't actually anonymous at all; they're cryptographic pseudonyms for the TPM's permanent 'name', the EK. But this certification protocol was designed to minimize the ability of observers to successfully associate any given AIK with a particular machine in any reliable fashion. If followed with dedication, it can even keep the CA who issued a certificate from knowing whether the certificate is legitimate . . . at least, until the CA sees the certificate being used later. Collusion between the CA and observers is required to trace an identity back to the original hardware, or to other identities associated with the same hardware.[15] This protocol thus doesn't provide absolute protection, but it does raise the bar, and it keeps every website you go to from being able to use your keys to reliably identify your machine.

Is that level of improvement worth the expense of implementing a custom protocol? Is pseudonymity even a desirable property? That depends heavily on your use cases. Most enterprises not only don't care about pseudonymity, they actively would prefer not to have it; their goal is to tie communications to particular hardware, more

---

without any really high-value content that is protected by the TPM in question. This is an entirely reasonable and rational set of trade-offs to make, and one that I often recommend as a transitional approach for enterprises which are rolling out TPMs in the field.

[15]At least, from a cryptographic perspective. Astute observers may be wondering 'Couldn't an adversary tell by inspecting traffic patterns?' In short: yes, the TPM can't protect an identity against an adversary who's watching all traffic in and out of your machine, or one with really good network analysis tools.

often than not. Those enterprises that do want pseudonymity usually want it only in an outward-facing direction: they want to be able to track their own machines, but they don't want everyone on the Internet to be able to track their employees. Either way, however, you have only two choices with a 1.2 TPM: use this protocol to certify your identity keys from a trusted EK, or certify your identity keys directly, as described in Section 5.2.2.

6.11.1.1   The AIK certification protocol

This clever little protocol takes advantage of what would normally be a weakness in a cryptographic exchange: the CA never knows the identity of the machine making the certification request. The participating CA is therefore often referred to as a Privacy CA, or PCA. The CSR contains the public half of a (supposed) EK and a (supposed) identity key, encrypted to the PCA; however, there is no proof that the requestor owns either key. This is deliberate: someone seeking strong pseudonymity who knows the public EKs of a number of TPMs can issue a whole stream of equally valid CSRs, each one claiming to associate a newly created identity key with a distinct TPM EK.

The PCA's response to this is also unusual: if the EK is legitimate, and the PCA has a certificate to prove it, it will always issue a certificate for the supposed identity key, certifying it as a legitimate TPM identity. However, unlike what we'd expect from a normal CA, this certificate is *not* public information! Instead, the certificate is encrypted to the EK in the request, and sent back to the requestor. The PCA has no idea if the identity is actually legitimate or on the same TPM as that EK. What the CA does know is that a legitimate TPM will never decrypt a certificate for an identity key it does not have.

When the TPM is passed the encrypted certificate using the TPM_Activate Identity command, it verifies not only that it can decrypt it successfully, but also that the certificate is issued for an identity key currently loaded into the TPM.[16] If the identity key is present, the decrypted certificate is provided back to the user, who can then treat it as a perfectly normal certificate (Figure 6.14).[17]

If you're used to standard certification protocols, this may feel backwards: the trust in the certificate's legitimacy doesn't come until well after it's issued, which can feel like a security risk. If the PCA reliably encrypts certificates to only trusted TPMs, however, this is at least as valid as any self-signed x509 request: invalid certificates will never be decrypted, can never be used, and are just junk data. If the PCA never encounters the decrypted certificate, it will never know which of the EK-identity pairs was actually valid.

Of course, there's a very easy way around the 'which is real?' problem, and it's one that most enterprises will be happy to use. If the PCA is run by the enterprise, which is normally the case, the PCA can just include the machine identifier associated with the EK in the identity credential, allowing any verifier to confirm

---

[16] Remember, the TPM doesn't know which keys it may have created in the past.
[17] This is a slight simplification. Technically, what's decrypted with TPM_ActivateIdentity is expected to be a symmetric key, which is used to decrypt the actual certificate. This allows certificates to be longer than the TPM's highly constrained input and output buffers.

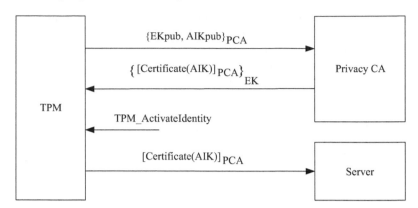

Figure 6.14   The AIK certification protocol. The first message, sent to the Privacy CA, is completely unauthenticated; anyone could produce it, and it contains no private information. The Privacy CA decides whether or not it trusts the EK to belong to a legitimate TPM, perhaps based on an Endorsement Credential passed along with the request. If it does, it will create a certificate for the identity key (AIK), claiming that it's a legitimate TPM identity. The CA has no idea if this is true or not at the time the certificate is created, so it encrypts the certificate to the trusted EK, knowing that it will be decrypted only if the association between the identity key and the EK is genuine. The AIK certificate must be kept secret by the Privacy CA until the encrypted message from the Privacy CA has been decrypted in order for the certification to be legitimate

that the key belongs not only to a legitimate enterprise TPM, but also to a specific enterprise machine.

One of the challenges of adding this certification protocol to enterprise CAs not designed to support it is that it relies entirely on the certificate being secret until decrypted using TPM_ActivateIdentity. Because many CAs treat certificate data as public information – which they normally are – adding this functionality as an add-on module can be difficult.

2.0 TPMs can support this protocol as well, although it's not as central to the 2.0 trust model. The TPM2_ActivateCredential command can be used in the same way as TPM_ActivateIdentity, with one critical difference: TPM2_ActivateCredential can verify the presence of any loaded TPM object, not just the restricted signing keys that directly parallel 1.2's identity keys. TPM2_ActivateCredential is used in Direct Anonymous Attestation (DAA) as well (see Section 9.3.4).

6.11.2   Certifying other TPM keys (1.2 and 2.0)

The certification of other TPM keys is extremely straightforward. The TPM offers certification commands: TPM_CertifyKey and TPM_CeritfyKey2 for 1.2 TPMs

Attestation data structure size in bytes
Attestation data structure:

Constant: TPM_GENERATED_VALUE
Attestation-type constant: TPMI_ST_ATTEST_CERTIFY
Unique name of the signing key
Nonce or other user-provided data
Clock info structure:

Clock value
resetCount value
restartCount value
Safe flag value

Firmware version identifier
Certify info structure:

Name of object
Qualified name of object

Figure 6.15   *The* TPM2B_ATTEST *data structure produced by the*
TPM2_Certify *command. While it looks as if there's not much*
actual object information here, the Name and Qualified Name fields
actually contain far more than they appear to. In 2.0 TPMs, object
names incorporate a hash of the entire public area of any object that
has one. This allows a verifier to confirm that the object being
certified is the same as the one they're establishing trust in. Qualified
names provide information about the entire hierarchy supporting
the object

and TPM2_Certify for 2.0. Each of these takes a key to be certified, and the handle of a key which will sign the certificate. The signing key must be an identity key for 1.2,[18] and a restricted signing key (a key with both the restrict and sign attributes) for 2.0. The key to be certified must have originated in the TPM and be non-migratable, or (for TPM_CertifyKey2) be a CMK. The TPM will create a certificate data structure (Figures 6.15 and 6.16), populate it with information about the key including the public key, the key type or attributes, any PCR constraints associated with the

---

[18] 1.2 TPMs will actually allow you to use a normal signing key to sign a TPM certificate. This is *never* a good idea. Do not do it, ever. The INFO-scheme signing keys were designed to allow this to be done safely, but have a cryptographic flaw. Never sign a TPM certificate with a signing key, and never trust a certificate signed with one. Remember, signing keys will sign user-provided data, and there's no way to tell which came from a user and which came from the TPM itself.

Constant tag: TPM_TAG_CERTIFY_INFO2
Constant filler byte: 0x00
Data structure version constant: 1.1.0.0
Key usage *(e.g. TPM_KEY_SIGNING)*
Key flags
Authorization data usage
Algorithm information
Public key digest
Nonce
Boolean indicating if any parent keys are PCR-constrained
PCR info structure size
TPM_PCR_INFO_SHORT structure:
PCR selection
Locality selection for key use
Digest of PCR composite for key use
Migration Authority size
Migration Authority digest (if any)

Figure 6.16   The TPM_CERTIFY_INFO2 data structure produced by the TPM_CertifyKey2 command and sometimes by the TPM_CertifyKey command (see Figure 6.17)

key, and so forth (Figures 6.15–6.17). It will then hash the data structure, sign the hash, and return the signature and the data structure to the user.

Much of the meaningful object information in a 2.0 certification structure is included in two non-obvious fields: the *Name* and *QualifiedName* fields.

The Name is a concatenation of a hash algorithm identifier, and the hash (using that algorithm) of an object's public data. That public data, as discussed in Section 6.4, includes the object type, its attributes (including, for keys, whether it is a restricted, signing, and/or decryption key, and whether it is duplicatable) and other parameters, and a unique identifier which for asymmetric keys is its public key.

The Qualified Name is a PCR-style hash chain combining the name of this object with the name of all parent objects. The Qualified Name of a primary key is the hash of the hierarchy handle concatenated with the name of the primary object. The Qualified

Data structure version constant: 1.1.0.0
Key usage *(e.g. TPM_KEY_SIGNING)*
Key flags
Authorization data usage
Algorithm information
Digest of public key
Nonce
Flag: any parent keys have PCR limits?
Size of TPM_PCR_INFO structure
TPM_PCR_INFO structure
PCR selection
Digest of PCR composite for key use
Digest of PCR composite at creation

Figure 6.17   The TPM_CERTIFY_INFO *data structure sometimes produced by
the* TPM_CertifyKey *command. See Figure 6.16 for the*
TPM_CERTIFY_INFO2 *structure returned by* TPM_CertifyKey2
or by TPM_CertifyKey *when the certified key has locality
constraints or PCR constraints for PCR indexes higher than 15.
(*TPM_CERTIFY_INFO *is designed to be backwards compatible with
1.1 TPMs.) See Figure 6.15 for the* TPM2B_ATTEST *structure
produced by the* TPM2_Certify *command*

Name of all other objects is the hash of the parent's Qualified Name concatenated
with that object's Name.

The net effect is that even though object properties cannot be derived from the
2.0 certificate structure, the certificate structure can be used to verify claims made
about the object and its parent objects.

6.11.3   Retrieving public portions of TPM keys

In many cases, we need to know the public half of a TPM key off-system. This
can be when we're creating a certificate for a TPM key without using the TPM's
secure but unique processes, when we want to verify a signature, or when we want
to encrypt data to a particular key. Public keys should always be verified before use,
but sometimes those verification methods require us to retrieve the public key by
itself.

Key parameters
TPM_KEY_PARMS data structure:

Algorithm ID
Encryption scheme used with key
Signature scheme used with key
Size of parameters field
Parameters field (byte array) based on algorithm; e.g. TPM_RSA KEY_PARMS data structure:

Key length
Number of primes
Exponent byte array size
Exponent byte array

TPM_STORE_PUBKEY data structure:

Public key length
Public key byte array (RSA public modulus)

Figure 6.18 The TPM_PUBKEY data structure returned by TPM_GetPubKey, at a high level. The details and all possible variations are described in section 10 of the 1.2 TPM Structures specification. (See Section 11.5.2 for where to find it.)

The 1.2 TPM_GetPubKey command exists for just this purpose. It takes the handle of a loaded key, and an authorization session for that key, and returns the public portion of the key in a TPM_PUBKEY data structure (see Figure 6.18).

In 2.0, we instead have the more generic TPM2_ReadPublic command, which retrieves the public area of any object, along with its name and qualified name, when you provide the corresponding handle. The public area returned is a generic TPM2B_PUBLIC structure (Figure 6.19), which itself contains the more detailed TPMT_PUBLIC structure and the size of that structure. TPMT_PUBLIC contains the public key, in the *unique* field, along with other useful information such as the key authorization policy (*authPolicy*), type of key or other object (*type*), and parameters (*parameters*). The exact data structures returned depend on the key type; an RSA key will have a TPM2B_PUBLIC_KEY_RSA in its *unique* field, for example, while an ECC key will have a TPM2B_ECC_POINT.

Of course, the public key is also contained within the key data structures, and can be retrieved by accessing the data structures the TPM returns directly. Note, however, that directly accessing TPM data structures can be harder than it looks; among the functions the various software libraries provide are resolving endianness

Size of TPMT_PUBLIC data structure
TPMT_PUBLIC data structure:

Type
Hash algorithm used to calculate object name
Object attributes
Authorization policy digest
Algorithm or structure parameters
Unique identifier (public key)

Figure 6.19   The TPM2B_PUBLIC *data structure returned by*
TPM2_ReadPublic. The exact data structures returned in the
fields depend on the type of the object. Section 12.2.3 of the Structures
section of the 2.0 TPM specification contains tables describing all
possible options. (See Section 11.6.2 for where to find it.)

conflicts and otherwise marshalling the TPM byte arrays into more usable data
structures.

6.12   Using keys created outside the TPM

In the rest of this chapter, we have talked exclusively about keys created in the TPM.
However, in some cases, you may want to import an externally created key into the
TPM. It might be a key that you've previously used, and would like to keep using with
added hardware protections. It might be because you want something that you can
use as a TPM key, but which doesn't come with the restrictions of a 1.2 key. It might
be because you're extremely picky about your sources of randomness and don't trust
the TPM's internal key store to generate something up to your standards.[19]

   1.2 TPMs are capable of loading keys created outside the TPM just as easily as keys created locally. Externally created keys must have their private halves
encrypted with a valid TPM parent key such as the SRK, and be structured as standard TPM_KEY data structures. When loading externally created keys, the migratable
flag (key->keyFlags->migratable) must be set to TRUE, or the TPM will
refuse to load the key. FIPS-compliant TPMs will refuse to load legacy keys, which
can perform both decryption and signing operations. Note that nothing actually prevents you from creating multiple key data structures for the same key, with different
key types; if you for some reason need to use the same externally created key for both

---

[19]In this case, however, you should consider instead using the TPM_StirRandom or TPM2_Stir
Random command (see Section 10.3) to add entropy from an external source to your TPM. Most people
who care that much about their randomness don't want to compromise on hardware protection or the
guarantees a TPM will provide about its keys.

signing and decryption on an FIPS-compliant TPM, you can create both a Signing and Binding version of the same key. There is a reason FIPS-compliant TPMs do not support these keys, however; reusing the same key for both kinds of operations can be dangerous.

Imported keys come with all of the downsides of migratable keys, plus one additional one: since the key wasn't created in a TPM, you *know* it existed for at least some period of time without hardware protections. Whether that matters to you depends on your goals; however, imported keys are not recommended for any high-security purpose.

Note that imported keys do not come out of the TPM as easily as they went in. If you want a key which is protected when not in use by the TPM, but which can be used by software (e.g. an e-mail encryption key), you're better off looking at the data protection options in Chapter 8.

In TPM 2.0, the `TPM2_LoadExternal` command has been provided to explicitly support the easy use of externally generated keys and objects. The command can be used to provide just a public key in the case of an asymmetric key, or the entire object, including secret data. The object must be in a TPM object structure, and must not have flags implying that it was created by a TPM. Importing keys can also be done with the `TPM2_Import` command, although with more work. This is the same command that's used for importing duplicate objects (see Section 6.6.3); there is, however, no requirement that the originating object must have come from another TPM.

6.13   The TPM's access control models

The TPM has a number of constraints that it will impose on the use of keys or other TPM resources. We'll talk about them in this chapter because the most common use cases for taking advantage of the TPM's access control mechanisms involve keys, and because when creating keys you are required to understand the access control model at least enough to be able to establish the null policy.

6.13.1   Physical presence

TPMs have a concept of physical presence: a way to indicate that someone is present at a machine. Physical presence mechanisms are intended to make sure that the physical owner of the machine is fundamentally in control of the TPM, to ensure privacy or to be able to use the TPM of a newly purchased machine. Physical presence can be triggered by hardware mechanisms, such as buttons, or by low-level software mechanisms, such as approval in the BIOS. It is not used to override password-based authorization; it is an entirely separate mechanism. In 1.2 TPMs, many commands are limited by physical presence, primarily those having to do with setting up a TPM or erasing existing contents, but users cannot force additional physical access checks to happen on demand. In 2.0 TPMs, physical presence is more smoothly integrated into the other access control mechanisms described below, although some commands may require physical presence in addition to other access control checks. Not all 2.0 TPMs are required to support physical presence.

6.13.2 TPM 1.2: user authentication, PCRs, and localities

In 1.2 TPMs, there are two fundamentally distinct forms of access control, although they are often used in combination. The first is authorization values, better known as passwords. When a key (or one of many other TPM objects, such as an allocated region of NVRAM) is created, a password string can be provided. That authorization value must be provided later on, every time the object is used. The intent of authorization values is to provide a mechanism for authenticating a user with a shared secret established during object creation. These authorization values can be changed later using the TPM_ChangeAuth command, which takes a key or data blob, the new authorization value for that key, and the current authorizations for both the key and its parent; however, it is critical to realize that the old blob will still work! TPM keys and other objects can have their old passwords invalidated only if every copy of the original blob is deleted.

As a result of the difficulty in guaranteeing that all copies of an old key data structure have been deleted, password rotation is often best accomplished by rotating keys instead. Frequent new keys are not considered burdensome in the infrastructure the TPM authors envisioned, since new certificates are easy to create and have very low overhead, so establishing trust in a new key is a simple and quick operation. Whether this is the case in the world in which most TPMs operate today is a different question entirely; picking strong authorization values is recommended for keys which will want a long lifespan of effective use.

The second kind of access control mechanism is based on the machine's state, and itself breaks down into two halves: PCR values and locality. PCRs are straightforward, and described in much more detail in Section 9.2; at a high level, they are a set of registers inside the TPM which are automatically zeroed on reboot, and which contain measurements of various system components or user data taken during the boot or operation of the platform. PCRs thus correspond loosely to machine state.[20] The TPM allows the object creator to choose PCR values to be bound to a given key or resource, so that the key can only be used or resource can only be accessed when exactly those values are in the specified registers. The TPM has 24 PCRs, and a key can be restricted to a value in one register, all 24, or anything in between.

Locality is rather more complicated, even though there are only five possible locality states. Locality is used to establish certain CPU execution states, which are intended to correspond to the DRTM, arbitrary trusted code executing in a secure CPU mode, a trusted OS, trusted applications, and unrestricted applications/user space (Section 9.1.3). (If you're familiar with the rings of protection model, in which kernels run in ring 0 and user applications in ring 3, this is the same idea with a slightly different implementation.) In theory, the locality value provided to the TPM at the

---

[20] How loose the correspondence is depends very heavily on what is producing the measurements and what is being measured; see Chapter 9 for a deeper exploration of the topic.

time a command is executed reflects not only the CPU state but the privilege or trust level of the code executing the command. In reality, significant OS support is required to distinguish between the OS, trusted application, and unrestricted application levels, and the systems on the market today execute all TPM commands from a single-device driver normally running in the unrestricted mode. This means that we effectively have only three localities to choose from: the DRTM locality, the locality used by code running in secure CPU mode, or an unrestricted locality. We'll cover the details in Chapter 9, but for now it's just important to note that the TPM can constrain use of keys with locality, as well as with PCRs. A key can be used in a single locality, in multiple localities, or in all localities.

PCR and locality constraints are defined together, as a single data structure. In 1.2 TPMs, PCR and locality constraints are permanent for the life of the key. (Why? Because they are included in the certificate for the key, so that a verifier can be confident that if the key is used, certain machine states must be reflected in the TPM. See Chapter 9 for how we can make use of this.) Again, if you want a key with different constraints, the expectation is that a new key will be created. It's worth noting, however, that measurements today are both extremely detailed and extremely primitive, and in most circumstances will change far more quickly than a normal person would want to change a password. That means that PCR-constrained keys in particular can be very fragile, and may become unusable unpredictably.

All keys must define authorization values and PCR and locality constraints, but the definition can be the null set if no actual controls are desired. The TPM has a particular string (all zeroes) which serves as the null password, called the WELL_KNOWN_SECRET.[21] PCR constraints are defined as a list of register index-value pairs, so a zero-length list indicates that no PCR constraints are to be enforced. The null locality constraints are defined differently: the TPM expects a list of localities in which a key may be used, so null constraints are indicated by a data structure with '1' for each locality bit, indicating that all localities are allowed.

6.13.3   TPM 2.0's Enhanced Authorization

TPM 2.0, unlike TPM 1.2, has a single unified authorization model called Enhanced Authorization, or EA, used not only for keys but also for data blobs, non-volatile storage[22] indexes, and all other TPM objects. It relies heavily on the same ideas of authorization values, PCRs, and locality used in 1.2 TPMs, but adds new ways of using them as well as new methods of authorization.

EA offers a number of features, including:

- A wide range of actual authorization mechanisms
- The ability to create authorization policies not just on objects, but on the uses of objects

---

[21] One of the best variable names ever.
[22] In 1.2 TPMs, you'll usually see this referred to as NVRAM; in 2.0 TPMs, this is often called NV storage instead.

- Keys, for example, can be constrained to be usable only with specific commands
- Objects can be constrained to be used with specific commands only if certain command parameters are present
- Composition of authorization policies with AND and OR
  - AND supports multiple-factor authentication; for example, requiring both a password and biometric identification
  - OR supports recovery options; for example, an IT department's recovery key to access a user's encrypted data
  - There is no limit to the depth and complexity of compositions; (A OR (B AND (C AND (D OR E)))) is a straightforward example, although it's not clear how often real-world policies need to get significantly more complex.
- Authorization policy updates are possible, if the policy allows it.

The following policy assertions are supported in all PCs; in each case, the description is followed by the command used to establish a particular assertion as part of a policy or policy session.

- Authorized using a different policy signed by a specific key (TPM2_Policy Authorize)
- Policy parameters are signed with a specific key (TPM2_PolicySigned)
- Authorized with the password/authorization value bound to the object (TPM2_ PolicyAuthValue, TPM2_PolicyPassword[23])
- Authorized with provided secret-based authorization session (TPM2_Policy Secret)
- Can be used for a particular command (TPM2_CommandCode)
- Can be used for a particular command, with specific input parameters (TPM2_ PolicyCpHash)
- The policy is used to authorize the duplication of an object (TPM2_Policy DuplicationSelect)[24] (see Section 6.6.3)
- Access is allowed within a particular time window according to the TPM's internal clock (TPM2_PolicyCounterTimer) (see Section 10.10.2)
- Executed in a particular locality (TPM2_PolicyLocality)
- A command is being executed on specific objects (TPM2_PolicyNameHash)
- A desired value is present in a section of non-volatile storage (TPM2_PolicyNV)
- Selected PCRs have a desired value (TPM2_PolicyPCR)
- A particular nonvolatile storage location has previously been written to by an authorized party (TPM2_PolicyNvWritten)

---

[23] It's important to note that the primary difference between authorization value and password authorizations is that password authorization is plaintext, and suitable only for well-known values or very unusual systems where all software is trusted.

[24] Why is this distinct from TPM2_CommandCode or TPM2_CpHash? To ensure that the extremely security-critical duplication operation must be handled as part of a distinct and carefully considered policy, rather than being included (potentially accidentally) in a broad policy.

- Duplication of an object to a particular new parent is authorized (Duplication-specific policy; TPM2_PolicyDuplicationSelect).

The following policy options are optional on PC TPMs, and may or may not be available:

- Someone has demonstrated, usually through use of the BIOS menu, that they are physically present at the machine.[25] Mandatory if a TPM implements physical presence. (TPM2_PolicyPhysicalPresence)
- Policy parameters have been previously authorized in a time-constrained ticket. The net effect is similar to TPM2_PolicySigned. (TPM2_PolicyTicket).

The initial empty policy that each of these commands modified as described below is created using the TPM2_StartAuthSession command with the TPM_SE_POLICY session type (see Section 6.10). The same TPM commands are used both to establish a target policy that should be enforced at some later point, and to create a policy session that will validate the conditions, although target policies can also be created using software that makes the same calculations as the TPM. To create a target policy (called *trial policy*), the session type provided to the TPM2_StartAuthSession command should be TPM_SE_TRIAL.

Enhanced Authorization works like PCRs' Extend operation: a policy digest (which the TPM uses both to establish a policy and to create policy sessions later that allow a user or other software to meet a policy) is the result of a series of hash operations, in which policy assertions are combined with the hashes of other assertions to produce a unique policy result. Each policy command changes the policy digest in a different way (Figure 6.20).

The boolean policy combination operations are straightforward. Policies combined with an AND operator, produced by passing one policy digest into another policy assertion command, are combined in exactly the same way as PCRs are extended: each new assertion is concatenated to the end of the digest of all prior assertions, and the result hashed. Thus, A AND B would become Hash (Hash (Initial, A), B). Policies combined with an OR operator, using the TPM2_PolicyOR command, concatenate the policy digests defining each branch, then hash the result. So P1 OR P2 would become Hash (P1, P2). In practice, TPM2_PolicyOR is very slightly more complicated: it takes a list of up to eight policy digests and a current policy session, and checks to see if the current policy digest matches anything on the list. If it does, it will change the current policy digest for the session to the concatenation of all digests on the list. Note that this has two interesting side effects: that the outcome of TPM2_PolicyOR will be the same regardless of which policy session it's run on as long as that session digest matches a digest in the list, and that the ordering of the list of allowed digests is critical in predicting the resulting policy digest.

Because of this hash-chain-based policy approach, the order of operations is critical both when defining policies and when creating policy sessions. A AND B

---

[25]It is important to note that this flag is set during boot, and remains set for the entire boot cycle. While this can be an extremely powerful tool, for example, to allow an on-site technician to perform recovery operations, it is also important that it be paired with a reboot after the expected operations are completed or the flag will remain on for the duration of normal operation.

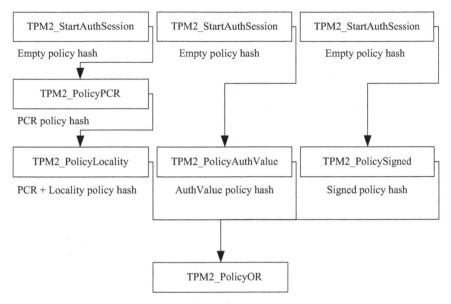

Figure 6.20 The process of construction of an Enhanced Authorization policy. For simplicity, the arguments to the commands have been ignored. In practice, the TPM2_PolicyPCR command would take a target PCR state, the TPM2_PolicySigned command would take a public key whose signature of other policies would be trusted, etc. You can see here that EA policies are built out of component hashes input to other commands. This particular policy is unusually complicated. A resource with this policy can be used in any of three cases: if both the PCR contents and TPM locality were correct; if the correct authorization value was provided; or if another access control policy signed by a trusted authority was met

is a different policy from B AND A, and the B AND A policy session will not be accepted by the TPM to meet the A AND B authorization policy.

Because policies can be long and complex, some TPM objects (including the hierarchies, as discussed in Section 3.2.2) have both an authorization value and an optional policy. Policies, once defined, can be reused easily for multiple objects. This also allows the use of precalculated policy components. An IT department could produce a precalculated recovery policy of 'use a policy signed by the IT department to authorize the TPM2_ObjectChangeAuth command', which could be combined using the TPM2_PolicyOR command with whatever additional policies a local user might want to use to protect their keys and data on an enterprise machine.

To retrieve the digest of a policy session, the TPM2_PolicyGetDigest command is used. This allows policies to be pre-computed, reused, and provided in a list to TPM2_PolicyOR.

6.13.3.1   Enhanced Authorization use cases

Some example policy combinations and use cases include:

- Allowing a password to be used for routine uses of a key, but requiring a public key's approval for high-sensitivity operations (a TPM2_PolicyCommandCode and a TPM2_PolicyCpHash combined with the TPM2_PolicyOR command and a TPM2_PolicyPassword, and the result of that is combined with TPM2_PolicySigned using TPM2_PolicyOR again)
- Allowing Jane and Bob to both use the same key with distinct passwords (Multiple TPM2_PolicyPassword or TPM2_PolicyAuthValue combined with TPM2_PolicyOR)
- Allowing a key to be used without a password early in the boot process, but requiring a password or other authentication method later (TPM2_PolicyPCR and TPM2_PolicyAuthValue combined with TPM2_PolicyOR)
- Allowing a key to decrypt data either if the PCR values are in a known good state, or if a recovery password is used (TPM2_PolicyPCR and TPM2_Policy AuthValue combined with TPM2_PolicyOR, and possibly TPM2_Policy CommandCode)
- Allowing anyone to use a key to quote a particular set of PCRs without needing a password, without allowing them to quote other potentially sensitive PCRs or certify objects with the same key (TPM2_PolicyCpHash)
- Provide all enterprise keys with a password recovery mechanism, where an IT department key can be used to authorize an authorization value change (TPM2_ PolicySigned and TPM2_PolicyOR, combined with whatever user policy is desired). Note that if the signed policy is not timed or deleted, it can be reused.

6.14   Key access control user stories

Note: Access control using PCRs and locality will be discussed at length in the attestation chapter (Chapter 9).

Alice has several keys for which she has to decide on access control. One is the identity or restricted signing key used to create system quotes. She would like this to be used in the background by system software without worrying about shared secrets, so she sets this to require only an authorization value and sets the authorization value to the well-known secret (all zeroes). Another is a binding or non-restricted decryption key used to distribute secure software updates. Alice doesn't want potential malicious software using this key freely, to prevent someone from creating a decryption oracle, so she has the user choose an authorization value that will be required to decrypt data. Since Alice isn't worried about data becoming unretrievable if a user leaves, she doesn't worry about setting up any kind of alternative access mechanism – if she needs to, she'll create a new key and resend the data to it instead.

Bob doesn't think his users ever need to use the TPM without the intervention of corporate software, and are much more likely to accidentally get themselves into trouble misusing keys. He assigns a standard password to each of them which is known to the corporate software. It's not highly secure, but it will keep users from signing things they shouldn't or accidentally encrypting data in a way that will mean the help desk's intervention is required to retrieve them.

Charlie is creating keys for his own use. He gives each key a different strong authorization value he knows.

Dana needs more complicated authorization options, because Dana's keys have very different use cases. The decryption key, used to receive financial data from customers, requires a password chosen by the user, but also has a policy that uses an authorization value Dana writes down in a secured location; that way, the user has to authenticate in order to decrypt the sensitive financial data, but the company will still have access if the employee becomes unavailable for any reason. The signing key also has a user-chosen password, but since this is used to indicate the formal approval of the employee in question for a given document, there is no policy for alternate access mechanisms. The restricted signing key, used by Dana to create audit records, has the *useWithAuth* value clear, so no password can be used to authorize the use of the key. Instead, Dana sets it up with a TPM2_PolicySigned policy that requires the use of the IT department's key, in order to reserve the use of the key for the formal audit process and prevent any unexpected leaks of potentially sensitive system information.

Elaine has acquired some TPM 2.0 machines, and wants to experiment with integrating them into her server farm. She wants to mimic the effect of a 1.2 CMK with 2.0 duplicatable signing keys, without losing the guarantee that duplication will be heavily locked down and approved by her organization. She creates an Enhanced Authorization duplication policy for the key by initiating a trial authorization session, then running TPM2_PolicyAuthorize with her Migration Authority public key and TPM2_PolicyCommandCode to tie the policy to the Duplication command. (Technically, she could skip the command code assertion here and just make sure she has an appropriate duplication-relevant assertion in her authorized policies in the future, but she doesn't want to let her Migration Authority key be used to authorize other commands for the server key.) She's happy to use authorization values for all non-duplication authorization on the key, so she doesn't bother using TPM2_PolicyOR to specify an authorization policy option for other circumstances.

To authorize duplication, Elaine first creates a new authorization policy on the migration authority machine using TPM2_PolicyDuplicationSelect, the object to migrate, and the duplication target, and then signs the policy with the migration authority key. On the machine whose key she wants to duplicate, Elaine uses TPM2_VerifySignature to verify the signature on the policy, which she'll then pass into her new session as an argument to the TPM2_PolicyAuthorize command. The policy session is structured a little differently than her first trial session: after starting the session, Elaine runs TPM2_PolicyDuplicationSelect to create a policy digest just like the one her migration authority approved, then TPM2_PolicyAuthorize with her verified ticket to show that the duplication selection policy should be considered authorized. Finally, she runs

TPM2_PolicyCommandCode. The resulting authorization session will let her run the TPM2_Duplicate command, but only for the object and duplication target the migration authority key was used to approve.

6.15   TSS 1.2 key management code examples

6.15.1   Background: using the SRK

Although we'll be talking about loading normal keys later in this section, it will help to know how to make use of the SRK at the beginning, since we'll be using it as our initial parent key when creating new keys. Because using the SRK is a common operation, I'm calling it out separately so it will be easy to find when you need it.

To load the SRK, which always exists in a defined location in the TPM, we use the Tspi_Context_LoadKeyByUUID command.

```
TSS_HKEY hSRK;

Tspi_Context_LoadKeyByUUID(hContext, TSS_PS_TYPE_SYSTEM,
  (TSS_UUID) TSS_UUID_SRK, &hSRK);
```

We'll frequently need to also set up the SRK's security policy, required to use its private half. In this example, the SRK is configured to use the well-known secret as its password, so as to be usable by anyone on the system. Note that we shouldn't need to set up the permissions to use the SRK when we set it as a parent key during key creation, since we're only using the public half.

```
// Set up SRK policy
Tspi_Context_CreateObject(hContext, TSS_OBJECT_TYPE_POLICY,
                          TSS_POLICY_USAGE, &hSRKPolicy);
// Set up SRK secret
BYTE wks[] =TSS_WELL_KNOWN_SECRET;
Tspi_Policy_SetSecret(hSRKPolicy, TSS_SECRET_MODE_SHA1,
                            sizeof(wks), wks);

// Associate policy with SRK object
Tspi_Policy_AssignToObject(hSRKPolicy, hSRK);
```

6.15.2   Key creation

The processes for creating keys in a 1.2 TSS program, as with a 1.2 TPM, differ for identity keys and other keys. However, there are some commonalities. In all cases, you will need a key object, and a loaded storage key to act as the parent key and encrypt the private half of the newly created key. In some cases, you will also want a security policy for the key and/or a set of PCR constraints to impose on the key's use.

Creating a standard wrap key – a signing, binding, storage, or legacy key – has two steps. The first is the use of the standard `Tspi_Context_CreateObject` command, where the object type is a `TSS_OBJECT_TYPE_RSAKEY`, and a pointer to the previously defined handle is the returned key object. The interesting part of the command is the third argument; a set of initialization flags. Any number of compatible initialization flags can be combined with | (OR); these flags will determine the details of the created key. The flags should include a key size and a key type, at a minimum. A full list of flags is available in section 2.3.2.2 of the TSS specification (see Section 11.1.1 on page 269), but some of the most helpful for routine use include:

TSS_KEY_TYPE_X: Where X is SIGNING, LEGACY, BIND, IDENTITY, or STORAGE.

TSS_KEY_SIZE_X: Where X is the RSA key size. 2048 is the recommended choice for most TPMs, although the software allows 4096 and higher if your TPM supports larger keys.

TSS_KEY_NO_AUTHORIZATION: The default authorization option if none is specified; no authorization information is required for the use of this key.

TSS_KEY_AUTHORIZATION: Authorization will be required for use[26] of the key. Note that if no authorization policy is associated with the key object during creation, this effectively becomes `TSS_KEY_NO_AUTHORIZATION` rather than producing an error.

TSS_KEY_NOT_MIGRATABLE: The key cannot be migrated for use outside this TPM. Default option.

TSS_KEY_MIGRATABLE: The key is migratable.

TSS_KEY_CERTIFIED_MIGRATABLE: The key is a certified migratable key, and the various CMK functions can be used with it.[27] For the HMAC of the owner approval of the migration authority, created with `Tspi_TPM_CMKApproveMA` or `Tspi_TPM_CMKCreateTicket`.

TSS_KEY_VOLATILE: The key must always be unloaded by the TPM on machine startup.

TSS_KEY_STRUCT_KEY12: The key is a 1.2 key (versus a plain STRUCT_KEY, which is a 1.1-compatible structure with reduced PCR and locality support)

The second step is to use the `Tspi_Key_CreateKey` command. The first argument is the key object you've just created, the second is the handle of the parent key which will encrypt the private portion of the key, and the third is an optional PCR

---

[26]In theory, there's a difference between `TSS_KEY_AUTHORIZATION`, which should require authorization for all key operations, and `TSS_KEY_AUTHORIZATION_PRIV_USE_ONLY`, which requires authorization for private key operations. In reality, some TSS implementations don't properly implement `TSS_KEY_AUTHORIZATION_PRIV_USE_ONLY` to require authorization at all, and public keys are available for any non-root keys anyway. Just using `TSS_KEY_AUTHORIZATION` if you want an authorization policy is the best choice.

[27]If this is used, other internal key data need to be set to use the key effectively; in particular, you will need to call `Tspi_SetAttribData` with the `TSS_TSPATTRIB_CMKINFO` flag and two different subflags: `TSS_TSPATTRIB_CMK_INFO_MA_DIGEST` to set the migration authority data digest, and `TSS_TSPATTRIB_CMK_INFO_MA_APPROVAL`

information data structure which contains any PCR or locality constraints that will be enforced on the key.

For example, to create a migratable signing key with no authorization or PCR values required for use and the SRK as the parent, one would use:

```
TSS_HKEY hSigningKey;
Tspi_Context_CreateObject(hContext, TSS_OBJECT_TYPE_RSAKEY,
                          TSS_KEY_SIZE_2048 | TSS_KEY_TYPE_SIGNING
                          | TSS_KEY_MIGRATABLE
                          | TSS_KEY_NO_AUTHORIZATION,
                                 &hSigningKey);
 result = Tspi_Key_CreateKey(hSigningKey, hSRK, 0);
```

In the next example, we create a storage key with PCR constraints and an authorization policy requiring the use of a password. I'll discuss why PCR constraints might be useful in much more detail in Chapter 9, but since the constraints are determined during key creation, I'll show how to set them up here.

```
TSS_HKEY hStorageKey;
TSS_HPOLICY hStoragePolicy;
TSS_HPCRS hStoragePCRs; // PCR data structure handle
BYTE* tempPCRVal;
UINT32 tempPCRLen;

/* Create key object. */
Tspi_Context_CreateObject(hContext, TSS_OBJECT_TYPE_RSAKEY,
                          TSS_KEY_SIZE_2048
                          | TSS_KEY_TYPE_STORAGE
                          | TSS_KEY_AUTHORIZATION
                          | TSS_KEY_NOT_MIGRATABLE,
                          &hStorageKey);

/* Create PCR data structure object. The third argument is
   optional,
 * for when a specific type of PCR data structure is wanted. */
 Tspi_Context_CreateObject(hContext, TSS_OBJECT_TYPE_PCRS, 0,
   &hStoragePCRs);

/* Retrieve current values of DRTM PCRs (17-19) and set
 * corresponding PCR constraints in PCR data structure */
Tspi_TPM_PcrRead(hTPM, 17, &tempPCRLen, &tempPCRVal);
Tspi_PcrComposite_SetPcrValue(hStoragePCRs, 17, tempPCRLen,
   tempPCRVal);

/* Freeing memory for tempPCRVal; because it's allocated by the TSS,
 * just overwriting it may cause memory issues. */
Tspi_Context_FreeMemory(hContext, tempPCRVal);

Tspi_TPM_PcrRead(hTPM, 18, &tempPCRLen, &tempPCRVal);
Tspi_PcrComposite_SetPcrValue(hStoragePCRs, 18, tempPCRLen,
   tempPCRVal);
```

```
Tspi_Context_FreeMemory(hContext, tempPCRVal);

Tspi_TPM_PcrRead(hTPM, 19, &tempPCRLen, &tempPCRVal);
Tspi_PcrComposite_SetPcrValue(hStoragePCRs, 19, tempPCRLen,
  tempPCRVal);
 Tspi_Context_FreeMemory(hContext, tempPCRVal);

 /* Setting authorization policy for storage key. Here, using a
    pop-up
  * to retrieve the desired password from the user.*/
Tspi_Context_CreateObject(hContext, TSS_OBJECT_TYPE_POLICY,
                         TSS_POLICY_USAGE, &hStoragePolicy);
Tspi_Policy_SetSecret(hStoragePolicy, TSS_SECRET_MODE_POPUP,
                     0, 0);
Tspi_Policy_AssignToObject(hStoragePolicy, hStorageKey);


/* Creating key using SRK as parent and PCR composite to set PCR
 * constraints */
Tspi_Key_CreateKey(hStorageKey, hSRK, hStoragePCRs);
```

The PCR constraints used above are the simplest kind we can create: a composite of the PCR values in several registers. For this kind of constraint, the type of PCR data structure used isn't particularly relevant, and we can use the default. In some cases, however, we want to use some of the specialized features that 1.2 PCR data structures added; most commonly, the use of locality to constrain the use of a key. For these, we want to explicitly create a PCR structure of TSS_PCRS_STRUCT_INFO_LONG, which has additional configuration options in addition to the Tspi_PcrComposite_SetPcrValue command we've introduced. Some of these options I won't discuss until we use those features in later chapters, but I'll show you how to set a locality constraint here, since it's part of the creation process.

```
Tspi_Context_CreateObject(hContext, TSS_OBJECT_TYPE_PCRS,
  TSS_PCRS_STRUCT_INFO_LONG, &hDemoPCRs);

Tspi_PcrComposite_SetPcrLocality(hDemoPCRs, TPM_LOC_THREE);
 /* Locality 3: Secure CPU mode code execution */
```

Note that the locality value is a bitmask, so putting in a numeric value for your desired locality may produce unexpected results. If you want a key to be usable in all localities, the correct value is 0x1f.

6.15.3 Creating identity keys

Identity keys in 1.2 TPMs are not created using the same command as other keys. Behind the scenes, I create identity keys using TPM_MakeIdentity, but it's worth calling attention to the TSS command name, since it's particularly non-intuitive: `Tspi_TPM_CollateIdentityRequest`.

The trickiest part of creating an identity key is that these commands require a Privacy CA public key. This is true whether or not you want to use the returned CSR; the TPM will not accept a null value, and requires a legitimate RSA public key. If you have a PCA and will be using the TCG-designed identity certification protocol, you presumably already have a key that you can incorporate (see Section 6.15.5 for more on managing public keys). Otherwise, you can create a local key (a legacy key with no constraints or usage requirements, e.g.) and pass its handle to the TPM as the 'PCA' key.

Note that creating an identity key requires owner authorization.

```
TSS_HPOLICY hTPMPolicy;
TSS_HKEY hAIK;
TSS_HKEY hPCA;
BYTE label[] = {}; // Optional string used to provide human-readable
    identity for the AIK
UINT32 labelLen = 0; // Length of label
BYTE *aikblob; // Data buffer to store the signing request in
UINT32 aikbloblen; // Size of signing request returned by TPM

/* Setting up the owner policy to authorize creating an identity
    key */
result = Tspi_Context_CreateObject(hContext, TSS_OBJECT_TYPE_POLICY,
    TSS_POLICY_USAGE, &hTPMPolicy);
result = Tspi_Policy_AssignToObject(hTPMPolicy, hTPM);
result = Tspi_Policy_SetSecret(hTPMPolicy, TSS_SECRET_MODE_PLAIN,
    strlen(pwd), pwd);

...

/* Set up Privacy CA key, hPCA. This can be a locally created key or
    an actual CA's public key. */
...

Tspi_Context_CreateObject(hContext, TSS_OBJECT_TYPE_RSAKEY,
                        TSS_KEY_TYPE_IDENTITY | TSS_KEY_SIZE_2048,
                        &hAIK);

/* The CollateIdentityRequest command requires the SRK handle as well
    as the TPM handle.
 * 3DES here is the algorithm the TPM will use to symmetrically
    encrypt the signing request contents
 * to the certificate authority, using an internally generated nonce.
    That nonce will then
 * be encrypted to hPCA.*/

Tspi_TPM_CollateIdentityRequest(hTPM, hSRK, hPCA, labelLen, label,
                        hAIK, TSS_ALG_3DES,
                        &aikbloblen, &aikblob);
```

The resulting identity key can be used just like any key created with `Tspi_Key_CreateKey`.

6.15.4   Key loading

The 1.2 TSS provides multiple options for loading keys.

The simplest to use, if you're using a key in the same program you've created it in, is `Tspi_Key_LoadKey`. This simply takes the handle of a key and the handle of its (loaded and authorized) parent key.

The TSS also has its own internal key storage database. A key can be added to the persistent storage using the `Tspi_Context_RegisterKey` command, which allows the user to assign the key a UUID. `Tspi_Context_GetKeyByUUID` can then be used to retrieve the key based on its UUID; the key handle can then be supplied to `Tspi_Key_LoadKey` in the same way as a key you've just created. If you don't have the UUID of a known registered key, you can also retrieve keys using `Tspi_Context_GetKeyByPublicInfo`, but this requires that you know the public key modulus. The `Tspi_Context_GetRegisteredKeysByUUID` can be used to retrieve information about all keys in persistent storage, if NULL is supplied instead of a UUID; the returned `TSS_KM_KEYINFO` structures contain the UUIDs of both a key and its parent, allowing `Tspi_Context_GetKeyByUUID` to be used.

Special keys that never leave the TPM, such as the SRK or keys stored long-term in the TPM (see section 10.6), can be loaded using `Tspi_Context_LoadKeyByUUID`. Unlike most other loading command, this one does not require a parent key; any required parents must not exist (e.g. for a root key) or be already available for loading from the TSS' persistent storage.

```
TSS_HKEY hSRK;
TSS_HKEY hBindingKey;


// Load SRK
Tspi_Context_LoadKeyByUUID(hContext, TSS_PS_TYPE_SYSTEM,
                           (TSS_UUID) TSS_UUID_SRK, &hSRK);

// Load binding key
Tspi_Key_LoadKey(hBindingKey, hSRK);
```

If you want to use the TSS' internal key storage, you can register a key for future use using the `Tspi_Context_RegisterKey` command. Once a key is registered, you can use the `Tspi_Context_GetKeyByUUID` or `Tspi_Context_GetKeyByPublicInfo` commands to retrieve a handle for the key. The latter allows the TSS's persistent storage to be searched by public key, rather than by a local reference such as a UUID. These commands will work in any programs using the same TSS on the same machine, without any need to pass data between programs.

If you're storing keys outside the TSS for later use, you'll usually want to use `Tspi_Context_LoadKeyByBlob`, which takes the key blobs created by `Tspi_Key_CreateKey`. The blob can be retrieved from the key object using the `Tspi_GetAttribData` command, and written to disk using normal file operations; all secret data in a key blob is encrypted. The `Tspi_EncodeDER_TssBlob` and `Tspi_DecodeBER_TSSBlob` commands can optionally be used to encode the key blob in a standardized format so that it can be read safely on different machines. Note that key blobs can be stored securely off-system, making this format particularly valuable for backup purposes.

```
UINT32 SigningKeyBlobSize;
BYTE* SigningKeyBlobData;
UINT32 EncodedBlobSize=600; // Input the maximum size for the
                               resulting encoded blob.
                            // Value will be updated with
                               actual size.
BYTE EncodedBlob[600];

Tspi_GetAttribData(hSigningKey, TSS_TSPATTRIB_KEY_BLOB,
                   TSS_TSPATTRIB_KEYBLOB_BLOB,
                   &SigningKeyBlobSize,
                   &SigningKeyBlobData);

Tspi_EncodeDER_TssBlob(SigningKeyBlobSize,SigningKeyBlobData,
                   TSS_BLOB_TYPE_KEY_1_2,
                   &EncodedBlobSize, EncodedBlob);
// Write EncodedBlob to disk
```

```
UINT32 blobLen = 600; // Input the maximum size of the output data.
                      // Value will be updated with actual size.
BYTE blob[600];
UINT32 EncodedBlobSize;
BYTE* EncodedBlob;
UINT32 blobType;

// Read EncodedBlob from disk

Tspi_DecodeBER_TssBlob(EncodedBlobSize, EncodedBlob,
                                 &blobType, &blobLen, blob);

switch(blobType) {
case TSS_BLOB_TYPE_KEY_1_2:
// Recognized 1.2 TPM key
  break;
case TSS_BLOB_TYPE_KEY:
// Recognized 1.1 TPM key
  break;
default:
```

```
// Not a recognized key, not safe to load
  return -1;
}

Tspi_Context_LoadKeyByBlob(hContext, hSRK, blobLen,
                           blob, &hKey);
```

In some cases, there is no key blob; the SRK, as we've previously discussed, has no blob to load, but needs to be loaded by the TSS in order for the software to know what key to use. In these cases, or in other cases where keys are permanently stored in the TPM (see Section 10.6), the `Tspi_Context_LoadKeyByUUID` command is used instead. To use this command, you need to know the location inside the TPM where the key is stored.

```
Tspi_Context_LoadKeyByUUID(hContext, TSS_PS_TYPE_SYSTEM, (TSS_UUID)
                           TSS_UUID_SRK, &hSRK);
```

6.15.5 Using public keys

We have several methods of retrieving a public key for a TPM key using the 1.2 TSS.

The `Tspi_Key_PubKey` command retrieves the public portion of a given loaded key, in the form of a `TPM_STORE_PUBKEY` object. This structure has two parts: a UINT32 length of the key field and a BYTE buffer of the specified length containing the RSA public modulus. The special owner-authorized command `Tspi_TPM_OwnerGetSRKPubKey` works identically, but only for the SRK. It is used when access to the SRK public key is restricted.

```
UINT32 pubKeyLength;
BYTE* pubKey;

Tspi_Key_PubKey(hBindingKey, &pubKeyLength, &pubKey);
```

We've discussed the use of the `Tspi_GetAttribData` command for retrieving the contents of a TPM key data structure. We can also use this command to retrieve the public subset of the key blob, again in the form of a `TPM_STORE_PUBKEY` data structure.

```
BYTE* SigningKeyPublicData;
UINT32 SigningKeyPublicSize;

Tspi_GetAttribData(hSigningKey, TSS_TSPATTRIB_KEY_BLOB,
                   TSS_TSPATTRIB_KEYBLOB_PUBLIC_KEY,
                   &SigningKeyPublicSize,
                   &SigningKeyPublicData);
```

These public key blobs may be useful for TPM functions, where we can use the equivalent SetAttribData in a key object and create a public-only key. They do not, however, provide all of the information we need to use the public key on another system, and require us to delve into TPM data structures.

The public modulus, exponent, and number of prime factors of a given key can also be retrieved individually, making them easier to import into other formats, such as openSSL library RSA keys.

```
UINT32 rsaExpSize, rsaModSize, rsaPrimes;
BYTE *rsaExp, *rsaMod;

Tspi_GetAttribData(hSigningKey, TSS_TSPATTRIB_RSAKEY_INFO,
                               TSS_TSPATTRIB_KEYINFO_RSA_EXPONENT,
                               &rsaExpSize, &rsaExp);
Tspi_GetAttribData(hSigningKey, TSS_TSPATTRIB_RSAKEY_INFO,
                               TSS_TSPATTRIB_KEYINFO_RSA_MODULUS,
                               &rsaModSize, &rsaMod);
Tspi_GetAttribUint32(hSigningKey, TSS_TSPATTRIB_RSAKEY_INFO,
                               TSS_TSPATTRIB_KEYINFO_RSA_PRIMES,
                               &rsaPrimes);
```

We can also load a public key using the reverse of the techniques we used to retrieve the data. For example, the following example creates a public signing key data structure usable for verifying signatures. Here, signingPubKeyLen and signingPubKeyBlob were retrieved using the `Tspi_Key_GetPubKey` command. Unfortunately, there is no corresponding SetPubKey function, so we have to use the `Tspi_SetAttribData` command instead. You may note that there are no TPM functions called here; public keys are never passed to the TPM except in very rare cases, such as for the `Tspi_TPM_CollateIdentityRequest` command discussed earlier.

```
TSS\_HKEY hSigningPub;

Tspi_Context_CreateObject(hContext, TSS_OBJECT_TYPE_RSAKEY,
                          TSS_KEY_SIZE_2048
                          | TSS_KEY_TYPE_SIGNING, &hSigningPub);

Tspi_SetAttribData(hSigningPub, TSS_TSPATTRIB_KEY_BLOB,
                   TSS_TSPATTRIB_KEYBLOB_PUBLIC_KEY,
                   signingPubKeyLen, signingPubKeyBlob);
```

6.16   TSS 2.0 key management code examples

6.16.1   Key creation

As we've previously discussed, there are two different commands for creating keys in TPM 2.0; TPM2_CreatePrimary for primary keys generated directly from the TPM's internal seeds which never leave the TPM, and TPM2_Create for normal keys which are stored encrypted outside the TPM and loaded later.

In the following example, TPM2_CreatePrimary is used to create a 2048-bit RSA primary key in the null hierarchy. The key will be a restricted decryption key, with a fixed TPM and fixed parent; in short, a primary storage key. The public parameters (in.inPublic) are what define a template.

```
CreatePrimary_In      in;
CreatePrimary_Out     out;
TPMI_SH_AUTH_SESSION  sessionHandle0 = TPM_RS_PW;
unsigned int          sessionAttributes0 = 0;
TPMI_RH_HIERARCHY     primaryHandle = TPM_RH_OWNER;
                        // Creating key in storage hierarchy
TPMI_ALG_HASH         nalg = TPM_ALG_SHA256;
const char            *keyPassword = NULL;
const char            *parentPassword = NULL;


...
/* Retrieve parent and key passwords from user */
...

    in.primaryHandle = primaryHandle;

    if (keyPassword == NULL) {
      in.inSensitive.t.sensitive.userAuth.t.size = 0;
        }
        else {
          rc = TPM2B_StringCopy(&in.inSensitive.t.sensitive.
              userAuth.b,
              keyPassword, sizeof(TPMU_HA));
            }
        }
    in.inSensitive.t.sensitive.data.t.size = 0;

    in.inPublic.t.publicArea.type = TPM_ALG_RSA;
    in.inPublic.t.publicArea.nameAlg = nalg;

    /* Set object attributes */
    in.inPublic.t.publicArea.objectAttributes.val = 0;
    in.inPublic.t.publicArea.objectAttributes.val |=
      TPMA_OBJECT_FIXEDTPM;
    in.inPublic.t.publicArea.objectAttributes.val |=
      TPMA_OBJECT_FIXEDPARENT;
    in.inPublic.t.publicArea.objectAttributes.val |=
      TPMA_OBJECT_SENSITIVEDATAORIGIN;
```

```
in.inPublic.t.publicArea.objectAttributes.val |=
  TPMA_OBJECT_USERWITHAUTH;
in.inPublic.t.publicArea.objectAttributes.val &=
  ~TPMA_OBJECT_ADMINWITHPOLICY;
in.inPublic.t.publicArea.objectAttributes.val |= TPMA_OBJECT_NODA;
in.inPublic.t.publicArea.objectAttributes.val |=
  TPMA_OBJECT_RESTRICTED;
in.inPublic.t.publicArea.objectAttributes.val |=
  TPMA_OBJECT_DECRYPT;
in.inPublic.t.publicArea.objectAttributes.val &= ~TPMA_OBJECT_SIGN;

/* Set auth policy */
in.inPublic.t.publicArea.authPolicy.t.size = 0;/* empty policy */

/* Set RSA key parameters */
in.inPublic.t.publicArea.parameters.rsaDetail.symmetric.
  algorithm = TPM_ALG_AES;
in.inPublic.t.publicArea.parameters.rsaDetail.symmetric.
  keyBits.aes = 128;
in.inPublic.t.publicArea.parameters.rsaDetail.symmetric.mode.aes =
  TPM_ALG_CBC;
in.inPublic.t.publicArea.parameters.rsaDetail.scheme.scheme =
  TPM_ALG_NULL;
in.inPublic.t.publicArea.parameters.rsaDetail.keyBits = 2048;
in.inPublic.t.publicArea.parameters.rsaDetail.exponent = 0;

/* Before the key is generated, the public key field is empty */
in.inPublic.t.publicArea.unique.rsa.t.size = 0;

/* Optional user-provided data for identifying the key */
in.outsideInfo.t.size = 0;

/* Optional set of PCRs to record in the creation data */
in.creationPCR.count = 0;

TSE_Execute((RESPONSE_PARAMETERS *)&out,
          (COMMAND_PARAMETERS *)&in,
          NULL,
          TPM_CC_CreatePrimary,
          sessionHandle0, parentPassword, sessionAttributes0,
          TPM_RH_NULL, NULL, 0);
```

We can retrieve the command results via the response parameters data structure:

```
TPMI_DH_OBJECT newKeyHandle = out.objectHandle;

if (verbose) TPM_PrintAll(''createprimary: public key,''
                              out.outPublic.t.publicArea.
                                unique.rsa.t.buffer,
                              out.outPublic.t.publicArea.
                                unique.rsa.t.size);
```

The TPM2_Create command works similarly, but can create a wider variety of objects, and requires a parent storage key. Here, we create an unrestricted signing key. A few helper functions with fairly intuitive functionality are used here, all included in the IBM TSS 2.0 utilities. Again, in.inPublic contains the public parameters which make up an object template.

```
TPM_RC                    rc = 0; // Return code
Create_In                 in;
Create_Out                out;

...
/* Retrieve key and parent passwords from user */
/* Retrieve loaded parent key handle from user */
/* Retrieve output filenames from user */
...

/* Record the key authorization value, if any, into the sensitive
 *data being passed to the TPM. */

if (keyPassword == NULL) {
    in.inSensitive.t.sensitive.userAuth.t.size = 0;
    }
else {
        TPM2B_StringCopy(&in.inSensitive.t.sensitive.userAuth.b,
                    keyPassword, sizeof(TPMU_HA));
        }

    in.parentHandle = parentHandle;

    /* Type of object being created; here, an RSA key */
    in.inPublic.t.publicArea.type = TPM_ALG_RSA;

    /* Hash algorithm to use when creating object name */
    in.inPublic.t.publicArea.nameAlg = TPM_ALG_SHA256

    /* Object attributes */
    in.inPublic.t.publicArea.objectAttributes.val |=
      TPMA_OBJECT_SENSITIVEDATAORIGIN;
    in.inPublic.t.publicArea.objectAttributes.val |=
      TPMA_OBJECT_USERWITHAUTH;
    in.inPublic.t.publicArea.objectAttributes.val &=
      ~TPMA_OBJECT_ADMINWITHPOLICY;
    in.inPublic.t.publicArea.objectAttributes.val |=
      TPMA_OBJECT_SIGN;
    in.inPublic.t.publicArea.objectAttributes.val &=
      ~TPMA_OBJECT_DECRYPT;
    in.inPublic.t.publicArea.objectAttributes.val &=
      ~TPMA_OBJECT_RESTRICTED;

    in.inSensitive.t.sensitive.data.t.size = 0;

    /* optional authorization policy */
```

```
if (policyFilename != NULL) {
  rc = File_Read2B(&in.inPublic.t.publicArea.authPolicy.b,
  sizeof(TPMU_HA),
  policyFilename);
}
else {
  in.inPublic.t.publicArea.authPolicy.t.size = 0;/* default empty
    policy */
}

in.outsideInfo.t.size = 0;
in.creationPCR.count = 0;

rc = TSE_Execute((RESPONSE_PARAMETERS *)&out,
        (COMMAND_PARAMETERS *)&in,
        NULL,
        TPM_CC_Create,
        sessionHandle0, parentPassword, sessionAttributes0,
        TPM_RH_NULL, NULL, 0);

/* save the private key */
if ((rc == 0) && (privateKeyFilename != NULL)) {
  rc = File_WriteStructure(&out.outPrivate,
  (MarshalFunction_t)TSS_TPM2B_PRIVATE_Marshal,
  privateKeyFilename);
}
/* save the public key */
if ((rc == 0) && (publicKeyFilename != NULL)) {
  rc = File_WriteStructure(&out.outPublic,
  (MarshalFunction_t)TSS_TPM2B_PUBLIC_Marshal,
  publicKeyFilename);
```

The output structure from TPM2_Create has two fields: outPrivate and outPublic. The contents of these will vary based on the object type, but we can generally treat them as black boxes.

6.16.2 Key loading

Loading a key requires the inputting of private and public data structures returned by TPM2_Create. Note that no interpretation is required if keys are just being created and loaded; the private and public portions can be treated as blobs.

```
Load_In                        in;
Load_Out                       out;


/* Read key data from file. */
File_ReadStructure(&in.inPrivate,
                    (UnmarshalFunction_t)TPM2B_PRIVATE_
                    Unmarshal,
                    privateKeyFilename);
```

```
File_ReadStructure(&in.inPublic,
                   (UnmarshalFunction_t)TPM2B_PUBLIC_
                   Unmarshal,
                   publicKeyFilename);

/* Set parent handle to already loaded storage key */
in.parentHandle = parentHandle;

/* Load key. Note that we only need to pass in the
   parent password; the key password, if any,
 * will be checked on use. */

TSE_Execute((RESPONSE_PARAMETERS *)&out,
            (COMMAND_PARAMETERS *)&in,
            NULL,
            TPM_CC_Load,
            sessionHandle0, parentPassword,
            sessionAttributes0,
            TPM_RH_NULL, NULL, 0);

    printf(''Handle %08x\n'', out.objectHandle);
```

6.16.3   Using public keys

Reading the public portion of a TPM 2.0 key uses the same command as reading the public portion of any other TPM-constructed data structure: TPM2_Read Public.

```
ReadPublic_In                in;
ReadPublic_Out               out;
TPMI_DH_OBJECT                   objectHandle = TPM_RH_
                                 NULL;

...
/* Retrieve object handle from user */
...

in.objectHandle = objectHandle;

TSE_Execute((RESPONSE_PARAMETERS *)&out,
            (COMMAND_PARAMETERS *)&in,
            NULL,
            TPM_CC_ReadPublic,
            TPM_RH_NULL, NULL, 0);
```

The out parameter here has three fields: *outPublic*, *name*, and *qualifiedName*. *outPublic* is the one that is of most interest to us. This is a TPM2B_PUBLIC data structure, which itself contains a UINT16 *size* and a TPMT_PUBLIC *publicArea* data structure, which actually contains the information that we're looking for. Note that the exact contents of this data structure will vary with the type of object being queried. For an RSA key, the public key (modulus) will be in the *unique* field, which in this case will be a TPM2B_PUBLIC_KEY_RSA structure. For an ECC key, the same field will instead contain a TPMS_ECC_POINT structure. If additional data about a key is required, it can generally be found in the *parameters* field, which again varies based on the type of key.

Note that the same *outPublic* data structure also contains information about an object's attributes and authorization policy, which can be useful. You can find all of the details, including how to interpret public data structures for non-key objects, in section 12.2 of the TPM 2.0 Structures specification. (See Section 11.6.2 on page 281.)

6.16.4 Enhanced Authorization policies

As discussed previously, setting up Enhanced Authorization policies can be quite complicated! This section won't provide you with comprehensive information on implementing every possible policy, but will give you a basic idea of how to build EA policies for your own use.

The first command you'll be using is TPM2_StartAuthSession. This has two effective modes for Enhanced Authorization: trial mode, which is used when building policy digests for key creation and other future use, and policy mode, which is used when actually trying to meet an authorization policy. (The command is also used for other authorization sessions, with a third mode.)

This command is also our first introduction to the rare IBM TSS 2.0 'extra argument'. You may have noticed that the third argument in all of our TSE_EXECUTE commands has been NULL; here, it won't be. This extra parameter contains the password used to calculate the session key.

Two values are returned by this command: the authorization session handle, which we'll pass to other policy commands (or other sequence commands, for HMAC sessions), and a TPM nonce, which is used to calculate the session key for this session. The session key is used to derive values for authorization and parameter encryption.

```
        StartAuthSession_In          in;
        StartAuthSession_Out         out;
        StartAuthSession_Extra       extra;
        TPMI_DH_OBJECT               tpmKey = TPM_RH_NULL;
/* salt key */
        TPMI_DH_ENTITY               bindHandle = TPM_RH_NULL;
/* default */
        const char                   *bindPassword = NULL;
        char                         seChar = 0;
/* session type */
        TPMI_ALG_HASH                halg = TPM_ALG_SHA256;
```

```
/* default */
    TPMI_ALG_SYM                     algorithm = TPM_ALG_XOR;
/* default symmetric algorithm */
    const char                       *nonceTPMFilename = NULL;
/* File to store returned nonce */

    ...
    /* Retrieve bindPassword,  nonceTPMFilename from user.*/
    /* Retrieve optional tpmKey handle: must be loaded decrypt key,
       used to decrypt optional salt.
     * Null handle is acceptable. If both bindHandle and tpmKey are
       null handle,
     * no session key will be used. */
    ...

    /* Establish the session type.
     * Other options:
     * TPM\_SE\_POLICY for starting an actual authorization session.
     * TPM\_SE\_HMAC for HMAC sessions. */
    in.sessionType = TPM_SE_TRIAL;

    /* salt key  */
    in.tpmKey = tpmKey;
    /* encryptedSalt (not required) */
    in.encryptedSalt.b.size = 0;
    /* bind handle */
    in.bind = bindHandle;
    /* nonceCaller (not required); sets nonce size for the session */
    in.nonceCaller.t.size = 0;
    /* algorithm used for parameter encryption */
    in.symmetric.algorithm = algorithm;
    /* hash algorithm used for session */
    in.authHash = halg;

    if (in.symmetric.algorithm == TPM_ALG_XOR) {
            in.symmetric.keyBits.xor = halg;
            in.symmetric.mode.sym = TPM_ALG_NULL;
/* none for xor */
        }
    else {            /* AES */
            in.symmetric.keyBits.aes = 128;
            in.symmetric.mode.aes = TPM_ALG_CFB;



    /* Pass the user-provided bind password to the TSE post processor
     * for the session key calculation. */
    extra.bindPassword = bindPassword;

  TSE_Execute((RESPONSE_PARAMETERS *)&out,
                      (COMMAND_PARAMETERS *)&in,
                      (EXTRA_PARAMETERS *)&extra,
                      TPM_CC_StartAuthSession,
                      TPM_RH_NULL, NULL, 0);
```

```
/* store the nonceTPM for future use */
File_WriteBinaryFile((uint8_t *)&out.nonceTPM.t.buffer,
                               out.nonceTPM.t.size,
                               nonceTPMFilename);

/* Return the policy session handle to the user, for use in other
   commands. */
printf(''startauthsession: handle %08x\n,'' out.sessionHandle);
```

The complexity of other policy commands varies widely. For example, here's TPM2_PolicyAuthValue, which says that the authorization value that would normally be used to do authorization-based access to the resource must also be provided when doing policy-based access. Because the authorization being checked belongs to the object the policy will be attached to, no additional information beside the policy session needs to be passed in. Note that there is no output for this command: the current hash value reflecting the sequence of policy commands run is part of the TPM's internal data for the policy session.

```
TPMI_SH_POLICY                policySession = 0;
PolicyAuthValue_In            in;


...
/* Retrieve policy session handle from user */
...

in.policySession = policySession;

TSE_Execute(NULL,
            (COMMAND_PARAMETERS *)&in,
            NULL,
            TPM_CC_PolicyAuthValue,
            TPM_RH_NULL, NULL, 0);
```

TPM2_PolicyOR is a little bit more complicated. In addition to the policy session handle, it takes a list of provided digest values, and checks to see if the current policy session digest matches a value in the list. If it does, the new policy digest for the session will be the concatenation of all of the digests in the list. Lists of digests provided to TPM2_PolicyOR should not be more than 8 digests long.

```
PolicyOR_In                   in;
TPMI_SH_POLICY                policySession = 0;
const char                    *pHashListFilename[8];
uint32_t                      count = 0;
```

```
...
/* Retrieve up to 8 file names containing policy digests
   from the user */
/* Set count to the number of file names retrieved */
/* Retrieve current policy session handle from the user */
...

in.policySession = policySession;
in.pHashList.count = count;
for (j = 0 ; j < count ; j++) {
    File_Read2B(&in.pHashList.digests[j].b,
                    sizeof(TPMU_HA),
                    pHashListFilename[j]);
}
TSE_Execute(NULL,
                (COMMAND_PARAMETERS *)&in,
                NULL,
                TPM_CC_PolicyOR,
                TPM_RH_NULL, NULL, 0);
```

At the much more complex end of the scale, we have commands such as TPM2_PolicySigned, which allows access if another policy which has been approved (signed) by a particular authority is met. Its most critical new argument is *authObject*, which is the handle of a public key for validating the authority signature; however, it also provides a number of new options. *cpHashA* is an optional parameter which takes a digest of command parameters which must be matched in order for the authorization to be used. (This allows, e.g., an IT department to create arbitrary policies for executing a TPM2_Quote on a given machine without allowing them to use the same restricted signing key to sign other data.) *policyRef* is an optional value that the signing authority may provide to identify policies or classes of policies; from the TPM's perspective, this is a black box. *expiration* is a time window defining how long this policy can be used. *auth* is a signed digest, and mandatory; the signature will not be checked if the current policy session is a trial session, however.

This is another command that requires an extra argument to TSE_EXECUTE; this time, it's a bit of an oddity, since it isn't actually used by the TPM. Instead, this particular IBM TSS 2.0 command combines the TPM TPM2_PolicySigned function and the actual signing of a policy digest using a software key. The extra argument is a callback function used for the signing of the policy digest.

The command produces two outputs, unlike most policy commands. One is a timeout value which indicates when the provided ticket expires. The other is a policy ticket structure, produced if the command succeeds and the expiration time has not passed.

```
PolicySigned_In          in;
PolicySigned_Out         out;
PolicySigned_Extra       extra;
```

```
TPMI_DH_OBJECT              authObject = 0; // Handle of object
                                for signature verification
TPMI_SH_POLICY              policySession = 0; // Policy session
                                handle
const char                  *nonceTPMFilename = NULL;
const char                  *cpHashAFilename = NULL;
const char                  *policyRefFilename = NULL;
const char                  *ticketFilename = NULL;
const char                  *timeoutFilename = NULL;
INT32                       expiration = 0;
TPMI_ALG_HASH               halg = TPM_ALG_SHA256;

...
/* Retrieve handles, filenames, and relevant passwords from user. */
...

        in.authObject = authObject;
        in.policySession = policySession;
        in.expiration = expiration;
        in.auth.sigAlg = TPM_ALG_RSASSA;
        in.auth.signature.rsassa.hash = halg;

        /* Read in optional arguments from files */
        File_Read2B(&in.nonceTPM.b,
                        sizeof(TPMU_HA),
                        nonceTPMFilename);
        File_Read2B(&in.cpHashA.b,
                        sizeof(TPMU_HA),
                        cpHashAFilename);
        File_Read2B(&in.policyRef.b,
                        sizeof(TPMU_HA),
                        policyRefFilename);

        /* signatureCallback is a function returning a signature
         * over a policy digest. In the IBM example code, it uses
           a software key
         * retrieved from the user. */
        extra.signatureCallback = signatureCallback;

        TSE_Execute((RESPONSE_PARAMETERS *)&out,
                        (COMMAND_PARAMETERS *)&in,
                        (EXTRA_PARAMETERS *)&extra,
                        TPM_CC_PolicySigned,
                        TPM_RH_NULL, NULL, 0);

        /* Note that the primary effect of this command, like other
           policy commands,
         * is to change the value of the session policy digest.
           The output values
         * are just potentially useful side effects. */

        File_WriteStructure(&out.policyTicket,
                                (MarshalFunction_t)TSS_TPMT_TK_AUTH_
                                Marshal,
                                ticketFilename);
```

```
File_WriteBinaryFile(out.timeout.b.buffer,
                                out.timeout.b.size,
                                timeoutFilename);
```

Once we've created the policy we want – or a policy we want to use as one of the inputs to TPM2_PolicyOR – we use the TPM2_PolicyGetDigest command to retrieve the current session digest.

```
PolicyGetDigest_In         in;
PolicyGetDigest_Out        out;
TPMI_SH_POLICY             policySession = 0;
const char                 *digestFilename = NULL;

...
/* Retrieve policy session handle and filename from user. */
...

in.policySession = policySession;

TSE_Execute((RESPONSE_PARAMETERS *)&out,
            (COMMAND_PARAMETERS *)&in,
            NULL,
            TPM_CC_PolicyGetDigest,
            TPM_RH_NULL, NULL, 0);

File_WriteBinaryFile(out.policyDigest.t.buffer,
                                out.policyDigest.t.size,
                                digestFilename );
```

Chapter 7

Machine authentication

Who are you?

7.1 What is machine authentication?

Authentication, in this context, refers to the verification of identity data in the form of a cryptographic key. Machine authentication is thus all about identifying a machine via its keys. This is particularly effective in a TPM context because the cryptographic keys are usable inside the TPM itself, and the TPM is attached to the motherboard; in some cases, the TPM is even a subset of the CPU. This means that if you can prove that a set of keys belonging to a given TPM was used, the machine that TPM is attached to must have been involved.[1]

Machine authentication is therefore a property we effectively get for free with many TPM applications. Any use case where a remote party is verifying a TPM key can be used for machine authentication.

7.1.1 Signing versus encryption

There are two primary approaches to machine authentication: signing-based authentication and encryption-based authentication. These approaches are based on the two operations that a remote party can verify cryptographically. If Alice signs a message and Bob can verify the signature, then Bob can prove that Alice's key has been used. And if Bob creates an encrypted message and Alice proves that she could read the contents, that similarly provides Bob with proof that Alice's key has been used. At a fundamental level, signing-based authentication identifies the sender, while encryption-based authentication verifies the recipient; however, protocols can be designed to allow either form of authentication to be used to authenticate any party in a transaction.

---

[1]Barring serious physical attacks where someone has removed the TPM from the motherboard, of course; see Section 1.3.7.3 for more information on the TPM's tamper resistance and Section 1.3.3 for more information on the TPM's threat model.

I break these approaches up into two sections because the protocols to use them look different, and the TPM commands and keys are different. The ideas behind both approaches are the same.

7.1.2   The limits of TPM-based machine authentication

It's easy to get caught up in the idea that since a key is in a TPM attached to a motherboard, any use of that key proves that the machine you're talking to is really the machine in question. The problem with this is man-in-the-middle attacks. These attacks can be on-system or network based.

In the on-system scenario, the man in the middle is operating on the TPM's platform. The authentication is genuine, but it is being used for bad purposes, such as providing a false identity for a different machine. The TPM is just a cryptographic chip. It has no idea what the context of the cryptographic operations it is performing might be, or should be. It will perform those operations equally well for user-approved software and for malware. Key passwords can reduce this risk, but not eliminate it, since targeted malware with the right system access can potentially intercept the password on its way from the user to the TPM software and then reuse it.

Even in an uncompromised machine, TPM keys do not provide perfect proof that a communications partner is the machine with the TPM, because of protocol-based flaws. If an attacker can fool a good machine into responding to a challenge from a malicious server, then the attacker can potentially masquerade as that good machine to a legitimate server by forwarding messages and data.

Note that in both cases, the genuine machine with the legitimate key *is* participating in the authentication process; however, it may not be participating in the way other people expect. When designing machine authentication systems, it is important to keep both potential problems in mind. I'll discuss some mitigation strategies later in this chapter.

7.1.3   What about user authentication?

This chapter is focussed on machine authentication, but one application that many enterprises are interested in is using the TPM for user authentication. In the most common variant of this case, the TPM – as part of the computer – is considered the 'thing you have' for two-factor authentication. It can also be used as part of complex access control mechanisms; for example, a company with extremely strict procedures might limit access to a database containing social security numbers to HR employees logged in to particular desktop machines in a locked-down room, thereby preventing those same employees from downloading the social security numbers on to a laptop to take home for weekend work.

The big challenge in using the TPM for user authentication is that the TPM doesn't know about users. Keys and other TPM objects such as encrypted data or key hierarchies can be tied to a particular user's password, but the TPM has no way of knowing the user's identity or reporting to an external party which password is authorized for a given resource. If we're going to trust a user identity based on TPM activity, therefore, one of two things needs to occur. Either a trusted party must provision TPM resources in such a fashion that they are user-constrained, or the cryptographic protocols used to verify user identity must tie that user identity to the TPM. Both of these present significant challenges. I will discuss user authentication in more detail in Section 7.4.

I'll discuss the provisioning of a TPM to provide evidence about its state – including user access – in Chapter 9. I'll discuss how to include user-provided data – which can include user identity information as well as application data – later in this chapter, in Section 7.2.3, and cover identity-specific challenges in Section 7.4.

7.2 Signing-based machine authentication

7.2.1 How it works

Cryptographic signatures form the basis of the most common and easiest to understand technique for machine authentication. A machine has an asymmetric cryptographic key; it uses that key to sign data; the recipient can then verify the signature was created using the correct key (Figure 7.1).

Any signing-based command that uses a TPM key can provide signing-based machine authentication. The most obvious – TPM_Sign or TPM2_Sign – sign user-provided data. It's important to call out here that the TPM doesn't usually sign the data directly; instead, as is standard for asymmetric signatures, the TPM signs a hash of the data. This is done because asymmetric signatures are highly expensive,

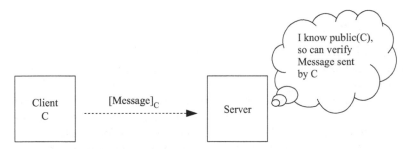

Figure 7.1   The basic concept behind asymmetric signing-based machine authentication. There are a few important things to note here. First, the server needs to know something about C's key in order to verify C's identity; the public key for asymmetric signatures, or the whole key for symmetric HMACs. Secondly, the server knows that C sent the message; it doesn't know that it hasn't passed through other entities between C and the server, or (without more context, such as the message contents) that C intended to send it to this server. Thirdly, the server doesn't know that the message originated at C, just that C sent it; if C is acting as a man in the middle, the contents could have been provided and even signed by some other party, with C replacing the original signature with its own

and the cost increases in proportion to the size of the data; in order to perform the operation reasonably, the content must be small. Using a hash gives us cryptographic verification of the original file without the size. For 1.2 TPMs, 20-byte SHA1 hashes are standard as input. 2.0 TPMs are flexible about the hashing algorithm used, in order to be more future-proof, but should support at least SHA1 and SHA256.

7.2.1.1 HMACs versus signatures

Symmetric cryptography can't be used to make what cryptographers refer to as a signature. It can, however, be used to create an HMAC, or Hashed Message Authentication Code. These serve a similar purpose to an asymmetric signature, in that a recipient can verify that the key was used to authenticate the message data; however, they are unlike an asymmetric signature, in that the recipient also must have a copy of the key in order to verify the message. This means that while HMACs can be used in many of the same places as the other authentication schemes we'll discussing, they will never truly authenticate a *single* machine. Rather, the HMAC must have been produced by *some* machine that knows the key. In some cases, when the only goal is to prove that a machine is a member of a trusted group, this can be useful, and HMACs are generally much faster to produce than an asymmetric signature.

HMACs will not be a focus of this section, because they generally meet a subset of signature use cases, do not provide true machine authentication, and are not supported by 1.2 TPMs. If you're designing an application that needs high speed message authentication, however, they're worth keeping in mind; just consider the trade-offs. HMACs are discussed in more detail in Section 7.2.3.2.

7.2.2   When to use it

Signing-based machine authentication is most useful when you have some data that you wish to associate with a machine. The data could be a file, a software-generated report, a transaction log – anything where it would be useful to verify that the data was present on a given machine. This form of machine authentication is very powerful for finding out where data came from, in real time or at a later date. Remember, however, that the signature only proves that the signed data was *present* on the machine, not that it originated there. While TPMs can be used for rough watermarking, the signatures are fundamentally an approximation of an actual proof of origination of the content: a TPM on a compromised machine or using a flawed communications protocol could potentially be tricked into signing data for a remote party.

When the data being signed is part of a cryptographic protocol – a session ID, for example, or a nonce – signing-based authentication just provides a straightforward and easy method for identifying a machine. In this case, the data itself is relevant only in context; outside the protocol, the signature is effectively meaningless. The most common use case here is challenge–response protocols, where a remote party provides a challenge and the machine being authenticated signs the challenge and sends it back.

It is particularly critical to watch out for situations where the same machine may be executing both signing-based cryptographic protocols and signatures for data authentication. It is all too easy to accidentally set up a situation where, for example, a remote party participating in a challenge–response protocol can send a challenge that results in output identical to a signature of locally generated data if one is not careful. It is therefore wise to use different techniques or different keys for signing-based authentication in cryptographic protocols from those you use for signing documents. Using a different key for each possible application is generally a good idea, especially if you're dealing with remote parties.

7.2.3 The TPM and signing-based authentication

The basic techniques for signing-based authentication are the same in 1.2 and 2.0 TPMs. In both cases, you can use commands which sign arbitrary data coming from outside the TPM, most notably the `Sign` commands, or commands which sign data stored inside the TPM. Different keys can be used depending on where the data being signed comes from.

The difference between TPM-stored data and externally provided data can feel very arbitrary for signing-based authentication, especially since the most common techniques we'll be discussing for TPM-stored data involve taking externally provided data and putting it into the TPM before signing it. The distinction is going to be far more critical when it comes to attestation, as discussed in Chapter 9, but it isn't meaningless here. In particular, the distinction can be very useful in two primary ways:

- Distinguishing between signatures verifying files and user-generated data from signatures verifying cryptographic protocols
- Providing additional verification that the data being signed was approved by someone on the system.

7.2.3.1 1.2 Techniques

Signing-based machine authentication techniques in a 1.2 TPM depend, first and foremost, on what kind of key is being used. As we discussed in Chapter 6, identity keys are used to sign data created by the TPM, while signing keys should be used only to sign user-created data. In both cases, the use of the key proves that the signed data came from the machine whose TPM signed the data, but for many use cases the data contents matter.

For signing keys, the most critical command is `TPM_Sign`. This lets the TPM sign arbitrary user-provided data, as long as it is in the correct format for the key: either a 20-byte SHA1 hash[2] for a SHA1-scheme key, or DER-coded information[3] whose maximum length is proportional to the key size for a DER-scheme key. The maximum length of data a DER-scheme key will accept is 117 bytes for a 1024-bit key and 245 bytes for a 2048-bit key.[4] Longer messages are signed by creating a hash or other digest of the message.

---

[2] Or other 20-byte content – the TPM can't tell a legitimate hash from any other 20-byte string.
[3] Again, the TPM won't check the validity of the format, just the length of the data.
[4] Why such arbitrary numbers? That's k-11 bytes (octets, in RFC 3447, the PKCS #1 RSA specification), where k is the length of the key in bytes.

The biggest advantage of using signing keys and TPM_Sign is that they require no custom TPM formats, and more than any other TPM function are usable as drop-in replacements for software signatures. That means that many programs which use signatures as part of an authentication protocol can be adapted to use full TPM-based machine authentication simply by sending the signature operation to the TPM instead of using a software library. Another advantage is simple flexibility: any piece of data can be tied to any machine with a TPM simply by signing the data or data digest. If there is a need to prove that the data is current, a nonce (fresh random value) can be included in the data, as I will discuss in more detail in Section 7.2.4.

In short, for the vast majority of signing-based machine authentication use cases with 1.2 TPMs, a signing key and TPM_Sign are the best choice.

- Signing keys can be created to sign 20-byte SHA-1 hashes, or up to 245 bytes of data with a 2048-bit DER-scheme key.
    - If you're using a 1.2 TPM and want stronger cryptography for digests, SHA-256 hashes can be signed with DER keys.
- Any data of any size can be signed by the TPM, although large data must be hashed or otherwise digested first.
- Signatures produced with the TPM_Sign command do not require any knowledge of TPMs to verify, allowing them to be used in a wide range of applications.
- Anyone who can verify the signature and certificates tying the key to the TPM can perform machine authentication on the signed data.

However, identity keys can also be used for signing-based machine authentication. Normally, this involves conveying information produced by the TPM: that a particular certificate was issued by given TPM and thus that the associated key is usable only on the associated machine, that the TPM's PCRs have certain contents, or that the TPM's tick counter has a particular value (see Section 10.9.4). In all cases, the use of the identity key still provides machine identification. Any command that takes a nonce (see Section 7.2.4) and produces signed data, including the nonce, can be used as part of a challenge–response protocol to confirm that the machine in question is on the other side of a remote connection, although it is important to protect against man-in-the-middle attacks (see Section 7.2.5).

TPM quotes, which will be discussed in much more detail in Chapter 9, have two useful properties when it comes to machine authentication. First, they take a nonce (see Section 7.2.4 for why this is important) and produce signed output including the nonce, which gives us a challenge–response protocol to prove freshness. Secondly, they include our choice of PCR contents; while we'll mostly be using this feature when discussing attestation of machine state, PCRs can also be extended with arbitrary data by a user. Although PCRs in a 1.2 TPM are only large enough to store a SHA-1 hash, that hash can be of anything: not only software, but also files, session identifiers, or other arbitrary data. Several PCRs are not used for measurements, and are free to be repurposed by user-level software. Some of them are *resettable*: they can be restored to their default value at any time, allowing them to be used to store individual values or short sequences without either requiring or revealing a full history since boot. Thus, user data stored in PCRs and included in a quote can give us a useful tool:

a TPM-signed data structure containing both a nonce and any number of user data hashes. Quotes can also be used to combine a signature of user data with attestation information about a machine's state at the time the data was signed, by quoting both a PCR extended with user data and PCRs containing state information. The downside of quotes is that the data structure is extremely TPM-specific, and requires either significant familiarity with the TPM or with a TPM library to verify. Quotes cannot be dropped into existing protocols or software without changing both the signing and verification ends.

It is also important to note that although the 1.2 `Quote` commands have an argument called 'user data', and the 2.0 command has the ambiguous 'qualifyingData' parameter, the associated field should *only* be used for random nonces, and should *never* be used for meaningful user data. Overloading the meaning of the nonce opens the door to an array of very nasty man-in-the-middle attacks if quotes are ever used without the meaningful nonce field. I'll discuss this further in Section 7.2.4.

Using identity keys for signing-based machine authentication thus has some pros and cons.

- Identity keys are used for machine authentication where the signed data is produced by the TPM.
- Many signed TPM data structures are designed for use with nonces to prove freshness of data.
- User data can be included by extending the data into a PCR and creating a Quote; the Quote can optionally also be used for attestation purposes.
- However, all TPM-created data structures require knowledge of TPMs or the use of a TPM library to verify. They are not suitable for many backwards-compatible applications, and upgrading software to use them is more complicated than with the corresponding Sign-based authentication.

7.2.3.2 2.0 Techniques

2.0 TPMs simplify the question of what kind of key can be used for signing-based attestation: any key with the signing attribute can be used, regardless of algorithm choice. Restricted signing keys are (slightly) more limited: they cannot be used to sign any user-provided data which would mimic a legitimate TPM-created structure. This makes them useful in place of 1.2's identity keys for any operation in which we want to trust data coming from the TPM, as discussed in detail in Chapter 9. Unlike identity keys, however, restricted signing keys may be used to sign almost all user-provided data as long as the TPM is used to calculate the digest, which makes them suitable for most general-purpose use as well. The exception is cases where the speed of the TPM when calculating digests would add too much of a time burden.

Signing keys in 2.0 can be asymmetric or symmetric. A symmetric signing key is one which can be used for calculating HMACs. These are not as useful for machine authentication as asymmetric signatures, because by definition every verifier must know the key in order to verify the HMAC, but I'll discuss them here because the basic ideas are similar.

The primary asymmetric signing operation in 2.0 TPMs is `TPM2_Sign`; this is almost identical to the 1.2 command, but has two new arguments in addition to the existing key handle and digest to be signed. The first new argument is an optional signature scheme, which can be provided per command if no scheme was defined for the key itself. The second is an optional validation check, which is used to prove that a given digest was produced by the TPM when a restricted signing key is used. When the TPM is used to produce the digest, it will return a validation value along with the digest; the validation value will allow the digest to be signed by a restricted signing key if the original content did not mimic a TPM-generated data structure. This can be done using the atomic TPM2_Hash command, or by combining the TPM2_HashSequenceStart, TPM2_SequenceUpdate, and TPM2_SequenceComplete commands, which produce a hash over all of the data in an incrementally updated sequence. These are described in more detail in Section 10.10.1.

The TPM2_HMAC command (or the set of TPM2_HMAC_Start, TPM2_SequenceUpdate, and TPM2_SequenceComplete) can be used to create an HMAC on user-supplied data. This command takes user-provided data, a hash algorithm to use, and the handle of a non-restricted, signing-capable symmetric key with the TPM_ALG_KEYEDHASH type, and returns the resulting HMAC. HMACs, like signatures, are useful for proving that a particular piece of data was present on a machine in possession of a particular key, and that someone with authorization to use the key created it. Unlike asymmetric signatures, HMACs can never uniquely identify a machine, because the verifier must know the key, although in practice the difference between 'only one machine knows this key' and 'only two machines know this key, I'm one of them, and I didn't sign this' can often be quite small. Note that because the key must be shared, a symmetric key which is created on the TPM and which is not duplicatable (see Section 6.6.3) is not useful for remote verification. For high-security verifiable symmetric keys, create them as duplicatable TPM keys and distribute them by encrypting them to the TPMs of the machines which will be producing or verifying HMACKs.

2.0 TPMs provide new commands to certify TPM-created data, including the time since the machine has rebooted, recorded by the TPM's internal clock, and creation information for TPM-created objects. These can all be used for machine authentication, like quotes, but I'll be covering them in more detail in the Attestation chapter (Chapter 9).

2.0 TPMs also introduce a new on-chip command for verifying signatures, allowing TPMs to be used for the verification side of machine authentication. The TPM2_VerifySignature command takes advantage of the fact that 2.0 TPMs can load public asymmetric keys for which they do not have the private data, although it can be used to verify either symmetric or asymmetric signatures. This command takes the handle of a loaded public or symmetric key, the digest that was signed, and the signature, and returns a successful verification message or an error.

7.2.4   Nonces: why they matter and how to use them

A common category of use cases for machine authentication involves identifying a machine we are currently communicating with. In these cases, it is critically important that I am able to distinguish between a signature made now, and a signature that has been replayed from a previous interaction, with us or someone else. This is what *nonces* are for.

> *Nonce: a freshly generated random (and therefore unpredictable) value.*

Because nonces are random numbers, if any reasonable generation function is used it will be vanishingly unlikely that an adversary could predict which value will be picked for a given transaction. This means that if a nonce is part of a challenge, and is received back as part of a signed response, the signature must have been generated as part of this transaction.

Time stamps are sometimes used as nonce alternatives, but are not safe for many applications. This is because an adversary can predict a time stamp, which makes it much more feasible for them to create a fake response at an earlier time and replay it; all they have to do is take advantage of a clock error or trick the signing machine into participating in a protocol which signs adversary-provided data, and include the time stamp. While this can be defended against by using different keys or signature types for each type of interaction, it is simplest to use nonces whenever possible. Session IDs made up of information contained within a particular protocol session can have similar problems, if the information is highly predictable.

Because nonce fields contain user-provided data, it can be tempting to overload them. One Trusted Network Connect protocol created by the TCG for using TPMs in an enterprise context did this, as shown in Figures 7.2 and 7.3. The challenger would provide a fresh nonce, the target would XOR the nonce with a hash of a file measurement, and the result would be used as the nonce for a quote. Unfortunately, these sorts of overloads can result in some very nasty, very subtle, and very easy man-in-the-middle attacks, especially in a context like this, where one party – the TPM – is

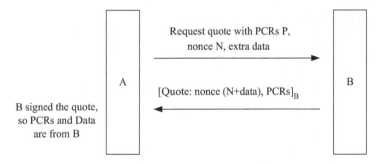

Figure 7.2   A real-world flawed protocol that uses nonces badly. A is using TPM quotes to verify B's state; in addition to the contents of the PCRs, A asks B to provide extra data, such as the current system report, so that software beyond what's being measured in the PCRs can be assessed. The extra data is hashed, and the hash combined with the nonce. Because A knows the nonce and can produce the hash of the data, A can verify the signature on the quote, as well as the validity of the data

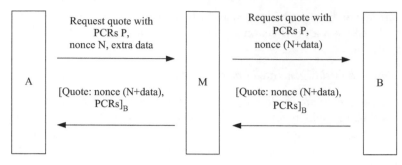

Figure 7.3   The attack on the previous protocol. Here, a man in the middle is taking advantage of the fact that B also will perform perfectly ordinary TPM quotes when requested. Since quotes are a standard TPM operation, this is a common scenario. From A's perspective, the results are identical to the expected behaviour. From B's perspective, they provided a routine quote with no additional data. Both parties acted reasonably, but the man in the middle was allowed to inject a completely arbitrary set of extra data and deceive A into believing it came from B. Because nonces are unstructured random data, B has no way of telling that the nonce the man in the middle provided contained additional meaning

not expecting the nonce field to carry meaning, and where multiple protocols using the same operation – like a TPM quote – may be running on the same network. If the challenger thinks that the target will modify the nonce, and the target thinks they're running a different protocol, which uses a challenger's nonce with no changes, then there's a mismatch in expectations that an adversary can take advantage of.

7.2.5   Mitigating man-in-the-middle attacks

One of the biggest risks of signing-based machine authentication is man-in-the-middle attacks. In these scenarios, an attacker masquerades as the machine being authenticated to the challenger, while masquerading as the challenger to the machine being authenticated. It is important to note that for machine authentication purposes, there are really two kinds of man-in-the-middle attack. One is the classic kind, where both parties are honest and the man-in-the-middle is forwarding and generating messages deceitfully between them. The second is where an adversary controls the machine being authenticated, usually via malware, and can forward requests to the controlled machine from other machines, causing those machines to appear to be the recognized machine. I'll call these 'control' attacks.[5] They can be highly problematic; for example, if an enterprise allows only recognized enterprise machines on to their network, expecting them to be running approved software, an adversary who can gain access to the authentication functions on a single machine can potentially use them to allow arbitrary other machines on to the network as well.

---

[5]This is not industry-standard terminology, just a convenience for this particular discussion.

It is far easier to prevent a classic man-in-the-middle attack than to prevent a control man-in-the-middle attack; however, there are a variety of mitigating techniques that can be used against one or both.

- Use encryption-based authentication (see Section 7.3). Protects against many classic attacks when used as part of a well-designed protocol.
- Make sure that the expected identities of both participants in a conversation are included in signed messages, preferably from both participants. Protects against classic attacks; must be combined with replay prevention, such as nonces, to be effective.
- Use a command which signs TPM-internal data, such as a quote (see Section 9.3.1) and enforce some level of access control on placing data into those TPM locations. This does not entirely prevent control attacks, but requires an attacker to have a higher degree of control over the machine and the TPM. Does not protect against classic attacks.
- Use software which requires active user confirmation to perform an authentication; for example, by requiring a password to be provided whenever a given key is used. Again, this does not entirely prevent control attacks, but it raises the bar for the attacker, especially if techniques are used to make keylogging more difficult during password input. Does not protect against classic attacks.

Why doesn't running signing-based machine authentication through an encrypted channel help against man-in-the-middle attacks? It can, in the right circumstances, but the problem rapidly becomes extremely complicated. How do you know who's on the other side of your encrypted channel? Many encrypted channels do not provide authentication of both participants. What if the party on the other end of the channel, who you trust, is also acting as a man in the middle – perhaps unknowingly, owing to compromised software – and is forwarding traffic on to a third party you're not even aware of? If you want to use encryption to protect data in transit, think about using the encryption-based machine authentication techniques described below, and then think about how you will establish trust in your communications partners.

7.3   Encryption-based machine authentication

In Section 7.2, I discussed how TPM-signed data can be used to authenticate a machine. In this section, I'll discuss a less common approach to machine authentication, using encryption.

7.3.1   How it works

Both signing and encryption-based authentication work because a remote party can prove that the private key corresponding to a given public key has been used. Thus, technically, encryption-based authentication should properly be termed decryption-based authentication: the verifier encrypts a secret, and if the recipient can prove they

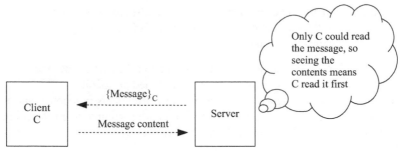

*Figure 7.4   Encryption-based authentication relies on two secrets: the one C
knows, such as a private key or shared secret with the server, which is
used to encrypt the data; and the one the server includes in the
message, which is usually a random nonce. Without a secret that the
server knows only C can use to read the message, encryption-based
authentication is impossible; however, the second secret is also
necessary, because otherwise the server cannot be certain that the
message has actually been accessed. The key feature of a message used
for encryption-based authorization is that some part of the message
must not be predictable, since otherwise an adversary could fake the
message decryption without ever seeing the true contents. Note that the
server knows only that C received and decrypted the message, and sent
out some of the contents; the server does not know, without additional
information, that C knew the message came from the server, or that the
message contents weren't received and modified by another party
between C and the server. Most encryption-based authentication
protocols include additional information, such as the server and client
names inside the encrypted messages, and a signature from the server
or an encryption to the server in the second message. One common use
of encryption-based authentication is to establish a shared session key,
which also acts as the second secret. Only the targeted recipient could
decrypt the message and retrieve the session key*

received the secret, they must have had access to the private key to decrypt the data
(Figure 7.4).

In the TPM 1.2 context, there are two kinds of keys which can be used for
encryption-based authentication. The first, and by far the simplest and most flexible,
is binding keys. Binding keys, unlike storage keys, allow a remote party to encrypt
data to a given TPM. The second, for using which outside its intended purposes much
more creativity is required, is the EK. Because this is such an unusual use case, I will
only discuss it briefly, later in this section.

Binding keys, as discussed in Chapter 6, are used with the Bind and Unbind
operations: but only TPM_Unbind is actually a TPM operation. Binding, unlike
Sealing, does not require the TPM's involvement, and can be executed in software by
anyone with access to the public half of the binding key. Bound data is constrained

only by any access controls on the binding key; there is no way to add additional constraints on the encrypted data itself. Full details on using Bind and Unbind can be found in Chapter 8.

In TPM 2.0, any key with the decrypt attribute can be used for encryption-based authentication, although non-restricted decryption keys are most useful. Restricted decryption keys, also known as storage keys, can only be used on TPM-formatted objects; their intended purpose is to protect TPM data, and while the TPM2_Import command, used to import duplicatable keys (see Section 6.6.3) can be used to import other keys using the same data structures, this is significant overhead for use cases involving a simple proof of possession. If the goal of the decryption-based machine authentication is to create a long-term shared secret, however, using the TPM's storage key and duplication infrastructure can be quite powerful.

Non-restricted decryption keys can be used with the fundamental primitives TPM2_RSA_Decrypt or TPM2_ECDH_ZGen.[6] These serve a similar purpose to the 1.2 TPM_Unbind command, in that they allow any party with access to a public key to encrypt data so that only the TPM can be used to access it, but unlike Binding, these fundamental primitives do not force the remote user to use TPM-specific data structures.

TPM 2.0's support for symmetric encryption also provides an additional option for decryption-based authentication, just as it does for signing-based authentication. As with signing-based authentication, symmetric key authentication will always be less strong than asymmetric key authentication, since the same key is used for encryption and decryption, and secure key distribution is required, using a mechanism such as duplication (Section 6.6.3). There is one way in which symmetric keys provide a potential advantage for authentication, however: because the key is required both for encryption and decryption, no additional signature is required to prove where the data originated as long as the key is shared only among trusted parties and there is no need to distinguish between them. The TPM2_EncryptDecrypt command can be used for both operations.

7.3.2 When to use it

Encryption-based authentication is most powerful when used to transmit data. Although it can be used in challenge–response protocols, encryption-based authentication allows a verifier to send data knowing that the authentication will be effective even if the verifier never receives a response. (Signing-based authentication has the reverse property, where the authenticated party knows that the authentication will be valid even if they never hear back from the verifier.) Encryption-based authentication can thus be used to do blind transmissions to trusted recipients, a particularly useful technique when connectivity is intermittent or data is being transmitted over physical media rather than a network.

Encryption-based machine authentication is useful *only* when the data being transmitted is secret. This means that it cannot be used to prove anything about the

---

[6]The equivalent encryption operations, which the TPM also supports, are TPM2_RSA_Encrypt and TPM2_ECDH_KeyGen. Note that the ECDH commands are very special purpose; see section 10.10.1.

identity of a machine outside of the context of a single interaction: once the secret is revealed, it can no longer be used to authenticate anyone. The interaction has no time limit, however.[7]

The identity key certification protocol described in Section 6.11.1 uses encryption-based authentication. The CA issues a secret certificate for a given untrusted identity key, knowing that only the target EK will be able to decrypt it. Authenticating the EK also provides trust in the behaviour of the associated TPM, causing the identity key to become trusted when the certificate is decrypted. The certification protocol is also the reason that the EK can be used for encryption-based authentication. The certification protocol does not require the EK to understand the contents of the signed 'certificate' provided by the CA; certificates can come in many formats, and the TPM is not verifying the signature. As far as the TPM is concerned when running the TPM_ActivateIdentity command, it is decrypting a black box which happens to be associated with a given loaded identity key. A creative user can create a custom 'certificate' data structure, just as a CA normally would, and include other authentication data; given the size of the data the TPM can decrypt, the supposed 'certificate' is often actually a symmetric key used to encrypt the real certificate, which will work just as well for encrypting other data. However, as this is a highly complicated procedure compared to a simple bind operation, and has no advantage except authenticating to the root key instead of another key on the same TPM, it is not recommended for practical use. The same caveat applies for TPM 2.0's TPM2_ActivateCredential command; a simple RSA decryption (TPM2_RSA_Decrypt) is vastly easier.

7.4   User identification versus machine authentication

As mentioned previously, while we have strong solutions for machine authentication which take advantage of the tight connections between keys and TPM and TPM and motherboard, we have less strong solutions for identifying users. In 1.2 TPMs, we have two choices to directly connect a user to a key: an authorization value (password), or finding a way to integrate user information into PCR values. 2.0 TPMs additionally allow the use of asymmetric keys to authenticate users. These bindings are not nearly as tight as the binding between key and machine: passwords can be stolen with keyloggers, the software that performs the asymmetric signatures can be hacked, or the key can be stolen. However, they can provide a reasonable approximation of user authentication, if the verifier has reason to believe that the key belongs to a particular user. For example, in an enterprise context, a user who creates a password-protected key with their TPM, registers its public key with the central database, and then calls their IT department to verify the fingerprint, is providing a fairly strong association between the user and the key, and one in which out-of-band mechanisms (such as notifying the user when their key is used to log in) can be used to catch key misuse.

Trusted software, particularly trusted OSes, can also be used to provide user authentication using the PCRs, by extending a username or other identifier into a

---

[7]If the secret is a shared key, the "interaction" lasts for as long as that key is trusted.

register when the user logs in. To be effective on anything other than a single-user system, however, it is necessary to make good use of the TPM's locality-based access control mechanisms for PCRs, discussed in much more detail in the attestation chapter, in Section 9.2. Otherwise, a user who was not the trusted OS could potentially extend a different identity into the PCR.

Another approach for user identification is to have a smartcard or other external cryptographic device owned by the user. In that case, the presence of the device could be used to verify the presence of the user. In a 2.0 system, using the smartcard's keys would be the most secure approach, but in a 1.2 system, extending a PCR with an HMAC produced by the card using a verifier's nonce can be an effective challenge–response system. Note that these solutions aren't perfect; they can be thwarted by an adversary using a man-in-the-middle-attack with software on both the computer with the TPM and a computer with the attached smartcard. It does, however, dramatically raise the bar for anyone seeking to forge a user's identity.

7.5   Machine authentication user stories

Alice wants to make sure that SecureCorp's HR and finance departments aren't opening the company up to an embarrassing breach if an employee takes data home on a laptop. Alice sets up the financial and HR databases to require not only user authentication but also machine authentication. Each user is only allowed to access the database from one of an approved list of desktop machines. When a user logs in, the database will verify that the machine the user claims to be logging in from is on the approved list, then will send a session key encrypted to that machine's TPM, using a pre-identified binding or non-restricted decryption key. Once the session key is decrypted, it is used to establish a secure channel, so that financial or personal identifying data can be sent only to the target machine. This doesn't entirely prevent breaches, since an employee determined to bypass the protections can copy the data once it's been received on the desktop, but it prevents accidental data leaks and means that an employee has to deliberately take an action to violate the data access policy.

Bob is aiming to upgrade Example, Inc.'s current TLS client-side authentication infrastructure, which uses software certificates created on each machine. Example, Inc.'s security department is concerned that client certificates make a prime target for an adversary, and would like to move towards hardware-based authentication. Bob has his coders update the corporate browser plug-in, so that clients with their TPMs set up use signing keys to sign the TLS CertificateVerify message; clients whose TPMs have not yet been provisioned, or clients without TPMs, will still use their software certificate. Once the transition period is over and all Example, Inc. client machines should have working TPMs, the software certificates will no longer be trusted. The only change Bob needs to make to his server code is in which certificates are accepted as valid. Some of Bob's users are agitating to continue to use Macs at work, which won't fit into Bob's handy transition plan; if the corporation decides the trade-off of user happiness for security is worth it, Bob will set up software TPM emulators on the corporate Macs, which will at least provide a standardized interface and features even if they lack the hardware security.

Dana has some users who would like to be able to sign documents for clients to verify without distinguishing between their laptop and desktop machines. After some consideration, Dana decides that the ease of use for customers is worth the slightly greater inconvenience in the event that a machine is lost and a key needs to be revoked. Dana has each user create a migratable signing key with an authorization policy that combines a strong password known only to the user (using `TPM2_PolicyAuthValue`) and a migration policy (using `TPM2_PolicyAuthorize` and `TPM2_PolicyDuplicationSelect`) that allows the key to be migrated to a trusted key distribution machine Dana runs, which has no network connection. Dana then has the user duplicate the key with the key distribution machine's storage key as the migration target, and uses a USB drive to bring the newly created keys to the key distribution machine. When a user wants to set up a new machine, they ask Dana to provision their signing key; Dana will re-duplicate the key using the new machine's storage key, allowing the user to sign data with the key. The signing key now provides a limited machine authentication (it is only available on the original machine, the off-line distribution machine, and the machines to which Dana has approved duplication) and a stronger user authentication (only the user who knows the password can use the key). Once the key distribution system is working, Dana decides to reuse it for decryption keys, so that clients can send data to a particular employee and have the data accessible on any of that employee's machines while still guaranteeing that access to the data will be limited.

Elaine wants each of her servers to send activity logs to a central repository for processing. Elaine has to meet compliance requirements for ensuring that logs haven't been tampered with, so she decides to make use of her server's TPMs again. She creates and certifies a non-migratable signing key on each machine. Every hour, when the logs are sent to the central repository, a hash of the log file is created and signed by the individual server's signing key. The repository can then verify that the signature is valid, which means the log file actually came from the server in question, and store it along with the data for future integrity checking. Elaine knows this doesn't protect against the log data being modified on each server before being sent out, but she is confident in her software administration practices and has put TPM attestation-based verification in place to deal with that threat separately.

Fatima is setting up a pilot project using 2.0 TPMs to enforce two-factor authentication to SecureCorp's network. She makes sure each user has a non-restricted signing key, which will be used as part of the VPN negotiations. The VPN uses an RSA-based key exchange, so the TPM key is substituted for the existing client key. Because this is part of a two-factor authentication scheme, she sets the access policy on the non-restricted signing keys to require both an authentication value (the thing you know) using `TPM2_PolicyAuthValue` and the signature from a smartcard attached to the machine (the thing you have) using `TPM2_PolicySigned`. This provides Fatima with some very strong guarantees about access to the internal corporate network.

An employee can't log in from their home machine even with their password and a copy of their VPN software's data files, because the TPM signing key cannot be transferred, and a thief who steals the laptop can't use it to log into the corporate network unless they've managed to both steal the user's smartcard and guess the user's password despite the on-system dictionary attack prevention mechanism. And because the key is tied to the hardware, all Fatima has to do to completely disallow a stolen machine is to remove the machine's keys from her trusted database.

Gabriel is maintaining a global network of both intranet and external-facing web servers for Example, Inc. Unfortunately, Example, Inc.'s budget for data centres is small, and some of the site offices which host servers have good local networks but badly overloaded Internet connections, so Gabriel's team has to maintain machines at the other end of all kinds of erratic and untrusted links. Gabriel needs to update a large set of SSL keys for the server network, so that Example, Inc.'s content can continue to be served in a trustworthy fashion, even if the connection back to the central repository can't maintain any kind of reasonable secure session. Gabriel encrypts the new SSL keys with a symmetric key, then encrypts the symmetric key to each web server's binding or unrestricted decryption key. The two encrypted files can now be sent at whatever pace the network connection can handle, or even via CD and the mail; only the target server can decrypt the bundle, which means that as long as the server software is secure, the SSL keys will continue to only authenticate approved Example, Inc. machines.

7.6   1.2 TSS machine authentication code examples

7.6.1   *Setting a signature scheme*

Signing-based attestation, of course, relies heavily on good use of signing keys. If you want to limit what a particular signing key can sign – the SHA1, DER, or INFO signature scheme settings described in Sections 7.2.3.1 and 6.4.2.1 – you can set that particular attribute of a signing key using the `Tspi_SetAttribUint32` command. Although the TSS specification does not clearly define a default signature scheme, the TrouSerS TSS uses SHA1 as the default. A SHA1-scheme key will not sign anything other than 20-byte data chunks (presumed to be a SHA-1 hash); a DER-scheme key will sign anything less than 245 bytes, including SHA-1 hashes. (Don't use the INFO signature scheme, it has vulnerabilities.)

```
// To set a signing key to only sign SHA1 hashes
Tspi_SetAttribUint32(hSigningKey, TSS_TSPATTRIB_KEY_INFO,
TSS_TSPATTRIB_KEYINFO_SIGSCHEME, TSS_SS_RSASSAPKCS1V15_SHA1);

// To set a signing key to sign any DER-compatible data
Tspi_SetAttribUint32(hSigningKey, TSS_TSPATTRIB_KEY_INFO,
TSS_TSPATTRIB_KEYINFO_SIGSCHEME, TSS_SS_RSASSAPKCS1V15_DER);
```

7.6.2   *Signing and verifying hashed data*

The trickiest part of signing data with the 1.2 TSS, once you've created your signing key, is to hash the data for signing. The TSS requires you to create a hash object, and then run either `Tspi_Hash_UpdateHashValue` or `Tspi_Hash_SetHashValue`, depending on whether you want the TSS to do the hashing for you or create your own hash (or hash-sized data).

```
BYTE* data = "TestDataHere";
UINT32 dataLen = sizeof(data);

// Create hash object
Tspi_Context_CreateObject(hContext, TSS_OBJECT_TYPE_HASH,
                          TSS_HASH_SHA1, &hHashedData);

// SetHashValue: set value of hash directly.
   updateHashValue: sha1 of data

// Set up hash for signing
Tspi_Hash_UpdateHashValue(hHashedData, dataLen, data);

// Sign a hash
Tspi_Hash_Sign(hHashedData, hSigningKey, &sigLength,  &sigData);
```

Verifying the signature is equally straightforward: input the hash and the public key to verify against, and the signature length and data. Examples of how to retrieve and load public keys can be found in the code examples in Chapter 6.

```
Tspi_Hash_VerifySignature(hHashedData, hSigningKey, sigLength, sigData);
```

7.6.3   *Encryption and decryption*

Examples of encryption and decryption code can be found in the Data Protection chapter (Chapter 8).

7.7   TSS 2.0 machine authentication code examples

7.7.1   *Signing*

One new question we need to deal with when signing data in TPM 2.0 is whether or not the data was TPM-generated. Because even restricted signing keys are capable of signing user data, we have verification values we may need to pass in to the TPM to confirm that a value is safe to sign (i.e., does not mimic TPM data structures). The ticketFilename in the code below and the in.validation data structure both refer to these validation values produced by the TPM's internal hashing commands.

```
    Sign_In                      in;
    Sign_Out                     out;
    TPMI_ALG_HASH                halg = TPM_ALG_SHA256;


...
/* Retrieve message input and signature output filenames */
/* Retrieve handle of loaded signing-capable key */
...
    File_ReadBinaryFile(&data,        /* must be freed by caller */
                       &length,
                       messageFilename);

    /* hash the file */
        digest.hashAlg = halg;
        sizeInBytes = _cpri__GetDigestSize(digest.hashAlg);
        rc = TSE_Hash_Generate(&digest,
                               length, data,
                               0, NULL);

    /* Handle of key that will perform signing */
    in.keyHandle = keyHandle;

        /* digest to be signed */
        in.digest.t.size = sizeInBytes;
        memcpy(&in.digest.t.buffer, (uint8_t *)&digest.digest,
           sizeInBytes);

        /* Signature scheme */
        in.inScheme.scheme = TPM_ALG_RSASSA;
        in.inScheme.details.rsassa.hashAlg = halg;


    if (ticketFilename == NULL) {
            /* No proof that digest was created by the TPM
               (NULL ticket) */
            in.validation.tag = TPM_ST_HASHCHECK;
            in.validation.hierarchy = TPM_RH_NULL;
            in.validation.digest.t.size = 0; }
    else {
          File_ReadStructure(&in.validation,
                             (UnmarshalFunction_t)TPMT_TK_
                             HASHCHECK_Unmarshal,
                             ticketFilename);}

    TSE_Execute((RESPONSE_PARAMETERS *)&out,
                (COMMAND_PARAMETERS *)&in,
                NULL,
                TPM_CC_Sign,
```

```
                    sessionHandle0, keyPassword, sessionAttributes0,
                    TPM_RH_NULL, NULL, 0);

      File_WriteStructure(&out.signature,
                          (MarshalFunction_t)TSS_TPMT_SIGNATURE_Marshal,
                          signatureFilename);
```

7.7.2   Verifying signatures

While signature verification can be done by any software crypto library that supports the relevant algorithms, 2.0 TPMs also provide built-in signature verification functionality.

```
      VerifySignature_In              in;
      VerifySignature_Out             out;

...
/* Retrieve signature filename, message filename */
/* Retrieve handle of loaded public key */
...

/* Read message file */
    File_ReadBinaryFile(&data,        /* must be freed by caller */
                        &dataLength,
                        messageFilename);

/* Create digest of message */
                digest.hashAlg = halg;
                sizeInBytes = _cpri__GetDigestSize(digest.hashAlg);
                rc = TSE_Hash_Generate(&digest,
                                        dataLength, data,
                                        0, NULL);

                /* digest to be verified */
                in.digest.t.size = sizeInBytes;
                memcpy(&in.digest.t.buffer, (uint8_t *)
                  &digest.digest, sizeInBytes);

/* Read in signature from file */
File_ReadBinaryFile(&buffer,        /* must be freed by caller */
                        &length,
                        signatureFilename);

/* Unmarshal data into recognizable TPM structure */
            buffer1 = buffer;
            rc = TPMT_SIGNATURE_Unmarshal(&in.signature, &buffer1,
                (INT32 *)&length, NO);
```

```
      /* Set verification key handle */
    in.keyHandle = keyHandle;

    TSE_Execute((RESPONSE_PARAMETERS *)&out,
                (COMMAND_PARAMETERS *)&in,
                NULL,
                TPM_CC_VerifySignature,
                TPM_RH_NULL, NULL, 0);
```

7.7.3   Encryption and decryption

Examples of encryption and decryption code can be found in the Data Protection chapter (Chapter 8).

Chapter 8
Data protection

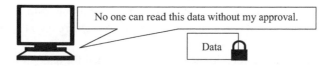

In today's marketplace, data protection is by far the most common use for TPMs. Windows' Bitlocker disk encryption system makes use of the TPM, on systems which have it, to protect user data stored on the hard drive. TPMs have been used by large companies as cheap smartcard replacements, providing two-factor authentication by protecting keys.

Data protection use cases for TPMs primarily fall into two related categories. The first uses the TPM as a hardware root of trust for disk encryption and other large-scale file protection. The second set use the TPM's internal storage directly for small-scale, high-value items.

Both of these use cases have numerous variations, taking advantage of the different kinds of TPM keys and key restrictions, the different types of storage available within the TPM, and the different commands the TPM provides to access internal data. In this chapter, we'll visit several use cases for data protection, and discuss how various TPM features and commands can be used.

8.1 The pros and cons of TPMs for data storage

One of the easiest sells for "why might I want a TPM?" is "provide hardware protection for your secret data." Disk encryption and encrypted key stores are already widely used, but concerns about data theft in the form of copied drives or large-scale data vacuuming can make the prospect of encrypting data with keys that software cannot steal extremely interesting.

The hardware-tied security of TPM keys can certainly lend strong protections to encrypted data. The caveat is that the TPM has no ability to use most data, and data that has been decrypted by the TPM for use by software is just as vulnerable to theft by running software as any other data. This means that although TPMs can be a very powerful tool for data protection, they do the most good when protecting data in smaller chunks which are unencrypted as needed, rather than doing bulk protection.

Bulk data protection, such as basing hard drive encryption on a TPM, is useful against drive copying attacks, evil maid attacks (where someone has access to a machine that is off for a short period of time) and other external attacks. It is not useful against software-based attacks such as malware that steals data.

In addition to encrypting data, the TPM can store a very limited amount of unencrypted data internally in its NVRAM, with limited access rights. This lets the TPM provide integrity-protected world-readable data to the system, which can be very useful for applications where the primary threat is malicious modifications to trusted system data, such as the trusted CAs or code-signing keys. This storage is primarily password protected; its advantage over OS-level access constraints is primarily in the inability of an OS administrator to overwrite it. Unlike most TPM data, however, the TPM owner is capable of overwriting all data stored in the TPM, so NVRAM storage should not be relied on in situations where the TPM owner is not trusted.

Machine state, as recorded in the PCRs, can be used for data protection as well as for attestation (covered in Chapter 9), so that data can be accessed not only on a single machine but on a single machine in a particular predictable state. This can be extremely powerful: for example, only allowing an application's data to be retrieved if the application is running in a trusted environment. However, PCR contents are highly volatile and this kind of constraint can often lead to accidental inability to access data, particularly in 1.2 TPMs where the authentication mechanisms do not support alternative access methods. Today's PCR contents, as discussed in more detail in Section 9.1, are also quite coarse, so that only the most predictable systems, built by people who are focusing on supporting system measurement, can reasonably use PCR contents for data protection at any level more detailed than "the system booted in the same configuration that it had yesterday." Keep in mind also that if the PCR contents change for a positive reason—for example, applying a system patch—the data will be just as inaccessible, so that it is particularly critical to back up data if using this approach. Using PCRs to constrain encrypted data is discussed in Section 8.8; backup techniques will be discussed in more detail in Section 8.3.

TPM 2.0 allows access to encrypted data to be limited by a wide range of additional criteria. The Extended Authorization model described in Section 6.13.3 can be applied independently to a TPM key used to encrypt data, or to an individual encrypted blob, allowing for a wide range of layered access control possibilities.

In short:

- The TPM can be used to securely protect data by encrypting it with TPM keys
- TPM-encrypted data is most secure if encrypted in small chunks corresponding to how the data will be used, rather than in large collections, since the unencrypted data is potentially vulnerable to on-system malicious software
- The TPM allows data to be state-locked, making it only accessible in specific PCR configurations; however, this is extremely fragile and not suitable for any systems but the most predictable
- Small quantities of data can be stored in the TPM's NVRAM. This is particularly useful for high-value data which needs integrity protection but not secrecy.

It's also worth mentioning again that the TPM's design goals are to protect against software-based attacks, rather than physical attacks. The TPM's data protection is more than sufficient to keep casual thieves from pulling data off of a stolen laptop, but it's not designed to protect against organized and technically skilled criminals or nation-states.

8.2 Basic TPM encryption features

In TPM 1.2, data encryption is divided into two categories: binding and sealing. Bind is not a real TPM command, but rather a function of software; it can be used to encrypt data, for either a local or remote TPM. (Remember, the 1.2 TPM only uses public key cryptography, and the encryption operation uses the public key; thus, Bind does not require any secrets to be present.) The corresponding TPM_Unbind command is used to decrypt bound data inside the TPM. In contrast, TPM_Seal[1] uses the TPM to encrypt data such that the data can only be decrypted by that same TPM; TPM_Unseal decrypts the sealed data. While sealing data is far more constrained than binding data, and cannot be used for many applications (notably, anything that involves encryption to a destination not on the same machine), it also comes with some benefits. Sealed data can be set so that a password, or an assurance that the TPM PCRs are in a given state, must be entered before the data can be decrypted. In addition, sealed data is guaranteed to have been encrypted on the same TPM that's unsealing it; for applications where integrity-based attacks, such as data substitution, are a serious risk, this assurance can be very powerful.

2.0's data encryption model is more complex. It provides simple cryptographic primitives suitable for many operations: TPM2_RSA_Encrypt, TPM2_RSA_Decrypt, and TPM2_EncryptDecrypt (for symmetric encryption and decryption). It also provides functionality similar to TPM 1.2's Seal functionality, where a TPM-specific data storage structure is created with certain access control guarantees and creation information. However, in 2.0, the creation of such a locally encrypted object is done with the TPM2_Create or TPM2_CreatePrimary commands, the same ones we used to create keys. Data objects should not have any of the restricted, sign, or decrypt attributes; the data to be protected is provided as part of the sensitive data in the input data structure. As with keys, these objects have either a parent key used to encrypt the sensitive data (which must be a storage key) or, for primary objects, a parent seed which is the hierarchy seed. To access the data, the created object must first be loaded with the TPM2_Load command, providing the parent authorization; its contents can then be accessed using the TPM2_Unseal command, providing the authorization information for the object. The full complexity of Enhanced Authorization policies can be applied to a data object; they can also be duplicatable, like keys, allowing them to be re-encrypted to parent keys on different machines when appropriate authorization is provided.

---

[1] Some TPMs may support the optional TPM_SealX command; this works exactly like TPM_Seal, but the data is required to be passed to the TPM via an encrypted transport session. Because it is both optional and effectively identical to TPM_Seal run with an encrypted transport session, I won't mention it again.

8.2.1   Storage hierarchies and data protection

Back in Chapter 6, I discussed key hierarchies and the dependencies between various keys for secret protection. Data protection uses the exact same concept; the security of any given encrypted object depends on the security of the key it is encrypted with, which may depend on other keys, and so forth. If a key that a given object is encrypted with can be duplicated or migrated to another platform, that object may also be decrypted on the new platform (Figure 8.1). (1.2 sealed objects, intended for use on a single platform, cannot be created using migratable keys, and contain their own encrypted proof value used to verify the originating TPM.)

If you're trying to create high-security encrypted data only usable on the local platform, be sure that all parent keys below it in the storage hierarchy have appropriately secure configurations, and none of the parent keys are migratable or duplicatable. In contrast, it can be very useful for backup purposes to have a single duplicatable or migratable storage key used to encrypt most data, allowing that duplicate key to be maintained in a secure storage location for data retrieval.

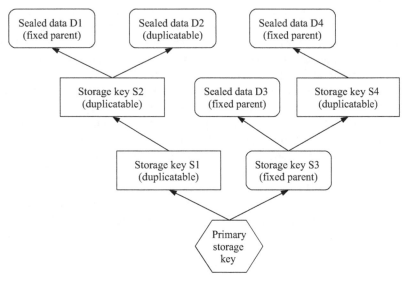

Figure 8.1   An example 2.0 storage hierarchy (also called a protection hierarchy in some TPM 2.0 documentation). The security of each piece of sealed data depends on the keys below it, and data encrypted with a duplicatable parent in its hierarchy can be duplicated along with its parent or parent hierarchy. Only D3 is not capable of being decrypted on another platform. D1 and D2 can be used on another platform if either S2 or S1 is duplicated, while D4 can only be duplicated if S4 is. D2 can also be duplicated on its own

8.3 Disk encryption, bulk data protection, and secure backups

The disk encryption scenario is, thanks to Bitlocker, one of the most widely used TPM data protection use cases. However, TPMs are not suitable for performing the bulk encryption themselves. 1.2 TPMs do not even support the symmetric ciphers suitable for bulk data encryption, and 2.0 TPMs have a limited buffer size for data input. In order to encrypt large quantities of data with the TPM, a two-step process is required. First, encrypt the bulk data with a symmetric key using software. Then encrypt the software's symmetric key with a TPM key, store the encrypted symmetric key, and delete the unencrypted symmetric key. After decrypting, the unencrypted symmetric key can again be deleted, since the encrypted symmetric key data still exists if it's wanted.

The symmetric key can either remain the same over time, or be rotated to a new key each time. Rotating the symmetric key is particularly useful in preventing rollback attacks, where an attacker substitutes an older version of the encrypted data for the newer version.

The two-stage process for large-scale data protection is both a slight vulnerability and a powerful tool for backing up data. The vulnerability from the process comes, simply, from the fact that if an adversary can acquire the symmetric key they don't need to engage with the TPM's protections, so application writers using this feature must take slightly more care. The power comes from the fact that you can efficiently provide multiple decryption options even in a 1.2 TPM, which does not support complex access control policies. A single symmetric encryption key can be encrypted with multiple TPM keys, or with multiple authorization values and access constraints applied to the encrypted data; it can even be encrypted to keys on multiple systems, supporting backup recovery in the event of the loss of the machine. Bitlocker uses this feature to provide two different mechanisms to decrypt the hard drive: one PCR-locked to the current expected boot software state, and one locked to a recovery password. An enterprise which wanted to use TPM-supported disk encryption while supporting data recovery could encrypt the data to both the local TPM, and to a TPM or other secure key on an off-line recovery system controlled by the IT department.

The backup techniques inherent to large-scale data are so powerful, in fact, that they should often be considered even for smaller-scale data. Encrypting data to multiple TPM keys or to keys on multiple systems is always a good idea if you're more concerned about maintaining access to data than about perfect secrecy.

The basic techniques used to protect large-scale data with a TPM can be used with any of the TPM encryption and decryption commands discussed elsewhere in this chapter.

8.4 Small-scale data protection

The TPM's strongest use case for data protection is for individual files or other small chunks of high-value data, such as key stores or password vault data. In these cases, keeping the data encrypted while not in use can provide protection not only against machine theft or disk copying but also many malware attacks or unlocked computer misuse. How much protection is provided varies depending on how often the data needs to be unlocked, and how long it stays in the clear on the system. A file full of tax information that is encrypted all year except for one day during which taxes are prepared has a significant window in which malware or unauthorized access can read system data but not the protected file data, while a key store that is decrypted into memory when a web browser is opened and remains open during almost the entire time the computer is in use will have very little TPM protection over full-disk encryption, since any malware presence or unauthorized access while the machine is in use can potentially be used to access the decrypted data. Thus, for optimal security, encrypting data in the smallest sections appropriate to the use case is a good idea. This applies even if the large-scale technique of encrypting the data with a symmetric key and encrypting the symmetric key with a TPM key is used: "small scale" on a human scale is often not the same as "small scale" in terms of what an RSA key can be used to encrypt. (RSA keys can only encrypt data up to the key size, minus padding, which can for some structures be moderately significant.)

The smaller scale of data protection divides into two main categories: on-system encryption and secure data transmission. On-system encryption covers all of the use cases in which we want to encrypt a file on the same system we'll eventually want to read it. Secure data transmission covers all of the use cases where we want to send data securely from one machine to another. There are also some hybrid use cases; on-system encryption with a remote backup, for example.

8.4.1   Small-scale local encryption

For local encryption of small amounts of data, such as keys or passwords, TPMs offer a range of choices: TPM_Seal/TPM_Unseal and TPM_Unbind (and the corresponding software bind operation) on 1.2 TPMs, and both the basic encryption/decryption commands, TPM2_Create, and even TPM2_CreatePrimary on 2.0 TPMs. On each version, there's a choice between a structure that provides additional TPM-enforced guarantees and information, and a structure that provides a pure encryption/decryption operation or something very close to it.

The pure encryption/decryption operations (TPM_Unbind, which uses a mere 5 bytes of padding (Figure 8.2), or none at all if a legacy key instead of a binding key is used; TPM2_RSA_Encrypt and TPM2_RSA_Decrypt; and TPM2_EncryptDecrypt) are primarily useful in cases where the TPM is solely being used as a trusted key repository, providing secrecy for the data. Note that integrity verification is *not* provided with these commands: if the encrypted data is modified, the TPM will happily provide the garbled decrypted data, and be none the wiser.

More interesting are the commands which offer TPM security guarantees of one sort or another. The TPM_Seal command on 1.2 offers several useful features, including an authorization value created when the data is encrypted and

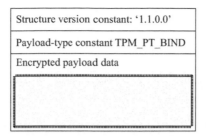

| Structure version constant: '1.1.0.0' |
| Payload-type constant TPM_PT_BIND |
| Encrypted payload data |

Figure 8.2 The simple TPM_BOUND_DATA *data structure used for bound data, decryptable with the* TPM_Unbind *command. The data structure can be created on any computer, including those with no TPM; TPM software libraries such as the TSS normally include a routine for creating these data structures. The structure is not required if a legacy key is used for decrypting the bound data. Note the limited overhead from the datastructure*

then required for decryption, records of the PCR state and locality at the time the sealed data blob was created, and optional constraints on PCR state and locality when the data is decrypted (Figure 8.3). Sealed data is also guaranteed to only be decryptable on the same physical machine, which makes it awkward for back-ups but very powerful for preventing data from leaving a given platform without authorization.

The TPM2_Create command can also be used to create sealed data objects, constrained using the complete TPM 2.0 Enhanced Authorization model discussed in Section 6.13. Creating a sealed data object uses the TPM_ALG_KEYEDHASH type in the data template, providing the data to be sealed as the input sensitive data. This data can be accessed by loading the resulting blob with the same TPM2_Load command as a TPM key, followed by the TPM2_Unseal command, which only requires the authorization of the data object since the data is already decrypted inside the TPM. (While technically TPM2_CreatePrimary can be used, primary objects never leave the TPM, which means the encrypted data would either be temporary or have to be configured to take up permanent space in the TPM; in either case, not really suitable for most storage use cases.)

Regardless of the command used to encrypt and decrypt data, additional constraints can be applied to the key used to store the data; a binding key with a password will require the password to decrypt data even though the data blob itself has no password. However, these constraints will remain the same each time the key is used, which may be an advantage or disadvantage. A TPM-enhanced password vault might want to apply no passwords to the individual data blobs, and instead have a single high-security password on a storage key, so the password is required when the vault is opened rather than when each secret is retrieved. An individual storing private information might want to use a different password for protecting the tax files shared with their spouse than for the financial data shared with a small business partner.

Structure tag constant: TPM_TAG_STORED_DATA12
Entity-type value: 0
Size of PCR info data structure in bytes
TPM_PCR_INFO_LONG structure See figure
Size of sealed data structure in bytes
Encrypted sealed data structure: Payload-type constant: TPM_PT_SEAL Authorization value for sealed data TPM internal secret random value Digest of TPM_TAG _STORED_DATA12 structure (minus sealed data size and contents) Data size in bytes Data

Figure 8.3   *The* TPM_STORED_DATA12 *data structure used for most sealed data in 1.2. If no PCR values are provided to the TPM to seal the data against, or if the PCR values are provided as a* TPM_PCR_INFO *structure, a slightly simpler* TPM_STORED_DATA *structure is used instead. It is almost identical to the structure shown here, except that the two initial constants are replaced with a single "1.1.0.0" structure version, and the* TPM_PCR_INFO_LONG *described in Figure 8.4 is replaced with the simpler and locality-free* TPM_PCR_INFO *structure. In both cases, the encrypted sealed data contains a TPM proof value, which is a random number generated by the TPM which never leaves; a sealed blob with the wrong proof value will not be unsealed successfully, so sealed data blobs are never creatable by any entity except the TPM which will eventually use them*

8.5   Secure data transmission

Secure data transmission overlaps very heavily with encryption-based user authentication, discussed in Section 7.3, since the primary difference is whether the emphasis is on the recipient receiving data or on the sender receiving confirmation that the data was received. In both cases, the sender must have a trusted key for the recipient. If the recipient is a 1.2 TPM, a binding key must be used. Software is used to encrypt the data, and the TPM uses TPM_Unbind to decrypt it. For secure data

TPM_PCR_INFO_LONG structure:

Constant tag: TPM_TAG_PCR_INFO_LONG
Locality at key or data creation
Locality selection for key or data use
PCR indexes to be measured at creation
PCR indexes to be measured on use
PCR values at key or data creation
Digest of PCR values required on use

Figure 8.4   The TPM_PCR_INFO_LONG *data structure. The same data structure is used for sealed data and 1.2 keys, in any situation where the user wants to take advantage of the two 1.2-specific features not available in the backwards-compatible* TPM_PCR_INFO: *locality, and distinct PCR index selections for object use versus the digest produced at object creation for later verification. The latter feature is primarily useful in sealed data scenarios where the same machine wants to send data securely between two very different states; for example, between a machine booted using the standard BIOS-launched OS vs. the same machine running a DRTM-launched trusted application. The full details of why these features are useful can be found in Chapter 9*

transmission to 2.0 TPMs, a non-restricted decryption key[2] must be used; however, that key can be an RSA key, an ECC key, or a symmetric key. For data transmission, the TPM2_RSA_Decrypt and TPM2_EncryptDecrypt commands are used to access the encrypted data on the receiving end.

Unlike a 1.2 TPM, 2.0 TPMs can be used to create the secure data to be transmitted, not just to decrypt received data, using the TPM2_RSA_Encrypt and TPM2_EncryptDecrypt operations. This is because 2.0 TPMs are capable of performing symmetric encryption and of loading public keys. The TPM2_RSA_Encrypt command can, of course, be replaced with equivalent software functionality, since there is no secret data being used.

Note that the commands used for secure data transmission do not support object-specific access control mechanisms. A password can't be required on a TPM object that will be decrypted with TPM_Unbind or TPM2_RSA_Decrypt, nor can PCR constraints or other standard TPM access controls be imposed directly on the object. If access control mechanisms are required, they need to be placed on the decryption key, not the data. Depending on the level of control the sender needs, this could mean anything from "the recipient machine certifies the decryption key's constraints using TPM_CertifyKey or TPM2_Certify" (see Section 6.11.2) to "the sender

---

[2]Which is to say, any key with the decrypt attribute, whether or not it is also capable of signing, although single-purpose keys are always recommended.

creates a migratable or duplicatable key with the constraints desired, and migrates the key along with the encrypted data to the destination."

8.5.1 Binding, legacy keys, and backwards compatibility

One of the challenges of using 1.2 TPMs is that their encryption and decryption operations expect TPM standard data structures, which makes secure data transmission using 1.2 TPMs challenging to integrate into existing environments. There is, however, an exception: when a legacy key is used instead of a binding key with the TPM_Unbind operation and the TPM_ES_RSAESOAEP_SHA1_MGF1 encryption algorithm is not selected, a simple RSA decryption operation is performed, and the output is returned with no data format verification. Legacy keys, as we mentioned earlier, can be used for both signing and decryption, and I rarely recommend their use; they aren't available at all on FIPS-compliant TPMs, and there are security risks involved in using them for both kinds of operations. However, this is the rare application where using a legacy key can provide a noticeable benefit, since they can provide drop-in TPM compatibility for existing applications. If you have a non-FIPS-compliant TPM and want to use legacy keys for remote data transmission, you can mitigate your risk by requiring a strong password for the legacy key and educating users about why not to use the key for signing operations.

8.6   Alternate backup techniques

The approach recommended in the large data section, where the data to be backed up is encrypted with a symmetric key and then the symmetric key is encrypted to multiple keys associated with both the local TPM and a remote machine, is not the only option for backup. One of the simplest is to use a migratable or duplicatable key to encrypt data; as long as the key has been migrated or duplicated before the original machine is lost, the encrypted data can be retrieved. Another approach, only suitable for small data such as the symmetric key originally discussed, is to encrypt the data once using local encryption techniques and a local key, and once using secure data transmission techniques and a remote key, either in a TPM or in another trusted device.

8.7   The TPM's internal storage (NVRAM)

The TPM also offers a *very* small amount of internal storage in its Nonvolatile RAM. This storage is referred to as NVRAM in 1.2 TPMs and NV storage in 2.0 TPMs, but for the purpose of this book we'll use the terms interchangeably. NVRAM is accessed using *indexes*, which the TPM uses to point to internally allocated sections, or spaces.

What's "very small?" In 1.2 TPMs, only 1280 bytes of total NVRAM are required, although in practice most seem to contain 2–6 kB of space. This means that in most systems, unless there is a single key or credential that is critical to keep inside the TPM, the NVRAM is most valuable when used to hold fingerprints, hashes, and other reference data to support integrity verification of objects on disk.

Why use data stored in NVRAM instead of just a signature for integrity verification? Rollback protection is one primary reason. (Another powerful tool for rollback protection, when used in combination with TPM signatures, is the TPM's monotonic counters, discussed in Section 10.5.) Software wanting to check that its saved data is the correct version can consult a hash of the expected data in the NVRAM and compare it to what's stored on disk.

Another primary reason to use NVRAM instead of signatures is that using signatures for integrity verification requires the verifier to know the keys they should trust, which may not always be the case. One use case for NVRAM is to establish trust in that initial key, or to establish trust early in the boot cycle when disk access is not available. For example, a system implementing boot-time software verification would need to check signatures of the software as it loads. In some cases, the initial key is built into the firmware or CPU, in which case the TPM is primarily useful if the manufacturer is not trusted to properly maintain key security, or if there are concerns about firmware-based attacks. In others, however, there is no good reference point, and the key is trusted because it is part of the BIOS or boot loader software. In these cases, it is particularly powerful to use the TPM as a reference to confirm the key's integrity, since a simple key substitution would undermine the security of the entire boot process.

Of course, it is important to note that any attack which actually changes software is capable of bypassing TPM-based integrity checks! Having a reliable reference point to detect key modification or rollback attacks can be very useful, but NVRAM provides a safe place to confirm that one is in a good state rather than a way to prevent a bad state from occurring.

NVRAM has several properties which make it not ideal for every use case that might spring to mind when "internal storage inside the TPM" is introduced.

- A limited number of write operations can be used before the NVRAM may become unreliable. This is guaranteed to be at least 10,000. For most applications the limit is not relevant, but it does mean that NVRAM should not be used for routine rollback prevention for applications with extremely frequent updates. Some TPMs implement rate limits on NVRAM write operations in order to minimize the risk of burnout.
- NVRAM space is allocated by the TPM owner, or, in TPM 2.0, the platform firmware. NVRAM can also be deallocated by the owner or firmware, allowing an owner to effectively override any write permissions on a location. The owner cannot use their privileged access to read data in NVRAM they could not otherwise read, however.
- 1.2 TPMs have no way to certify the contents of NVRAM; NVRAM checks are only useful for on-system verification, where the TPM's secure communications protocols (see authorization sessions) provide a sufficient guarantee of data accuracy. (2.0 TPMs can certify NVRAM contents for external verifiers using the TPM2_NV_Certify command.)

TPM 2.0 introduced several new NVRAM capabilities. Along with the ability to certify NVRAM contents previously mentioned, NVRAM can be allocated and configured to behave like a monotonic counter (see Section 10.5) or PCR (see Section 9.2). It also introduced new access control options. Allocated indexes can be assigned authorization values (passwords) and Enhanced Authorization policies (see Section 6.13.3), which can be assigned separately for read and write access.

Optionally, an index may be configured to also allow the platform or owner authorization to be used for read or write access. Temporary write and read locks are possible, where the platform or owner can cause a specific index or pre-configured selection of indexes to be unwritable or unreadable until the next boot. These are particularly useful when early boot software wishes to provide information for later-running programs without fear of their being modified, without the complexity of managing passwords or policies. These locks are not universally usable; to allow a given index to be write locked, for example, it must already have the TPMA_NV_WRITE_STCLEAR or TPMA_NV_WRITEDEFINE attribute bit set. These attributes, along with the various data types and access control options, are part of a given NV index's parameters, set as part of the initial creation using TPM2_NV_DefineSpace.

8.7.1   Using NVRAM in 1.2

The first step in using NVRAM is to establish a named space using the TPM_NV_DefineSpace command, which requires owner authorization and which establishes the parameters of a given NV area. These parameters include the index to be used, size of the area, and, for each of reading and writing, the PCR constraints (if any), and authorization (if any). 1.2 NV areas can either use the owner authorization, an alternate authorization, or no authorization, and reading and writing are defined separately. It is important to note that NV areas which use non-owner authorization are *not* cleared with the rest of the TPM's contents. It is also important to note that one of the TPM's flags, nvLocked, can cause the TPM to not enforce any authorization checks on NVRAM use. See Section 10.4 for more information.

Although the owner can choose the index to be used, the TPM has some reserved indexes maintained for the use of the TPM or the manufacturer. These indexes include locations for the manufacturer-provided endorsement credential (TPM_NV_ INDEX_EKCert) and platform credential (TPM_NV_INDEX_ PlatformCert).

To write data to an NVRAM index, the TPM_NV_WriteValue or TPM_NV_WriteValueAuth commands are used; the first is used if the index is set to require either no authorization or owner authorization for write access, while the second is used if non-owner authorization is required for write access. These commands allow writing of any continuous subset of the NV area, not just the full area: the writer provides a chunk of data and the offset from the index to which to write the data. Reading data uses the TPM_NV_ReadValue or TPM_NV_ReadValueAuth commands. Again, the first command is used if the index requires no authorization or owner authorization, while the second is used for non-owner authorization, and both can read a subset of the data area if desired.

In all cases, the PCR values at the time the command is run are also verified against the PCR requirements specified when the index is created. Note that these values cannot be changed after the space is defined without redefining the space, which may (if the TPM is designed for high-security operations, or is in FIPS mode) overwrite the existing contents. Given the fragility and instability of PCRs (see Section 9.2), it is rarely a good idea to put PCR constraints on NV indexes for operations which you wish to perform, unless the goal is to make a given index only available early in the boot process when some PCRs are still empty.

Table 8.1 *TPM 2.0 NV attributes, bits 0–15. Each bit in the TPMA_NV UINT32*
assigns a specific attribute to the NV index. Not all attributes can be
used in combination; providing an invalid set of attributes (e.g. both
*TPMA_NV_COUNTER and TPMA_NV_BITS) will cause TPM2_NV_*
DefineSpace to return a TPM_RC_NV_ATTRIBUTES error

Bit	Name	Description
0	TPMA_NV_PPWRITE	If set, platform authorization can be used to allow writing to the index.
1	TPMA_NV_OWNERWRITE	If set, owner authorization can be used to allow writing to the index.
2	TPMA_NV_AUTHWRITE	If set, an HMAC session or password can be used to authorize a user writing to the index.
3	TPMA_NV_POLICYWRITE	If set, a policy session can be used to authorize a user writing to the index.
4	TPMA_NV_COUNTER	If set, the index contains an 8-octet value that acts as a monotonic counter and is changed using TPM2_NV_Increment.
5	TPMA_NV_BITS	If set, index contains an 8-octet value that is used as a bit field and changed using TPM2_NV_Setbits.
6	TPMA_NV_EXTEND	If set, index acts in the same way as a PCR
7–9	Reserved	Must be zero
10	TPMA_NV_POLICY_DELETE	If set, the index authorization policy must be provided in order to undefine the index.
11	TPMA_NV_WRITELOCKED	If set, index cannot be written to.
12	TPMA_NV_WRITEALL	If set, any write to the index must be the same size as the space. If not set, partial writes are allowed.
13	TPMA_NV_WRITEDEFINE	If set, TPM2_NV_WriteLock can be used to prevent further writes to the index.
14	TPMA_NV_WRITE_STCLEAR	If set, TPM2_NV_WriteLock can be used to temporarily prevent writes to the index until the next reboot.
15	TPMA_NV_GLOBALLOCK	If set, TPM2_NV_GlobalWriteLock can be used to prevent writes to the index until the next reboot.

To remove an NVRAM index, use the TPM_NV_DefineSpace command again, and overwrite the existing index. Note that whether or not this will actually overwrite the data depends on implementation, so for high-security content, it may be wise to overwrite the contents yourself first.

8.7.2 *Using NVRAM in 2.0*

Using NVRAM in a 2.0 TPM also begins with the TPM2_NV_DefineSpace command, but there are more options available for the NV attributes (Tables 8.1 and 8.2), and NV space can be used for additional kinds of functionality. New options include

*Table 8.2   TPM 2.0 NV attributes, bits 16–31. Each bit in the TPMA_NV UINT32
assigns a specific attribute to the NV index. Not all attributes can be
used in combination; providing an invalid set of attributes (e.g. both
TPMA_NV_COUNTER and TPMA_NV_BITS) will cause TPM2_NV_
DefineSpace to return a TPM_RC_NV_ATTRIBUTES error*

Bit	Name	Description
16	TPMA_NV_PPREAD	If set, platform authorization can be used to allow the index to be read.
17	TPMA_NV_OWNERREAD	If set, owner authorization can be used to allow the index to be read.
18	TPMA_NV_AUTHREAD	If set, an HMAC session or password can be used to authorize a user reading from the index.
19	TPMA_NV_POLICYREAD	If set, a policy session can be used to authorize a user reading from the index.
20–24	Reserved	Must be zero
25	TPMA_NV_NO_DA	If set, authorization failures for the index don't activate the dictionary attack protections, and dictionary attack lockouts don't prevent access to the index.
26	TPMA_NV_ORDERLY	If set, the state of the index is only required to be saved when the TPM shuts down in an orderly fashion. If not set, the state must be saved every time an update command is run.
27	TPMA_NV_CLEAR_STCLEAR	If set, TPMA_NV_WRITTEN is cleared on each reboot.
28	TPMA_NV_READLOCKED	If set, the index cannot be read until the next reboot. Set by TPM2_NV_ReadLock.
29	TPMA_NV_WRITTEN	If set, the index has been written.
30	TPMA_NV_PLATFORMCREATE	If set, the index may be undefined using platform authorization, but not owner authorization. If not set, owner authorization and not platform authorization can be used. Must be the same as the authorization used to define the index.
31	TPMA_NV_READ_STCLEAR	If set, TPM2_NV_ReadLock may be used to lock the index temporarily.

declaring the space to be a monotonic counter (TPMA_NV_COUNTER), a PCR-like extendable area (TPM_NV_EXTEND), or an 8-byte bit array (TPM_NV_BITS), although a traditional generic readable and writable data area of flexible size is still the default option.

Some other attributes of interest:

- TPMA_NV_OWNERREAD and TPMA_NV_OWNERWRITE allow the owner authorization to be used for read and write operations, respectively.
- TPMA_NV_PPWRITE and TPMA_NV_PPWRITE allow the platform authorization to be used for reading and writing operations, respectively.

- TPMA_NV_AUTHREAD and TPMA_NV_AUTHWRITE allow an HMAC session or password to be used to authorize read or write operations, respectively. This authorization value, if any, is provided as one of the arguments to the TPM2_NV_DefineSpace command, or is set with the TPM2_NV_ChangeAuth command. If multiple authorization values are desired, or different authorization values should be used for different commands, use an Enhanced Authorization policy instead.

- TPMA_NV_POLICYREAD and TPMA_NV_POLICYWRITE allow an Enhanced Authorization policy to be used to authorize read or write operations, respectively. This access policy is set in the same TPMS_NV_PUBLIC data structure which defines the attributes.

- TPMA_NV_CLEAR_STCLEAR is particularly relevant for extendable areas. If this bit is set, an extendable area's contents will be reset to the zero digest on each reboot just like a PCR would, while if this is not set, the hash chain history will be maintained for the duration of the area's existence.

- TPMA_NV_ORDERLY determines whether the TPM is allowed to wait until an orderly shutdown to write any changes permanently into NVRAM, or if an update to the stored contents should happen whenever an update command is run. This choice is relevant because the life of NVRAM is determined by the number of write operations; an area which is updated frequently and which is tolerant of potential rollbacks in the event of an unexpected hardware problem should have this bit set in order to preserve the NVRAM's working life. If the NVRAM content updates are highly relevant to maintaining the integrity of other components such that a rollback could cause a security failure, this bit should not be set.

The TPM2_NV_DefineSpace command requires either the owner or platform authorization. It takes a TPMS_NV_PUBLIC data structure which defines the attributes (Figure 8.5). The handle must be chosen in advance; trying to define an NV index using an existing handle will cause the command to fail. Handles are all unsigned 32-bit integers; the most significant octet of all NV index handles is 0x01. One approach to selecting a free index is to simply increment through index values until the command succeeds. Another is to use TPM2_GetCapability to retrieve

Size of TPMS_NV_PUBLIC data structure
TPMS_NV_PUBLIC data structure:
NV index handle
Hash algorithm used to calculate name and auth policy
Index attributes (TPMA_NV)
Auth policy digest
Data area size

Figure 8.5   TPM 2.0 TPMS_NV_PUBLIC data structure, used when requesting new NV space using TPM2_NV_DefineSpace. For the complete list of attributes, see Tables 8.1 and 8.2

the list of currently defined handles[3] as described in Section 10.4.2, and select a handle value not on that list.

At least one read attribute and at least one write attribute must be set. Unlike a 1.2 TPM, any number of read or write attributes may be set simultaneously, in which case any one of the options may be provided to successfully access the defined NV index. Once an NV index is created, its attributes are static; the only way to change them is to undefine the space and redefine it with the new attributes. Note that this will lose all data stored in the index.

The commands for changing the contents of NV space depend on the type of the space. Each command requires the authorization set up as part of the original definition for that index. For traditional data areas, the TPM2_NV_Write command is used. As with the 1.2 version, this command overwrites a portion of the allocated data area; it takes the index, the data to write, and the offset from the index. The TPM2_NV_Increment command is used to increment a counter by one; we discuss counters more in Section 10.5. TPM2_NV_Extend is a simplified version of TPM2_PCRExtend (in fact, it's closer to the 1.2 TPM_Extend command); it takes the index and a digest, and changes the contents of the space to the hash of the concatenation of the old data and the digest. The hash algorithm used is the one set in the TPMS_NV_PUBLIC data structure provided in the original TPM2_NV_DefineSpace command. These can be used to create what is effectively additional user-defined PCRs for a system, although the NVRAM imitations cannot be reset and are a bit trickier for a remote verifier to establish trust in. TPM2_NV_SetBits is used to change bit field indexes; it changes the contents of the area to the bitwise OR of the old contents and the input data.

Indexes, regardless of the type, are read using the TPM2_NV_Read command, which requires the authorization defined when the space was originally allocated. This command takes an index, the amount of data to be read, and the offset into the space. NV contents can be used as part of an Enhanced Authorization policy (see Section 6.13.3); using the TPM2_PolicyNV command as part of a policy session is also effectively a read of the relevant index, which means that an appropriate read authorization must be provided. The final, and most powerful, way of reading an NV index is with the TPM2_NV_Certify command. This command takes an NV index, a signing key (which should be restricted, since this command is providing TPM internal data), a user-provided nonce (called qualifyingData in the specification), an optional signing scheme if the signing key does not specify one, and the section of the NV area to sign. It requires read authorization for the NV index and use authorization for the signing key. It will return an attestation data structure including the NV contents and the nonce, and the signature over the data structure. This allows a remote party to verify the current contents of a TPM's NVRAM. If an extendable NV index is being used as a pseudo-PCR, the Certify capability provides comparable functionality to a Quote command.

Information about indexes can be retrieved with the TPM2_NV_ReadPublic command. This command, unlike other NV commands, does not require any

---

[3]An NV index in TPM 2.0 is just a subtype of handle, which means anything that asks for a handle without specifying type can be applied to NV indexes.

authorization, since the public information about an index is considered non-sensitive. This can be used to retrieve the index name,[4] attributes (including what type of space it is, and whether the owner, platform and/or other authorization options can be used to access it), access policy hash, and size. This can be very useful when one is trying to figure out what indexes are in use and how to access them, especially if the name or policy information is stored for reference anywhere.

An index can be created to be *lockable*: the TPM2_NV_ReadLock command can be used to prevent any further reads from this index until the next reboot, or the TPM2_NV_WriteLock commands can be used to prevent any further writes to that index until the next reboot. To create a temporarily lockable index, the TPMA_NV_READ_STCLEAR or TPMA_NV_WRITE_STCLEAR attributes should be set when the space is defined. The TPMA_NV_GLOBALLOCK attribute can also be set, in which case the TPM2_NV_GlobalWriteLock command will cause all indexes with that attribute to be temporarily write-locked until the next reboot. An index can also be configured to be permanently lockable with TPM2_NV_WriteLock if the TPMA_NV_WRITEDEFINE attribute is set. Temporarily lockable indexes are useful if the index is intended to only be used by early boot software or during system setup; permanently write-locked indexes are useful in cases where a reference value is meant to be maintained in an integrity-protected state for extended periods of time.

To undefine an NV index, the TPM2_NV_UndefineSpace command is generally used. This command requires owner or platform authorization, depending on which was used to define the space originally. If a particular index should require a non-owner or non-platform authorization policy for deletion, the TPMA_NV_POLICY_DELETE attribute should be set, in which case the TPM2_UndefineSpaceSpecial command (which uses Enhanced Authorization policies instead of the owner or platform authorization) is used to delete the index. If an index is deleted and then redefined, its old contents will no longer be present, having been overwritten. Once an index has been undefined, TPM2_NV_DefineSpace can once again be called with that index.

8.8 Conditional data access

For both TPM-encrypted data and data stored in NVRAM, it is possible to use the TPM's access control to constrain who can access the data, and when.

For data encrypted by the TPM, we have two different ways to limit access. One is by limiting the use of the key being used to perform the decryption and encryption operations. This is particularly useful if we're going to want a large number of objects with the same access constraints or if we want to set constraints on the decryption of an object that we're encrypting on a different system. We can also set access controls directly on the encrypted data itself, if it's created on the same platform

---

[4]This is not a human-readable or human-created name: this is a unique identifier which is a hash of the object's public area including index, using the hash algorithm specified in that public area. This is the same sort of name we discussed for keys back in Section 6.9.

as the TPM; this is particularly interesting in 2.0 TPMs, where sealed data objects can be duplicatable, just like keys. Adding an Enhanced Authorization policy to our encrypted data objects allows us to enforce access control on the data on a remote system without requiring the recipient to set up and certify a new key—at least as long as we make sure we only duplicate the data to trusted TPMs. On either version of TPM, the data-specific access control lets us limit access to individual pieces of data, change the access control easily over time as the data is decrypted and re-encrypted, or use a single generic encryption key for a wide range of encryption needs.

In 1.2 TPMs, we have three options for access control, which we can use in any combination.[5] As discussed in Section 6.13, these are an authorization value, or password; PCR contents; and locality, or CPU state. Authorization values are usually the correct choice when we want to limit data access to certain human users. PCR contents, if our system is predictable enough, can be used to limit access to particular software states. Locality constraints are either extremely powerful or completely useless, depending on whether we're making use of secure processing modes such as Intel's TXT or AMD's SVM. If we are, then we can constrain arbitrary data to be usable only when our CPU is in secure mode and is executing particular software, which makes data theft by malware extremely infeasible. However, if we're not, we can't use locality meaningfully at all.

In 2.0 TPMs, our options are much more varied, although all of the 1.2 options are still available. Enhanced authorization is discussed in detail in Section 6.13.3; here, I'll focus on some of the specific Enhanced Authorization policy options which are particularly interesting in a data protection context.

- The clock or timer options allow data to only be accessed within a particular time window. This creates data which automatically expires.
- The counter option allows data to only be decrypted a certain number of times if system software is designed to update the counter in coordination. This is not quite comprehensive DRM, since decrypted data can be used freely by whatever software is running and an interruption in counter updates will allow data to be used indefinitely, but can be used as part of a DRM solution. It can also be used as an extreme form of rollback prevention, in architectures where data is intended to be single use.
- The private key plus data option, intended for use with biometric devices, can in some cases be used to require biometric identification or the presence of a specialized dongle to access high-sensitivity data.

8.9   Data protection user stories

Alice needs to make sure that high-value files being worked on by SecureCorp employees are both kept secure and not modified. The files could be anything, including text files, images, and spreadsheets; regardless, they will be much too large for the TPM to

---

[5]Technically, we're using all of them all of the time, but in each case there is a null constraint option.

directly encrypt. Although SecureCorp already uses basic full-disk encryption, Alice wants to be sure that even if malware gets onto an employee's computer, as little sensitive data is compromised as possible, giving the IT department more of a chance to notice and respond to a breach in time to protect secrets. Alice has her coders create a file encryption program which will take an arbitrary user-provided file, encrypt it with a fresh symmetric key, then encrypt the symmetric key with a TPM key. Alice wants to be sure that files can be recovered if the machine is lost, so makes sure that in addition to encrypting to a local storage key she also encrypts to a trusted remote backup key, which is stored off-line. Alice would like to make use of her system measurements someday, so she has the encryption program use TPM_Seal or TPM2_Create, which allow her to eventually add PCR constraints and in the meantime record the PCR status of the TPM at the time the file was encrypted. Alice is also concerned about integrity protection, because an adversary modifying the encrypted files could be a different kind of serious threat, so makes sure that a signing key is used to sign a digest of the encrypted file. To keep the signing key from being trivially misused by an on-system adversary, Alice makes sure that the signing key requires a password to use.

Bob is using Bitlocker to set up full-disk encryption for all of his Windows users in the easiest way he can. Bitlocker encrypts the data with a symmetric key used for bulk encryption, then uses TPM_Seal[6] to encrypt the symmetric key. Bob uses the default Bitlocker settings, which use the sealed data's PCR information to verify that the machine's software has not been modified unexpectedly since the last boot.

Charlie is securing his password vault. The open-source application he's using isn't TPM specific, and thus uses the simplest of the TPM's encryption functions: a software TSS_Bind combined with a TPM_Unbind. Charlie doesn't think he needs the full PCR constraints that using TPM_Seal would give him, but he doesn't want someone who steals his laptop to be able to just use the binding key to decrypt his password data. So Charlie modifies the code slightly to make sure that the software prompts for a password to be passed to the TPM to authorize each use of his binding key. That way, he has the TPM's dictionary attack protections and password requirements in place as well as the software's existing protections.

Dana has accountants who need to routinely receive files full of sensitive financial data from clients. Dana takes advantage of the fact that the TPM2_RSA_Decrypt function does not expect TPM-specific data structures, and makes sure each accountant has a password-protected non-restricted RSA decryption key. These keys are duplicatable, and distributed on each computer an accountant needs to be capable of working on so that files can be opened regardless of location. Dana issues certificates for each of the public keys, using the TPM2_Certify feature and an endorsement-hierarchy primary key to establish trust in the keys at Dana's corporate CA.

---

[6]While Bitlocker supports 2.0 TPMs, their public documentation has not been updated as of the time of writing to include details of which approach to TPM encryption is used on 2.0 machines.

The resulting certificates are posted on the corporate website. Clients seeking to send data to their accountant can simply pull the public key from the certificate, create a symmetric key to encrypt their data, and encrypt the symmetric key with the accountant's public key, never knowing that there are TPMs in use on the receiving side.

Fatima would like to ensure that the computers participating in the secure VPN pilot project only trust SecureCorp VPN servers and DNS servers. She stores the keys for the VPN servers and the DNSSec trust anchors in TPM NVRAM on each machine in the pilot project. Because the pilot project is only using 2.0 TPMs, she uses TPM2_NV_DefineSpace and the owner password (the Storage hierarchy authorization) to define two NVRAM spaces. Because she wants these to be highly trusted spaces, she sets the TPMA_NV_OwnerWrite attribute, so that only the owner password can be used to update the data stored inside either area. She does not want any restrictions on who can read the data stored, but is required to set a read attribute; so she uses TPMA_NV_AuthRead with a null password. She then uses TPM2_NV_Write and the owner password for each machine to store the trusted VPN server keys and DNSSec trust anchor keys. The VPN program is modified to use TPM2_NV_Read to retrieve the trusted VPN server keys from the known NVRAM location, and to shut down the connection if there is a mismatch. The machine's DNSSec libraries are updated to refer to the relevant NVRAM location to retrieve trust anchor information, and to provide a user-visible error if there are any problems.

Han is running a pilot program in two-factor authentication for domain access for Example, Inc., where the TPMs serve as an alternative to smartcards as the "thing you have" for lower-security machines. Smartcard authentication has been piloted elsewhere in the company, but Example, Inc. is big and smartcards are an added expense. While TPM keys could be used directly as a smartcard replacement, and would provide the strongest association with the physical machine, Example, Inc. previously invested in proprietary software that doesn't use standard cryptographic library interfaces. Han determines that, for compatibility, the private keys will need to be directly accessible to the proprietary software, but he still wants to tie the keys to the machine with the TPM as much as is possible. He uses the TPM_Seal and TPM2_Create commands to encrypt the software keys, because Example Inc.'s user TPM keys are not password protected and Han wants to make sure that the encrypted software keys require a password to access. The password will be established during the initial setup portion of the application, and known only to the user; in the event of termination, the keys should no longer be usable, as they are part of user authentication. The keys will be decrypted by software on each use, and then the unencrypted keys will be deleted. This requires the user to input the password on every key use, but the smartcard authentication is infrequent enough that the user burden is minor while the security benefits of not keeping the unencrypted keys around any longer than necessary is something Han wants to prioritize.

Ingrid is setting up a distributed sensor network as part of a local utility energy-efficiency effort. She knows that TPMs don't provide the full tamper protection she'd like for her widely distributed and physically accessible machines, but her budget is limited and her goal is to make tampering more difficult and more expensive rather than impossible. Ingrid wants to ensure that firmware updates sent to the sensors are distributed only to the sensors, since the contents could be used to look for flaws in the utility system and thus should be treated as sensitive, and to ensure that all firmware updates are signed by the utility. Her sensors use 1.2 TPMs, as they are cheap, easily available in bulk, and well supported by the Linux-based OS her sensors are using. For each sensor, Ingrid creates a binding key, which she certifies using TPM_Certify and an identity key previously established for each sensor before they leave the utility's facilities. The binding key is associated in a utility database with a device identifier, and maintenance workers in the field report devices they encounter which are missing, damaged, or obviously tampered with. When a new firmware update is created, Ingrid encrypts it with a symmetric key and sends the encrypted file to all of the IP addresses believed to contain utility sensors. Then Ingrid encrypts the symmetric key with the binding key for each sensor, retrieved from the database, and sends that blob to the destination. Only sensors with the correct TPM and binding key will be able to decrypt the symmetric key and thus the firmware. Ingrid debates using a distinct symmetric key for each machine, since the existing approach means that a single tampered machine could retrieve the symmetric key and decrypt other firmware bundles destined for different machines, but decides that since the firmware is not tailored for individual machines the additional work wouldn't provide any security benefits: in either case, the result is that an adversary gets access to the complete firmware for a given update.

Ingrid also wants to make sure that firmware updates are signed by the utility. She allocates a region of NVRAM using TPM_NV_DefineSpace, and sets it to be owner writable (since the utility is the owner and has previously established a secure password for each sensor, stored in a central location) but readable without authorization, and large enough to hold the public key used by the utility to sign firmware updates. This gives her a safe space to store a key, while having flexibility to update it if need be. The firmware is then written to look in NVRAM using TPM_NVReadValue to verify the public key and then check the appropriate signature before decrypting the symmetrically encrypted firmware data bundle. Failure to verify signatures will result in an error back to the utility.

8.10   TSS 1.2 data protection code examples

8.10.1   Binding and unbinding

It's worth emphasizing again that binding data does not actually require the use of a TPM. However, since the TSS provides us a convenient interface to bind data regardless of whether or not a TPM exists on our system, I'll show both binding and unbinding here. Bound data must be encrypted to a binding key on the destination system, whether local or remote. Here, we assume the binding key (or public key, for a remote system) has already been loaded.

```
BYTE* data = ''TestDataHere'';
UINT32 dataLen = sizeof(data);

result = Tspi_Context_CreateObject(hContext, TSS_OBJECT_
   TYPE_ENCDATA, TSS_ENCDATA_BIND, &hBoundData);
debug ("Creating bound data object", result);

result = Tspi_Data_Bind(hBoundData, hBindingKey, dataLen,
   data);
debug("Binding test data", result);
```

To retrieve the bound data, we have an even simpler operation. Again, we assume the binding key has already been loaded.

```
result = Tspi_Data_Unbind(hBoundData, hBindingKey,
   &outDataLen, &outData);
debug("Unbinding test data", result);
```

8.10.2   Sealing and unsealing

Sealing data requires the use of a storage key. We can use the SRK for this, or create a new storage key, depending on what access restrictions we want for the sealed data. It's worth noting again that there are two different points during the unsealing process that we can enforce access control: on the use of the storage key protecting the data, or on the sealed data itself. Unlike binding, sealing data also requires that the storage key's access control constraints be met, which can be used to gather information about the state of the machine or presumed user when the sealed data was created.

There are two different access control choices that must be made when creating sealed data using the TSS: an access control policy containing a required authorization value, and a set of PCRs to constrain the data to, which may be null (0). Note that although one can usually call the Tspi_Policy_SetSecret command with TSS_SECRET_MODE_NONE, that will cause errors when sealing data; instead, if you want sealed data to not require a password to access, use the well-known secret as shown here. This example features sealed data with no data-specific access constraints.

```
BYTE wks[] =TSS_WELL_KNOWN_SECRET;

// Set policy for object to be sealed. Setting a policy
   with a secret is
// mandatory, and TSS_SECRET_MODE_NONE causes errors.
result= Tspi_Context_CreateObject(hContext, TSS_OBJECT_
                     TYPE_POLICY,
                     TSS_POLICY_USAGE,  &hSealPolicy);
debug("Creating policy for sealed data", result);
```

```
result = Tspi_Policy_SetSecret(hSealPolicy,
   TSS_SECRET_MODE_PLAIN, sizeof(wks), wks);
debug("Setting null secret policy for data", result);

result= Tspi_Policy_AssignToObject(hSealPolicy, hSealData);
debug("Assigning policy to sealed data object", result);

TSS_HPCRS hSealingPCRs = 0; // For this example, not sealing
                                         to PCR constraints

result = Tspi_Data_Seal(hSealData, hStorageKey, inDataSize,
   inData, hSealingPCRs);
debug("Sealing data", result);
```

It's worth noting that when choosing the PCRs to use when sealing data, we have more choices than we normally do. `TSS_HPCRS` objects have an attribute defining the TPM data structure being used behind the scenes. We usually don't care about this attribute; however, if we use a `TSS_PCRS_STRUCT_INFO_LONG`, we have the option of defining a different PCR selection to be used at creation than at release. The PCRs at release are a concept we've used repeatedly: the data will not be unsealed unless the value of the selected registers matches the specified composite. The PCRs at creation are something else entirely. Each sealed blob contains a record of the PCR state of the machine when the blob was created; the PCRs at creation determine which PCRs are included. By default, these selections are the same. The other major difference is that the long structure includes locality information; again, different locality selections can be chosen for creation and release.

To set the PCR info structure, the structure type can be specified during object creation as one of the initialization flags. Otherwise, the `Tspi_SetAttribUint32` command is used, with the attribute `TSS_TSPATTRIB_PCRS_INFO` and the subattribute `TSS_TSP_ATTRIB_PCRSINFO_PCRSTRUCT`. The same choices can be made when creating PCR info structures for use with keys and other objects. An example is shown in Section 6.15.2.

8.10.3   Using NVRAM

Even those who don't intend to use NVRAM as part of their routine TPM use may want to perform one simple NVRAM operation: looking to see if their TPM includes an Endorsement Credential signed by their manufacturer. This uses the standard command for reading content in NVRAM: `Tspi_NV_ReadValue`. Note that we cannot simply provide the numeric index we want; the command is expecting a TSS object which happens to include the index. This can seem a bit ridiculous when you're just reading the contents of a given space, but it will make more sense in a little while when we start using the same structure to define new NVRAM spaces.

Although you can use the numeric indexes listed in Table 5.1 to access manufacturer-created content, the TSS provides handy predefined constants. In this case, we're using TPM_NV_INDEX_EKCert to access the EK certificate, but there are a few other useful indexes to know about if your manufacturer is especially good about including credentials: TPM_NV_INDEX_PlatformCert, and for those interested in conformance credentials (primarily useful to those working with governments), TPM_NV_INDEX_TPM_CC and TPM_NV_INDEX_Platform_CC. It is important to note that just because these indexes are defined in the standard doesn't mean they're actually in use in any given TPM; if the manufacturer did not include a particular credential, the TPM will return a bad index error.

Reading indexes created locally works the exact same way as reading manufacturer-created indexes, but the index in question will have been defined by software.

```
TSS_HNVSTORE hEKCert;
TSS_HNVSTORE hNVData;
UINT32 EKDataLen = 1024;
BYTE* EKCertData;

result = Tspi_Context_CreateObject(hContext,
  TSS_OBJECT_TYPE_NV, 0, &hEKCert);
debug("Creating EK Cert handle object", result);

/* Set to defined index for EK Cert (0x000F000) */
result = Tspi_SetAttribUint32(hEKCert,
  TSS_TSPATTRIB_NV_INDEX, 0, TPM_NV_INDEX_EKCert);
debug("Setting NV Index value", result);

/* Read certificate out, if present. */
result = Tspi_NV_ReadValue(hEKCert, 0, &EKDataLen,
  &EKCertData);
debug("Reading NV contents for EK Cert", result);
```

To create our own NVRAM space, we begin by defining the index and its attributes, using the same kind of TSS_OBJECT_TYPE_NV object we created to read an index. However, we need to additional attributes besides the index to create a space: the command will fail unless we have specified access permissions and data size.

When choosing an index to write to, the TSS gives us a major advantage over just using the TPM directly. The TSS_NV_DefineSpace command we'll be using will return an error if the index already exists, allowing us to safely test for existing indexes just by checking failures without worrying about overwriting good data. Behind the scenes, both TSS_NV_DefineSpace and TSS_NV_ReleaseSpace use TPM_NV_DefineSpace, but the TSS helpfully does not automatically and silently overwrite existing indexes.

```
result = Tspi_Context_CreateObject(hContext,
  TSS_OBJECT_TYPE_NV, 0, &hNVData);
debug("Creating NV Data handle object", result);
result = Tspi_SetAttribUint32(hNVData, TSS_TSPATTRIB_NV_INDEX,
  0, 0x0100000);
debug("Setting NV Index value", result);

/* Setting index to owner-only read and write, and
   writeall (must
 * completely be overwritten on each write) */
result = Tspi_SetAttribUint32(hNVData,
                              TSS_TSPATTRIB_NV_PERMISSIONS, 0,
                              TPM_NV_PER_WRITEALL |
                              TPM_NV_PER_OWNERWRITE |
                              TPM_NV_PER_OWNERREAD);
debug("Setting NV Permissions value", result);

result = Tspi_SetAttribUint32(hNVData,
  TSS_TSPATTRIB_NV_DATASIZE, 0, 20);
debug("Setting NV Data Size value", result);
```

To actually define the NVRAM space, we must provide owner authorization. Only the owner or an owner delegate (see Section 10.9.3) can define new NVRAM spaces, although depending on the permissions configured for a given index, non-owner parties may be able to read or write the contents.

```
/* Set up owner authorization, required to define NVRAM space */
TSS_HPOLICY hOwnerPolicy;
result= Tspi_GetPolicyObject(hTPM, TSS_POLICY_USAGE,
                             &hOwnerPolicy);
debug("Getting owner policy", result);

/* Set owner secret using whatever method is appropriate */
result= Tspi_Policy_SetSecret(hOwnerPolicy, TSS_SECRET_MODE_PLAIN,
                              strlen(pwd), pwd);
debug("Setting owner secret", result);

/* Define the new space we previously configured.
 * Second and third arguments are optional TSS_HPCRS objects
   specifying
 * the PCR constraints associated with reading and writing
   respectively. */
result = Tspi_NV_DefineSpace(hNVData, 0, 0);
debug("Defining NV space", result);
```

There is one special case for TPM_NV_DefineSpace: writing to TPM_NV_INDEX_LOCK. This index is used to set the nvLocked flag (discussed in more detail in Section 8.7.1) which determines whether or not the TPM enforces access control on NVRAM. Unlike all other TPM_NV_DefineSpace uses, this one index does not require owner authorization to write. Once written, it is set for the life of the TPM unless the EK itself is successfully revoked (see Section 10.2.1).

8.11 TSS 2.0 data protection code examples

8.11.1 Creating a sealed blob

In Chapter 6, we showed how TPM2_Create can be used to create a key, but it is also used to create the sealed data blobs used for storing encrypted data. Here, the object attributes are entirely different: it is a data blob, and it cannot be used for signing, cannot be used for decryption, and has a fixed parent (is only duplicatable if a key in its parent hierarchy is duplicatable). We also set it without the restricted attribute; this attribute has no meaning for non-key objects, and must not be set. Because this is a sealed blob, where we are providing the data to be encrypted rather than having the TPM generate the secret data, the sensitiveDataOrigin attribute must also not be set.

```
Create_In                   in;
Create_Out                  out;
TPMI_DH_OBJECT              parentHandle = 0;
TPMI_SH_AUTH_SESSION       sessionHandle0 = TPM_RS_PW;
unsigned int                sessionAttributes0 = 0;
TPMI_SH_AUTH_SESSION       sessionHandle1 = TPM_RH_NULL;
unsigned int                sessionAttributes1 = 0;

...
/* Retrieve parent key information, authorization values, and
   authorization policies as appropriate. */

/* Retrieve filenames containing data to be sealed (dataFilename) and
   to store output. */
...

  {

    in->inPublic.t.publicArea.type = TPM_ALG_KEYEDHASH;
    in->inPublic.t.publicArea.nameAlg =  TPM_ALG_SHA256;

    /* Establish object attributes */
    in->inPublic.t.publicArea.objectAttributes.val &=
      ~TPMA_OBJECT_SIGN;
    in->inPublic.t.publicArea.objectAttributes.val &=
      ~TPMA_OBJECT_DECRYPT;
    in->inPublic.t.publicArea.objectAttributes.val &=
      ~TPMA_OBJECT_RESTRICTED;
    in->inPublic.t.publicArea.objectAttributes.val &=
      ~TPMA_OBJECT_SENSITIVEDATAORIGIN;
```

```
in->inPublic.t.publicArea.objectAttributes.val |=
  TPMA_OBJECT_USERWITHAUTH;
in.inPublic.t.publicArea.objectAttributes.val |=
  TPMA_OBJECT_FIXEDPARENT;
in->inPublic.t.publicArea.objectAttributes.val &=
  ~TPMA_OBJECT_ADMINWITHPOLICY;

/* While sealed blobs have the same object type as keyed hashes,
   they have no associated signing method. */
in->inPublic.t.publicArea.parameters.keyedHashDetail.scheme.
  scheme = TPM_ALG_NULL;

/* The unique identifier for a sealed blob requires data that
   will be filled in by the TPM, so its initial value is 0. */
in->inPublic.t.publicArea.unique.sym.t.size = 0;

/* If we wanted to set an external identifier for the data being
   sealed, we could fill it in in in.outsideInfo. Here,
   we don't. */
in.outsideInfo.t.size = 0;

/* If we wanted to establish a PCR selection to record the
   TPM register state when the object was created, we
 * could use creationPCR. Here, we don't. */
in.creationPCR.count = 0;


/* Set password for sealed blob. */
if (keyPassword == NULL) {
  in.inSensitive.t.sensitive.userAuth.t.size = 0;}
 else {
  rc = TPM2B_StringCopy(&in.inSensitive.t.sensitive.userAuth.b,
                        keyPassword, sizeof(TPMU_HA));}

/* Input data to be sealed. */
if (dataFilename != NULL) {
  rc = File_Read2B(&in.inSensitive.t.sensitive.data.b,
  MAX_SYM_DATA,
  dataFilename); }
 else {
    printf(``Sealed data object needs data to seal.\n'');}

/* Use an encrypted input session, so sensitive data being passed
   in is protected in transit.  */
sessionAttributes1 |= TPMA_SESSION_DECRYPT;

rc = TSE_Execute((RESPONSE_PARAMETERS *)&out,
                 (COMMAND_PARAMETERS *)&in,
                 NULL,
                 TPM_CC_Create,
                 sessionHandle0, parentPassword, sessionAttributes0,
                 sessionHandle1, NULL, sessionAttributes1,
                 TPM_RH_NULL, NULL, 0);

/* Save the private portion of the sealed data returned
   by the TPM. */
```

```
if ((rc == 0) && (privateKeyFilename != NULL)) {
    rc = File_WriteStructure(&out.outPrivate,
                         (MarshalFunction_t)TSS_TPM2B_PRIVATE_
                         Marshal,
                         privateKeyFilename);
}
/* Save the public portion of the sealed data returned
   by the TPM. */
if ((rc == 0) && (publicKeyFilename != NULL)) {
    rc = File_WriteStructure(&out.outPublic,
                         (MarshalFunction_t)TSS_TPM2B_PUBLIC_
                         Marshal,
                         publicKeyFilename);}
```

8.11.2   Decrypting a sealed blob

Unsealing is much more straightforward than creating sealed data. The only input required is the object handle, and the only output is the contents of that object's sensitive data field. An appropriate authorization session may be required if the sealed blob requires a password or authorization policy to access.

```
/* Since we're retrieving encrypted data from the TPM,
   set the session attributes *
 * to encrypt.
*/
sessionAttributes1 |= TPMA_SESSION_ENCRYPT;

rc = TSE_Execute((RESPONSE_PARAMETERS *)&out,
                (COMMAND_PARAMETERS *)&in,
                NULL,
                TPM_CC_Unseal,
                sessionHandle0, password, sessionAttributes0,
                sessionHandle1, NULL, sessionAttributes1,
                TPM_RH_NULL, NULL, 0);

/* Write resulting data to file. */
if ((rc == 0) && (outDataFilename != NULL)) {
    rc = File_WriteBinaryFile(out.outData.t.buffer,
                            out.outData.t.size,
                            outDataFilename);}
```

8.11.3   Using NV storage

Our first step in using NV storage is to decide how we will define our space. Each NV index we establish using TPM2_NV_DefineSpace has a certain set of attributes which determine how that section of NV index can be used. The full list of attributes can be found in Tables 8.1 and 8.2. Note that in the IBM TSS 2.0 library, the variable names which are listed as bits in the specification as TPMA_NV_XXXX are implemented as full UINT32 values with the naming scheme TPMA_NVA_XXXX. The example code uses TPMA_NVA_NO_DA, which ensures that authorization failures for accessing the index do not trigger the TPM's dictionary attack protection, as the original attribute value to which other attribute values can be combined using bitwise OR operations. High security operations which do want to use the TPM's built-in dictionary attack protection mechanisms to protect an index can, of course, use any of the TPMA_NV_XXXX values as the initial attribute set.

For example, to create an ordinary NV index, used for reading and writing data, which can be written to and read from only by the owner, one would use:

```
TPMA_NV                              nvAttributes;

/* default values */
nvAttributes.val = TPMA_NVA_NO_DA;

nvAttributes.val |= TPMA_NVA_ORDINARY |
   TPMA_NVA_OWNERWRITE | TPMA_NVA_OWNERREAD;
```

While to create a PCR-style NV index which can only be read or extended by someone with the appropriate authorization value, one would instead use:

```
nvAttributes.val |= TPMA_NVA_BITS | TPMA_NVA_AUTHWRITE
   | TPMA_NVA_AUTHREAD;
```

One can, of course, mix and match; creating a space which is writable by the owner but readable by anyone who meets a particular authorization policy (which could be a completely trivial one, if you want the index to be widely readable) would involve combining TPMA_NVA_OWNERWRITE with TPMA_NVA_POLICYREAD. If you want a space to be readable either by people with a password or people with a policy, you can combine TPMA_NVA_AUTHREAD and TPMA_NVA_POLICYREAD. There is no limit to the number of attributes that can be selected, as long as none of them are mutually contradictory.

Policies and authorization values are passed in as part of the TPM2_NV_DefineSpace arguments along with the attributes. The authorization value, if any, is provided as its own argument(auth); this is not the authorization value to create the NV space, which is provided with an existing authorization session, but the authorization value referred to in the TPM_NV_AUTHREAD and TPM_NV_AUTHWRITE attributes. Other arguments, including attributes, size of the space, and index handle, are passed in as part of the `TPM2B_NV_PUBLIC` structure `nvPublic`.

```
    NV_DefineSpace_In          in;
    TPMI_RH_NV_INDEX           nvIndex = 0;

...
/* Collect authorization value and file containing policy
   values, if any. */
...

      /* Set desired password to access NV index, if any. */
      if (nvPassword == NULL) {
        in.auth.b.size = 0;
      }
      else {
         TPM2B_StringCopy(&in.auth.b,
         nvPassword, sizeof(TPMU_HA));
      }

      /* Optional authorization policy, read from policyFilename */
      if (policyFilename != NULL) {
        nvAttributes.val |= TPMA_NVA_POLICYWRITE | TPMA_NVA_
          POLICYREAD;
        File_Read2B(&in.publicInfo.t.nvPublic.authPolicy.b,
        sizeof(TPMU_HA),
        policyFilename);
      }
      else {
         in.publicInfo.t.nvPublic.authPolicy.t.size = 0;
/* default empty policy */
      }


      in.publicInfo.t.nvPublic.nvIndex = nvIndex;
/* the handle of the data area */
      in.publicInfo.t.nvPublic.nameAlg = nalg;
/* hash algorithm used to compute
   the name of the Index and used
   for the authPolicy  */
      in.publicInfo.t.nvPublic.attributes = nvAttributes;
/* the Index attributes */
      in.publicInfo.t.nvPublic.dataSize = dataSize;
/* the size of the data area */

      rc = TSE_Execute(NULL,
                       (COMMAND_PARAMETERS *)&in,
                       NULL,
                       TPM_CC_NV_DefineSpace,
                       sessionHandle0, parentPassword,
                       sessionAttributes0,
                       TPM_RH_NULL, NULL, 0);
```

Once we've established our NV storage space, we can write content to it. For an ordinary index, we use the TPM2_NV_Write command:

```
NV_Write_In                    in;
TPMI_SH_AUTH_SESSION           sessionHandle0 = TPM_RS_PW;
unsigned int                   sessionAttributes0 = 0;

...
/* Retrieve index to write, authorization information,
   data to write from user. */
...

  /* Set the authorization handle to use. The authorization
     session will contain the actual authorization value,
     if any.*/
  if (hierarchyAuthChar == 'o') {
    in.authHandle = TPM_RH_OWNER;
  }
  else if (hierarchyAuthChar == 'p') {
    in.authHandle = TPM_RH_PLATFORM;
  }
  else {
    in.authHandle = nvIndex;
  }

  /* Set data to be written to NV index, either from file
     or string */
  if (data != NULL) {
    TPM2B_StringCopy(&in.data.b, data, MAX_NV_BUFFER_SIZE);}
  if (datafilename != NULL) {
    File_Read2B(&in.data.b, MAX_NV_BUFFER_SIZE,
    datafilename);}

  /* Set index to write to, and the offset bytes to use
     when determining where in
     the NV space defined by that index to write. Offset
     will be 0 when overwriting
     the complete contents. */
  in.nvIndex = nvIndex;
  in.offset = offset;

  /* Call TSE to execute the command. Note that there is no
     ''out'' structure here, because
     TPM2_NV_Write does not return data. */
  TSE_Execute(NULL,
              (COMMAND_PARAMETERS *)&in,
              NULL,
              TPM_CC_NV_Write,
              sessionHandle0, nvPassword, sessionAttributes0,
              TPM_RH_NULL, NULL, 0);}
```

8.11.4   *Reading NV contents and manufacturer certificates*

```
    NV_Read_In                    in;
    NV_Read_Out                   out;
    uint16_t                      offset = 0;
/* default 0 */
    uint16_t                      size = 0;
    TPMI_RH_NV_INDEX              nvIndex = 0;
    const char                    *nvPassword = NULL;
/* default no password */
    TPMI_SH_AUTH_SESSION          sessionHandle0 = TPM_RS_PW;
    unsigned int                  sessionAttributes0 = 0;

...
/* Retrieve index, size, and offset (if applicable). */
/* Retrieve authorization information. */
...

        if (hierarchyAuthChar == 'o') {
            in.authHandle = TPM_RH_OWNER;
        }
        else if (hierarchyAuthChar == 'p') {
            in.authHandle = TPM_RH_PLATFORM;
        }
        else if (hierarchyAuthChar == 0) {
            in.authHandle = nvIndex;
        }
        in.nvIndex =nvIndex;
        in.size = size;
        in.offset = offset;

        TSE_Execute((RESPONSE_PARAMETERS *)&out,
                    (COMMAND_PARAMETERS *)&in,
                    NULL,
                    TPM_CC_NV_Read,
                    sessionHandle0, nvPassword,
                    sessionAttributes0,
                    sessionHandle1, NULL,
                    sessionAttributes1,
                    sessionHandle2, NULL,
                    sessionAttributes2,
                    TPM_RH_NULL, NULL, 0);

        File_WriteBinaryFile(out.data.b.buffer, out.data.b.
          size, datafilename);
```

In many cases, you will want to retrieve the manufacturer Endorsement Credentials even if you're not otherwise using NV storage. The range of possible NV indexes these credentials could be stored in are listed in Table 5.1 on page 57.

If you're not sure what authorization value an index is expecting, or the allocated size, you can retrieve the public data using the TPM2_NV_ReadPublic command. The data returned is the same TPM2B_NV_PUBLIC data structure we created for use in TPM2_Create.

```
NV_ReadPublic_In            in;
NV_ReadPublic_Out           out;
TPMI_RH_NV_INDEX            nvIndex = 0; /*
                            Placeholder index */

...
/* Retrieve index to be accessed. No authorization
   information is required, because
   the ReadPublic command only retrieves public data. */
...

    in.nvIndex = nvIndex;

    TSE_Execute((RESPONSE_PARAMETERS *)&out,
                (COMMAND_PARAMETERS *)&in,
                NULL,
                TPM_CC_NV_ReadPublic,
                TPM_RH_NULL, NULL, 0);

    printf(''nvreadpublic: name algorithm %04x\n'',
    out.nvPublic.t.nvPublic.nameAlg);
    printf(''nvreadpublic: attributes %08x\n'',
    out.nvPublic.t.nvPublic.attributes.val);
    printf(''nvreadpublic: size %d\n'', out.nvPublic.
    t.nvPublic.dataSize);

    /* Print policy and name buffers using IBM TSS
       2.0 helper function. */
    TPM_PrintAll(''nvreadpublic: policy'',
                out.nvPublic.t.nvPublic.authPolicy.
                t.buffer,
                out.nvPublic.t.nvPublic.authPolicy.
                t.size);
    TPM_PrintAll(''nvreadpublic: name'',
                out.nvName.t.name, out.nvName.t.size);
```

Chapter 9

Attestation

Who are you?

Attestation, as we discussed briefly in Chapter 2, is the presentation of verifiable evidence about machine state to an *appraiser*, who can decide whether or not the state is acceptable. Our focus will be on *remote attestation*, where the appraiser is on a different machine, for two reasons. First, the vast majority of interesting attestation use cases are those where we want a machine to prove to an external party that it is trustworthy. Second, local attestation often presents a unique challenge: if one is trying to decide whether one can trust the machine one is using, how can you be certain your ability to determine what state is acceptable has not been modified? As a result, local attestation tends to take two forms: boot-time protections, where the state of the next piece of software to load is being assessed and the boot process may be halted if the software is not approved, and the very rare temporal attestation, where one is verifying the state of the machine at some previous time when some particular action was taken.

9.1 Machine state and the TPM

TPMs have no insight into the state of the machine they are installed on. Instead, the measurements of machine state stored in the TPM are generated outside, by components of the *measurement trust chain*. This is a *chain of trust* consisting of the RTM, and software launched by that root.

9.1.1 Measurement chains of trust

The Roots of Trust for Measurement, or RTMs, are the components of a system which we trust to take the initial measurements of the system. The measurements here are not complicated. These are small and simple components, so as to be maximally trustworthy, and take a simple hash of the next component to boot before handing off control, forming a trust chain as shown in Chapter 3; this hash is placed into the TPM PCRs. This next component, because it has been measured, is considered to be trusted, in the trusted computing sense of the word which really means "we have evidence we can use to evaluate its expected behavior." This trusted component is the next link in the chain of trust. It can then measure another component before handing off control, and so forth until we have a chain of trust consisting of many components, each of which has been measured by a previous component going back to the root of trust.

Although the chain metaphor implies that these chains of trust must be linear, this is not actually required; any component that is measured before it is launched, and where the measuring components have themselves been measured, is part of a chain of trust. A trusted OS could easily measure dozens of applications before they launch, bringing them into the chain of trust without requiring each application to measure other applications.

Because the trust in the whole chain of measurement relies on the root of trust at the bottom, it is important to understand the differences between the available RTMs and choose one that is appropriate for your use cases.

9.1.2   The Static Root of Trust for Measurement

The **Static Root of Trust for Measurement**, or **SRTM**, refers to a small piece of BIOS/UEFI code, the boot block. It is "static" because it only measures (hashes) one thing: the rest of the BIOS. Exactly which parts of the rest of the BIOS are measured depends heavily on implementation; in some cases, critical pieces of code are not measured, and in others irrelevant data such as installation timestamps are included. This can mean that in some systems the SRTM measurements are both extremely unpredictable (the exact same BIOS code will have different measurements on different systems) and not going to catch a number of BIOS-based attacks. For high-security systems, this means that wherever possible, it's worth investing in learning more about the details of your BIOS, and potentially in making modifications to it. For everyday users, this isn't much of a concern, as low-level BIOS attacks are uncommon and it's often sufficient to check that a machine is in the same state as it was yesterday rather than checking for the presence of a trusted "golden" image. Modern UEFI firmware is designed to be more modular and predictable than old-fashioned BIOSes, and the SRTM may as a result produce more reliable and predictable measurements; however, not all of the problems with BIOS SRTMs are fixed in UEFI firmware.[1]

One of the biggest downsides of the SRTM is that it is implemented by BIOS vendors, who are often small companies about whom very little is known, and with whom an individual or enterprise has no direct relationship. Trust can be very difficult in such circumstances, and an untrustworthy SRTM—either because of malice or simple lack of attention—can be a notable vulnerability for people who care deeply about security. Some SRTMs have been determined to not be well-protected against firmware updates and other unauthorized changes, even aside from the original vendor's trustworthiness. BIOS vulnerabilities are becoming more widely known,[2]

---

[1] https://www.mitre.org/sites/default/files/publications/bios-chronomancy.pdf

[2] http://www.legbacore.com/Research_files/2015_ShmooCon_BIOSBugs.pdf shares a few examples, but there's plenty of information out there.

making this a real concern even for people not concerned about nation-state level attackers such as the NSA.

The SRTM's advantages lie in usability. If your machine boots and is designed to use the TPM, the SRTM will execute and store the values it measures in the TPM's PCRs. For this reason, it is sometimes called the *Core Root of Trust for Measurement*, or *CRTM*. No expertise or additional work is required to use its measurements, and the chain of trust it launches (Figure 9.1) will, depending on the OS, automatically run up until the boot loader; some boot loaders may continue further in the boot process, such as the Windows boot loader, which measures the kernel. If your boot loader does not measure your OS kernel or other higher level resources, you may need to install a custom boot loader such as Trusted Grub or tboot (see Section 11.8.5), which will measure the OS kernel before it boots and provide the option of measuring other critical system files. Some OS extensions may even let you extend measurements into the running OS; the Linux IMA, for example, will take a hash of application binaries before launching them and extend those measurements into the TPM.

9.1.3   The Dynamic Root of Trust for Measurement

The *Dynamic Root of Trust for Measurement*, or *DRTM*, is an alternate root of trust for measurement designed to avoid trust in the BIOS code or vendors. The DRTM is very different from the SRTM: it does not launch automatically, but instead is started by software initiating a special trusted CPU mode and passing it a region of memory to be executed. (A DRTM CPU mode is part of Intel's TXT technology, as well as AMD's SVM.) When the CPU enters the secure mode, it pauses all other running processes and goes into a single-threaded mode. Then the CPU automatically runs a check to ensure that the DRTM code is signed by the CPU vendor, and measures and launches the DRTM code. The DRTM code will measure the user-provided region of memory by taking a hash of it and putting it into the TPM, then pass control to the point in the memory indicated by the user. The memory region can contain anything: executables, data, even a full OS. Because the entire memory region is chosen by the user and then measured, this approach provides extreme flexibility: the content passed to the DRTM can be exactly what the user wants to be able to trust, including an executable and its configuration or input files, or a trusted OS and applications.

The DRTM allows for much greater precision and predictability in measurements, since the user (or IT department) chooses what is measured. However, this approach requires significantly more knowledge and effort than using the SRTM. The secure CPU mode must be entered, and then carefully exited: in the full secure mode, programs are single threaded and only the code provided to the DRTM may execute, so many of the restrictions imposed must be turned off or secure mode ended for normal computing operations to proceed.

There are two primary approaches to using the DRTM, which are mutually incompatible for reasons we'll discuss in detail in Section 9.2. The first is to use the DRTM to put a system into a trusted execution state (trusted OS, measured applications, etc.)

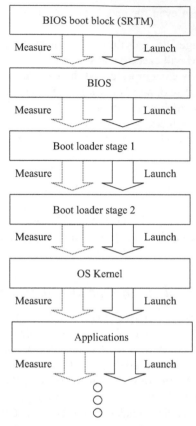

Figure 9.1   An example SRTM boot chain rooted in the BIOS boot block. In practice, there are several common variants. First, many modern systems use UEFI firmware instead of a BIOS; because BIOS code is often highly obscure, customized, and adapted from older systems, while UEFI is (at least in theory) more modular and better organized, UEFI firmware may provide better measurements. Second, each step in the chain must be TPM-aware and designed to participate in the measurement chain for it to continue; some boot loaders measure the OS kernel, while others do not, and very few OSs today continue the measurement chain to measure applications. Nor do most applications measure their configuration files, user-provided code, or other information that might affect system security. Third, while this is depicted as a chain for simplicity, chains of trust can actually be trees of trust, especially at higher levels. For example, the boot loader might separately measure the OS kernel, OS kernel modules, and files on the OS such as security-critical libraries. An OS capable of measuring applications, such as Linux with the Integrity Measurement Architecture (IMA) extensions (Section 11.8.5.1), will measure each application separately before launching, effectively providing dozens or hundreds of parallel "links" in the last step of the chain

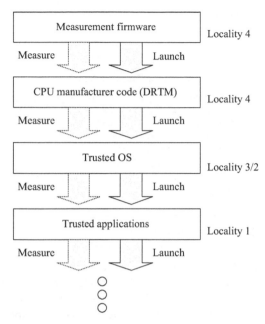

Figure 9.2   An example of a trusted OS launch sequence using the DRTM. Here, the length of the trust chain is much shorter than in the SRTM case, and there are fewer trusted parties involved in creating the relevant firmware and software. In fact, the distinction between the actual CPU measurement and signature verification action and the manufacturer-signed code which measures and launches the OS is rarely necessary to make; from the perspective of higher level software, both of these can largely be lumped together as "the DRTM." The trusted OS has two localities listed (discussed in more detail in Section 9.1.3.1) because although it initially executes in the CPU-supported high-trust state, a modern OS requires functionality (such as multithreading) not available in secure mode, and so the locality will change as the OS restores normal operation. Note that localities 2 and 1 here are established and enforced solely by the trusted OS and TPM driver, not by the CPU or the TPM

without relying (much) on an untrusted BIOS.[3] In this case, the DRTM is used once at system startup, and the normal boot sequence is just used to launch the DRTM. Here, the measurements created by the DRTM cover the OS and associated trusted files. An example is shown in Figure 9.2.

---

[3] Eliminating all trust in the BIOS is impossible, as the BIOS or UEFI firmware launches other low-level firmware the system uses to communicate with installed devices.

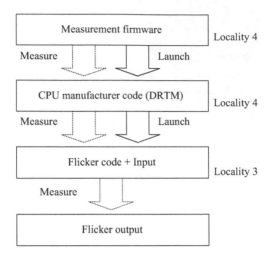

*Figure 9.3   An example of the extremely short chain of trust involved in a
DRTM-launched trusted application that executes entirely in secure
mode, and which uses the DRTM measurements and secure mode
locality protections to allow a remote party to verify the application
code, input values, and output*

The second approach to the DRTM is to execute temporary trusted applications
or operations, in a secure mode where the less trusted OS and applications cannot
interfere. An example is the Flicker program created by CMU (see Section 11.8.4.1),
which is depicted at a high level in Figure 9.3. Here, the DRTM is passed a single,
usually limited-function executable and its inputs. The DRTM measurements cover
the executable, its input, and often the executable output, which is extended into the
TPM by the executable while secure mode is running. This allows the user to prove to
external parties that the trusted executable ran, in a trusted environment, with given
input and output. In this approach, the DRTM may be executed repeatedly during a
given boot cycle, since it's used every time the high-trust operations are performed.

The reason we can use the DRTM for multiple high-trust operations in a single
boot cycle is the same reason we can't use the DRTM both to launch a secure OS
and to run trusted applications. Every time the DRTM is launched, all measurements
from prior DRTM executions are erased and replaced with the new measurements.

9.1.3.1   Locality and establishing trust in the DRTM

For the DRTM to work, we need to be certain that certain measurements actually
originated in the DRTM. We can't rely on the SRTM assumption, which is that it
will always be the first thing on the platform to boot and will therefore be capable of
measuring into the first PCR without interference. This is where *locality* comes into
play. We covered locality briefly back in Section 6.13.2, where we established that it
provides a very coarse-grained access control based on CPU state. Its real purpose
is to support the DRTM, using a special bus whose value changes based on the CPU
state and flags on the pages of memory being executed.

Table 9.1   How the Trusted Computing Group designed localities to be used, and how they're used in practice today

Locality	Intended meaning	Common use
4	Trusted Hardware/DRTM	DRTM
3	Auxiliary Components/DRTM	Software launched by DRTM
2	Trusted OS	Not used
1	Trusted Applications	Not used
0	SRTM/Legacy	STRM, Default

When the DRTM is executing, the locality sent to the TPM with each command is set to 4, indicating that the command was issued to the CPU by the DRTM firmware. When the DRTM passes control to user-provided code, but the CPU is still in secure mode, commands are sent to the TPM with locality 3. Normal execution uses locality 0. Localities 1 and 2 are controlled by the OS, based on the memory page the code is being executed from Table 9.1. Because using locality 1 and 2 meaningfully in a standard workstation relies both on having high trust in your OS's enforcement mechanisms and on having a trusted TPM driver capable of operating in multiple localities, they're not used on commercial systems today. However, the two additional localities can provide interesting opportunities in certain circumstances; for example, a company heavily invested in virtualization could use distinct localities for the hypervisor or for requests coming from VMs. Locality is the same in 1.2 and 2.0 TPMs.[4]

Locality gives us a few powerful features. First and foremost, the way we can determine that measurements were created by the DRTM or DRTM-launched code is by looking at the specific PCRs which can only be extended in localities 4 or 3 (see Figure 9.8). These PCRs are automatically reset (set to a known value) when the DRTM is entered. Second, this lets us create keys which can only be used while DRTM-launched code is executing in secure mode, by constraining them with to the DRTM-launched locality. A DRTM-protected banking application could have a binding key only accessible while the banking app is running in secure mode, allowing secure transmission of data to the specific application. A malware detection program that takes advantage of the paused system state during secure mode to look for rootkits and other low-level attacks could have a constrained signing key with which to sign its reports, allowing external parties to confirm that the report came from the trusted software and was generated while no other programs could interfere with it. The illustrations in Figures 9.2 and 9.3 show the localities used at various points in some example trusted boot operations.

When using the DRTM for individual applications generating trustworthy output for a single transaction, it is often simplest to have the application extend the input and output of the application into the locality-limited PCRs rather than using a locality-limited signing key to sign the results. This is for two reasons. First, it

---

[4]The 2.0 TPM specification does support an extended locality feature, intended for use with vTPMs and other use cases where additional software localities may be desired, but the feature is not in use today.

is much faster: the slow RSA signing operation used to verify the PCR contents happens outside of secure mode, which is useful since the entire system is paused during secure mode, while the extend operation that occurs while in secure mode is a quick hashing operation. Secondly, it means that if the application measurements are not consistent, a single Quote (see Section 9.3.1) will provide attestation of both the application and the output without needing a new key, certification for the new key, and the signed data. Why might a trusted application not have consistent measurements? The DRTM allows for an unusual kind of challenge–response system, where a trusted appraiser can send the machine being verified not only simple input data but also an entire executable to run in secure mode. An enterprise with a widely distributed server network, which wishes to periodically assess the system health of the servers without fully shutting them down and rebooting them, might choose to send randomized health-testing challenge executables to each machine, which will execute in the DRTM mode and inspect a distinct region of the running machine's memory each time. This kind of randomized challenge can be useful for keeping malware from hiding effectively without taking the time required to inspect the entire system memory every time. Remember, however, that using the DRTM does pause the machine for as long as the user-provided executable is running; some OSes, such as Windows, are sensitive to unexpected and extended pauses and may behave in unpredictable ways.

9.2   Using the PCRs

I introduced the PCRs briefly back in Section 3.6, and talked about how we could use them to limit access to keys and other system resources in Section 6.13.2. To refresh your memory, the PCRs are a set of registers in the TPM's internal storage which are used to store system measurements and other data. The contents of all PCRs are set to known values on every reboot, and rather than being overwritten by the user, PCRs can only have data added using some very specific operations. As a result, PCRs contain hash chains that we can use to verify everything that has been added to the register, making it impossible for a malicious party to forge good measurements. In this section, I'll cover PCRs in much more detail, including what we expect them to contain, where that information comes from, and how we can use them creatively to certify more than just system measurements.

9.2.1   Essential PCR operations

The two most basic PCR operations are extend (TPM_Extend and TPM2_PCR_ Extend) and reset (TPM_PCR_Reset and TPM2_PCR_Reset). The extend operation, as shown in Figure 9.4, takes a new value and a PCR index, hashes the new value with the current contents of the register with that index, and sets the register's new value to be the result of the hash operation. Sequences of extend operations form hash chains allowing a verifier to confirm all values extended into the register since the register was reset. The reset operations shown in Figure 9.5, which are only available on some PCRs (see Sections 9.2.4 and 9.2.5), take a PCR index, erase all

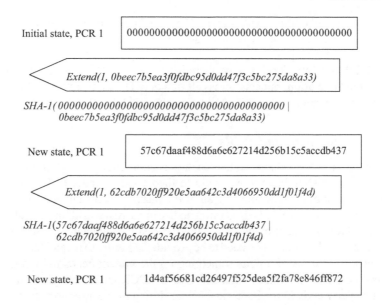

Figure 9.4 *As previously shown in Figure 3.4, sequence of PCR extend operations. Each time a digest is extended into PCR 1 (first the hash of "foo," then the hash of "bar"), the TPM concatenates the old value and the new value, takes the hash of the result, and makes that hash the new PCR value*

Figure 9.5 *The PCR reset operation. Regardless of the contents of the PCR, the reset operation will overwrite all bits in the register with ones or zeroes, according to the default for that register. The reset operation happens automatically for all registers on boot, and for registers 17–22 whenever the DRTM is launched. Some registers may be reset deliberately by software using the* TPM_PCR_Reset *and* TPM2_PCR_Reset *commands, as discussed later in this chapter*

previous contents of the register at that index, and set it to a standard value of either all ones or all zeroes, depending on the register and implementation. PCRs are also reset automatically on other occasions; most notably, when the machine first boots, all PCRs are reset to their default values. Launching the DRTM will also reset a number of PCRs: all of those which are used by the DRTM or by the measured launch environment it creates. I'll discuss the details of which PCRs are involved later in this chapter.

TPM 2.0 also introduces a new operation, `TPM2_PCR_Event`; it works just like the extend operation, but acts across all of a new TPM 2.0 feature of PCR banks. PCR banks and the event operation will be discussed in detail in Section 9.2.5.

9.2.2   Measurement and PCRs

Because PCRs use hash chains so that each measurement extended into the register is added to the existing history, we could in theory use a single PCR to record the entire boot record of the machine, and all of the measurements taken during the boot process. However, this would be frustrating to use in the real world for several reasons.

First and foremost, although hash chains are easily recalculated by someone who knows the inputs, those inputs do need to be provided. In order to recalculate a complex hash chain with dozens of inputs, something on the system needs to be responsible for recording all of the values extended into the PCR, and there just isn't such a responsible party early in the boot sequence or during the secure mode that launches the DRTM. A single file could be used to track a series of measurements, and this is in fact used by the Linux IMA security extensions, but establishing a single, easily findable location outside of the TPM (whose storage is just too small to be used for this purpose) which can't be modified by a malicious party but which is easily extended by any component which needs to add to the system measurement record rapidly becomes a highly complex decision, especially since some PC TPMs can be found in decidedly non-PC environments. (Want a TPM for your microcontroller? You can buy them, and they'll use the PC TPM specification.)

Second, in many use cases we'd like to be able to distinguish between measurements that almost never change and measurements that change frequently, because we may want to monitor only the more predictable measurements. On a system where measurements went all the way up to the application layer, a browser measurement might change weekly while the BIOS measurement would hopefully never change without a very rare and centrally required firmware update. If we tied all of the measurements together in a single PCR, there would be no way to usefully tie resource access to PCR values, since the values would be changing constantly from all of the different variables, and no way to easily alert on unexpected changes to predictable components.

Instead, the PC client specification calls for measurements of each distinct component in the SRTM, and each stage of a hypothetical DRTM trusted OS launch, to be recorded in distinct PCRs (Figure 9.6). There are a number of under defined registers, some of which have an official expected use but which are under utilized today, and others which have no TCG-defined use but which are in active use by software.

The basic mapping of measurements to PCRs is the same for both 1.2 and 2.0 TPMs, to make comparability easier.

When using measurements, either for quotes or to impose constraints on the use of keys (Section 6.13.2) or data (Section 8.2), we often wish to make use of the values

PCR	TCG defined use	Other uses
0	SRTM, BIOS, Host Platform Extensions, Embedded Option ROMs	
1	Host Platform Configuration	
2	Option ROM Code	
3	Option ROM Configuration and Data	
4	IPL Code (usually Maste Boot Record) and Boot Attempts	MBR and stage 1 (trusted GRUB)
5	IPL Code Configuration and Data	
6	State Transitions and Wake Events	
7	Host Platform Manufacturer Specific	
8	For use by static OS	Bootloader stage 2 part 1 (Trusted GRUB)
9	For use by static OS	Bootloader stage 2 part 2 (Trusted GRUB)
10	For use by static OS	Default application measurement register (Linux IMA)
11	For use by static OS	
12	For use by static OS	Command line arguments for boot loader (Trusted GRUB)
13	For use by static OS	Measurements of user-specified files (Trusted GRUB)
14	For use by static OS	Loaded files; kernel, modules, initrd, etc. (Trusted GRUB)
15	For use by static OS	
16	Debug	
17	DRTM component measurements[a]	
18	Measurements of signing authorities for DRTM components[a]	
19	Measurements of DLME[b], or measurements of signing authorities	
20–22	Reserved for use of DLME.	
23	Application Support	

[a]The values in 17 and 18 can be reversed using the `PCR_AuthoritiesChanged` DRTM resources table flag. Users will usually not want to change the value of this flag, but it's worth noting that your DRTM implementation could use either ordering.
[b]Dynamically Launched Measured Environment, the formal term for the user-provided code and data block which the DRTM launches.

Figure 9.6   *The official PC client expectations of PCR contents. It's easy to see here that there's lots of room to maneuver. The PC Client implementation specification (see Section 11.7) has more detail about what is and is not required to be measured at different steps. However, even with that additional information, two different manufacturers are likely to include very different content in their measurements, and not all BIOS manufacturers are concerned with perfect compliance. It is not uncommon to see several low-numbered PCRs with identical contents, which is usually a sign that a placeholder value was extended into the PCR, preventing malicious software from forging arbitrary values but not containing meaningful system information. The "Other Uses" column highlights some more concrete uses that well-documented software makes of specific PCRs; it is not comprehensive, but may provide useful places to look for understanding system measurements*

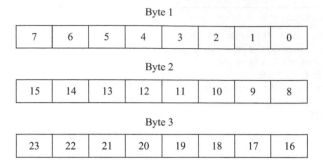

*Figure 9.7   The PCR indexes indicated with a given bit in a standard 3-byte PCR
selection. For TPMs with larger numbers of PCRs, the pattern continues*

in multiple PCRs at once. To indicate which PCRs we want to use, we create PCR
selections. When interacting with the TPM, these structures are bitmaps, although
many software libraries provide helpful abstractions for handling them. It can be
important to know how to interpret the TPM's data format, however, since for many
applications you will want to verify that the correct PCRs are being included.

The standard PCR selection is a 3-byte array; however, in 2.0 TPMs with additional allocated PCRs (or an extremely unusual 1.2 TPM with more than 24 PCRs)
longer arrays are possible. Each PCR index is indicated with one bit of the array. The
algorithm for calculating the bit corresponding to a given index makes some sense
mathematically, but ends up looking pretty non-intuitive when you look at the data
structure as a whole. For a given PCR index, we calculate the byte in the array by
dividing the number by 8, while the bit in the array is the remainder after division
with the *least* significant bit in a given byte defined as bit 0. So PCR 5 would be in
byte 0, bit 5, and PCR 16 in byte 2, bit 0. Most humans would generally expect the
first or last bit in an array to be bit 0; instead, it's bit 7, as shown in Figure 9.7.

9.2.3   Beyond measurements: creative uses of PCRs

Although PCRs contain measurements automatically propagated during system boot
or DRTM launch, there are many more uses for PCRs.

- Users wishing to extend the chain of trust into an OS or application may wish
  to create their own measurements and extend them into a PCR. Note that these
  measurements do not have to be simple hashes of a binary file; a smart measurement might hash particularly sensitive configuration files such as a browser's
  certificate store, hash both the binary and critical library files, hash a set of malware signatures a program has been assessed against, or even perform complex
  calculations to verify that a program's code has not been tampered with and hash
  the output. Even long and complex reports can be usefully extended into a PCR,
  as long as the original report is available for verification by an appraiser.
- A TPM-aware OS could extend the username of anyone who logs in into a PCR.

- An OS configured to use the TPM for audit purposes could extend the id of each user who performed a sudo or administrative action into a PCR, along with the action taken. In this case, the PCR is serving as a tamper detection mechanism for the on-disk log, since a malicious administrator could modify the log but could not force the PCR to match the modified log.
- A particular communications session can be tied to PCR measurements by extending the session identifier or a hash of messages sent into a PCR, and including that along with the measurement PCRs in a quote.
- A file generated by a trusted program on the machine could have its hash extended into a PCR, to certify that the file was created when the machine was in a trustworthy state. This can allow a quote to be used in place of a standard signature, associating the file with the state the machine was in when the quote was created.

When using PCRs to store measurements or other data, there are two critical features to consider: whether the PCR can be *reset*, and who can *extend* the PCR.

Resettable PCRs are powerful tools for some purposes, and dangerously weak tools for others. These PCRs can be set by an authorized user (determined by locality; for more information see Sections 9.2.4 and 9.2.5) to a well-known value of all zeroes or all ones, erasing all prior contents. Resettable PCRs are very useful when we don't wish to provide an appraiser with all state changes since boot: session identifiers used when setting up VPN sessions, for example, should only include data from that single transaction, and not from every session initiated since the machine booted. An audit log, however, needs to not be resettable; otherwise, a malicious party could overwrite the log and replace the PCR contents with a freshly generated false history.

Very few PCRs are limited in who can extend them in 1.2 TPMs; this feature is primarily useful for verifying that certain content was generated by the DRTM or by DRTM-launched code. TPM 2.0, however, allows new PCRs beyond the basic 24 to be created with their own authorization values or distinct access policies, allowing for much more fine-grained usage constraints. In TPMs which support additional PCRs, these can be used in the same way we use the DRTM-constrained PCRs, to derive information about the origin of content in the register. In 2.0 TPMs that support the PCR authorization feature, both reset and extend can be associated with the full complexity of an Enhanced Authorization policy, so that a PCR could require a password to reset or could only be extended in the first 5 min after boot. TPMs that support PCR authorization values will require the authorization value for any operation on that PCR. Note that for the feature to be supported, there are three critical requirements: that the TPM have the internal space to support PCRs beyond the basic 24; that the TPM support the optional `TPM2_PCR_SetAuthPolicy` or `TPM2_PCR_SetAuthValue` commands; and that the platform firmware (which controls the platform hierarchy authorization) supports the use of the `TPM2_PCR_Allocate`, `TPM2_PCR_SetAuthPolicy`, and/or `TPM2_PCR_SetAuthValue` commands.

Because these features are both new and optional, they are unlikely to be common in early 2.0 TPMs; however, ask your TPM manufacturer. They can be very powerful, however, when available. For example, a TPM could have a PCR extendable only with

PCR Index	Alias	pcrReset	pcrResetLocal for Locality 4, 3, 2, 1, 0	pcrExtendLocal for Locality 4, 3, 2, 1, 0
0–15	Static RTM	0	0,0,0,0,0	1,1,1,1,1
16	Debug	1	1,1,1,1,1	1,1,1,1,1
17	Locality 4	1	1,0,0,0,0	1,1,1,0,0
18	Locality 3	1	1,0,0,0,0	1,1,1,0,0
19	Locality 2	1	1,0,0,0,0	0,1,1,0,0
20	Locality 1	1	1,0,1,0,0	0,1,1,1,0
21	T/OS Controlled	1	0,0,1,0,0	0,0,1,0,0
22	T/OS Controlled	1	0,0,1,0,0	0,0,1,0,0
23	Application Specific	1	1,1,1,1,1	1,1,1,1,1

Figure 9.8   This chart illustrates several different features of each 1.2 PCR (see Section 9.2.4)

the use of a public key held in a smartcard or dongle, requiring both that physical device is present and recognized software is running for certain data to be accessed. Different applications running on the same trusted OS[5] could be given distinct application PCRs for use in reporting their own data. Virtual machines could each be given their own set of state registers in the TPM, allowing resources to be locked to a single VM as long as the hypervisor is trustworthy. A PCR could even be allocated which only a trusted remote authority could extend, creating a locally enforceable notion of central approval.

9.2.4   1.2 PCR design

The formal specification of 1.2 PCRs for a PC TPM, as described in the PC Client TPM Specification (see Section 11.7), is as follows:

Figure 9.8 lays out the properties of each PCR in a 1.2 TPM as described in the PC Client TPM Specification (see Section 11.7), according to the following layout:

Index: Each PCR is referred to by a numeric index. There are 24 PCRs in a 1.2 TPM.

Alias: This is just a name; the shorthand for what the designers expected it to be for. I'll discuss shortly how things work in practice.

pcrReset: Each PCR is either resettable or not. A non-resettable PCR is reset only when the machine reboots: on reboot it is always set to all zeros, and all values extended into the PCR will remain part of the hash chain until the next reboot. A resettable PCR can be reset by a user command, although there may be restrictions on when such a command can be issued.

pcrResetLocal: Which localities are allowed to reset each resettable PCR. In particular, it's worth noting that 17–20 are resettable by Locality 4: these PCRs will automatically be reset when the DRTM is launched.

pcrExtendLocal: Which localities are allowed to extend each PCR. PCRs 17–20 are intended for DRTM use, while the low-index PCRs (0–16) can be extended freely by anyone.

---

[5]The OS must be trusted in this scenario, since an untrusted OS could leak any secrets known to one application to other applications.

The default value for PCRs 0–16 and 23, both on boot or after a reset, is all bits set to zero. The boot value of PCRs 17–22 is all bits set to one (referred to in the TCG specifications as -1); when the DRTM is launched, 17–22 are automatically reset to all bits being zero, and any reset operations allowed by user code will also reset all bits to zero, allowing easy checks for whether the DRTM has been used.

9.2.5 2.0 PCR design

The default behavior of PCRs in PC 2.0 TPMs is very similar to the 1.2 behavior. There are, at a minimum, 24 PCRs sized for SHA-1 hashes, with almost identical default extend and reset constraints to a 1.2 TPM (there were some minor changes in which PCRs could be reset by the DRTM and DRTM-launched code), and the same default values for initial boot state and reset. No authorization policy or password is required to use these PCRs. The primary difference is that 2.0 TPMs are designed to be more flexible when it comes to hash algorithm than 1.2 TPMs were, to prevent future problems if a given algorithm is discovered to be weak. Although only 24 SHA-1 PCRs are required to exist, the TPM is also required to support 32-byte registers supporting SHA-256.

2.0 TPMs introduce the idea of PCR **banks**: groups of PCRs supporting a single hash algorithm. Each bank uses an index-based numbering scheme, and the same index will always have the same access control permissions and capabilities regardless of bank. Thus, PCR 17 in a SHA-1 bank and PCR 17 in a SHA-256 bank will have the same resettability properties, the same extendibility limitations, and the same authorization policy or password. When a TPM quote is being requested, or a policy is being created which relies on PCR state, the banks are specified (by hash algorithm) along with the PCR indexes. In the case of SHA-256 support, the TPM specification recommends providing both a SHA-1 and a SHA-256 bank, but allows a TPM to be manufactured with a single PCR bank that is initially SHA-1 and which can be reallocated as SHA-256 by the platform firmware.

Other PCR-related changes in TPM 2.0 include:

* TPM2_PCR_Extend now takes a list of tagged digests, rather than a single digest. Each entry in this list includes the PCR index and bank. This can be used to extend multiple banks with equivalent digests created using different hash algorithms, as well as to extend multiple PCRs in a single bank with one command.
* The new TPM2_PCR_Event command (see Figure 9.9) provides an alternative to the traditional TPM2_PCR_Extend. Where Extend takes the pre-computed digest, Event takes data up to 1024 bytes and a PCR handle (index). The TPM will perform the necessary hashes to extend the value into that PCR in all available banks, and return a list of the digests produced. *If you use multiple PCR banks, using the TPM2_PCR_Event command as your standard mechanism for extending PCRs is good practice, as it will minimize the risk of banks becoming out of sync.*
* A counter of the number of times PCRs have been extended since reboot exists, although some PCRs (16, 21, 22, and 23 in the default configuration) are designed for more frequent use and do not increment the counter. This counter

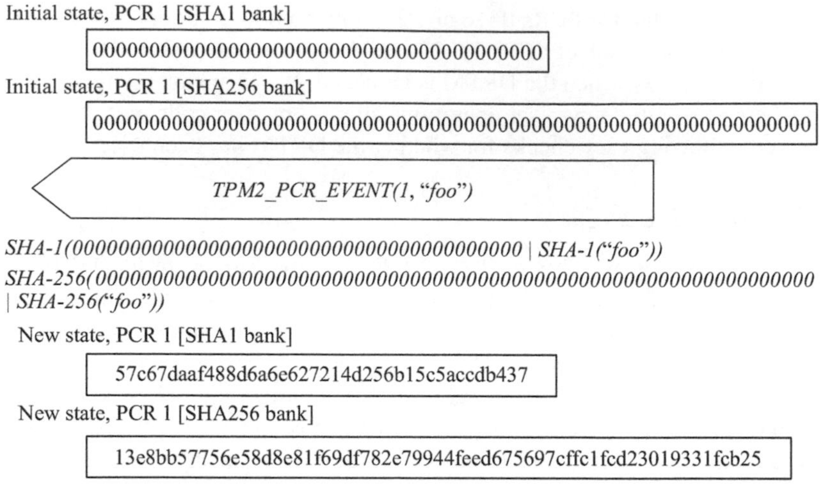

Initial state, PCR 1 [SHA1 bank]

> 0000000000000000000000000000000000000000

Initial state, PCR 1 [SHA256 bank]

> 0000000000000000000000000000000000000000000000000000000000000000

> *TPM2_PCR_EVENT(1, "foo")*

SHA-1(0000000000000000000000000000000000000000 | SHA-1("foo"))
SHA-256(0000000000000000000000000000000000000000000000000000000000000000
| SHA-256("foo"))

New state, PCR 1 [SHA1 bank]

> 57c67daaf488d6a6e627214d256b15c5accdb437

New state, PCR 1 [SHA256 bank]

> 13e8bb57756e58d8e81f69df782e79944feed675697cffc1fcd23019331fcb25

*Figure 9.9   The new TPM2_PCR_Event command provides a useful alternative to
the TPM2_PCR_Extend command in 2.0 TPMs. There are two major
differences with TPM2_PCR_Event: instead of being limited to a
digest for input, TPM2_PCR_Event takes up to 1024 bytes of data,
and creates digests itself; and TPM2_PCR_Event is designed to work
well on TPMs with multiple banks of PCRs, producing one digest for
each hash algorithm and then extending that digest into the
corresponding bank's PCR at the chosen index. Note that when a PCR
index is chosen with TPM2_PCR_Event, all banks will always be
updated. If using multiple PCR banks to support both older
applications that expect SHA-1 PCR values and more modern
applications that want to use the more secure SHA-256, replacing all
system TPM2_PCR_Extend operations with TPM2_PCR_Event
will reduce the chances of the two banks becoming out of sync*

is used by the TPM2_PolicyPCR command to ensure that PCRs cannot be
changed without forcing a re-evaluation of the policy, and can be retrieved directly
using the TPM2_PCR_Read command. Note that this value cannot be retrieved
with any of the commands which produce signed PCR data, such as a quote or
the creation data from objects.

- The platform authorization can allocate PCRs using the TPM2_PCR_Allocate
command. This can be used to reallocate a bank from SHA-1 to SHA-256, as
well as to potentially add additional banks or additional PCRs beyond the basic
24, if there is sufficient space. This is only rarely useful, since these registers are
not part of the standard, so most software won't try to use them, and adding these
registers requires that you be writing your own firmware; however, in rare cases
where a platform is being custom-built, it can be very useful for creating PCRs
with unique reset properties or access requirements.

- Some TPMs may support adding Enhanced Authorization policies or authorization values (passwords) to PCRs beyond the basic 24 using the TPM2_PCR_ SetAuthPolicy or TPM2_SetAuthValue commands. This also requires platform authorization. When available, this feature can be used to provide trusted hardware with a reliable reporting mechanism, using public key authorization to guarantee that only the trusted hardware can use the PCR in question.

PCRs in 2.0 are somewhat dynamic: additional PCRs (either beyond the basic 24 within an existing bank, or in additional banks to support different hash algorithms) can be allocated out of the TPM's available NVRAM using the Platform Authorization (see Section 3.2.2) by early boot firmware using the TPM2_PCR_Allocate command. In addition, PCRs (like other NVRAM locations) can have authorization values or even full authorization policies associated with them. This means that instead of the coarse locality-based access control of 1.2 PCRs, 2.0 TPMs can—at least in theory—have finer-grained control based on passwords, public keys, locality, or even biometrics, as previously discussed in Section 9.2.3. And as discussed in the Enhanced Authorization section (Section 6.13.3), policies can limit not only the mechanisms with which access is gained, but also what actions can be taken.

Dynamic PCR allocation is not hugely useful in consumer systems, where simple PCR access policies to enable basic platform attestation are the only predictable option. However, it can be tremendously powerful for enterprises capable of investing in boot-time firmware. If your enterprise controls the Platform Authorization, you can use the custom PCR policies in very powerful ways. For example, a USB input device with a known key that was capable of speaking the TPM's authentication protocol could be trusted to verify a user with anything from a fingerprint to a PIN, and extend the PCR with the user's identity. A tamper-detection device with a trusted key that was installed in the machine chassis could extend a PCR on boot, or whenever the chassis state changed unexpectedly. A card reader could have an associated PCR which would be extended whenever a user's smartcard was inside, and reset when it was removed. In short, this feature can be used by those with significant influence over the hardware composition of a platform to tie the TPM's reporting capability to any input device that can be provisioned with a known key. For those willing to trust some of their software to maintain secrets from other software, it can also be used to authenticate specific software components, although this is a riskier proposition. Any authentication method known to one piece of software will be available to the OS, and potentially to other software on the system in the event of a compromise.

Another feature of 2.0 PCRs is that a counter of the number of times PCRs have been modified since the last platform reboot (the pcrUpdateCounter) exists. Not all PCRs will cause this counter to increment, but this feature can be used to detect the effects of PCR resets even if the PCR is then extended back to its original value. It can also be used to limit access to resources to early in the boot cycle.

9.2.6 Choosing PCRs to use

The full list of expected PCR uses defined by the TCG is shown in Figure 9.6. In practice, there are some simple guidelines that can be used when interpreting PCRs, or choosing which PCRs to consider reporting for attestations (Section 9.3), although you should always refer to the actual PCRs when determining what's meaningful for your own system.

- The standard SRTM uses PCRs 0–7 on most systems; however, only a subset contain real content. Which subset may vary from system to system.
- If you have a TPM-aware boot loader or OS, it may use additional PCRs in the 8–15 range. The Linux trusted boot loader uses 8, 9, and 12–14. The IMA Linux kernel extension uses 10.
- The DRTM code itself is measured into PCR 17. PCR 18 will contain a measurement of the code launched by the DRTM. PCRs 18, 19, and 20 can be used by applications launched by the DRTM, although only 18 guarantee that the contents were produced while the secure mode was executing.

If you're choosing PCRs to extend for your own application, the choices get a little more interesting. The first question is how many applications will be using the PCR, either for reporting or for storing data. A corporation creating a comprehensive attestation infrastructure where all attestations are verified by a single, central authority has a lot of flexibility to add meaning to any PCR it likes, since it will be responsible for all verification. An individual user writing an open-source application meant to be used in a wide range of environments has to pay more attention to not causing unexpected behavior.

Some useful rules of thumb when extending PCRs:

- Always remember to record the data you extended into a PCR, for verification purposes. Don't just extend and forget.
  - When possible, if a single PCR is being used to record activity for multiple applications, use a single log so the verifier has a single, ordered list of what content should have been extended into the hash chain.
- When designing your own application for a specific enterprise, use a PCR not otherwise in use on your systems if you can. Coordinating extend logs between applications can be complicated. Commercial software developers storing data in PCRs should be certain to document both which PCRs are being used, and where the log of extended values is stored.
- If you don't explicitly want a record of past activity—if you're signing a single piece of data, or creating a quote to authenticate session identifiers, for example— use a resettable PCR, such as 16 or 23. This minimizes the potential complications of multiple applications using the same PCR, from unverifiable hash chains full of unexpected data to maintaining control of the TPM interface for a very small number of commands.
- If you do require an audit-worthy record of activity, never use a resettable PCR.

9.2.7   PCRs beyond the PC

Although this book is focused very heavily on PC TPMs, it is worth calling out PCRs in particular as a place which will vary dramatically on different kinds of platforms, even if command selection is similar. A mobile TPM or automotive TPM will expect radically different measurements to be placed in their PCRs, and are likely to even have different numbers of PCRs. A virtual TPM may have additional localities and PCRs assigned beyond the standard PC set, allowing for backwards-compatible applications to use the TPM without being virtualization aware, but providing additional measurements of the virtualized environment for applications and appraisers who understand the architecture.

9.3   Basic attestation techniques

Attestation with the TPM comes in two primary forms. The first is the *quote*: a signed data structure, created by the TPM, containing a nonce and the contents of the user's choice of PCRs. The second is the use of certifiable keys with PCR constraints, as described in Chapter 6. Any key with PCR constraints can be used to create an attestation. In both cases, a remote party receiving the attestation knows that at the time the attestation was produced, the PCR state of the TPM matched the contents of the quote or the constraints on the key, respectively. The PCR contents, if chosen correctly, provide information about either the boot state of the machine, the code most recently run in the DRTM, or user-generated state. More advanced and useful information requires better measurement capabilities, as discussed in Section 9.4; but the techniques for reporting on PCR contents are the same regardless of the quality or nature of the measurements.

9.3.1   Quotes

TPM quotes, created with the `TPM_Quote`, `TPM_Quote2`, or `TPM2_Quote` command, all follow the same basic structure. The user requests a quote, providing a nonce, a suitable loaded key, and a selection of PCR indexes. The TPM responds with a data structure containing the current PCR contents for the chosen indexes and the nonce, along with a signature over the data structure (Figure 9.10). The nonce allows a verifier to confirm the freshness of the data (see Section 7.2.4 for more on how to use nonces well).

Quotes should only be signed using identity keys in 1.2 TPMs, and restricted signing keys in 2.0 TPMs. This is to prevent a user from creating an imitation quote structure, using the TPM to sign it, and passing it off as a legitimate report on PCR contents. Quotes can be created using legacy or signing keys in 1.2 TPMs, or non-restricted signing keys in 2.0 TPMs; however, these are insecure and cannot be remotely verified to contain data from the TPM instead of the user, and so should never be used to quote or trusted to sign quotes.

Why are there two different quote commands for 1.2 TPMs? `TPM_Quote` was designed to be backwards-compatible with the 1.1 TPMs, which only had 16 PCRs and no concept of locality. `TPM_Quote2` uses a slightly larger data structure which contains locality information, and which makes the problem of verifying that the correct PCRs were selected for the quote much easier.

One of the challenges of using quotes in 1.2 TPMs is that verification can be complex. 1.2 TPMs do not return the complete quote data structure, just the signature

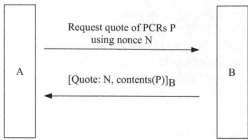

Figure 9.10   *An extremely abstracted view of how quotes are designed to be used.*
An appraiser (A) is seeking to verify a remote machine (B). The
appraiser selects a set of PCR indices (P) which contain the
measurements A is seeking to evaluate, and generates a fresh random
nonce (N). The attestation target (B) may or may not have software
which decides whether or not to respond to quote requests, based on
whether the appraiser (not authenticated in this sample transaction) is
trusted or whether the PCRs chosen are considered acceptable
information to release. If B chooses to provide A with a quote, B's
TPM will assemble a quote data structure containing the nonce and a
hash of the current PCR contents from the chosen indexes, then sign
the data structure. A can then evaluate the result; if the nonce is the
same and a good random value was used, then A knows that the quote
was generated after A's initial request and is therefore current, and if
the key used for signing is a trusted identity or restricted signing key
belonging to B the quote came from B's TPM. Once that verification
has succeeded, A can decide whether or not the measurements are
acceptable. In practice, it often helps to have B return an unsigned
report of the individual PCR values along with the quote, so that A
can evaluate individual measurements as well as the single composite
digest

and the TPM internal PCR data. This means that the data structures (shown in Figures 9.11 and 9.12) must be reconstructed in order to be verified. While the TPM_Quote command returns a complete PCR data structure, with the values of each PCR selected included in an array. TPM_Quote2 does not; instead, TPM_Quote2 returns only a composite hash of the included PCRs. It includes locality information that the basic quote does not, but reconstructing the individual PCR contents at the time the quote was produced requires using the TPM_PCRRead or TPM_Quote commands to retrieve the contents of each quoted PCR and assemble them into the composite hash used in verification.

2.0 quote structures use a standardized attestation data structure which incorporates the TPM's notion of current system time, a nonce, and the firmware version, in addition to the quote-specific PCR information. PCR contents are presented as a calculated digest, produced by iterating through the PCR selection and updating the

Data structure tag constant: TPM_TAG_QUOTE_INFO2
Structure-type constant: 'QUT2'
User-provided data (nonce)

Structure version constant: '1.1.0.0'
Structure-type constant: 'QUOT'
SHA-1 hash of PCR composite data structure:

PCR selection
Size of PCR value array, in bytes
Array of PCR values, in order specified by selection

User-provided data (nonce)

(a)

Short PCR info data structure:

PCR selection
Locality Quote2 command executed in
SHA-1 hash of PCR composite data structure:

PCR selection
Size of PCR value array, in bytes
Array of PCR values, in order specified by selection

(b)

Figure 9.11 *The quote data structures produced and signed by 1.2 TPMs. The highlighted selections (the PCR composite data structure and the PCR short information data structure, respectively) are returned by the TPM and must be integrated into a full quote data structure by the verifier to check the signature. (a) Quote data structure signed by the* TPM_Quote *command. (b) Quote data structure signed by the* TPM_Quote2 *command. Includes locality information and a more readable PCR selection*

digest with each value according to the appropriate hash algorithm. This is the same type of digest used to set PCR-based authorization policies (see Section 6.13.3) and returned as part of object creation data. In order to verify individual PCR values, the TPM2_PCRRead command must be used, and the contents assembled using the same techniques the TPM uses. Details can be found in section 8.6.3.21 of the TPM 2.0 Supporting Routines specification (see Section 11.6.2).

One of the most powerful features of quote-based attestation is that the PCR contents do not have to be predictable in advance. A quote can be provided alongside a record of values extended into each PCR, allowing an appraiser to evaluate the trustworthiness of a platform from much richer data than a mere hash. These extended values could be as simple as an unpredictable sequence of hashes, such as that produced by the Linux IMA extension, in which each binary that is launched is hashed beforehand. They could also be arbitrarily complex. A comprehensive report on the configuration of a system intended for human evaluation and consumption could also be extended into a PCR and quoted, producing a verifiable record of the configuration at the time which could be interpreted later as needed.

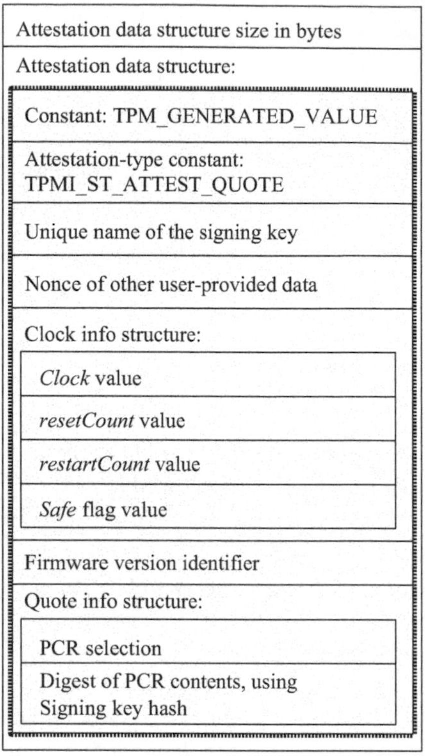

Attestation data structure size in bytes
Attestation data structure:

Constant: TPM_GENERATED_VALUE
Attestation-type constant: TPMI_ST_ATTEST_QUOTE
Unique name of the signing key
Nonce of other user-provided data
Clock info structure:

Clock value
resetCount value
restartCount value
Safe flag value

Firmware version identifier
Quote info structure:

PCR selection
Digest of PCR contents, using Signing key hash

Figure 9.12   TPM 2.0 quote data structure

9.3.2   Verifying quotes

There are, broadly speaking, two approaches to verifying TPM quotes. One provides much greater accuracy and more detailed information; the other is simpler to implement quickly but only suitable in very specific circumstances.

The optimal approach, for organizations willing to put in the effort, is to use the unsigned TPM_PCRRead and TPM2_PCR_Read commands to retrieve the contents of the PCR indexes being quoted, and reconstruct the full PCR selection and digest data structure produced by the TPM and included in the quote. In 1.2 TPMs, the digest is produced by hashing a simple concatenation of PCR contents; for 2.0 TPMs, which have multiple PCR banks, the operation can be more user dependent, as the banks are concatenated in the order requested by the user (see section 17.5 of the TPM 2.0 Architecture specification for details) before hashing. This way, verifying the quote signature verifies not only the complete digest but also the individual PCR values. While this approach makes the information sent to the appraiser by the target machine noticeably larger and increases the complexity of the verification operation, it allows the contents of each PCR to be evaluated independently. This is powerful for several reasons. First, it means that if the full digest is not an expected value, it is possible to determine which PCRs contained unexpected values, and thus where the chain of trust broke down. It also makes it easier to evaluate systems where there are a large number of acceptable values for individual PCRs without needing to track a combinatorics explosion in acceptable digest values.[6] This is also the only approach that will work for applications where the contents may change frequently; for example, if file contents, session information, or other unpredictable information is included in a quote, digests will have to be calculated afresh for each transaction to be verified.

In some cases, where only a small number of highly predictable PCR values are accepted, it is possible to take a shortcut. Here, the PCR digest for a given selection is treated as a single black-box system measurement; if one "good" quote for the machine has been received and stored, the structure can be verified later just by switching out the old nonce for the new and checking the signatures. This approach is primarily useful when the goal is change detection rather than measurement *per se*: an enterprise that has centralized tracking of all expected software changes might not care about making sense of PCR contents, but still want to raise an alert with the IT department if measurements have changed without a corresponding software update.[7] Note that, unless the machines have very predictable "gold images" all the way down to the BIOS (which is unusual unless you're purchasing with that goal in mind, and not always possible with some BIOSes even then) individual machines' expected measurement will need to be tracked.

9.3.2.1 Signing user data with quotes

In some circumstances, it is desirable to use a quote to sign data that contains no system PCR measurements. This is most common as part of a staged deployment, where measurements are expected to eventually be integrated; for example, using a quote to sign the output of a local audit program with the intent of eventually including system measurements to show that the audit program is itself trustworthy. In very rare cases where a system only has an identity key, and creating a signing key or establishing trust in it is infeasible, this technique can be used to sign user data. It can also be used to tie a signature to a particular point in time via the quote's nonce, although it is more common and much easier to simply include the nonce in an ordinary signature; for example, by concatenating the nonce and the desired message to be signed before taking the hash to sign.

When using quotes to sign data, it is critical to extend that data into a freshly reset resettable PCR, rather than including the data in the "user data" field which contains the nonce. This is true even if the goal is to create a long-term signature,

---

[6]On a system with five acceptable values for each of 10 tracked PCRs, evaluating the individual PCRs would require maintaining a list of 50 possible acceptable values. Tracking all possible quoted digests, which combine all 10 PCRs, would require 5^{10} acceptable values, or a whopping 9,765,625. Given that five acceptable options are actually a pretty small amount of variation for desktop systems using today's hash-based measurements, avoiding the combinatorial explosion can be necessary rather than merely convenient.

[7]It's worth noting that the default measurements on PCs today never reaches the application level, and sometimes doesn't even reach the OS kernel; when considering how frequent an expected measurement-visible change might be, firmware updates or Microsoft's monthly Patch Tuesday are a more realistic schedule than the Flash/Office/browser update of the day.

where no real nonce is provided. See Section 7.2.4 for more information about why proper separation of nonces and data to be signed is important.

9.3.3   Constrained key attestation

A good rule of thumb for attestation is that any machine authentication activity, when performed with a state-constrained key, provides attestation. A signing key with state constraint X will, when used, provide proof that at the time an object was signed, the PCR contents were compatible with X. An encryption key with state constraint Y will only decrypt the data if the PCR contents are compatible with Y.

Why do we say "compatible with X," rather than "the state was X?" Because most realistic PCR constraints don't cover the full set of PCRs: most applications can only make sense of a small number of registers, and don't care about the rest. This is particularly true with regards to the choice of DRTM or SRTM; many applications will want to know about either the most recent DRTM execution or the SRTM boot sequence results, but not both.

The use of key constraints for attestation can be highly powerful, at least in theory. If I know that a particular key can only be used when a given trusted program is running, then I may be willing to send content to a machine that I need the trusted program to protect. If I know that a set of logs were signed while my trusted audit program is running, I may be more willing to believe that they're up to date and accurate. However, the measurement capability we have today makes this sort of scenario difficult except in a few limited circumstances, both because our measurements do not cover every variable which might affect our trust in a given platform, and because measurements change so often that creating a trusted key for each trusted state can be difficult. In practice, key-based attestation is most useful in two situations: when the DRTM is being used to launch predictable trusted programs, or when the entire system is using unusually predictable and limited software (a "golden image").

Key-based attestation can also be used to gain a picture of the system's evolution over time, by combining PCR constraints and parent–child relationships, as discussed in Section 6.4.1 and shown in Figure 9.13.

9.3.4   Direct anonymous attestation

DAA is a set of techniques intended to provide the assurances of attestation (that a given set of evidence was produced by a legitimate TPM, and as part of a trusted platform architecture) without any kind of machine authentication. The goal of DAA is to provide complete, guaranteeable privacy to a machine or machine owner, while allowing a verifier to trust a machine's software state. The use cases here are intended primarily for the consumer market, where being able to prove your trustworthiness without giving away your identity is, at least in theory, a powerful tool. Given the many difficulties of remotely verifying even a well-known and well-understood machine's software integrity, as we'll be discussing shortly, the real-world utility of DAA is unclear. However, there are niche cases where an identity-free attestation in a world of complex measurements may still be useful; for example, when verifying that a machine has executed a particular piece of code such as a bank's secure signing

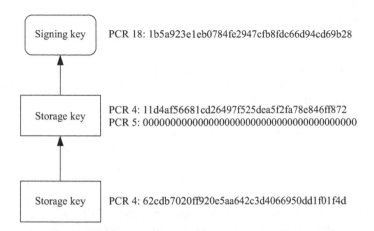

Figure 9.13   A parent–child key hierarchy in which all three keys have PCR constraints. In order for the signing key to be used, the PCR 18 value must be met. However, in order for the signing key to be used, it must first be loaded, which will require the use of the two storage keys in order. This means that if I receive a value from the signing key, I know that at some point in the past, PCR 4 must have had first one known value, then a second; that PCR 5 must have been empty at the same time that PCR 4 had its second value; and that the time when PCR 18 had the signing key's value was after the first two points in time

utility using the DRTM and associating that code with a given output, or to allow the use of TPMs for DRM or software verification in specialized consumer devices without creating a consumer tracking system. Despite its niche utility, DAA is a required feature in TPMs in order to support European privacy regulations. It is also the most mathematically complicated operation in a TPM and presents a number of practical implementation challenges; if this functionality is not of interest to you, you may want to skip straight on to Section 9.4. The DAA protocol relies heavily on zero-knowledge proofs, which if you aren't familiar with are discussed briefly in the cryptography review in Appendix A.8.

DAA in 1.2 TPMs is a highly complex operation. While there are only two commands, TPM_DAA_Join to establish credentials with an external authority and TPM_DAA_Sign to perform an anonymous signing operation, each command is designed to be run repeatedly with different arguments in order to perform different stages of processing for the zero-knowledge proofs, which would overwhelm the TPM's resources if performed simultaneously. I refer to each distinct combination of command an argument as a stage; TPM_DAA_Join has 24 stages that must be run to perform a single join operation, while TPM_DAA_Sign has 15. Any errors will invalidate the entire operation, and require the full sequence of stages to be started again from the beginning. Interrupting the sequence of operations with other commands will also cause the state to be lost and require the sequence to be restarted, although the

TPM_SaveContext and TPM_LoadContext commands can be used to save the DAA state and allow it to be restored later. Because of this overwhelming complexity, fragility, and the DAA feature's limited utility, I will not be covering how to use these commands. If you would like to learn more, section 33 in the 1.2 TPM Design Principles specification and section 26 of the 1.2 TPM Commands specification (see Section 11.5) have the full details.

In 2.0 TPMs, using DAA requires fewer TPM actions, but noticeably more complex activity on the part of the associated applications. The 2.0 TPM supports ECDAA—direct anonymous attestation based on ECC. (In academic literature, this is often referred to as ECC DAA, with various punctuation choices.) The TPM only implements the most critical operations used in the ECDAA protocol, however: those involving the use of the secret key. Other operations, including quite a few calculations and the communications protocols used between the TPM and external parties, are up to the software implementation to perform. It's not yet clear whether any 2.0 TSS will provide the software support to use ECDAA easily.

There are two challenges to explaining the software ECDAA operations in detail. The first is that there is no single defined set of expected operations in the specifications; the second is that to understand the operations even at a fairly high level requires quite a bit of mathematical background. If you're interested, the book *Trusted Computing Platforms* (see Section 11.3.3) has a very thorough explanation, but you'll really want to have brushed up on the mathematics behind ECC and zero-knowledge proofs before reading it. Note that even there, the protocol is described with attention focused on the mathematical properties and does not include any information about message format or data structures.

At an extremely high level, ECDAA involves five stages:

- *Setup*: The certificate issuer creates a group key; the private portion will be used to create group credentials, while the public portion will be used as the group public key.
- *Join*: The TPM creates an ECDAA key and proves to the certificate issuer that the key belongs to a legitimate TPM by associating it with the TPM's EK. The TPM receives a group certificate from the issuer.
- *Sign*: The TPM uses the ECDAA key with the TPM2_Commit command in combination with another TPM signing command to create an anonymized signature, which is sent to the verifier along with the group certificate. The signature optionally includes information linking this key to specific other signatures by the same key.
- *Verify*: The verifier confirms that the signature was produced by some valid key that is covered by the certificate.
- *Link*: If two signatures were created to be linkable, the verifier can run an algorithm to confirm that both signatures were produced by the same signer. The verifier cannot tell the difference between two non-linkable signatures created by the same party, and two signatures created by different parties.

Of course, that summary is so high level that it is in many ways inaccurate (in practice, several of these steps are performed as interactive protocols, e.g.) but it gives you a general idea of how the whole concept works. A trusted authority knows that a given TPM has a ECDAA key; depending on the exact protocol used, it might have a clear association between the ECDAA key and the TPM key, or it might only know a pseudonym for the ECDAA key. The recipient of the certificate knows only that the key being used is part of a group trusted by the CA. Groups can be large and low on information (e.g., 2.0 TPMs) or small and specific (e.g., 2.0 TPMs in computers issued to a particular corporate site). The CA should include in the certificate relevant properties of the group which the TPM shares, such as TPM version or corporate affiliation, so that the recipient can make a reasonable trust decision. Relevant properties will vary by use case.

An interesting property of ECDAA is that the user can decide whether they want two distinct signatures to be correlatable by the verifier. This allows for user-controllable consistent pseudonyms to be created while using the exact same key for entirely anonymous (within the certificate group) operations. Consistent pseudonyms allow for better audit trails for a given application, while still preventing the correlation of activities between applications.

ECDAA keys will often be primary keys in the endorsement hierarchy, so that the keys can be certified once in a trusted manufacturer environment, issued an appropriate manufacturer certificate, and recreated as needed, just like any primary key. However, some use cases will rely on certificates issued by a more local authority. A device vendor could issue certificates for all valid devices they manufacture, allowing the devices to talk to a number of app vendors without making those communications correlatable. An enterprise could certify computers belonging to it, without allowing external parties to track its employees individually. In these cases, it is critical that the ECDAA key being certified is reliably tied to the recognized TPM, just as with any other certification operation. The TPM2_ActivateIdentity command can be used here, using a protocol similar to the one we used for verifying AIKs back in Section 6.11.1.1. Of course, an ECDAA key can be certified using TPM2_Certify just like any other TPM key, but this produces a tight binding between TPM identity and ECDAA key for the certifier. In any use case where real anonymity is desired or the CA is not entirely trusted, using the identity certification protocol is probably a better choice, but it's important to note that there are operations which can be performed to transform an ECDAA credential into something even the issuer can't associate with a particular key while still allowing for verification.

ECDAA keys can be used in any command that creates a signature to produce truly anonymous signatures (where the same signer's activity cannot be correlated) and pseudonymous signatures (where a given identity's activity can be correlated, but distinct identities cannot be). ECDAA keys are still certified by CAs like normal keys; however, the credential and public key both have random data mixed with them before being sent to the verifier, so the verifier cannot identify them, even though the TPM can prove that it has a valid key and credential. The anonymous identity can then be used to certify other keys, as AIKs were in 1.2 TPMs, to produce anonymized certificates proving that a given object is a TPM key without identifying the TPM. TPMs cannot verify ECDAA signatures.

ECDAA keys are created as normal TPM keys, using `TPM2_Create` or `TPM2_CreatePrimary`; they should be signing keys with the `TPM_ALG_ECDAA` signature scheme. Because they are certified by an authority which needs to be able to confirm that the TPM is legitimate, it may be advisable to create these as primary keys, to allow them to be recreated even after a TPM is cleared and minimize the need to re-provision them. Each set of credentials, associated with a given ECDAA key, is effectively creating a pseudonym.

To sign data with an ECDAA key, a two-phase operation is used. First, the TPM commits to a (pseudo)random value and creates an intermediate signing value using the `TPM2_Commit` command. This command returns values which can be verified by a remote party, along with a counter that the TPM uses to reference the created random value. In a later signing or attestation command (`TPM2_Sign`, `TPM2_Quote`, `TPM2_Certify`, and other commands that produce an attestation structure), the counter is returned as a field in the scheme parameter, allowing an external verifier to connect that signature with the earlier commit message. When creating an attestation structure for a DAA key, the TPM will not include portions of the data structure that could identify the TPM. The credential for the ECDAA is sent along with the signature, but the supporting application is expected to perform some cryptographic operations that combine the credential with a fresh random number to prevent association between signatures using the credential. The operations allow signature verification despite this randomization.

It's worth calling attention to the fact that an ECDAA key can be used to sign the output of a `TPM2_Certify` command. This allows an entire key or object hierarchy to be created and certified without allowing it to be associated with other keys from the same TPM. It also means that once the initial certification has been performed, later operations can use the simpler interfaces and more varied functionality of normal TPM keys without compromising anonymity.

Revocation with ECDAA is possible, but somewhat complex. An entire group can be revoked at once by changing the issuer key and revoking the original one, then recertifying any trusted members of the group. A verifier can also maintain a local revocation list, containing the private portions of untrusted keys, and verify that a particular signature was not created by that key. In the event that consistent pseudonyms are being used, a verifier can also check to see whether a particular untrusted pseudonym is being used; note that this form of revocation can easily be bypassed by changing the pseudonym identifier, so it is only suitable for cases where new pseudonyms are verified in a way that would detect whatever problem cause the revocation to occur.

In short, DAA in either 1.2 or 2.0 TPMs can provide privacy-protecting functionality unlike anything else in the TPM specifications. However, using it in a real-world system requires committing to a significant amount of implementation complexity. The 2.0 ECDAA scheme is poorly specified and relied heavily on the implementer fully understanding some very complex mathematics in order to not make potentially dangerous mistakes. Most TPM experts do not expect it to be frequently used despite its potentially interesting functionality.

9.4 Machine state measurement in theory and reality

The design behind PCR-based attestation is elegant. We create a complete record of the machine's state, starting at boot; when we launch the OS or even trusted applications, measurements continue to be recorded into the PCRs, so that malware or other malicious activity will be recorded and will be unable to usefully falsify the records to hide their actions. Meaningful actions will be recorded, providing us with a clear picture of the trustworthiness (or lack thereof) of a system.

Unfortunately, this is much more difficult in practice than it is in theory. This approach relies heavily on two assumptions.

The first assumption is that software has predictable measurements. In practice, much software contains data that is both irrelevant to the trustworthiness of its actions and will throw off easy measurements. Hash-based measurements, which is what we rely on today, are extremely fragile; they are designed to change if the input is even trivially different. This is approximately as effective as relying on facial recognition software that thinks you're a different person because you changed your shirt. For example, a program that records the time stamp of its installation or the hostname of the machine as part of its internal configurations will have a different hash on every system, even though the configuration settings which actually affect its behavior are the same. In many cases, information that changes regularly (such as the last-changed date of a file) is included, making consistent measurements even on a single system very hard unless the measurer is deeply familiar with exactly what data is being recorded where, and is willing to take the time to do more than simply hash a file.

The second assumption is that we can recognize "good" values when we see them. In many contexts, such as enterprises where users are allowed to install their own software or change their computers' configurations—let alone in a consumer context!—the profusion of possible "good" measurements rapidly becomes impossible to track.

This means that today, the only scenarios in which we can gain anything like the full power attestation promises us are those in which systems have a limited and predictable set of possible "good" states, or where we've invested significant effort in distinguishing between the meaningful "good" information and irrelevant information for our measurements. For practical purposes, unless highly customized software is an option, this means true attestation is possible for either relatively small programs run using the DRTM, or large enterprises capable of producing a predictable "golden image" on nearly identical hardware. In other circumstances, attestation is most useful for change detection: if the measurements are not the same as they were yesterday, and no changes were expected to have been made to the system, something may be wrong.

9.5 Attestation user stories

Notes: Because attestation depends heavily on measurement quality, and because so many of today's measurements don't live up to the potential of attestation's most powerful use cases, each user story here will be labeled with a feasibility level. "Today" means the use case has been successfully implemented in an enterprise context. "Research" means that prototypes have been built as of 2015, but the technology has not yet been scaled up to support large deployments or a wide range of systems. "Future" means that the TPM has been designed to support similar use cases, but significant support is required from software that does not yet exist as of 2015, and there are both design and implementation challenges involved. All three are included because imagining future possibilities is important when shaping long-term direction, but don't plan on deploying anything in the "Research" or "Future" categories without (potentially significant) research beyond this book.

Alice wants to set up monitoring for unexpected changes to low-level software on SecureCorp user systems. She sets up a central repository to hold measurement data for each machine, along with a server which will act as the communications interface, and adds a software hook to the login process on each machine. When the user logs in, the machine will initiate a measurement action and connect to the central server. The server will provide a nonce, which the machine will use in combination with a non-restricted signing key or identity key to generate a TPM quote which is returned to the server. The signature is verified against an expected machine's key, the nonce is checked to confirm that the quote is current, and the quote contents are compared to the previously stored value for that machine. Any change will be flagged, and fed into the corporate alert processing system to be correlated with any expected software updates. Unexpected changes will cause an alert at the corporate help desk, which will follow up with the user and check for potential attacks. [Today]

Charlie wants to experiment with using Flicker to input a master password for his password vault. He creates a program designed to be launched by Flicker, which will perform both password input and verification for the password vault, and extend PCR 19 with either a value indicating that the verification has succeeded or a value indicating that it failed. Charlie can then create a sealing key to use with the password vault which is constrained to PCRs 17, 18, and 19: it will only be usable to decrypt keys if Flicker has launched, run the password input program, and password verification has succeeded. Using this program, Charlie can be confident that no keyloggers can access his master password. Of course, if Charlie takes no extra precautions, once the password verification has been completed in a given boot, the sealing key can be used freely; highly convenient for usability, but not much protection against malware. Adding a password to the sealing key would require that both the securely input master password and the TPM key password must be used, but if Charlie is primarily concerned about keyloggers would not add much security. Using Flicker with different input would change the values in PCRs 17–19, however, effectively locking Charlie out of his password vault until the password program is run again. [Research]

Dana's accountants would like to maintain detailed audit and forensics information by providing information about the software running on the machine at the time their financial files were produced. However, software updates happen frequently enough that using PCR-constrained keys would require creating and tracking large numbers of keys. Dana instead has the accountants use the TPM2_Quote command to sign the file information. Rather than using the file digest as the quote nonce, which would provide a dangerous conflict with other uses of quotes in the company, Dana sets up a program which will first use the TPM2_PCR_Event command to extend the selected file's hash into the resettable PCR 16, and then run a quote including both 16 and the PCRs containing software measurements of interest, with no nonce. The quote can then be stored in a central audit location; verifying the machine state at the time the file was signed requires simply verifying the signature, then confirming that both the file digest and software measurements are as expected. [Feasibility depends on measurements in question; research to future]

Fatima is setting up the TPM-aware VPN for SecureCorp's network. She would like machines using the VPN to be connected either to the full corporate intranet or to a DMZ[8] that only provides access to the corporate patch and antivirus servers, depending on whether or not the machine's software is up to date. She updates the VPN software to require a current quote from a recognized TPM, including the full set of PCR values created during the machine's boot. The VPN server will provide the nonce for the quote once the initial secure connection to the machine has been established. A current quote that corresponds to up-to-date measurements and the correct machine will cause the VPN server to grant full access. All other machines are permitted to only access the limited DMZ. [Research; future, if application-level measurements such as antivirus updates are included]

Gabriel wants to make sure that his server secrets are distributed only to machines running trustworthy software. Because the only machines Gabriel is verifying are servers that are created and centrally controlled by Example, Inc., Gabriel doesn't have to worry about a lot of the variability of end user system measurements. Instead, Gabriel has a handful of "gold image" measurements, corresponding to the default initial installation software and the most recent software versions, running on the three standard server hardware models. When a server wants to prove its suitability to receive updated secrets, it contacts the central server, which issues a nonce as the challenge; the remote server then provides a TPM quote. If the quote comes from a trusted machine and matches a golden measurement, the encrypted secrets will be sent to that machine; if not, the machine will be flagged in the network operations center for follow-up, and no secrets will be distributed. [Today]

Han, who is running Example, Inc.'s TPM-as-smartcard program, would like confirmation from the OS that the user logged into a given machine is the same one as the machine is registered to in certain cases. Han doesn't think that the measurements in the TPM will be of any use to him; after all, Enterprise, Inc. allows users to run a wide range of software on highly varied hardware and does not require upgrades on any particular schedule, and tracking the full set of measurement combinations would be

---

[8]Demilitarized zone; a common term for a constrained network region with limited privileges.

impossible. Instead, Han sets up a login script on Example, Inc.'s Windows machines, which will simply extend the username of the active user into the otherwise unused PCR 10 and maintain a log of all usernames used since the last boot. In situations where he would like to confirm that the logged in user matches the credentials being presented, the server will present a nonce for a TPM quote and request the machine's list of users who have logged in since the last boot. On receiving the quote, the server will verify that the quote is current, valid, and matches the provided username list, and that the most recent username is the same one whose credentials are being used. [Today]

Ingrid would like her sensors to confirm on each contact which version of the software they're running. She would like to upgrade existing communications protocols to take advantage of the TPM, because some of her software components are off-the-shelf. Ingrid decides that it won't be too hard to switch the software to use TPM signing keys instead of software keys, but integrating quotes would be difficult. However, because her sensors use very predictable hardware and software, they only have one expected set of PCR values at a given point in time. And because firmware updates are uncommon, Ingrid can use PCR-bound TPM keys and only need to change them and go through the key certification process on rare occasions. Because the signing key can only be used when the PCR values match the expected current firmware, receiving a signature as part of the normal protocol implies that the values on the sensor's TPM match the PCR values defined for the key and included in the key's certificate. Thus, as long as Ingrid keeps her list of acceptable keys up to date, ordinary signature verification provides her with confirmation that a sensor's firmware was correct as of its last boot. [Research]

José is creating a trusted cloud server hosting a number of virtual machines for third parties. He wants to give the VM owners reason to trust both the hypervisor which is managing the virtual machines and the virtual machines themselves. José decides that the server TPM can be used for both. Josè wants to make sure that the hypervisor is running in a trusted state, and that verifiers do not need to trust the BIOS and boot loader vendors, so uses the DRTM to measure the trusted hypervisor and its VM access control policies and launch the trusted hypervisor. When a verifier requests a quote about a particular VM, the hypervisor will use a resettable PCR (23) to store the measurement of the VM image, first running `TPM_PCR_Reset` or `TPM2_PCR_Reset` followed by `TPM_Extend` or `TPM2_PCR_Event` with a digest of the VM image file that was loaded and the VM name it's accessed with. The verifier can establish trust in the hypervisor and its protections between VMs using the DRTM measurements, and if it trusts the hypervisor can trust that the VM measurement corresponds to the actual loaded image. High security VMs can use the system TPM to seal data to the trusted hypervisor and VM-specific PCRs, minimizing the risk of unauthorized VMs or hypervisors accessing the VM's data, although a remote backup should always be maintained to keep a software update from making the data unavailable. [Research]

Kameko is worried not just about boot-time measurements but about the runtime state of her machine. She's part of SecureCorp's research division, and is willing to put in the resources to do the job properly. She starts with a Linux kernel and a boot loader that will measure the kernel, kernel modules, access control policy, and critical system libraries. She uses the Linux IMA to measure each executable that launches, and modifies a few high trust executables such as her antivirus software to operate in Locality 1 and use the Locality 1 PCR to record their current input files and output. [Basic boot measurements and IMA: today, although interpretation on an enterprise scale is still closer to research. Using the TPM to record application state is research-future.]

9.6 TSS 1.2 attestation code examples

9.6.1 Reading PCR contents

Reading PCR contents is very simple with the 1.2 TSS.

```
UINT32 pcrLen;
BYTE* pcrVal;

Tspi_TPM_PcrRead(hTPM, 0, &pcrLen, &pcrVal);
Tspi_TPM_PcrRead(hTPM, 13, &pcrLen, &pcrVal);
```

The `Tspi_TPM_PcrRead` command takes four arguments: the TPM handle established during setup, the index of the PCR to be read, a pointer to a UINT32 which will contain the size of the returned PCR contents, and a pointer to a byte array which will contain the value of the specified PCR. You can read the complete set of PCRs by looping through indexes 0–23.

A PCR reading program is one of the simplest introductory TSS programs. It's doubly useful for sanity checking if you're developing code on Linux, since you can easily read the PCR contents from the OS as described in Section 5.2.1.1 and compare the results to confirm that your code is working.

9.6.2 Extending PCRs

Extending a PCR is a bit more complicated than reading one. The `Tspi_TPM_PCR_Extend` command is used to extend data into a PCR, but it takes more than just the TPM handle, PCR index, and input data. In addition, it contains three output arguments: an optional pointer to a `TSS_PCR_EVENT` data structure which will be filled in and added to the TSS' internal log of PCR events, the length of the final PCR contents after the command is executed, and the final PCR contents. In order to be useful, the `TSS_PCR_EVENT` structures need to be used on every single extend operation. If you're not using the TSS' event logging, you can just pass in NULL.

The data extended into the PCR cannot be of arbitrary length; it has to be the length of a SHA-1 hash, 20 bytes. Normally, we want to store the measurements of larger data; the data must be hashed first, either by the user or using the TSS' built in hash functions.

```
BYTE* extendData = ''The data to extend into a PCR goes here.
  It doesn't need to be a string.''
UINT32 extendLen = strlen(extendData); // size of data
  to extend
TSS_HHASH hExtendHash;
BYTE* extendHash;
UINT32 extendHashLen;
BYTE* extendOutput;
UINT32 extendOutputLen;

// Create hash object
Tspi_Context_CreateObject(hContext, TSS_OBJECT_TYPE_HASH,
                                 TSS_HASH_SHA1, &hExtendHash);
// Use UpdateHashValue to add the hash of our arbitrary data
  to the hash object
Tspi_Hash_UpdateHashValue(hExtendHash, extendLen, extendData);
// Retrieve the resulting hash value for use in extend command
result = Tspi_Hash_GetHashValue(hExtendHash, &extendHashLen,
                                 &extendHash);

Tspi_TPM_PcrExtend(hTPM, 16, extendHashLen, extendHash,
                   NULL, &extendOutputLen, &extendOutput);
```

9.6.3   Resetting PCRs

Resetting PCRs is straightforward with the 1.2 TSS. First, you'll need to create a PCR composite object indicating which PCRs to reset. For this command, the composite should be a `TCPA_PCR_INFO` structure. Individual PCRs are selected using the `Tspi_PcrComposite_SelectPCRIndex` command, which only takes two arguments: the PCR composite object and the index of the PCR to reset. If you want multiple PCRs to be selected, just run the command multiple times on the same composite object.

The `Tspi_TPM_PcrReset` command will return an error if any PCRs in the composite are not resettable.

```
TSS_HPCRS hResetSet;

// Create a TCPA_PCR_INFO struct
Tspi_Context_CreateObject(hContext, TSS_OBJECT_TYPE_PCRS,
  TSS_PCRS_STRUCT_INFO, &hResetSet);
```

```
// Select relevant PCR indexes.
Tspi_PcrComposite_SelectPcrIndex(hResetSet, 16);

// Reset the selected PCRs
Tspi_TPM_PcrReset(hTPM, hResetSet);
```

9.6.4   Creating and verifying a quote

As mentioned earlier, there are two different TPM functions used to retrieve quotes. The `Tspi_TPM_Quote` command is the simplest to use, and retrieves the simpler `TPM_QUOTE_INFO` structure as the signed output. The `Tspi_TPM_Quote2` command has more options, and returns a `TPM_QUOTE_INFO2` structure containing the more complex `TPM_PCR_INFO_SHORT` data structure. Figure 9.11 illustrates the difference between the two; most notably, the `Tspi_TPM_Quote2` output includes locality information and a PCR selection outside of the PCR composite digest. We'll be referring to those data structures when verifying the returned quotes.

`Tspi_TPM_Quote` takes four arguments: the TPM handle, the handle of the loaded identity key which will be used to sign the quote, the set of PCRs to be quoted, and a pointer to a `TSS_VALIDATION` data structure. The `TSS_VALIDATION` structure will be filled in for the quote output, but must also be partially filled in before running the command with the "external data"—i.e., the nonce used to calculate the quote and verify its freshness. The PCR set here is a `TSS_PCRS_STRUCT_INFO` data structure just like the one we created when resetting PCRs, and is filled in the same way.

In order to provide the quote operation with its nonce, the `ulExternalDataLength` and `rgbExternalData` fields of the `TSS_VALIDATION` structure must be filled in with the nonce length and nonce data, respectively.

```
TSS_HPCRS hQuoteSet;
TSS_VALIDATION QuoteResult;
UINT32 nonceLen = 20;
BYTE* nonceData = nonce; // 20 bytes of random data passed in

QuoteResult.ulExternalDataLength = nonceLen;
QuoteResult.rgbExternalData = nonceData;

Tspi_TPM_Quote(hTPM, hAIK, hQuoteSet, &QuoteResult);
```

`Tspi_TPM_Quote2` is a more complex command, with far more arguments. In addition to the TPM handle and identity key handle, Quote2 provides a new option: whether to return the TPM version as well as the quote response. TRUE will return TPM version information, FALSE will not. The fourth argument is the PCR selection, but unlike the one we used in `Tspi_TPM_Quote`, it must be specified as a `TSS_PCRS_STRUCT_INFO_SHORT` or the command will fail. This more complex structure requires different commands to modify, as described below. The fifth argument is a `TSS_VALIDATION` data structure, which as in

`Tspi_TPM_Quote` should contain the nonce information in the external data fields. The last two arguments provide the length and byte array for the returned version information, if any. (If no version information is desired, they can be pointers to 0 and NULL, respectively.)

Creating a suitable PCR selection for Quote2 involves a normal `Tspi_Context_CreateObject` command, with the type `TSS_OBJECT_TYPE_PCRS` and subtype `TSS_PCRS_STRUCT_INFO_SHORT`. To select the PCRs to be quoted, the `Tspi_PcrComposite_SelectPcrIndexEx` command is used. This takes one additional argument besides the PCR structure and index that `Tspi_PcrComposite_SelectPcrIndex` used: either `TSS_PCRS_DIRECTION_RELEASE` or `TSS_PCRS_DIRECTION_CREATION`. When creating the structure for a Quote2 (or any SHORT PCR data structure), only `TSS_PCRS_DIRECTION_RELEASE` will work.

```
TSS_HPCRS hQuoteSet;
TSS_VALIDATION Quote2Result;
UINT32 nonceLen = 20;
BYTE* nonceData = nonce; // 20 bytes of random data passed in
BYTE *versionInfo = NULL;
UINT32 versionInfoLen = 0;

Quote2Result.ulExternalDataLength = nonceLen;
Quote2Result.rgbExternalData = nonceData;

result = Tspi_Context_CreateObject(hContext, TSS_OBJECT_TYPE_PCRS,
                                   TSS_PCRS_STRUCT_INFO_SHORT,
                                   &hQuoteSet);

Tspi_PcrComposite_SelectPcrIndexEx(hQuoteSet, 1,
                                   TSS_PCRS_DIRECTION_RELEASE);
Tspi_PcrComposite_SelectPcrIndexEx(hQuoteSet, 2,
                                   TSS_PCRS_DIRECTION_RELEASE);
Tspi_PcrComposite_SelectPcrIndexEx(hQuoteSet, 3,
                                   TSS_PCRS_DIRECTION_RELEASE);
Tspi_PcrComposite_SelectPcrIndexEx(hQuoteSet, 4,
                                   TSS_PCRS_DIRECTION_RELEASE);

result = Tspi_TPM_Quote2(hTPM, hAIK, FALSE,
                         hQuoteSet, &Quote2Result,
                         &versionInfoLen, &versionInfo);
```

Verifying the signature of a quote can be done outside of the TSS, of course, but the same functionality the TSS uses to verify signatures over any hash can be used here. The exact same commands can be used for both Quote and Quote2 output: the differences in the returned data structures are just part of the hash we're verifying.

The `QUOTE_INFO` data structures—the content which has been signed— are stored in the `rgbData` field of the `TSS_VALIDATION` structure returned by a quote command, with `ulDataLength` containing the length of the data field. The signatures themselves are stored in `rbgValidationData`, with `ulValidationDataLength` holding the signature length.

```
TSS_HHASH hQuoteHash;

Tspi_Context_CreateObject(hContext, TSS_OBJECT_TYPE_HASH,
                                    TSS_HASH_SHA1, &hQuoteHash);

Tspi_Hash_UpdateHashValue(hQuoteHash, QuoteResult.ulDataLength,
                                    QuoteResult.rgbData);
Tspi_Hash_VerifySignature(hQuoteHash, hAIK,
                            QuoteResult.ulValidationDataLength,
                            QuoteResult.rgbValidationData);
```

Of course, simply verifying the signature over the hashed quote data structure doesn't tell us whether the quote contents are what we expect.

In this example, we check the contents of a `TPM_QUOTE_INFO` returned by `TPM_Quote`.

```
// Set up data structures for quote contents
BYTE* quoteNonce;
BYTE* quoteInfoStructure;
UINT32 quoteInfoLength;
BYTE structfixed[4]; // String for comparing with the
   returned data structure
structfixed[0] = 'Q';
structfixed[1] = 'U';
structfixed[2] = 'O';
structfixed[3] = 'T';
TPM_STRUCT_VER version;
TPM_COMPOSITE_HASH composite;
TPM_NONCE nonce;
TPM_STRUCT_VER ver;
TPM_QUOTE_INFO *testquote;

// Basic sanity checking: does the TPM think it gave
   us back something reasonable?
if (QuoteResult.ulExternalDataLength != 20){
  printf("Invalid response nonce length in quote\n");
  return -1;
}
quoteNonce = QuoteResult.rgbExternalData;
quoteInfoLength = QuoteResult.ulDataLength;
quoteInfoStructure = QuoteResult.rgbData;
  // TCPA_QUOTE_INFO

testquote = (TPM_QUOTE_INFO*) quoteInfoStructure;

version = testquote->version;
```

```
printf("Version of quote: %x.%x.%x.%x\n", version.major,
   version.minor, version.revMajor, version.revMinor);

/* Verify data structure tag */
if (memcmp(testquote->fixed, structfixed, 4))
  printf("Quote info structure unrecognized\n");

/* Verify correct nonce */
  if (memcmp(testquote->externalData.nonce, quoteNonce, 20))
    printf ("Unexpected nonce value");

/* Retrieve PCR composite digest.
 * Note that compositeHash is a quirk of TrouSerS; in
   the TPM spec, the field
 * is digestValue. */
  composite = testquote->compositeHash;
```

The `TPM_QUOTE_INFO2` retrieved from `TPM_Quote2` is much more complicated to verify, because the assumptions the TPM makes about how to construct a
data structure are not what every compiler uses. As a result, simply casting a byte
array to the desired data structure can cause comprehensive and mysterious problems.
In particular, many modern compilers assume that fields in a data structure will end
on some nice round number of bytes; often a multiple of four. The compiler will
automatically add padding to its own internal representations of the data structure.
The TPM, however, is a limited-memory device with no such assumptions; each field
is concatenated to the one before it with no regard to elegance. That means that if
you don't have a cooperative compiler, verifying the structure becomes a complex
process of byte-by-byte reconstruction.

For added fun, many of the additional fields in the `TPM_QUOTE_INFO2` are
not byte arrays, which means that questions of whether the TPM's endianness matches
the rest of the system come into play. If you're getting strange results from fields whose
values you think you know, try reversing the byte order and see if they look better.

```
TPM_QUOTE_INFO2* testquote2;
BYTE structfixed[4]; // String for comparing with the returned
   data structure
structfixed[0] = 'Q';
structfixed[1] = 'U';
structfixed[2] = 'T';
structfixed[3] = '2';

/* Casting works for the initial sections of the structure,
   because
 * the bytes produced by the TPM are still in alignment
   with what the
 * compiler expects. */
testquote2 = (TPM_QUOTE_INFO2*) quote2InfoStructure;
```

```
if (memcmp(testquote2->fixed, structfixed, 4))
  printf("Quote info2 structure unrecognized\n");

if (memcmp(testquote2->externalData.nonce, nonceData, 20))
  printf ("Unexpected nonce value in quote2\n");

/* Reverse endianness of tag to match demo system */
TPM_STRUCTURE_TAG temptag = testquote2->tag;
if (bswap_16(temptag) != TPM_TAG_QUOTE_INFO2)
  printf("Unexpected tag %x in Quote2, expected %x\n", bswap_16
    (temptag), TPM_TAG_QUOTE_INFO2);

/* After the nonce, we go directly into a TPM_PCR_INFO_SHORT.
 * Its first field is a TPM_PCR_SELECTION. */
/* Setting pointer directly, since compiler causes padding
 problems in
 * this data structure.  2-byte tag + 4-byte fixed + 20-byte
   nonce
 * -> offset 26 bytes */

BYTE* pcrselectpointer = quote2InfoStructure+26;
TPM_PCR_SELECTION* paddingselect = (TPM_PCR_SELECTION*)
  (pcrselectpointer);
/* Correct for endianness again */
UINT16 selectionSize = bswap_16(paddingselect->sizeOfSelect);
printf("Size in bytes: %d\n", selectionSize);

/* Read PCR selection, switching endianness */
BYTE* testselect = (BYTE*)malloc(sizeof(BYTE)*selectionSize);
BYTE* TPMendianselect = (BYTE*)malloc(sizeof(BYTE)
  *selectionSize);
for (i=0; i<selectionSize;i++){
  testselect[selectionSize-i] = pcrselectpointer[i+2];
  TPMendianselect[i] = pcrselectpointer[i+2];
}
printf("PCR selection: %02x%02x%02x\n",
       testselect[0], testselect[1], testselect[2]);

// Locality: after PCR selection.
// Located 2 (selection size) + size bytes into structure.
BYTE paddinglocality = *(pcrselectpointer+5);

printf("Locality from quote2: %x\n", paddinglocality);
switch(paddinglocality){
case TPM_LOC_FOUR:
  printf("Locality 4\n");
  break;
case TPM_LOC_THREE:
  printf("Locality 3\n");
  break;
```

```
case TPM_LOC_TWO:
  printf("Locality 2\n");
  break;
case TPM_LOC_ONE:
  printf("Locality 1\n");
  break;
case TPM_LOC_ZERO:
  printf("Locality 0\n");
  break;
case 0x1f:
  printf("All localities selected\n");
  break;
default:
  printf("Unrecognized locality %x.\n", paddinglocality);
}


/* PCR composite is final data after single-byte locality
   selection */
TPM_COMPOSITE_HASH* digestAtRelease;
digestAtRelease = (TPM_COMPOSITE_HASH*) pcrselectpointer+6;
```

9.7   TSS 2.0 attestation code examples

9.7.1   Creating a PCR selection

One piece of functionality that will be used over and over again in attestation functions is creating a PCR selection data structure. As such, I'll explain it once here and just refer to it in later code examples.

In this particular example, the PCR selection data structure is accessed via in.PCRselect (as used in a quote); however, in other commands, the name of the data structure will be different. The contents, however, will have the same structure and meaning.

```
    TPMI_DH_PCR                    pcrHandle;

    /* Hash algorithm, which determinesPCR bank */
    in.PCRselect.pcrSelections[0].hash  = TPM_ALG_SHA1;

    /* Bytes in PCR selection bitmap; 3 (24 PCRs) unless new
       PCRs allocated */
    in.PCRselect.pcrSelections[0].sizeofSelect = 3;

    /* PCRs selected from bitmap. Byte = index/8.
     * Bit in byte is remainder after division by 8.
     * 0 = no PCRs selected. */
    in.PCRselect.pcrSelections[0].pcrSelect[0] = 0;
```

```
in.PCRselect.pcrSelections[0].pcrSelect[1] = 0;
in.PCRselect.pcrSelections[0].pcrSelect[2] = 0;

/* pcrHandle here is a single index received from caller.
 * This code automatically calculates a bit value from an
   index.*/
in.PCRselect.pcrSelections[0].pcrSelect[pcrHandle / 8] =
  1 << (pcrHandle % 8);
```

9.7.2 Reading PCR contents

```
PCR_Read_In                    in;
PCR_Read_Out                   out;

/* Set up PCR selection in in.pcrSelectionIn  */

TSE_Execute((RESPONSE_PARAMETERS *)&out,
            (COMMAND_PARAMETERS *)&in,
            NULL,
            TPM_CC_PCR_Read,
            TPM_RH_NULL, NULL, 0);

/* Write results to file. pcrValues contains a list of
   digests, one for each PCR. */
File_WriteBinaryFile(out.pcrValues.digests[0].t.buffer,
                     out.pcrValues.digests[0].t.size,
                     datafilename);
```

9.7.3 Extending PCRs

Although the TPM2_PCR_Extend operation can be used, it is generally a safer choice in 2.0 TPMs (which may have multiple banks of PCRs) to use TPM2_PCR_Event instead, which will simultaneously extend content to all banks at once, using the hash algorithm appropriate to the bank.

For data larger than the TPM's input buffer for a single parameter, use the event sequence commands. (See Section 10.10.1.)

```
PCR_Event_In                   in;
PCR_Event_Out                  out;

/* Read data input buffer from file provided by user.
 * 1024 is the guaranteed input buffer size TPMs will
   accept,
 * although some may be larger.*/
File_Read2B(&in.eventData.b,
            1024,
            datafilename);
```

```
/* While authorization sessions are used for this
   command,
 * since locally created PCRs can be set up to use them,
 * the default set of PCRs have no authorization
   requirements besides
 * the command locality. Thus, a null password
   authorization session.*/
TSE_Execute((RESPONSE_PARAMETERS *)&out,
                    (COMMAND_PARAMETERS *)&in,
                    NULL,
                    TPM_CC_PCR_Event,
                    TPM_RS_PW, NULL, 0,
                    TPM_RH_NULL, NULL, 0);
```

The command also returns a complete list of all of the digests used to extend individual PCRs in the out.digests field, for verification purposes.

```
for (c = 0 ;  c < out.digests.count ;c++) {
    switch (out.digests.digests[c].hashAlg) {
      case TPM_ALG_SHA1:
        if (verbose) printf(``Hash algorithm SHA-1\n'');
        if (verbose) TPM_PrintAll(``Digest'',
                                 (uint8_t *)&out.digests.
                                 digests[c].digest.sha1,
                                 SHA1_DIGEST_SIZE);
        break;
      case TPM_ALG_SHA256:
        ...
```

9.7.4 Resetting PCRs

Resetting is one of the most minimal TPM functions; its only input is the PCR to reset, and no output is returned.

```
PCR_Reset_In                    in;
TPMI_DH_PCR                     pcrHandle;

...
/* Retrieve PCR index from user. Handle = index. */
...
        in.pcrHandle = pcrHandle;

        TSE_Execute(NULL,
                    (COMMAND_PARAMETERS *)&in,
```

```
                      NULL,
                      TPM_CC_PCR_Reset,
                      TPM_RS_PW, NULL, 0,
                      TPM_RH_NULL, NULL, 0);
```

9.7.5 Creating and verifying quotes

In this selection, we set up a PCR selection to feed into the quote. For simplicity, the setup for authorization session information and variable retrieval from the user has been removed from this example.

```
Quote_In                    in;
Quote_Out                   out;

/* Handle of key that will perform quoting */
in.signHandle = signHandle;

/* RSA signature scheme */
in.inScheme.details.rsassa.hashAlg = TPM_ALG_SHA256;

/* Number of PCR selections to be quoted.
 * Multiple selections allowed since 2.0 TPMs may
   have multiple PCR banks. */
in.PCRselect.count = 1;

/* Define each PCR selection as described above. */

/* Nonce data, supplied by caller. Here pulled from
   file. */
if (qualifyingDataFilename != NULL) {
       File_Read2B(&in.qualifyingData.b,
                    sizeof(TPMT_HA),
                    qualifyingDataFilename);}
else {
       in.qualifyingData.t.size = 0;}

/* call TSE to execute the command */
TSE_Execute((RESPONSE_PARAMETERS *)&out,
                 (COMMAND_PARAMETERS *)&in,
                 NULL,
                 TPM_CC_Quote,
                 sessionHandle0, keyPassword,
                   sessionAttributes0,
                 TPM_RH_NULL, NULL, 0);


/* Write attestation data structure to file */
File_WriteBinaryFile(out.quoted.t.attestationData,
                           out.quoted.t.size,
                           attestInfoFilename);
```

```
/* Write signature data (over attestation structure)
   to file. */
File_WriteStructure(&out.signature,
                              (MarshalFunction_t)
                              TSS_TPMT_SIGNATURE_Marshal,
                              signatureFilename);=
```

The signature can be verified using the same TPM2_VerifySignature code we discussed back in Chapter 7.

Of course, merely retrieving a quote and the verifying signature over it is not sufficient for most purposes: we need to understand the quote contents. This is more difficult to show in working code, since it involves the less stable API for marshalling and unmarshalling of data structures, but here's a simple example of code which checks to see whether the nonce (qualifyingData) provided by the caller is the same as the nonce included as part of the quote.

```
TPMS_ATTEST                    tpmsAttest;
BYTE *tmpBuffer = out.quoted.t.attestationData;
INT32 tmpSize = out.quoted.t.size;
TPMS_ATTEST_Unmarshal(&tpmsAttest, &tmpBuffer,
  &tmpSize);

BOOL match;
match = TPM2B_Compare(&in.qualifyingData.b, &tpmsAttest.
  extraData.b);
if (!match)
    printf("quote: failed, extraData !=
      qualifyingData\n");
```

Chapter 10
Other TPM features

10.1 The smorgasbord

In this chapter, we'll be discussing many of the TPM's small but useful features that didn't fit well elsewhere in this book. Nothing in this chapter is critical for making use of the TPM; however, everything here serves a useful purpose in certain circumstances. We'll begin with the functions with the broadest applicability, including clearing the TPM of data, using the TPM's RNG, managing the TPM's internal configuration information, and creating an archive. Later in this chapter, we'll cover more special-purpose features such as monotonic counters, delegation, and timing capabilities.

10.2 Clearing the TPM

When a machine with a TPM in it is being transferred to a new owner or disposed of, the TPM should be *cleared* to erase its secrets. Clearing the TPM erases the current owner's changes and keys, and restores the TPM to the manufacturer's default state, with a few small exceptions.

In a 1.2 TPM, clearing the TPM will erase the SRK, causing all keys created by the TPM to become unusable, and all data encrypted by the TPM to be irretrievable. It will also erase the owner authorization, any delegations set up (see Section 10.9.3), and a number of TPM internal values used to verify that keys or encrypted blobs were created inside this TPM. Flags and other configuration values are reset to their default values. Clearing also deallocates some (but not all) allocated NVRAM storage areas: those which are readable or writable by the TPM owner, and which were not created to be permanent during the TPM's manufacturing process (see Section 8.7.1). Other NVRAM storage must be individually deallocated using TPM_NV_DefineSpace.

Running the command requires either owner authorization (for the TPM_Owner Clear command) or physical presence (for the TPM_ForceClear command). Either (but not both) can be disabled using the TPM's flags; see the end of this section. In enterprises where the owner authorization is widely known, disabling TPM_OwnerClear may be a good idea unless the enterprise wants to retain the ability to remotely clear a TPM and has reason to believe it can gain the necessary remote access. BIOS menus use the TPM_ForceClear command; disabling that may be appropriate if your primary threat model is evil maids or other short-term untrusted physical access to the machine.

Many automated tools which clear the TPM, such as the Windows tpm.msc and some BIOS options, automatically disable the TPM as well; in these cases, the TPM must be turned back on before being used again.

In a 2.0 TPM, clearing the TPM will erase all non-seed objects in the Storage and Endorsement hierarchies,[1] replace the SPS so that data and keys encrypted by this TPM become irretrievable, reset the authorizations and policies set during provisioning,[2] remove all NV storage indexes allocated by the owner, and reset a number of internal values to their default state. Clearing the TPM in 2.0 requires either platform authorization (probably provided by a BIOS option or other manufacturer firmware) or lockout authorization, using the TPM2_Clear command.

For both 1.2 and 2.0 TPMs, clearing the TPM does not reset the PCR values; these values are reset only on reboot, to prevent someone from being able to forge 'good' PCR values by clearing a running TPM. The EK (1.2) and EPS (2.0) are also not reset, since these are what the manufacturer uses to certify that the TPM is legitimate and since other keys are used to actually identify the TPM to other machines.

The clear operation, with its ability to render user data unreadable and keys unusable, is one of the most high-sensitivity operations that TPMs offer. An unwanted clear is an effective denial of service attack. That means that the security of the authorizing passwords – the owner authorization for 1.2 systems that don't explicitly disable TPM_OwnerClear, and the lockout authorization for 2.0 systems – needs to be considered during the provisioning process (see Chapter 5) in view of the risk of DoS from accidental or hostile clear commands.

1.2 TPMs offer two different commands to disable the different clear commands. Only one can be active at any given time; you can't completely eliminate the ability to clear the TPM. TPM_DisableForceClear prevents someone with physical presence from clearing the TPM; its state is reset on every boot, so if you intend to use it regularly, it's best to build it in early in the system startup sequence. Note that unless you're writing your own BIOS, any BIOS clear options will take effect before you can disable force clear. TPM_DisableForceClear does not require any authorization to run, and can thus be run easily in firmware if desired. TPM_DisableOwnerClear has a longer-term effect; once set, the only way to clear a TPM is with physical access, and it remains set until the TPM is next cleared. TPM_DisableOwnerClear requires owner authorization to run.

In 2.0 TPMs, the TPM2_ClearControl command can be used to change the value of the TPM's permanent disableClear attribute. To set disableClear, which prevents TPM2_Clear from being run, either the lockout authorization or platform authorization may be used. To clear disableClear, allowing TPM2_Clear again, only the platform authorization may be used. The general expectation is that the lockout authorization will be used to prevent any software clearing of the TPM, while the BIOS or other low-level firmware can reset the attribute as needed to allow a clear by someone with physical access to the machine.

---

[1] Note that primary objects in the Endorsement Hierarchy can be recreated using TPM2_CreatePrimary and the original template.
[2] The owner, endorsement, and lockout authorizations and policies.

10.2.1 Revoking trust in an EK

If the EK for a given TPM was created using `TPM_CreateRevocableEK` (see Section 5.2.1.2), `TPM_RevokeTrust` can be used to erase the EK. The `TPM_RevokeTrust` command requires that the same authorization value defined in `TPM_CreateRevocableEK` be provided, and that physical presence was asserted. Note that this is *not* the owner authorization: it's a single-purpose value used solely for revoking the EK. `TPM_RevokeTrust` acts like a more thorough version of `TPM_OwnerClear`. In addition to all of the actions of a standard clear, `TPM_RevokeTrust` erases the internally stored EK, changes the internal data used for DAA, and removes all NVRAM indexes that are set as part of the manufacturing process, such as those containing certificates.

10.2.2 Clearing user stories

Alice wants to make sure that decommissioned SecureCorp machines not only no longer have potentially secure SecureCorp data on them but also cannot be mistaken for SecureCorp machines in the future. For 1.2 TPMs, this means deallocating all NVRAM indexes which are not owner-linked using `TPM_GetCapability` to retrieve the indexes in use as described in Section 10.4 and the `TPM_NV_DefineSpace` command to deallocate them, then using either `TPM_OwnerClear` or the `TPM_ForceClear` command supported by the BIOS. Since clearing NVRAM requires owner permissions anyway, Alice creates a TPM clearing script to preform both the NVRAM cleanup and `TPM_OwnerClear` operations. The script can be executed locally or remotely. Since each machine has a unique owner password that only SecureCorp's IT department knows, and which is protected by the TPM's usual dictionary attack prevention methods, Alice isn't worried about unauthorized parties misusing the utility. For SecureCorp's 2.0 TPMs, Alice decides to go beyond the simple `TPM2_Clear` operation and also reset the TPM's EPS using the `TPM2_ChangeEPS` command; this has the unfortunate side effect of invalidating any manufacturer-issued certificates for the TPM, but Alice is willing to slightly lower the utility of decommissioned machines that are near end of life in order to guarantee that no SecureCorp machine can possibly be tricked into trusting a decommissioned machine based on out-of-date information about its TPM.

Dana is using TPM keys to identify users, and has allowed their users to create their own keys. After confirming that all encrypted data from a departed user's machine has been retrieved, Dana uses the `TPM2_Clear` command via the BIOS' built-in option to erase the storage hierarchy, thus automatically invalidating any user-created keys as well as the storage hierarchy keys Dana created to identify the user.

10.3 Random number generation

TPMs have RNGs, which are intended to provide higher quality randomness than software-based pseudo-RNGs. The primary purpose of the TPM's RNG is to create TPM keys without the potential weaknesses that can result from insufficient randomness. However, there are two features worth noting.

The first is that the TPM's RNG can also produce randomness for other applications using the `TPM_GetRandom` or `TPM2_GetRandom` commands. This allows software to take advantage of the TPM's RNG, or lets an OS update the seed using its RNG. If using this feature, it is worth noting that because many TPMs use hardware RNG, extensive use of the feature can result in slow responses while sufficient randomness is generated.

The second is intended for high-security use cases, and enterprises which care deeply about how their randomness is generated. TPMs do not come with strong guarantees about the strength of their random number generators; the quality will depend on the manufacturer's implementation choices. If an additional source of high-quality random bits is available, this extra randomness can be mixed into the TPM's store of random bits using the `TPM_StirRandom` or `TPM2_StirRandom` commands. The number of bytes of randomness that can be added is implementation-specific in 1.2 TPMs, although at least 256 bytes must be accepted; in 2.0 TPMs, only 128 bytes of randomness may be added with a given `TPM2_StirRandom` call. Because the TPM uses its RNG to generate keys, this technique can be used to improve the quality of keys for particularly high-security applications when a high-quality source of randomness is available. Unless you have reason to believe that your TPM has insufficiently good randomness or that you have an especially high-quality entropy source, however, this feature can largely be disregarded.

10.3.1   Random number user stories

Alice would like to ensure that her users have the option of using the TPM's random number generator to generate seeds for OS or software pseudo-random number generators. She creates a convenient command-line utility which runs `TPM_GetRandom` or `TPM2_GetRandom` as appropriate, and makes it available on SecureCorp's default user images. The default installations of the OpenSSL library are configured to use the TPM's RNG to seed its random number generator function, since that is the most common cryptographic library used in SecureCorp.

Lemar is setting up TPM-enabled computers for a government agency which wants to be entirely confident of the quality of the random numbers used to generate keys. The agency has its own high-quality hardware entropy generators. Lemar uses `TPM_StirRandom` on the 1.2 TPMs before taking ownership to provide data from the agency entropy generators to the TPM, in order to ensure that the SRK, which is so critical for protecting other TPM keys, is created using high-quality randomness. If a 1.2 TPM has no existing EK, Lemar waits until after the `TPM_StirRandom` command has been executed to create one. For 2.0 TPMs, the agency would rather have the guarantee of high randomness than the assurance provided by the manufacturer's certification, so Lemar runs `TPM2_StirRandom` to add high-quality entropy before running `TPM2_Clear` to clear the SPS and `TPM2_ChangeEPS` command to change the EPS, so that the critical random seeds of the user hierarchies are as random as possible. Users interested in creating their own TPM keys later who wish to refresh the entropy of their TPMs may request high-quality randomness and run the appropriate `StirRandom` command again at any time in the future.

10.4   TPM configuration

TPMs have a variety of configuration options. In 1.2 TPMs, these primarily consist of flags which are set by either the manufacturer or the TPM owner; in 2.0 TPMs, there is a much wider range of possible configurations, owing to the new key hierarchy structure.

10.4.1   Configuration in 1.2

The 1.2 TPM has a range of internal *capabilities* or *flags*. Some of these are configurable either by the manufacturer or by the owner; others aren't truly variable, and instead merely describe a particular TPM's capabilities, but use the same infrastructure for reading out the current values.

The most relevant and useful flags in most enterprises are:

FIPS: This flag is set by the manufacturer and forces the TPM to adhere to a higher baseline of security. An FIPS-enabled TPM will not allow 512-bit or legacy keys, for example, and will always overwrite key data with zeroes when the TPM is cleared. Note that a TPM with the FIPS flag set is not technically FIPS-compliant, despite the name, but does meet a number of requirements that a non-FIPS-enabled TPM is not guaranteed to meet. A non-FIPS-enabled TPM may take the actions of an FIPS-enabled TPM in most cases, but is not required to do so.

nvLocked: This flag determines whether authorization checks are performed on NVRAM. It intended to allow manufacturers to write certificate data into NVRAM without authorization; but some manufacturers have been known to not set the flag to require authorization before the TPM leaves the factory. Users who intend to make use of NVRAM features should check to ensure it has been set correctly. Unlike other flags, this one is set using the `TPM_NV_DefineSpace` command, targeting the index `TPM_NV_INDEX_LOCK` with no authorization and no data.

disableOwnerClear: If this flag is set, the owner cannot use the `TPM_OwnerClear` command, and will get an error when they try to. This cannot be set if `disableForceClear` is set. This is used to prevent software with access to the owner password from clearing the TPM, particularly relevant if the owner password is shared between machines.

disableForceClear: If this flag is set, physical presence cannot be used to clear the TPM, preventing BIOSes and other firmware clear options from working. This cannot be set if `disableOwnerClear` is set. This is used to disable evil maid attacks that could clear the TPM.

allowMaintenance: Indicates whether the TPM is capable of creating a maintenance archive (see Section 10.9.2). This will normally be set if the TPM supports the maintenance archive commands, and not if it does not; however, the flag can be set to false in order to ensure that a TPM with maintenance archive capability does not use it.

Values of these flags and others (Table 10.2) are retrieved using the `TPM_GetCapability` command, and set (where possible) using the owner-authorized `TPM_Set Capability`. (While a `TPM_GetCapabilitySigned` command was defined in the 1.2 specification, to allow remote parties to verify the TPM's settings, it is explicitly removed from the PC client version which defines all of the 1.2 TPMs on the market today.) Not all capabilities can be set by the user or TPM owner, and some (such as the TPM's permanent flags) require other commands to be used.

In addition to the flags mentioned above, there is extensive information about the TPM's settings, history, and capabilities that can be retrieved using `TPM_GetCapability`. Although primarily useful for those building low-level drivers or software stacks, this may be of interest to those seeking to fully utilize their TPMs. Table 10.1 shows some of the more useful; the full list, along with details of how to use them, can be found in section 21.1 of the Structures section of the 1.2 TPM specification (see Section 11.5.2). Each capability in the 1.2 TPM has a name, and in some cases, a *subcapability* which specifies which information in a given category should be accessed.

10.4.2 Configuration in 2.0

To read the TPM's internal configuration information in a 2.0 TPM, the `TPM2_GetCapability` command is used. It takes a *capability* parameter, which defines the category of data, just as in 1.2; it also takes a *property* parameter, which is the first value in that category which will be returned, and a *property count*, which specifies how many of the relevant properties will be returned. If a requested property does not exist, the next property will be returned, if there is one; if the property count is above the number of properties present, the TPM will return all remaining properties in a given category. The command's other returned value, a YES/NO `TPMSI_YES_NO` data structure, will indicate whether there is more data of a given category available, allowing software or a user to determine whether additional queries should be run to retrieve further properties.

If you want to retrieve the complete set of properties associated with a given capability, providing 0 as the property parameter will access the first value in the category. A large property count, especially with attention to the returned moreData value, can be used to ensure that all available properties are returned.

Available capabilities include:

TPM_CAP_ALGS: Provides a list whose elements are an algorithm ID and a set of algorithm properties.

TPM_CAP_HANDLES: Provides a list of handles of objects currently in the TPM, based on the handle type of the provided property value. Useful handle types include:

TPM_HT_NV_INDEX: Handles of NV indexes currently defined.

TPM_HT_TRANSIENT: Handles of transient objects such as data and keys currently loaded in the TPM.

TPM_HT_PERSISTENT: Handles of objects that have been made persistent in the TPM (see Section 10.6).

TPM_HT_PCR: Handles of available PCRs.

Table 10.1 Most frequently useful capabilities in 1.2 TPMs. The full set of capability inputs can be found in section 21 of Part 2 of the TPM 1.2 standard

Capability name	Sub-capability	Description
TPM_CAP_ALG	A valid TPM_ALGORITHM_ID as defined in the Structures specification	Indicates whether or not that algorithm is supported by the TPM.
TPM_CAP_PID	A valid TPM_PROTOCOL_ID as defined in the Structures specification	Indicates whether or not that particular communications protocol is supported by the TPM. These protocols are not network protocols but the TPM's secure communications protocols.
TPM_CAP_FLAG	TPM_CAP_FLAG_PERMANENT	Returns a structure with the full set of TPM permanent flags, including the FIPS flag, the NVLocked flag, and the allowMaintenance flag (Table 10.2).
TPM_CAP_PROPERTY	TPM_CAP_PROP_MANUFACTURER	Returns the manufacturer ID for the TPM.
TPM_CAP_PROPERTY	TPM_CAP_PROP_MAX_KEYS	Returns the number of 2048-bit keys that can be simultaneously loaded. This is primarily useful if OwnerEvict (Section 10.6) is being used, as most software libraries will manage loading and unloading keys behind the scenes.
TPM_CAP_PROPERTY	TPM_CAP_COUNTERS	Number of available monotonic counters
TPM_CAP_NV_LIST		Lists all NV index values currently allocated.
TPM_CAP_DA_LOGIC	A valid TPM_ENTITY_TYPE	(Optional) Retrieves information about the TPM's dictionary attack logic, including the type of response. If fully enabled, also includes information about the threshold and current failure counts.

Table 10.2   The complete set of boolean flags in the TPM_PERMANENT_FLAGS data structure, returned by running TPM_GetCapability with the TPM_CAP_FLAG and TPM_CAP_FLAG_PERMANENT subcapability. Flags listed in the 'Can Set?' column can be changed command, although there are often constraints as described in the comments column

Flag	Description	Can Set?	Comments
disable	Determines if TPM is disabled	Y	Owner auth using TPM_OwnerSetDisable or physical presence required.
ownership	Determines if the TPM has an owner	Y	Physical presence required, using TPM_SetOwnerInstall
deactivated	Determines if TPM is deactivated	Y	Physical presence required
readPubek	Determines if owner authorization is required to read the public EK data.	Y	Owner auth required, using TPM_SetCapability
disableOwnerClear	Disallow owner authorized clear	Y	Owner auth required. Starts FALSE; can only be set to TRUE using TPM_DisableOwnerClear. Will reset on successful TPM clear.
allowMaintenance		Y	Can be set only to FALSE, using TPM_KillMaintenanceFeature. Only changing owner returns to TRUE.
physicalPresenceLifetimeLock	If set, the state of the other physical presence flags cannot be changed for the life of the TPM.		Set by manufacturer.
physicalPresenceHWEnable	Enables hardware indication of physical presence.		Set by manufacturer.
physicalPresenceCMDEnable	Enables a software command, TSC_PhysicalPresence, for indicating physical presence.		Set by manufacturer.
CEKPUsed	Indicates whether the EK was created using the TPM_CreateEndorsement KeyPair command (TRUE) or by the manufacturer (FALSE).		

Flag	Description	Auth	Notes
TPMpost	Determines whether the TPM must perform an immediate self-test of all commands and return a result when a self-test is executed (TRUE) or can perform a dynamic self-test after the command returns and produce a result to query later (FALSE).		Set by manufacturer.
TPMpostLock	Deprecated		
FIPS	Determines if the TPM operates in FIPS mode (TRUE) or not (FALSE).		Set by manufacturer.
operator	If TRUE, an operator has been set using TPM_SetOperatorAuth.		The operator is allowed only to temporarily deactivate the TPM for a single boot. This flag defaults to FALSE, and is reset to FALSE on a clear.
enableRevokeEK	Determines whether the EK can be revoked with the TPM_RevokeTrust command.		Set by manufacturer.
nvLocked	If TRUE, all NV authorization checks are active. If FALSE, no NV authorization checks are performed.		
readSRKPub	Determines if TPM_GetPubKey can (TRUE) or cannot (FALSE) be used to retrieve the SRK public key.	Y	Owner authorization required, using TPM_SetCapability.
tpmEstablished	Determines whether the machine is in the DRTM-launched secure mode.		The DRTM launch sequence sets this to TRUE; TSC_ResetEstablishmentBit called with localities 3 or 4 sets it back to FALSE.
maintenanceDone	Indicates whether a maintenance archive has been created or loaded since the last TPM clear.		Set by the relevant maintenance commands.
disableFullDALogicInfo	If TRUE, only a limited amount of information will be returned when requesting TPM_CAP_DA_LOGIC	Y	Owner authorization required, using TPM_SetCapability

TPM_CAP_COMMANDS: Returns command codes implemented by the TPM, starting with the command code provided as the property parameter. If any vendor-specific commands are implemented, they will be listed after the base commands.

TPM_CAP_PP_COMMANDS: Provides a list of those commands which require physical presence in addition to other authorization, starting with the command code provided as the property parameter. This list can be changed using the TPM2_PP_Commands command, which itself requires physical presence and the platform authorization.

TPM_CAP_AUDIT_COMMANDS: Provides a list of command codes currently set to be included in the command audit (see Section 10.7).

TPM_CAP_PCRS: This will always return the complete current allocation of PCRs, and the property parameter should be zero.

TPM_CAP_TPM_PROPERTIES: Returns properties and their current values. Properties are grouped, and the TPM will return only values in the same group, regardless of how large the property count provided is. Unlike other capabilities, the property value here is very important. Useful properties include:

    TPM_PT_REVISION: The specification revision that this TPM implements, multiplied by 100 to be a whole number. (Revision 01.16 would thus be returned as 116.)

    TPM_VENDOR_STRING_1, TPM_VENDOR_STRING_2, TPM_VENDOR_STRING_3, TPM_VENDOR_STRING_4: Combined, these are the characters of the vendor ID string (Figure 10.1).

    TPM_PT_FIRMWARE_VERSION_1, TPM_PT_FIRMWARE_VERSION_2: A vendor-specific value indicating the version number of the TPM firmware.

    TPM_PT_NV_COUNTERS_MAX: The number of monotonic counters that can be allocated (see Section 10.5).

    TPM_PT_HR_NV_INDEX: The number of currently defined NV indexes.

    TPM_PT_NV_INDEX_MAX: The maximum size of an NV data area (see Section 8.7.2).

    TPM_PT_MAX_AUTH_FAIL: The number of authorization failures allowed before dictionary protections cause a temporary lockout.

    TPM_PT_LOCKOUT_INTERVAL: The number of seconds before the TPM will decrement the count of recent authorization failures as part of the dictionary attack protections.

    TPM_PT_LOCKOUT_RECOVERY: The length of time required after a failed attempt to use the lockout authorization to reset dictionary attack protections before the lockout authorization can be attempted again.

    TPM_PT_NV_WRITE_RECOVERY: The milliseconds required between commands which will modify the TPM's NVRAM. This value is an approximation, but may be useful in certain circumstances for debugging unexpected failures of NV commands.

TPM_CAP_PCR_PROPERTIES: The property for this command should be a given PCR property. (For example, TPM_PT_PCR_RESET_L4 for PCRs which

Assigned to:	ASCII	Hex
AMD	`'AMD'`	0x41 0x4D 0x44 0x00
Atmel	`'ATML'`	0x41 0x54 0x4D 0x4C
Broadcom	`'BRCM'`	0x42 0x52 0x43 0x4D
IBM	`'IBM'`	0x49 0x42 0x4d 0x00
Infineon	`'IFX'`	0x49 0x46 0x58 0x00
Intel	`"INTC"`	0x49 0x4E 0x54 0x43
Lenovo	`'LEN'`	0x4C 0x45 0x4E 0x00
National Semiconductor	`'NSM'`	0x4E 0x53 0x4D 0x20
Nationz	`'NTZ'`	0x4E 0x54 0x5A 0x00
Nuvoton Technology	`'NTC'`	0x4E 0x54 0x43 0x00
Qualcomm	`'QCOM'`	0x51 0x43 0x4F 0x4D
SMSC	`'SMSC'`	0x53 0x4D 0x53 0x43
ST Microelectronics	`'STM'`	0x53 0x54 0x4D 0x20
Samsung	`'SMSN'`	0x53 0x4D 0x53 0x4E
Sinosun	`'SNS'`	0x53 0x4E 0x53 0x00
Texas Instruments	`'TXN'`	0x54 0x58 0x4E 0x00
Winbond	`'WEC'`	0x57 0x45 0x43 0x00
Fuzhou Rockchip	`'ROCC'`	0x52 0x4F 0x43 0x43

Figure 10.1   The table in this figure provides the complete list of TPM Vendor IDs as of September 2015. When you use either TPM_GetCapability or TPM2_GetCapability to request the manufacturer/vendor information, the TPM will return the hex value on the right, which corresponds to the manufacturing company listed in the 'Assigned To' column. Not all companies are actively selling TPMs

are resettable in locality 4, or TPM_PT_PCR_EXTEND_L0 for PCRs extendible in locality 0; a full list is available in section 6.14 of the TPM 2.0 Structures specification.) It will return a selection of PCRs for which that property is true. The properties for the first 24 PCRs are defined by the standard (see Section 9.2) but this can be useful in implementations where additional PCRs have been defined by the platform firmware.

TPM_CAP_TPM_ECC_CURVES: Returns a list of the ECC curves currently available for use.

A full list of capabilities and properties can be found in sections 6.12 and 6.13 of the TPM 2.0 Structures specification (see Section 11.6.2).

10.4.3   Configuration user stories

Alice would like to ensure that all SecureCorp TPMs are FIPS compliant; however, many machines already out in the field were purchased before Alice started her effort to bring SecureCorp's TPMs up to date, so she did not have a chance to work with manufacturers to ensure that her requirements were met. She knows many of the machines will not be up to her standards, and she would like to prioritize replacing those which are not FIPS-compliant as the opportunity presents itself. She creates a survey utility that will run on all SecureCorp machines and report back to a central server, to check if 1.2 TPMs have the FIPS-compliance flag set. The utility executes the TPM_GetCapability command with the TPM_CAP_FLAG capability and TPM_CAP_FLAG_PERMANENT subcapability, then looks at the resulting structure and reads the value of the TPM_PF_FIPS flag. TPMs where the FIPS flag is false are not compliant, will be phased out over time, and are certified with a different key in case SecureCorp needs to change its trust policies quickly.

Bob is considering adding some additional keys to his users' TPMs to support new applications, but still wants to make sure that his users can't cause massive problems by deleting stored key blobs off the disk. Bob decides that he should find out just how many keys it is safe to store as OwnerEvict keys in his 1.2 TPMs. He uses TPM_GetCapability with TPM_CAP_PROPERTY and TPM_CAP_PROP_MAX_KEYS to retrieve the maximum number of loaded keys available in his TPMs. Subtracting two from that number, since the TPM won't allow the last available slots to be locked down, gives Bob his answer.

José is considering some design choices for his trusted virtualized system which would be much easier if he had access to additional PCRs to store virtualized machine state information, or additional monotonic counters to track changes. He uses TPM2_GetCapability with the TPM_CAP_TPM_PROPERTIES capability and the TPM_PT_NV_COUNTERS_MAX property to determine how many monotonic counters his 2.0 TPM supports. Since only one value is expected to be returned, José inputs 1 for the property count. When the command returns, José retrieves the more-Data value, which indicates that there is no further data, and the capabilityData value, which contains the number of monotonic counters the TPM can support. He also wants to retrieve information about the PCRs implemented on this TPM; for this, he uses TPM2_GetCapability with the TPM_CAP_PCRS capability. Here, he wants to retrieve the full set of PCRs but doesn't know how many they are; he uses 0 as the property, and UINT_MAX for his property count. The returned capabilityData is a list of TPMS_PCR_SELECTION data structures.

10.5   Monotonic counters

The TPM's monotonic counters are intended primarily to support anti-rollback measures by providing a frequently updatable, externally verifiable value which is guaranteed to never decrease. Unlike the TPM's NVRAM, which is write-limited, the monotonic counters are required to be frequently updatable (in 1.2, 7 years of increments every 5 seconds) without causing the TPM to burn out.

TPMs support multiple monotonic counters, although how many will depend on the vendor, and in some cases there are limits to when they can be used. 1.2 TPMs are required to support at least four, but only one can be incremented during any given boot. 2.0 TPMs, which use a hybrid implementation in which counters are allocated as part of NVRAM, allow for the provisioning of as many counters as there is room for.

Monotonic counters are most useful for applications which rely on time moving forward, but which may not trust the system clock. Updating the monotonic counter every time rollback needs to be prevented provides an application-specific 'clock'. Including the current value of the monotonic counter inside signed, stored data prevents an adversary from substituting old content.

Monotonic counters in 1.2 TPMs are created with the TPM_CreateCounter command, which also sets an authorization value (password) for the counter and returns its handle. The TPM_IncrementCounter command requires that authorization, and updates the given counter value by one. The TPM_ReadCounter command retrieves the current value of a counter, and does not require any authorization. TPM_ReleaseCounter eliminates a counter, such that no further reads or writes to that counter handle will succeed. Reuse of counter handles is not a useful attack, because new counters will always be initialized to the highest value any counter has ever reached. When the TPM is cleared, all counters will be deallocated, but the count value will continue to go up from the maximum value previously reached.

In 2.0 TPMs, monotonic counters are created as any other NV index, using the TPM2_NV_DefineSpace command, as discussed in detail in Section 8.7.2. To create a monotonic counter, the TPMA_NV_COUNTER attribute bit must be set. Newly created counters will be set to a value greater than any previously used count value for any counter on this TPM. Incrementing the counter is done using the TPM2_NV_Increment command. Counters that update frequently and which are tolerant of unexpected changes may wish to set the TPMA_NV_ORDERLY attribute, which allows the TPM to maintain the current counter value in RAM and only write the current value into NV storage intermittently, when the difference between the current value and the last written value is too large, or during an orderly shutdown. This will never cause a counter's monotonic increasing property to be violated, as a non-orderly shutdown will cause the TPM to set the counter's value to the maximum it could have been without being written again to NVRAM; however, it may cause a counter's value to be something other than the last value software expected it to be. This feature is useful for minimizing the number of writes to the TPM's NVRAM, which has a lifespan limited by number of writes. To read a counter's current value, the TPM2_NV_Read command is used. To provide a remotely verifiable attestation of a counter's state, the TPM2_NV_Certify command is used. Details of how to use these commands are discussed in Section 8.7.2.

10.5.1 Monotonic counter user stories

José wants to prevent rollback of virtual machine images on his trusted virtualized system, in order to ensure that changes to passwords and other access control settings are protected. He decides to include the value of a TPM monotonic counter in each saved image, and increment the counter when the image is replaced. Because José expects this machine to have only a small number of VMs over its lifetime, he opts for the simplest but most resource-intensive design option, in which each VM is assigned its own monotonic counter, created using `TPM_CreateCounter` on 1.2 machines or `TPM2_NV_DefineSpace` with the `TPMA_NV_Counter` bit set. Because José is willing to accept some chances of counter discrepancies in exchange for a longer machine life, and expects some VMs to be updated frequently, he also uses the `TPMA_NV_ORDERLY` bit when defining the 2.0 counter, to minimize the number of NV write operations.

Whenever a new image is saved, the monotonic counter value is incremented using `TPM_IncrementCounter` or `TPM2_NV_Increment`, providing the counter handle; read out using `TPM_ReadCounter` or `TPM2_NV_Read`, since the value will not be reported to a third party; and included in a signature along with the hash of the image file, which is stored locally. When the hypervisor loads an image, the signature is checked against the image file and current monotonic counter value. In the event of a failure, the user is notified and given the option of booting or not booting the potentially problematic image, in order to prevent a malicious actor or software bug from making images unusable. An adversary who attempts to replace a software image with an old version, or replace the hypervisor's record of current software images, would fail the sanity checks later unless the adversary can also use the hypervisor's key to fake a signature. This is a particularly powerful technique if the primary concern is replacement of data when the machine is booted into an untrustworthy state, and combines well with Josè's plan of booting the hypervisor using the DRTM and using a TPM key constrained to the DRTM PCR values for signing the hypervisor's image data.

If there were more VMs on the machine than reasonable numbers of monotonic counters, José could use a more complex scheme he designed in which the hypervisor uses a single monotonic counter to track all updates. However, this would require the hypervisor to maintain a record of the current value of all images, and then both verify the old signatures and issue new signatures each time any VM image was updated. For the systems where he can, José would rather use more counters than add additional complexity to the hypervisor.

10.6　Storing extra keys in the TPM

Although most TPM keys are stored outside the TPM and loaded as needed, it is sometimes desirable to keep a key loaded inside the TPM indefinitely, even over reboots. This can be particularly useful when keys are being used by early boot firmware that may not have easy disk access, or if the same key is being used constantly. 2.0 generalizes this to any loadable object. This is called setting an object to *owner evict*: only the owner is capable of evicting the object. (2.0 also has a concept of *platform evict*, where only the platform key can be used to evict an object; this serves the same purpose, but is intended for use by boot-time firmware.)

To use this feature, the key (or other object) must already be loaded into the TPM, and loading it must not have required any PCR or locality states to have been met. This is to ensure that the owner evict feature cannot be used to bypass what would otherwise have been limitations on the use of the key resulting from constraints on any parent keys.[3]

In 1.2, the `TPM_KeyControlOwner` command is used on a loaded key. The command requires that the public portion of the key, not just the handle, be used to identify it, to prevent handle-substitution attacks from causing the wrong key to be affected. The same command is used both to set and unset the `TPM_KEY_CONTROL_OWNER_EVICT` bit; when the bit is set to true, the key will remain loaded in the TPM until the bit is unset or the TPM is cleared. The command will fail if the key or any parent keys would have required PCR or locality constraints to be loaded, to prevent the bypassing of constraints. It will also fail if there would be space for fewer than two keys to be loaded simultaneously afterwards, in order to ensure that all TPM commands can be run.

In 2.0, the `TPM2_EvictControl` command is used; it requires either owner or platform authorization. If called on a valid transient object, such as a loaded key which did not require state dependencies to be loaded, it will make the object persist in the TPM. If called on a valid persistent object, such as an evict controlled key, the object will be removed from persistent memory. In other words, the same `TPM2_EvictControl` command is used both to make an object remain in the TPM's memory, or to evict an object the command has already been called on. As with 1.2 TPMs, the command will fail to make an object persistent if there would be insufficient space afterwards to hold two transient objects, to ensure all commands can be run.

10.6.1 Persistent key user stories

Alice creates a primary storage key in the storage hierarchy of her 2.0, which will be used to protect other non-primary keys, and wants to ensure that it doesn't need to be recreated each time the machine reboots or when too many other keys are loaded. Alice uses `TPM2_EvictControl`, providing the handle returned by `TPM2_CreatePrimary`. The primary key will then remain available at that handle until the key is explicitly removed using `TPM2_EvictControl`, allowing software to create child keys without needing to recreate the primary storage key.

Bob wants to ensure that the user's storage and signing keys which have been centrally approved are available even if the user decides to delete unrecognized files from their machine's hard drive, or install a new OS. After Bob creates the keys and loads them, his script uses `TPM_KeyControlOwner` or `TPM2_EvictControl`, providing the owner authorization and key handle, to ensure that the keys stay loaded even through reboots. The handles will be sufficient to use the keys in the future, without any additional loading actions.

---

[3]As we discussed in Chapter 6, constraints on the key itself are verified on use, but constraints on the parent are verified when the child key is loaded.

10.7 Command auditing

In some cases, it may be valuable to track when certain high-sensitivity TPM commands are executed, and with what arguments. The command auditing functionality in the TPM, for TPMs which support it, is designed to support this functionality using the TPM as a trusted verifier. The TPM does not maintain the audit log itself, since such logs can become lengthy and the TPM has limited storage space; instead, the TPM maintains a digest, which (much like a PCR) provides a hash chain which is added to every time a new auditable command is run. It also maintains an audit counter, which tracks how many audit logs have been produced, in order to catch adversaries who might cause an audit to be missed. Software is expected to track the expected value of the digest and audit counter by creating associated logs.

When a command is audited in a 1.2 TPM, the TPM records two sets of information into the digest; you can think of this as performing two extend operations into a PCR. The first 'extend operation' adds a digest of the command input, including the command ordinal. The second adds a digest of the command output, including both the command ordinal and the return code (Figure 10.2). These digests are the same ones used to verify the integrity of command parameters.

In 2.0 TPMs, the audit digest is updated (extended) after the audited command completes. The new audit digest is the hash of the concatenation of the old digest value, the command parameter hash, and the response parameter hash. The hash algorithm used is specified with the same command used to add commands to the audited list, as discussed later in this section.

In TPM 1.2, the TPM_SetOrdinalAuditStatus command is used to either start auditing or stop auditing a given command (ordinal). It requires owner authorization. To retrieve the digest data, two commands are available: TPM_GetAuditDigest, and TPM_GetAuditDigestSigned. TPM_GetAudit

Command run	Audited?	Digest after	Audit counter
		000..000	8
TPM_Sign(*In*)	Y	$h(digest|$TPM_Sign(*In*))	8
		$h(digest|$TPM_Sign(*Out*))	8
TPM_Unbind(*In*)	N	*digest*	8
TPM_GetAuditDigest(*In*)	N	*digest*	8
TPM_GetAuditDigestSigned(*In*)	N	000...000	9

Figure 10.2 An illustration of an example 1.2 command audit sequence and how it affects the audit digest and counter. Here, TPM_Sign is on the command audit list and TPM_Unbind is not. Note that running one audited command causes the digest to change twice: once when the input is added, and a second time when the output is added. This is different from 2.0 command audits, where both input and output are included in a single digest change. The parameters here are abstracted for legibility; h represents a hash algorithm, and digest is the value of the audit digest before the command was run

Digest is purely informative: it provides the current digest value, along with the audit counter value indicating which audit log has been provided. TPM_Get AuditDigestSigned produces a signature over a more complex set of data, including a user-provided nonce, the audit digest, the audit counter value, and a digest indicating which ordinals are being audited. While any signing-capable key can be provided, an identity key is the only trustworthy choice for relying on the provided data. TPM_GetAuditDigestSigned is also the command used to reset the digest and increment the audit counter: if the boolean closeAudit argument is set to true, and an identity key is provided for signing the data, then the digest will be reset to zero and the audit counter will be incremented. It is important to note that the list of audited commands provided by TPM_GetAuditDigestSigned is the current state at the time the digest was created; there is no way for a remote party to verify when those audited commands may have changed. This means that the owner must be trusted by the verifier to maintain a reasonable audit log and not to hide commands. However, since the general expectation of a 1.2 TPM is that the owner has arbitrary control over what information about a TPM to reveal to an external party, this is within the expected usage model.

In TPM 2.0, the list of commands to be audited is updated using the TPM2_SetCommandCodeAuditStatus command, which requires either owner or platform authorization. This command can both add and remove commands to and from the current list to audit; it can also change the hash algorithm used for the audit digest. The TPM2_SetCommandCodeAuditStatus command is itself always audited.

The TPM2_GetCommandAuditDigest command is used to retrieve the audit digest. This command requires the privacy administrator's authorization. It returns the digest, the audit counter, a digest of the currently audited commands, and the current hash algorithm as part of an attestation structure. As with other attestation structures, a nonce and an optional signature scheme (for signing keys which one did not define during creation) are also accepted as arguments. This structure is signed using a provided key, which must be a signing key, and which should be a restricted signing key to avoid forgery of the TPM data structure; the signature is returned along with its associated structure. The attestation structure, if used with a nonce for freshness (see Section 7.2.4) and a restricted signing key to guarantee that the structure originated in a particular TPM, allows remote parties to verify software-produced audit logs of TPM activity. Using TPM2_GetCommandAuditDigest resets the digest and increments the audit counter, starting a new log.

Certain events can cause the audit digest to be reset outside a log delivery. These include changes to the audit hash algorithm and non-orderly shutdowns of the TPM. Audits use the TPM's NV storage, which means that extensive command auditing can cause NVRAM burnout, and overuse of the NV storage can cause audits to become unreliable. (See Section 8.7 for more information on NV storage.)

While it may at first glance seem advantageous for high-security use cases to audit all commands, there are definite exceptions. The commands used to establish transport sessions in 1.2 TPMs are prone to causing complications when tracking audit digests. Auditing the commands required to set up an authorization session is rarely going to add knowledge that the use of the authorization session does not. And the more commands that are audited, the more complicated it becomes to analyse the results to make sure that the behaviour is what's expected. In practice, limiting an audit to commands which are of particular interest to an auditor is the best choice.

10.7.1 Command audit user stories

Dana wants to track all documents that have been signed using a given accountant's key. Because the command audit record includes not only the command but the command and result parameters, Dana knows they can track the signed documents if they have a set of reference values to go along with the input. Dana does two things. First, she sets the command audit to include TPM2_Sign, using TPM2_SetCommandCodeAuditStatus. Dana also checks to see what other commands are being audited, using TPM2_GetCapability with the TPM_CAP_AUDIT_COMMANDS capability, a property parameter of zero, and a property count of 300, to be certain of retrieving the entire set. Dana will not clear any of these audited commands; if they're recorded by default, she thinks they might as well be monitored. Dana then modifies the TPM software stack code to provide an on-disk audit log of the command parameters and response parameters for each executed command that should be audited. Monthly, a script will run to verify the command audit on each machine. The parameter log will be sent along with the results from TPM2_GetCommandAuditDigest to the server, which will verify the logs against the signed digest and record a list of all hashes signed. The list of hashes can be correlated with a list of expected signed documents, so discrepancies can be noted and tracked down during audits.

Fatima wants to ensure that no unexpected changes are made to the NVRAM used to store the SecureCorp VPN server and DNS server public keys. She gets the privacy administrator authentication information from IT security, then uses TPM2_SetCommandCodeAuditStatus to change the set of monitored commands. Since no one else at SecureCorp is using the command audits or NVRAM, Fatima sets the hash algorithm to SHA-256, the commands to be audited to TPM2_NV_Write and TPM2_NV_DefineSpace, and the list of commands not to be audited to all other commands. This will limit the audits to only the commands which could be used to erase or change the reference keys, as well as the TPM2_SetCommandCodeAuditStatus command. Periodically, the VPN server will challenge the VPN client to produce a current audit for a machine, using the TPM2_GetCommandAuditDigest command. The central server will verify that the digest contains no unexpected entries, which in this case should mean any not connected to a known key rotation, and that the audit counter is the expected value for the machine, showing that no audits have been missed.

10.8 Field upgrades

Some TPMs may support field upgrades to firmware. These commands are optional, but where supported, allow the TPM's internal code to be upgraded in the event of a patch or the release of additional functionality. (For example, a 2.0 TPM might take a firmware upgrade to support additional cryptographic algorithms.)

1.2 field upgrades use the TPM_FieldUpgrade command; this command is manufacturer-specific, and the only constant is that it requires owner authorization.

In 2.0 TPMs, TPM2_FieldUpgradeStart is used to validate the firmware signature from the manufacturer, and confirm that the platform policy authorization has been provided. The key to verify the signature against is a loaded public key; the command requires platform authorization, and may also require physical presence. Once the upgrade has been confirmed, the TPM2_FieldUpgradeData command is used to provide blocks of data until the complete sequence that matches the original signature has been provided. No authorization is required for the TPM2_FieldUpgradeData command, since each block of data must correspond to the previously provided data and the original signed digest. TPM internal data, including primary seeds, hierarchy authorization policies and values, persistent objects, NV storage, and clock information, are preserved through a firmware update. The TPM2_FirmwareRead command can be used to retrieve the currently installed firmware, in a format which can be provided back to the TPM as a field upgrade in the event of a failure.

10.9   1.2-exclusive features

10.9.1   Temporarily deactivating the TPM

In some use cases, primarily focussed on maintaining user privacy, it may be desirable to give a user of a machine a way to temporarily deactivate the TPM without requiring that they be capable of successfully turning it back on again in the BIOS. The TPM *operator authorization* exists for this purpose. It can be set at any time, with no authorization, if someone has asserted physical presence on that boot of the machine, using the TPM_SetOperatorAuth command. The operator authorization is used for only one command: TPM_SetTempDeactivated, which can also be executed any time that physical presence has been asserted. When TPM_SetTempDeactivated is used, the TPM is deactivated until the next boot.

10.9.2   Maintenance archives

A feature manufacturers may choose to support in 1.2 TPMs is the creation of a maintenance archive. Maintenance archives are designed to provide backup capabilities for data protected by the TPM. When a maintenance archive is created, it stores the TPM's SRK in an encrypted form, to be decrypted on a destination TPM. Maintenance archives are the only way in which SRKs can ever leave the TPM, and the only way to provide comprehensive backup for lost or destroyed hardware. Maintenance archives are also potentially dangerous if used carelessly, since they effectively allow the duplication of every key except the EK. If maintenance archives are supported on a given TPM, the TPM will also support the TPM_KillMaintenanceFeature command, which will prevent archives from being created until the TPM is next cleared.

Maintenance archives require the active cooperation of the TPM or platform manufacturer. The manufacturer is responsible for injecting a permanent public key, which will be used along with the owner authorization or a new TPM-created random value to protect the archive data. The archive can only be retrieved if the owner of the associated private key decrypts it and delivers it to a new destination, and that destination either shares the same owner authorization or knows the random value. Normally, the archive key injected into the TPM would belong to the TPM or platform manufacturer, although it is conceivable that very large enterprises might be able to work with a manufacturer to establish an enterprise archive key. This requirement of manufacturer cooperation in the archive process is one reason maintenance archive support is rare.

If the TPM supports maintenance archives, `TPM_CreateMaintenance Archive` is used to create an archive; this command requires owner authorization, and takes a boolean argument which determines whether owner authorization (if false) or a random value (if true) will be used to protect the data. If random values are used, the TPM's RNG will be used to generate random data; either a 198-bit random number or an equivalent-length pseudo-random value generated from the owner authorization will be XORed with the secret archive data before being encrypted to the manufacturer's archive public key. The random value, if one is created, is returned along with the encrypted archive. On a receiving TPM, a decrypted archive from a manufacturer is loaded using the `TPM_LoadMaintenanceArchive` command; this also requires owner authorization. Unlike most TPM commands, the one for loading a maintenance archive does not have a fully defined command interface. It includes an unknown number of vendor-specific parameters, which must at a minimum include a mechanism for inputting random data to be used to decrypt archives. Maintenance archives encrypted using owner authorization can be loaded only on TPMs with the same owner authorization. Loading the archive will overwrite the new TPM's SRK, change the owner authorization to the original TPM's authorization value, and set the TPM's internal 'proof' value so that data created on the original TPM will be recognized on the new TPM. Note that loading a maintenance archive effectively clears the new TPM, in terms of its effect on accessing previously created data, and replaces it with the ability to access the old TPM's data.

10.9.2.1   Maintenance archive user stories

Charlie would like to ensure that in the event of a hardware failure or machine loss, he can still decrypt all of the data created on his TPM. He is lucky enough to have a TPM which provides the maintenance archive features, and whose manufacturer provides a public key and support for archive retrieval. Charlie uses `TPM_CreateMaintenanceArchive`, using the owner authorization value so that he doesn't have another secret to potentially lose; after all, he hopes to never use the archive, and if he does have to it may not be for several years. He stores the maintenance archive in his off-line backups. In the event that his equipment fails, is lost, or is destroyed, Charlie will contact his manufacturer and request that the archive be transferred to the TPM on a newly purchased machine. The manufacturer will request certification of the new TPM, showing that it is a legitimate TPM from the same manufacturer, and will then provide Charlie with a decrypted version of the archive, containing the old TPM's SRK and internal data XORed with a pseudo-random number seeded from the old TPM's owner authorization.[4] Charlie uses `TPM_LoadMaintenanceArchive` on his new machine to replace the current SRK with the SRK from the old TPM; this allows Charlie to load his disk backups and retrieve all of his TPM-encrypted secrets.

10.9.3 Delegation

Because so many unrelated capabilities are assigned to the TPM owner, the 1.2 specification provides for *delegation* capability, in which a new authorization value (password) is created to allow a non-owner entity to act as though they were the owner when performing specific actions. Delegation is imperfect; among other problems, because the TPM has no concept of identity beyond authorization values, the owner must know the authorization value being delegated to. Delegation is also complicated, requiring multiple commands to be run to establish even a single-privilege delegation, and using layered data structures whose purpose is not intuitive. It was thus removed in 2.0, since the multiple key hierarchies serve a similar purpose.

Delegation can be a powerful tool in certain situations, particularly in an enterprise context where an IT department may be the owner for a TPM and want to allow the user limited permissions (such as the ability to create identity keys) or give trusted software the ability to read sensitive data (such as certain capabilities, which require owner authorization). It can also be used to give a key a secondary authorization value which can be used to authorize only certain commands.

The most complicated part of delegation is setting it up in the first place. This requires the use of the `TPM_Delegate_Manage` command to set up a *family table* inside the TPM. Each delegation is created as an entry in one of these families, and a delegation family can be enabled or disabled as a group. Families have an identity, and the `TPM_Delegate_Manage` command performs a variety of operations on them, based on the operation argument passed in. `TPM_FAMILY_CREATE` creates a new family, to which we can then assign delegation permissions. Families are used to group sets of delegations, so that they can easily be invalidated together, or so that old delegations can easily be declared obsolete and replaced simultaneously. `TPM_FAMILY_ENABLE` enables or disables a family's delegation permissions. `TPM_FAMILY_INVALIDATE` eliminates a family and all of its delegation permissions. `TPM_FAMILY_ADMIN` is used to lock a given family, preventing changes to that family's delegation permissions until the next TPM clear.

The `TPM_Delegate_CreateOwnerDelegation` command is the most powerful and flexible of the delegation commands; it allows the TPM owner to delegate the ability to execute a single TPM command requiring owner authorization to another authorization value. Note that this is a single command in the sense of a

---

[4]Manufacturer procedures here are hypothetical, but this is an example of the sort of process a manufacturer might follow. The owner authorization or random value is the TPM owner's secret, preventing unauthorized parties from using the manufacturer to retrieve the archive contents.

Structure tag constant: "TPM_TAG_DELEGATE_PUBLIC"
Delegate label: (TPM_DELEGATE_LABEL)
Constraints on delegation use: TPM_PCR_INFO_SHORT structure / NULL <table><tr><td>See TPM_PCR_INFO_SHORT diagram</td></tr></table>
Permissions this delegation allows: TPM_DELEGATIONS <table><tr><td>Structure tag constant: 'TPM_TAG_DELEGATIONS'</td></tr><tr><td>TPM_DEL_OWNER_BITS or TPM_DEL_KEY_BITS</td></tr><tr><td>Permissions: UINT32 bit field indicating commands</td></tr><tr><td>0 (UINT32, reserved for future use)</td></tr></table>
Family this delegation is part of (TPM_FAMILY_ID)
Verification counter for the family at the time of creation

Figure 10.3   The TPM_DELEGATE_PUBLIC data structure, used by
TPM_Delegate_CreateOwnerDelegation and
TPM_Delegate_CreateKeyDelegation. The
TPM_PCR_INFO_SHORT diagram can be found in Figure 10.4

single command ordinal (such as TPM_MakeIdentity or TPM_OwnerClear) rather than a single execution of a command. Each time the TPM_Delegate_ CreateOwnerDelegation command is run, the owner has the option to incre-ment a validation counter which will invalidate all previous delegations for that family and require delegation permissions for the family to be individually re-approved by the owner. The permissions to be delegated are passed in using a TPM_DELEGATE_PUBLIC data structure (Figure 10.3), which itself contains a TPM_DELEGATIONS structure defining the commands allowed. The commands allowed are selected using a bitmap defined in a reference table. (20.2.1 in the TPM 1.2 Structures specification for owner delegatable commands, 20.2.3 for key delegat-able commands. See Section 11.5.2 on page 276 for where to find the specification.) TPM_Delegate_CreateOwnerDelegation returns a delegation blob, which I'll explain how to use shortly.

Delegation can also be used outside an owner context, although it would be even more unusual. Keys with multiple authorization values can be supported in 1.2 TPMs using the TPM_Delegate_CreateKeyDelegation command, which allows someone with a loaded key's authorization information to set a new valid authorization value that can also be used for the key in question. A TPM owner can also create a key that works only on specific commands when a given authorization value is provided; for example, if an owner wanted to give a user the ability to use an identity key to sign quotes but not to certify new TPM keys, they could create a key delegation allowing only the TPM_Quote2 command to be used when a particular password is used

TPM_PCR_INFO_SHORT structure:

PCR selection to be included in digest
Locality selection
Digest of PCR values at selected indexes

Figure 10.4   The structure of the TPM_PCR_INFO_SHORT *data structure*

to authorize the key. As with the TPM_Delegate_CreateOwnerDelegation command, this returns a delegation blob structure.

Delegations are not actually functional until the blob returned by either of the delegation creation commands is loaded into the TPM. Because the TPM has limited internal storage, only a limited number of simultaneous delegations are allowed to be active; however, any number of delegation blobs can exist and be loaded as needed, with a couple of caveats. First, loading the delegation requires owner authorization; a user with delegated privileges can't simply provide the blob and their authorization value to get access to the delegated commands. Secondly, the delegation lock created for a given family by TPM_Delegate_Manage and TPM_FAMILY_ADMIN also prevents any new delegation blobs for that family being loaded. This is particularly relevant because delegation blobs are not loaded generically, like keys, with a handle returned by the TPM. They're loaded into user-specified rows in an internal delegate table, and future loads into the same row will overwrite the previous data. Loading a delegation blob for a particular family, locking the family, and then overwriting that delegate table entry will effectively prevent the family from being used; a new family with the same purpose would need to be created. Each table row has its own verification value, which is based on the family verification value at the time that the delegation was loaded by the owner. These verification values are used to make both blobs and existing loading delegations obsolete; the owner can increment the family verification value using TPM_Delegate_CreateOwnerDelegation, at which point any blob with an older value will be rejected. Individual blobs and delegate table rows can be updated by the owner using TPM_Delegate_UpdateVerification, allowing them to be used after a value change.

Delegation blobs are loaded using the owner-authorized TPM_Delegate_ LoadOwnerDelegation command. This command can itself be delegated, but delegated owner permissions can only be used to load blobs from the same family as the delegated user. In addition to the delegation blob and authorization, the caller supplies the index into the delegate table that the delegation should be written to. The public delegation and family table contents (i.e. everything but the authorization values) can be read out by any TPM user with the TPM_Delegate_ReadTable command, which takes no arguments and returns an array of family table entries, and another array of delegate table indexes and the associated TPM_DELEGATE_PUBLIC structures. The delegate table is non-volatile; it will be reset when the TPM is cleared, but not on reboots.

Once a delegation blob has been loaded by the owner, it can be used for authorization for as long as the verification index is valid. (Incrementation of the index for a family can be used to rapidly invalidate large numbers of delegations.) This requires the use of a special kind of authorization session (see Section 6.10), TPM_DSAP, which takes a (loaded) delegation blob and associates it with either the owner or a given key. For as long as the authorization session is valid, a user can provide the alternative authorization value specified in the delegation blob to commands, and the command will be allowed if the blob indicated that it should be. DSAP sessions are terminated automatically if any command using the session returns an error, or if a number of delegation-related or owner-related commands are run; it can also be explicitly terminated using any of the authorization session termination commands.

For a convenience, TPMs that support delegation provide the TPM_Delegate_VerifyDelegation command. This command is used to determine whether a delegation blob is valid; anyone can run it, as there are no effects on the internal TPM state. The command checks the validity of the family as well as the verification value and blob integrity.

10.9.3.1   Delegation user stories

Lemar's government agency is relying on the integrity of data stored in the TPM's NVRAM, and wants to minimize the number of people who have access to the data. However, the agency also wants its employees to be able to freely create new cryptographic identities for their machine. Employees may be involved in a number of different projects that want cryptographic signatures but not a correlatable identity. Normally, creating new AIKs in 1.2 TPMs is an owner privilege; however, employees should not have the owner-level access to the NVRAM contents. Instead, Lemar sets up high-security owner passwords on each machine, which will be kept securely off-line, and establishes a set of delegation authorizations authorized to create identity keys. He uses TPM_Delegate_Manage with the TPM_FAMILY_CREATE operation to create a new family table. Next, he uses TPM_Delegate_CreateOwnerDelegation to create a secondary authorization value and select the owner commands he'd like it to allow: TPM_MakeIdentity, TPM_ActivateIdentity, and TPM_ReadPubek, which cover everything his users should need to create new identity keys and get them certified. He then runs TPM_Delegate_LoadOwnerDelegation, using his owner authorization, to load the resulting delegation blob into the delegate table. The user of each machine is provided with the secondary authorization value, rather than the owner authorization value; the value can be used for those three commands in place of the owner authorization. The users' software is configured to use the delegation-specific authorization sessions and supply the delegation blob as needed.

10.9.4   Tickstamps

Tickstamps are 1.2 TPMs' primitive clock replacement. The idea behind the tick counter is simple: each TPM, when powered on, produces an oscillating 'tick' at a rate that will be reliable for a given TPM. So TPM A may tick 30 times per second, and TPM B from the same manufacturer 50; but the tick rate will always be the same for TPM A, allowing ticks to be calibrated with external clocks. When the machine reboots, the TPM will usually do two things: create a random value that represents the current **tick session**, and reset the tick counter to a random value which will then increment every time the TPM ticks. Tickstamps can be signed with an identity key in combination with a nonce, producing a remotely verifiable relative 'time' for a given system. This can be useful for determining the time a given operation took on a remote system without network delays coming into consideration, if the TPM ticks can be calibrated.

Although the current tickstamp can be retrieved using the TPM_GetTicks command, that command provides an unauthenticated record of the tickstamp and is useful for local reference only. The TPM_TickStampBlob command is designed to allow remote verification of the tickstamp. It requires a key handle for a signing-capable key, which should always be an identity key, and takes both a nonce and a digest which will be included in the signed output structure. It returns the signature over a data structure incorporating the tickstamp, nonce, and digest; however, only the tickstamp and signature are returned, requiring the verifier to reconstruct the data structure to confirm the signature. This functionality allows a remote verifier to use a nonce-based challenge–response system to establish a clock equivalence for a given TPM. In addition, the inclusion of the digest allows a log file, for example, to be correlated with both a verifier-provided nonce and a locally-produced timing tick. Once a basic timing equivalence has been established, a sequence of signed tickstamp blobs with digests can provide evidence about a file's presence on-system between remote attestations, as well.

It is worth noting that although the tick session and tick counter usually reset on reboot, they are not guaranteed to do so. Tickstamps cannot be used as reliable reboot detectors.

10.9.4.1 Tickstamp user stories

Kameko would like to use some timing-based attestation techniques to measure software on her machines and ensure that they are working correctly. Timing-based attestation uses detailed knowledge of a processor, environment, and algorithm execution time to produce a result which will return in the expected time frame only if it is following the known code path; any forged measurements will take longer to compute than the original algorithm required. Unfortunately, the network connection between her central audit server and the machines being measured is lossy and unreliable, and the timing-based attestation technique she's using requires that she get a reasonably precise measurement of how long the software takes to execute on the measured machine. The network variability will dwarf any differences she'd like to see. Instead, Kameko has her software run TPM_TickStampBlob before and after the execution of the timing-based attestation code, and send both signed blobs back to the audit server along with the attestation results. In order to prevent an adversary on the machine from artificially shortening the execution time reported, Kameko has the audit server supply a nonce which is fed directly into the first tickstamp and the attestation code, but uses a hash of the output of the attestation code (which includes the nonce) for the second tickstamp 'nonce'. This ensures that an adversary can't pre-compute the second tickstamp. If Kameko has previously calibrated the ticks from this TPM with her standard clock, she can use the paired before and after tickstamps to determine the maximum time it could have taken for the remote algorithm to run.

Lamar would like to use a TPM in combination with a smartcard reader, to produce both machine and user attestations. Unfortunately, since there is no direct hardware connection between the smartcard reader and the TPM, the TPM has no way of verifying that the reader is on the same device as the TPM. Lamar is concerned about adversaries using one compromised machine with a smartcard reader and valid card to fake legitimate user activity on other compromised machines and gain access to sensitive data by forwarding challenges and responses to the remote machine with the valid card. While this attack can't be easily prevented, Lamar can bracket the smartcard authentication with two `TPM_TickStampBlob` operations, in the same way as Kameko did. This makes it easier to detect unexpected delays, which might be caused by an adversary forwarding data between machines, and alert IT security personnel.

10.10 2.0-exclusive features

10.10.1 Cryptographic primitives

2.0 TPMs offer a comprehensive set of cryptographic primitive operations. We've discussed many of these previously in the book, but not all, and it's worth at least briefly mentioning them again, since this is one of the most powerful new features in TPM 2.0. These primitives allow the TPM to be used as a true secure cryptographic coprocessor, albeit one which is not very fast. Primitives are available for both symmetric and asymmetric operations, and for a range of supported algorithms.

Cryptographic primitives include:

TPM2_EncryptDecrypt: This command performs symmetric encryption or decryption, depending on a provided flag. It is usable with any symmetric algorithm supported by your TPM.

TPM2_RSA_Encrypt: This command requires that the public portion of an RSA key be loaded into the TPM, using the `TPM2_LoadExternal` command. If the key handle does not specify a padding scheme, one can be selected with this command, from the options of OAEP, RSAES, or no padding.[5] An optional label can be included as part of the padding. The message length is limited depending on the padding scheme chosen; it can be no longer than the RSA public key, and may need to be smaller. It will produce encrypted data with no custom TPM formatting.

TPM2_RSA_Decrypt: This command performs a straightforward RSA decryption using a loaded key, and returns the unencrypted data. As with the encryption

[5]Padding is used to determine how a message is prepared for encryption. The padding schemes are defined in IETF RFC 3447; OAEP is defined in section 7.1, and RSAES in section 7.2.

operation, if the key in question does not specify a padding scheme, the user must select one.

TPM2_ECDH_KeyGen: This command, part of an elliptic curve Diffie–Helman key exchange, creates an ephemeral key pair, based on the parameters of a loaded public ECC key. The private portion of the key does not need to be loaded to run the command. It returns a public point, to be sent to the remote party whose public key was used, and a Z point, which will be the shared secret.

TPM2_ECDH_ZGen: This command, the second half of an elliptic curve Diffie–Helman key exchange, takes a public point and a loaded ECC key with the unrestricted decrypt attributes. It will return the Z point, which is the shared secret.

TPM2_EC_Ephemeral: This command creates a single-use ECC key for use in two-phase key exchange protocols in combination with TPM2_ZGen_2Phase. It takes information about an ECC curve, and outputs the ephemeral key's public key and a counter usable to regenerate the ephemeral key.

TPM2_ZGen_2Phase: This command takes another party's long-term and ephemeral public keys, a key exchange scheme to use, and a counter from a previous call to TPM2_EC_Ephemeral. It returns an appropriate key based on the selected exchange scheme.

TPM2_ECC_Parameters: This command is used to retrieve the parameters of an elliptic curve known to the TPM. The TCG-assigned curve ID is used to identify the curve.[6] This is particularly useful in cases where TPM ECC cryptography is being used to communicate with non-TPM systems. The mandatory set of curves for PC 2.0 TPMs is NIST P-256 (TPM_ECC_NIST_P256) and BN P-256 (TPM_ECC_BN_P256), although manufacturers may include additional curves.

There are also several functions, as discussed briefly in Section 7.2.3.2, which let the TPM create hashes and HMACs. In the case of hashes, there is no functional difference between a hash created by the TPM itself and one created by software outside the TPM; however, a restricted signing key can be used only to sign hashes created by the TPM, in order to prevent an adversary from forging TPM responses such as quotes or certificates.

TPM2_Hash: Takes data up to the maximum size of the TPM's input buffer, and hashes it according to the selected hash algorithm. (e.g. TPM_ALG_SHA256.) Also takes a hierarchy that will be used for a ticket showing that the resulting hash was not created from data that imitates a TPM data structure; TPM_RH_NULL indicates that no ticket is desired. Will return the hash and, if applicable, the ticket. The hierarchy is used to determine which TPM internal proof value will be included in the ticket, as described later in this section.

TPM2_HMAC: Takes the handle of a non-restricted symmetric signing key (type TPM_ALG_KEYEDHASH, sign attribute set, restricted attribute not set), a buffer of data up to the maximum size the TPM will accept, and a hash algorithm to use to create the HMAC if the key does not specify one. Returns the appropriate HMAC.

---

[6]There are a number of standard elliptic curves used in ECC, defined by public parameters.

The sequence commands are provided to support use cases where the data being hashed or HMACed is longer than the TPM's input buffer. TPMs are required to support a buffer size of at least 1024 bits, but individual TPMs may have larger capacity. In the sequence commands, data is provided to the TPM in chunks using a special sequence handle with its own authorization value. When all data has been provided, the sequence completes and returns the final value to the user. Once complete, sequences are no longer stored in the TPM; partial sequences cannot be held inside the TPM for future reuse.

In addition to normal hash and HMAC sequences, whose functionality adds up to much the same effect as the simple TPM2_Hash and TPM2_HMAC commands, a third sequence type also exists: event sequences. Event sequences are designed to support the use of multiple PCR banks. As discussed in Section 9.2.5, 2.0 TPMs have parallel sets of PCRs, each of which uses a different hash algorithm. This is intended to support legacy applications expecting SHA-1 PCR values and newer applications which want to use the more secure SHA-256, or other algorithms that their TPM may support. It is therefore convenient to have a method for simultaneously calculating the expected values which would be found in each bank given the same initial input. It can also be convenient to have a simple method to calculate hashes of all appropriate lengths which can be extended into each PCR bank. Event sequences serve this purpose.

TPM2_HMAC_Start: This command is used to create HMACs for data longer than the TPM's maximum input buffer. Unlike TPM2_HMAC, no data is provided to this command; instead, an authorization value is provided which will authorize later use of the HMAC sequence. If the hash algorithm provided is TPM_ALG_NULL, the TPM will begin an event sequence (see above). It returns a sequence handle to be provided to TPM2_SequenceUpdate or TPM2_SequenceComplete.

TPM2_HashSequenceStart: This command is used to create hashes for data longer than the TPM's maximum input buffer. It takes only the hash algorithm to use and an authorization value which will authorize later use of the sequence; the data and hierarchy to use for a ticket will be specified in later commands. It returns a sequence handle to be provided to TPM2_SequenceUpdate or TPM2_SequenceComplete. TPM2_SequenceUpdate.

TPM2_SequenceUpdate: This takes a sequence handle (which should be associated with an authorization session) and buffer of data to be added to the hash or HMAC in progress. It returns only a success or failure code. It can be run any number of times on a sequence.

TPM2_SequenceComplete: This takes a sequence handle and a final buffer of data to add to a sequence, along with a hierarchy value to be used for validation tickets if the sequence is a hash sequence. It returns the resulting digest from the complete sequence, and a validation ticket if applicable. For HMAC sequences, this is a NULL ticket.

TPM2_EventSequenceComplete: This command takes a sequences handle, a final buffer of data to add to a sequence, and the handle (index) of a PCR which will be extended with the event data. This will cause the selected PCR index to be extended in all banks the TPM supports. Using `TPM_RH_NULL` as the PCR handle will cause it to not extend any PCRs. It returns a list of digest values corresponding to the sequence input, one for each PCR bank.

Commands that create hashes take a somewhat unexpected argument: a hierarchy. Hierarchies are used to create part of the ticket which the hash commands return to prove (if applicable) that a given set of data can be signed by a restricted signing key. Restricted signing keys will not sign any data which could be mistaken for legitimate TPM output. The hierarchy is used to determine which hierarchy proof value is included in the ticket. The proof value just confirms that a ticket was produced by the same TPM; however, different proof values are associated with each hierarchy, and are reset when the equivalent hierarchy primary seeds are erased. In general, unless you are changing seeds or clearing the TPM regularly, the choice of hierarchy isn't particularly relevant. There are two cases where it *is* relevant. The first is that if you use the endorsement hierarchy, hashes produced by the TPM can still use the same tickets to prove that they can be safely signed by a restructured signing key, even if the TPM is cleared, resulting in a reset of the owner hierarchy proof. The second is that if you aren't planning on having the hash signed with a restricted signing key, you can skip the ticket entirely and instead use `TPM_RH_NULL` as your input hierarchy. When the null hierarchy is passed in, the returned ticket will also be NULL.

It's worth noting that if the sequence commands are used for either creating a digest or making an HMAC, the interim state is stored inside the TPM until the sequence is complete or the machine is rebooted. This means that there is a limited number of storage spaces in the TPM for such ongoing sequences. These *sequence contexts* have handles, which are created by the sequence start command and are provided to the later commands. The TPM allows these contexts to be saved and restored, using the `TPM2_ContextSave` and `TPM2_ContextLoad` commands; while this is primarily useful for those writing drivers, who may wish to manage the TPM's internal space, it can also be used to replay a partial sequence as long as the replaying party has appropriate authorization permissions. In unusual cases where long sequences with the same initial data are being hashed repeatedly, small increases in speed may be achievable by saving a sequence context containing the common data and reloading it, instead of rerunning the entire hash sequence from the beginning.

10.10.2   Clocks and attesting to local time

2.0 TPMs have a more sophisticated idea of time than 1.2 TPMs, although the TPM's clock is nothing like a normal computer clock. 2.0 TPMs have two different internal timing mechanisms: a timer which resets on any system startup and measures the time since boot (called *Time*), and a clock which works something like the 1.2 tick counter or a monotonic counter, providing a universal sense of 'time' that can (mostly) only advance (called *Clock*). 2.0 also solves one of the major missing information problems of 1.2 TPMs by providing two counters which track relevant system events: *resetCount*, which is incremented whenever the TPM starts up cleanly (a system reset, rather than a suspend-resume cycle), and *restartCount*, which increments whenever other events that may cause time discontinuities to occur, such as suspends and resumes or DRTM executions (see Section 9.1.3). *resetCount* is zeroed only when the TPM is cleared, but `restartCount` is zeroed on a full system reset event as well.

Clocks can be used as part of attestations, to allow a remote party to verify a system time when some action took place or to correlate an external interaction with system time. This allows for both timing-based attestations, as discussed earlier in Section 10.9.4.1, and for more routine functionality, such as tying system audits or program output to a particular point in time.

Clocks can also be used as part of Enhanced Authorization policies (see Section 6.13.3), to gate access to particular resources to a given time window according to the internal timer, clock, or counter. This allows policies such as 'Allow access to this key only for the next hour' or 'This data can be decrypted only during the next machine boot cycle'.

Because the current value of *Clock* is maintained in volatile storage and only intermittently written to NVRAM to prevent excessive writes causing burnout, disorderly shutdowns (where the TPM loses power without going through a full shutdown operation) may cause the clock to roll back for up to an hour. The *Safe* flag, provided in all time data structures, indicates whether the TPM guarantees that the current clock value is not a repeat of a previous value.

There are two commands, new to TPM 2.0, that can adjust clock behaviour. Both require either owner or platform authorization. One is `TPM2_Clock RateAdjust`, which changes the rate at which *Clock* and `Time` increment using pre-defined abstract change rates, as defined in Figure 10.5. The rate of change cannot be set to be outside the frequency tolerance set by the manufacturer; at worst, this should be within 15% of real time. The intent of this command is to allow the system owner to tweak the TPM's internal clock speed to match real time. It is important to note that these clock adjustments may not persist across TPM power cycles. If your TPM clock speed is off, the expectation is that the system will automatically adjust it on each boot.

The other clock adjustment command is `TPM2_ClockSet`, which advances *Clock*'s value to an arbitrary new time. The new time cannot be before the current

Name	Value	Comments
TPM_CLOCK_COARSE_SLOWER	−3	Slow the *Clock* update rate by one coarse adjustment step.
TPM_CLOCK_MEDIUM_SLOWER	−2	Slow the *Clock* update rate by one medium adjustment step.
TPM_CLOCK_FINE_SLOWER	−1	Slow the *Clock* update rate by one fine adjustment step.
TPM_CLOCK_NO_CHANGE	0	No change to the *Clock* update rate.
TPM_CLOCK_FINE_FASTER	1	Speed the *Clock* update rate by one fine adjustment step.
TPM_CLOCK_MEDIUM_FASTER	2	Speed the *Clock* update rate by one medium adjustment step.
TPM_CLOCK_COARSE_FASTER	3	Speed the *Clock* update rate by one coarse adjustment step.

Figure 10.5   The available clock adjustment constants in TPM 2.0

time, and cannot be so large that it triggers overflow prevention protections.[7] The intent of TPM2_ClockSet is that it will be used to catch the TPM up on whatever time has passed while the TPM was powered off.

The TPM2_ReadClock command retrieves the current time information, including *Time*, *Clock*, and the reset and restart counters. This command provides no authentication; it is solely for informational purposes, and intended to provide convenient functionality for on-system software.

TPM2_GetTime, in contrast, is designed to attest to the current time and reboot counters for the use of a remote party. A nonce or other user data is provided, along with the necessary signing key (a restricted signing key should be used, since a TPM data structure is being created) and the Privacy Administrator's authorization. The Privacy Administrator's authorization is required because the information included in the response is considered sensitive. The signed data structure which is returned includes not only *Time*, *Clock*, *resetCount*, *restartCount*, and the *Safe* flag, but also the firmware version.

Unusually, the exact data returned will vary depending on which hierarchy the provided signing key is in (see Section 3.2.2), owing to a duplication of the firmware and time information within the attestation data structure. A signing key in the endorsement or platform hierarchy will provide plaintext information about the platform firmware and system time in both places in the data structure. A signing key in the storage hierarchy or no hierarchy will use standard obfuscated values in the primary data structure and plaintext values in the interior data structure. This allows the Privacy Administrator to decide which recipients should be able to correlate the plaintext content with the standard, obfuscated information provided in most attestation data structures.

---

[7]The maximum value *Clock* can be set to would prevent a clock from overflowing to zero for several thousand years, even at advancement rates noticeably faster than real time. Because this is safely over the expected lifetime of the TPM, software should not need to take precautions against TPM clock overflow.

Chapter 11
Software, specifications, and more: Where to find other TPM resources

This book is designed as an introductory text to the world of TPMs and trusted computing, but it's far from the whole story. In this chapter, we'll discuss where to find additional resources of many kinds. These resources include software libraries to support use of the TPM, which are useful for implementing simple applications and generally giving TPM use a try; books and other materials that will help you learn more about related topics; and, for those who need to delve deeper, the specifications themselves, with an account of how to get the most out of them.

Because so many of the resources referred to here are online, there is a high probability that some of the links will become obsolete at some point during the lifetime of this book. Updated links, along with other errata and additional content, will be available at http://digital-library.theiet.org/content/books/pc/pbpc013e.

11.1 1.2 Programming tools

11.1.1 1.2 Trusted/TCG software stacks (TSS)

These interfaces are designed to be compliant with the TCG 1.2 TSS standards; they are sometimes referred to as Trusted Software Stacks (TSS), sometimes as TCG Software Stacks. They implement the TSS standard discussed in detail in Section 11.5.1, providing both a standardized API and a back end support stack which provides partially automated handling of TPM sessions, keys, and other details that may otherwise be annoying to implement. The code provided in the 1.2 TSS examples throughout the book should be supported in any standards-compatible TSS implementation.

For Linux systems, the open-source TrouSerS TSS is available in the vast majority of distributions, although the packages required vary. In all cases, the trousers package must be installed. You will usually additionally want either the trousers-devel(Red Hat), trousers-dbg (Debian) or libtspi-dev package (Ubuntu), which contain useful header files, debugging symbols, and documentation for the TSS; you can usually find these in /usr/include/tss. The webpage for the TrouSerS project, which is not as well maintained as the software, can be found at http://trousers.sourceforge.net; while out of date at the time of writing, it still provides links to some useful documentation.

Windows TSS support is less well developed, but there are multiple projects providing ports of the Linux TrouSerS code to Windows, including TORSEC (http://security.polito.it/trusted-computing/trousers-for-windows/) and the more recently updated TrouSerS for Windows sourceforge project (http://sourceforge.net/projects/trouserswin).

The NTRU TSS is a commercially available and supported 1.2 TSS for Windows and Linux. It is, at the time of writing, not sold individually to users, and instead is licensed in bulk to software vendors and manufacturers. Some Windows systems which come with manufacturer-provided TPM support software may have one already installed. As of the end of 2015, more information can be found at https://www.securityinnovation.com/products/encryption-libraries/tss.html.

As mentioned in Chapter 5, Windows users planning on using code built using a TSS implementation should avoid using the integrated Windows services to take ownership of their TPM, as the resulting owner password cannot be easily used in TSS applications due to poorly documented differences in password encoding.

11.1.2   Microsoft's TBS

Microsoft provided a TBS interface to 1.2 TPMs starting in their Vista and Windows 2008 OSes. This interface is not actually a standard TSS API; instead, it provides a centralized interface to submit commands directly to the TPM, and must be used in conjunction with the TPM specification (Section 11.5.2). More information should be available at https://www.securityinnovation.com/products/tss.

It is important to note that the TBS is not a simple pass-through interface to the hardware; it does make some modifications to data passing through it. Reading the documentation in detail before using it is highly recommended.

11.2   2.0 Programming tools

While the TCG has two defined APIs for the 2.0 TSS at the time of this writing, they are not yet in common use, and there are no commercially available implementations of the TCG specifications discussed in Section 11.6. However, some independent efforts have produced helpful tools for those programming for 2.0 TPMs.

11.2.1   IBM TSS 2.0

Ken Goldman, one of the primary authors of the original 1.2 TSS implementation, has also produced an early TSS for TPM 2.0, available at http://sourceforge.net/projects/ibmtpm20tss/. Although it is called a TSS, it does not provide the TCG's published APIs; it is similar in some ways to the TCG's System API, but is much simpler for the user. The IBM TSS 2.0 provides a largely invisible interface to the 2.0 TPM which closely resembles the specification while handling the annoying details of session management and data structure marshalling internally.

It works on Windows and Linux, and with both hardware TPMs and simulators. At the time of writing, it is being actively developed, but already offers a comprehensive interface to a 2.0 TPM.

We discuss the basic techniques for using the IBM TSS for programming in Section 4.2. Because it is designed to closely reflect the underlying TPM command structure, users of this interface will be using the hardware specification discussed in detail in Section 11.6.2, particularly Part 3, as a primary reference.

The IBM TSS 2.0 also comes with an extensive collection of utility functions, which serve a triple role as test suite, sample code, and userspace TPM utilities. These programs are all open source, and released under the licence in Copyright Notices. While I include many relevant highlights from these programs in this book, I encourage anybody interested to look at the full functions for examples of how to put this library into effective practice, or to consider making use of the pre-written utilities. They are all designed for easy use as userspace command line programs, and are named after the corresponding TPM 2.0 command. If you encounter a command in this book you'd like to experiment with, or learn more about, it may be worth installing the IBM TSS 2.0, even if you don't intend to code with it, just to work with the utilities.

11.2.2 2.0 TSS.Net and TSS.C++

Microsoft Research has a TPM Software Stack (TSS.Net and TSS.C++) for Windows 8, designed to work with a TPM 2.0 or their TPM 2.0 simulator. Their libraries are available at `https://github.com/Microsoft/TSS.MSR`. While a tremendously valuable resource for those seeking to develop TPM 2.0 code on Windows, it is also not compatible with the TCG TSS standard. It was designed to adhere closely to the TPM hardware commands, with enough abstraction to make software writing straightforward. Documentation is included in the package. A more up-to-date version can be found by searching Microsoft Research's website for TSS.Net.

11.3 Books, courses, and other digested material

11.3.1 TPM 1.2 concepts

The original two-day *Introduction to Trusted Computing and TPMs* course which inspired this book is available online at `http://opensecuritytraining.info/IntroToTrustedComputing`. The site includes all of the slides and handouts, as well as video recordings of the original version of the class. While none of the material in the class will be new to a reader of this book, and some parts of it have become obsolete, it may still be useful to those with different learning styles.

11.3.2 TPM 1.2 programming

A Practical Guide To Trusted Computing, by David Challener, Kent Yoder, Ryan Catherman, David Safford, and Leendert Van Doorn provides the most comprehensive guide to programming for 1.2 TPMs. In addition to providing instruction on using the

1.2 TSS, there are chapters on lower-level topics such as talking to the TPM from the BIOS, and higher-level topics, such as creating TPM programs to be compatible with other security standards such as PKCS #11. It does not cover as much of the 'why' as this book, but provides more in-depth explanations of how to use the TSS, both by itself and as part of more complex functionality, as well as quite a bit of practical example code.

For those looking for a quicker introduction to programming with the 1.2 TSS than a full book, David Challener also put together a freely available short course. The handout and slides are available at `https://www.cylab.cmu.edu/tiw/slides/challener-handout.pdf` and `http://www.cylab.cmu.edu/tiw/slides/challener-TPM.pdf`. It lacks a full explanation of how the TSS works and how to use it, but provides practical advice and useful sample code for a variety of functions, and makes a great quick start guide if you're comfortable using boilerplate code and are building simple applications.

11.3.3   TPM 2.0

Trusted Computing Platforms, by Grame Proudler, Liqun Chen, and Chris Dalton, is an excellent resource for those seeking to understand TPM 2.0 in detail, and provides historical and legal context for some of the decisions that may be surprising to a casual observer. It focusses more on what specific TPM operations do and less on how to use them than this book does, and goes into significant technical detail. If you're looking for a deeper reference to use when implementing a TPM 2.0 system without diving straight into the specifications, it is a great choice. It also includes some context for the entire trusted computing ecosystem back through manufacturers, the best explanation of TPM 2.0's DAA approach available (written by the researcher who developed the protocols in question), and a chapter on using the hardware TPM to support virtual machines.

A Practical Guide to TPM 2.0: Using the Trusted Platform Module in the New Age of Security, by Will Arthur and David Challener, provides much less-specific technical detail than *Trusted Computing Platforms*, and will be less useful to the low-level implementer, but is an easier read for the less experienced or implementation-focussed user who's looking for context and detail of TPM 2.0 features beyond what this book provides. It also contains more information about commercial applications available for TPM 2.0.

11.3.4   Other trusted computing topics

David Grawrock's *Dynamics of a Trusted Platform* is an extremely detailed book on the design and implementation of Intel's Trusted Execution Technology (TXT). It covers the goals and history of trusted computing, and does a very deep dive into the roots of trust for measurement as well as how the TPM interacts with the platform and CPU. If you're planning on using the DRTM it's an invaluable resource, but it's also potentially of interest to anyone looking for a low-level perspective on trusted computing.

11.4   Community

11.4.1   The TCG

The TCG, as discussed in Section 1.2.3, is the large industry working group creating the specifications on which TPMs and many other trusted computing technologies are based. Their website, http://www.trustedcomputinggroup.org, has extensive information on trusted computing topics, including TPMs, Trusted Network Connect, and a wide variety of other technologies. However, the website has a very diverse audience and years' worth of content. Many of the documents are intended more for marketing than for conveying technical information, and the titles don't always clearly show which are which. The 'Developer' sections are usually most helpful for implementers or people seeking technical details, and include specifications as well as some talks and white papers about how to use the relevant technologies.

The TCG is also worth discussing as one of the primary communities for those interested in trusted computing. The TCG is an industry collaboration, with a voting membership made up of contributing companies and other institutions, and a lengthy list of non-voting liaison partners who help with the development and analysis of standards. Companies who want to invest in trusted computing technology may find membership worthwhile, especially if there arc future features you're particularly interested in seeing, and academic institutions and other research groups can join the free liaison program if they want to provide expert consulting on ongoing designs and future specifications.

There are three primary benefits to joining the TCG, even as a non-voting member: access to TCG Work Groups, access to the twice-yearly TCG meetings, and the chance to provide feedback on new specifications before they are finalized. The TCG Work Groups are committees of interested parties working to develop new standards or new standardized solutions to widespread industry problems, making use of existing standards. The TCG meetings are primarily intended as a chance for Work Group members to meet in person and get a sense of what the whole range of Work Groups are doing, but they're also invaluable as a way to meet other people with interest and practical experience in trusted computing. Whether advance feedback on draft specifications is useful will depend heavily on your circumstances. Voting members additionally have the opportunity to vote on draft specifications to determine if they become official.

11.4.2   TrouSerS-users mailing list

The TrouSerS-users mailing list was created years ago for discussion and questions about TrouSerS and the 1.2 TSS API in general. The archives are available online, and anyone can sign up to join. The list information, including a link to the complete archives and the list signup, can be found at https://lists.sourceforge.net/lists/listinfo/trousers-users.

11.5   1.2 Specifications

In a lot of computing fields, people using pre-existing libraries rarely need to refer to the original standard specifications; sadly, that is not the case in trusted computing. Although this book attempts to convey as many of the subtle details and surprises as it can, serious implementers are extremely likely to need to go further.

There are three categories of 1.2 specification. The first, and the most useful for those implementing higher-level software, is the TSS specification. The TSS specification does not contain very much detail about what the commands do, making familiarity with the underlying TPM capabilities tremendously helpful; however, it does contain a complete API for the TSS commands.

The TPM specification, which is itself broken into multiple documents, is useful for those implementing low-level TPM software, including those writing device drivers, using Microsoft's TBS, or implementing code to run as part of the DRTM. The TPM specification is also useful for those who wish to better understand the TPM's capabilities and design goals, particularly Part 1, and for those implementing higher-level software functionality not directly supported by the TSS; it is a particularly frequent reference for people who are trying to get the most out of data structures returned by the TPM.

The Platform Specification, intended to specify how TPMs interact with their PC environment and the requirements for PC TPMs, is most useful for those who want to understand PCR use, how TPMs are implemented in reality, and which optional features actually exist. There can, in theory, be non-PC platform specifications; in practice, none are in use for 1.2 TPMs.

11.5.1   1.2 TSS specification

The full TSS specification, which contains all of the commands available for the high-level software API implemented in TrouSerS, is available at `http://www.trustedcomputinggroup.org/resources/tcg_software_stack_tss_specification`. It defines not only the API but also many of the requirements of software implementing the API. In addition to the TSPI API we've used in our code examples in this book, it also defines multiple APIs for lower-level abstractions, which are closer to the TPM's expected inputs and outputs (Figure 11.1).

In some ways, the 1.2 TSS specification is really three specifications in one: three different APIs, at three different abstraction levels, with a multilayered architecture of software supporting them.

The TCG Service Provider, or TSP interface, is object oriented. It is intended for applications, and is designed to let the programmer focus on high-level functionality and the objects the programmer really cares about, rather than worrying about TPM-specific details. It is designed to support multi-threaded processes cleanly, and is the only required interface for TSS implementations. It also provides access to a number of software-only functions which support standard TPM operations, such as binding or signature verification. Its commands all begin with the 'Tspi' prefix.

Tspi_Key_CertifyKey

This method signs a public key using TPM_SS_RSASSAPKCS1v15_SHA1 .   It requires some extra data if the certification procedure has to do with CMK (see remark).

Definition:

```
TSS_RESULT Tspi_Key_CertifyKey
(
    TSS_HKEY          hKey,             // in
    TSS_HKEY          hCertifyingKey,   // in
    TSS_VALIDATION*   pValidationData   // in, out
);
```

Tcsip_CertifyKey

Tcsip_CertifyKey allows a key to certify the public portion of certain storage and signing keys.

C-Definition:

```
TSS_RESULT Tcsip_CertifyKey
(
    TCS_CONTEXT_HANDLE  hContext,          // in
    TCS_KEY_HANDLE      certHandle,        // in
    TCS_KEY_HANDLE      keyHandle,         // in
    TCPA_NONCE          antiReplay,        // in
    TPM_AUTH*           certAuth,          // in, out
    TPM_AUTH*           keyAuth,           // in, out
    UINT32*             CertifyInfoSize,   // out
    BYTE**              CertifyInfo,       // out
    UINT32*             outDataSize,       // out
    BYTE**              outData            // out
);
```

Figure 11.1   The same command at two different abstraction levels of the 1.2 TSS. The first, at the TSP layer, has very few arguments, while the second calls out explicitly authorization values, a nonce, and a context. The data being passed in at the two levels are not actually so different as they may initially look, but the two abstractions are organized very differently. The TSP layer is almost object oriented; In the TSP layer, authorization values are associated with the corresponding keys before this command is ever called, and nonce information is passed in via the same TSS_VALIDATION data structure used to retrieve the output, In fact, command information (whether TPM_CertifyKey or TPM_CertifyKey2 is used) is also passed in the TSS_VALIDATION data structure, based on which kind of CERTIFY_INFO structure is provided inside it. The TCS layer, in contrast, provides a much thinner layer of syntactic sugar over the underlying TPM commands

The TCG Core Services interface, or TCS, provides a simple C-style interface to the TSS. Some programmers may find it an easier tool to use, if the multithreading support the TSP provides is not required for their application and their TSS supports it. The TCS commands tend to more closely reflect TPM functionality. Many functions that are not actually provided by the TPM, such as binding, are not supported by the TCS either, although the TCS does support a PCR event log and some local key management. Its commands all begin with the 'Tcsi' prefix; commands which cause a call to the TPM begin with 'Tcsip'.

The TCG Device Driver Library, or TDDL, interface, is not designed to be used by most implementers. This API is intended to be called exclusively by TCS implementations, and serves as a manufacturer-agnostic interface to TPM device drivers.

When using the TSS specification, there are a few useful tips to remember.

- There is no good way to use both TCS and TSP calls in the same application. Stick to one abstraction. You may sometimes find functionality easily in the TCS layer (which uses the TPM command naming scheme) but not in the TSP layer; this doesn't mean the functionality doesn't exist, but rather that it may have been moved from a TPM-centric command with TPM-standard naming to an object-centric command with a more function-centric name.
- Most of the time, you'll be able to get by with just the TSS-defined data structures. However, if you're going to be looking at the contents of data returned by the TPM – for example, quotes, tick stamp blobs, and certificates – the TSS data structures won't give you access to the contents. You'll need to reach beyond the TSS specification and to the TPM data structures specification. (You'll also need to include the `tss/tpm.h` header file in your code.)
- The TSS error codes provide a limited amount of information about where in the TSS or TPM an error occurred. This can be useful when dealing with some errors, especially since Part 3 of the TPM specification provides exact instructions for when various error codes are returned. Any errors actually returned from hardware can often be narrowed down by looking up the relevant command in the TPM specification. See Chapter 12 for some of the hazards.

11.5.2   1.2 TPM specification

The 1.2 TPM specification, also known as the TPM Main Specification, can be downloaded from the TCG's website: `http://www.trustedcomputinggroup.org/resources/tpm_main_specification`. It comes in three parts. In order to make full use of the specification, you will need all three.

Part 1: Design Principles
This section provides high-level context for understanding the TPM, such as the basic architecture and the goals the TPM was designed to meet. It also contains information about the TPM's access control model and how it is enforced, explanations of major concepts, and a number of extremely useful charts which map out how various commands and structures interact. Look here for high-level overviews, architectural

requirements (such as which components must be present in a TPM), manufacturing requirements (such as the number of times monotonic counters must be writable, or the minimum size of storage areas), and behavioural requirements which are not command-specific (such as the TPM's dictionary attack prevention mechanisms or how the TPM checks PCR values).

Part 2: TPM Structures
This section, as the name suggests, contains all of the TPM's data structure definitions. Because the TPM uses so many custom data structures as part of its input and output, this section is much more important than it sounds, and is often used in close conjunction with the Commands section. Many of the TPM's data structures are multilayered, which makes understanding data structure contents critical in understanding just what information is passing in and out of the TPM.

Part 3: TPM Commands
This section defines all of the commands that a TPM will respond to, including their arguments, their output, and what actions the TPM will take. Note that because so many arguments and outputs are themselves complex data structures, you will need to have a copy of Part 2 on hand to make practical use of this section. However, this is by far the most useful of the three parts when trying to figure what the TPM can do. The informative comments at the beginning of each command, while not always comprehensive, are particularly valuable for understanding what each command does.

While Part 1 is primarily text, and Part 2 is generally self-explanatory as long as you're willing to flip back and forth inside it, Part 3 can be non-intuitive, especially when you're trying to figure out which details you need to really care about, so it's worth going into a little more detail about how it's structured.

Each command begins with an informative comment (highlighted in gray), and has at least three normative (i.e. required to meet the specification) sections: the incoming operands table which shows what the TPM is expecting to receive (Figure 11.2), the outgoing operands table that shows what the TPM will return (Figure 11.3), and an actions section describing what the TPM does when it receives the command. Some commands additionally have a normative description section, which usually details additional requirements on the command that are not included in the actions.

The actions section is, sadly, not entirely comprehensive; certain routine actions, such as verifying that the PCR and locality constraints imposed on a key are checked each time the key is used, are not included in the step-by-step list for each command. These exceptions are rare, however, and the actions section can be an invaluable guide when you need to know exactly what operations the TPM is performing or what could have generated a particular error message. It is worth noting that manufacturers are not required to strictly follow the ordering of operations in the list when it comes to error checking, but that rarely makes a difference when debugging.

Figure 11.2 contains the complete Incoming Parameters table for an example command (TPM_Sign). The leftmost columns under 'PARAM' detail the order in which arguments are passed to the TPM, and the size of the argument in bytes, respectively. The 'HMAC' columns similarly detail the order parameters are included

| PARAM | | HMAC | | Type | Name | Description |
#	SZ	#	SZ			
1	2			TPM_TAG	tag	TPM_TAG_RQU_AUTH1_COMMAND
2	4			UINT32	paramSize	Total number of input bytes including paramSize and tag
3	4	1S	4	TPM_COMMAND_CODE	ordinal	Command ordinal: TPM_ORD_Sign
4	4			TPM_KEY_HANDLE	keyHandle	The keyHandle identifier of a loaded key that can perform digital signatures.
5	4	2s	4	UINT32	areaToSignSize	The size of the areaToSign parameter
6	<>	3s	<>	BYTE[]	areaToSign	The value to sign
7	4			TPM_AUTHHANDLE	authHandle	The authorization session handle used for keyHandle authorization
		2H1	20	TPM_NONCE	authLastNonceEven	Even nonce previously generated by TPM to cover inputs
8	20	3H1	20	TPM_NONCE	nonceOdd	Nonce generated by system associated with authHandle
9	1	4H1	1	BOOL	continueAuthSession	The continue use flag for the authorization session handle
10	20			TPM_AUTHDATA	privAuth	The authorization session digest that authorizes the use of keyHandle. HMAC key: key.usageAuth

Figure 11.2   The Incoming Parameters table for the TPM_Sign *command*

| PARAM | | HMAC | | Type | Name | Description |
#	SZ	#	SZ			
1	2			TPM_TAG	tag	TPM_TAG_RSP_AUTH1_COMMAND
2	4			UINT32	paramSize	Total number of output bytes including paramSize and tag
3	4	1S	4	TPM_RESULT	returnCode	The return code of the operation
		2S	4	TPM_COMMAND_CODE	ordinal	Command ordinal: TPM_ORD_Sign
4	4	3S	4	UINT32	sigSize	The length of the returned digital signature
5	<>	4S	<>	BYTE[]	sig	The resulting digital signature
6	20	2H1	20	TPM_NONCE	nonceEven	Even nonce newly generated by TPM to cover outputs
		3H1	20	TPM_NONCE	nonceOdd	Nonce generated by system associated with authHandle
7	1	4H1	1	BOOL	continueAuthSession	Continue use flag, TRUE if handle is still active
8	20			TPM_AUTHDATA	resAuth	The authorization session digest for the returned parameters. HMAC key: key.usageAuth

Figure 11.3   The Outgoing Parameters table for the TPM_Sign *command*

in the HMACs used as part of transport session security, and the parameter size. Users not implementing transport and authorization sessions can ignore them.

The first parameter in every command input is a tag indicating the type of communication and the expected authorization sessions for the command. The second is the total size, in bytes, of the command input. The third is the command name (ordinal). Unless you're actually creating your own command structures to be passed to the TPM, you can ignore these.

The interesting parameters – those which vary from command to command, and which you're most likely to be looking up – are those between the ordinal and the thin double line (here, between parameters 6 and 7). Some commands, which take no arguments, may not have any.

Below the double line are parameters which have to do with the TPM's session handling. Unless you're creating your own command structures to be passed to the TPM or handling your own authorization sessions, you can ignore all of these. You can see some patterns here, if you look for them; this is where authorization sessions (which we use to provide passwords to the TPM) are connected to the use of the associated resources. A command which does not require authorization will not have a double line or parameters below it.

Figure 11.3 contains the complete Outgoing Parameters table for TPM_Sign, which is structured very similarly to the Incoming Parameters table. Again, the left-most 'PARAM' and 'HMAC' columns show the ordering of and size of parameters; again, we have a tag and the size of the total output. Again, everything below the double line has to do with authorization session management, and can be ignored by most users. The third argument in each response can be ignored when reading the specification but is important in implementations: this contains the return code, which will either be TPM_SUCCESS or an error code produced by the command.

Once again, the most interesting part of the table is the lines after the return code and before any double lines; this is where the command output is described.

This means that for most users, what can at first glance look like a lot of large and complicated tables actually turns out to contain an easy-to-identify and easy-to-read subset that you can use as a simple reference: the Type, Name, and Description columns of parameters 4+, up to any double lines. Those will tell you everything you need to know as a higher-level software developer about what the TPM expects to receive, and what the TPM expects to return. The action description will tell you how the former is used to generate the latter, if you need to understand the finer details of what is contained in various data structures and how that information is used or generated.

11.6 2.0 Specifications

Even more than with 1.2, 2.0 implementers are likely to find themselves consulting the specifications regularly. Although the TCG TSS specifications may be useful once implementations are available, anyone going beyond the minimalist FAPI will be relying heavily on the underlying specifications; the lower-level TCG TSS API is defined by reference to the hardware commands. Users of the IBM TSS 2.0 will find themselves regularly consulting the hardware specifications as well.

11.6.1 TCG TSS (TPM Software Stack) specifications

TPM 2.0 has a more complicated set of TSS specifications than 1.2 did. (The complexity is not helped by the fact that neither the IBM TSS implementation used in this book nor Microsoft libraries with TSS in their names follow any of the TCG TSS specifications.) In particular, because the 1.2 TSS's complexity made it hard for novice users to use even the most common functionality without unwanted overhead, and forced users to pay more attention to the abstraction levels than was optimal, there was a desire to take a different approach. The 2.0 TSS solved the conflict between power and usability by having two entirely distinct APIs: one that offers the most commonly used commands simply, and the other of which provides comprehensive access to the 2.0 TPM. A third API, meant to provide a comprehensive but easier to use interface, has not yet been released.

As of the end of 2015, no implementations of any TCG TSS specification have been publicly released.

11.6.1.1   TSS (TPM Software Stack) FAPI

The FAPI was designed for the vast majority of users who need only a tiny subset of the TPM's features. It is intended to be much simpler and easier to use than the 1.2 TSS, in part because it hides many of the TPM's functions and options from the user. It has a very limited set of available functions, and relies on predefined profiles and key types to hide many of the complex decisions (such as key algorithms and constraints, or hash algorithm to use for PCRs) from the user. It provides a selection of predefined standard policies and authorization values, so novice users are not required to write their own custom security policies to make a program work, but allows for more complex policies to be created.

Some features and limitations of the FAPI:

*   Key hierarchies, key handles, and non-volatile storage locations are made explicit and easy to use with consistent path descriptors. Key path descriptors also determine whether a key is available system-wide or only to a single user (enforced by the OS), and whether a key can be duplicated for use on a new system or not.
*   Automatic creation of access policies using XML input definitions.
*   Functionality includes signing, quoting and PCR operations including verification, encryption and decryption, and non-volatile storage operations.
*   Only a subset of key types are available; besides the root keys, only unrestricted storage keys, restricted signing keys, and HMAC keys can be created.

The full TSS FAPI specification can be found at `http://www.trustedcom putinggroup.org/resources/tss_feature_api_specification`.

11.6.1.2   TSS system-level API and TPM Command Transmission Interface

The System Level API (SAPI) and TPM Command Transmission Interface (TCTI) were intended for those building low-level software who might not want the intermediate layers required to implement the FAPI, and for those who need the full power of the TPM rather than merely its most commonly used functions. These are stateless interfaces, unlike the other TSS variants we've discussed. Applications using them are required to maintain most state themselves, including state involving communication sessions with the TPM.

Most applications will use the SAPI, which is the layer intended to be exposed to even low-level users, such as BIOS and firmware authors. It allows access to all TPM 2.0 commands, with an interface designed to mimic the TPM hardware commands as closely as possible, so that the TPM 2.0 specifications (see 11.6.2) can be used as a reference. In fact, it does not define specific APIs for individual commands, but rather the rules for how to transform hardware commands into the associated SAPI commands. The SAPI's most valuable feature is that it performs the work of marshalling and unmarshalling output so that C structures with appropriate endianness are used as input and output, rather than byte arrays which may contain surprises.

The full TSS System API specification, along with the specification for the TPM Command Transmission Interface intended for communications directly with the hardware, can be found at `http://www.trustedcomputinggroup.org/resources/tss_system_level_api_and_tpm_command_transmission_interface_specification`.

11.6.2   2.0 TPM specifications

The specifications defining 2.0 TPM functionality are collectively referred to as the TPM Library. At the end of 2015, they were approved for publication as International Standard ISO/IEC 11889:2015, Parts 1-4.

As with 1.2, the 2.0 TPM specification consists of several different parts. However, there are several important differences between the 1.2 and 2.0 specifications. First and foremost, the 2.0 specification is written in C with extensive English commentary, to minimize problems 1.2 had with differing interpretations of requirements. The output of the code, excluding any bugs,[1] defines the correct behaviour of the 2.0 TPM. Secondly, and largely as a result, the 2.0 specification is divided into four somewhat differently organized parts, compared to the three of 1.2. The complete specification can be found at `http://www.trustedcomputinggroup.org/resources/tpm_library_specification`.

Part 1: Architecture
The Architecture section of the specification, much like the Design Principles section of the 1.2 specification, covers the core ideas used in TPM 2.0, as well as the components included in the TPM. However, the Architecture section covers many more details critical to TPM implementations, such as how the policy hashes for Extended Authorization are calculated, or the details of block cipher modes. Those seeking to fully understand the 2.0 TPM will want to be familiar with this section of the specification at least at a high level.

Part 2: Structures
The Structures section of the specification contains the data structures used by the TPM, as well as definitions for various constants and parameters. This section is rarely used in isolation; rather, it is most useful in combination with Parts 3 and 4.

Part 3: Commands
This section defines all of the TPM 2.0 commands. For each command, there is a high-level description, a table similar to those used in 1.2 covering the command input and output (see Figures 11.4 and 11.5), and the C code defining exactly what should happen when the command is executed (see Figure 11.6). However, most commands rely heavily on function calls which are defined in Part 4; Part 3 can only

---

[1]The designers were realistic – in any coding project of this magnitude, there will be bugs, and they reserve the right to fix them without implementations needing to be bug-compatible with prior versions.

TPM2_GetTime Command

Type	Name	Description
TPMI_ST_COMMAND_TAG	tag	TPM_ST_SESSIONS
UINT32	commandSize	
TPM_CC	commandCode	TPM_CC_GetTime
TPMI_RH_ENDORSEMENT	@privacyAdminHandle	handle of the privacy administrator (TPM_RH_ENDORSEMENT) Auth Index: 1 Auth Role: USER
TPMI_DH_OBJECT+	@signHandle	the *keyHandle* identifier of a loaded key that can perform digital signatures Auth Index: 2 Auth Role: USER
TPM2B_DATA	qualifyingData	data to tickstamp
TPMT_SIG_SCHEME+	inScheme	signing scheme to use if the *scheme* for *signHandle* is TPM_ALG_NULL

Figure 11.4   A selection from the TPM 2.0 command specification showing the command input. The top three arguments, above the striped line, are the command header; all commands will have a similar structure. Below the striped line and above the heavy divider are handles; most commands use one or two, but some have none and some have more. Note that these handles may be key handles, policy session handles, or handles for roles such as that of the policy administrator or owner. Below the heavy divider are other command parameters. Note that this structure is informative about what information the TPM will require to execute the command, and accurately reflects what many software APIs will use for input, but cannot be used as-is to construct data to be sent directly to the TPM: it is missing the authorization session information. Commands such as this one, with the TPM_ST_SESSIONS *tag in the header, have authorization session information included between the handles and the command parameters. This authorization session information consists of a 32-bit value which is the size of the authorization area in bytes, and then an authorization area containing authorization session information. The full details of command and response structure are described in section 18 of Part 1 of the TPM 2.0 specification, and the handling of authorization sessions in command input and response is described in section 4.4 of Part 3. A complete code implementation using this function has been included in Appendix C.2.2 for comparison*

be used without Part 4 if you're looking for general command descriptions. Input and output parameters use data types defined in Part 2.

Part 4: Supporting Routines
This section contains all of the header files, structure definitions, functions, and other code required to make the 2.0 specification into a working reference implementation.

TPM2_GetTime Response

Type	Name	Description
TPM_ST	tag	see clause 6
UINT32	responseSize	
TPM_RC	responseCode	.
TPM2B_ATTEST	timeInfo	standard TPM-generated attestation block
TPMT_SIGNATURE	signature	the signature over *timeInfo*

Figure 11.5   A selection from the TPM 2.0 command specification showing the command response. As with the command input, command responses start with common header information, followed by command-specific parameters. Command responses only provide the listed parameters in the event of a successful result; each command lists the errors that can be produced. If a command which has the TPM_ST_SESSIONS tag completes successfully, the TPM's response will also include authorization information not listed in this diagram. For responses, a hidden 32-bit parameter size field exists between the header and any handles returned, and the parameters; authorization session information is provided after the listed parameter information, and the response size field includes both the listed parameters and the unlisted authorization session information. A complete code implementation for the IBM TSS 2.0 using this particular function has been included in Appendix C.2.2 for comparison

Because the core functionality of many commands was implemented as function calls to keep the command code short, modular, and comprehensible, these 'supporting routines' often contain code which is critical to understanding the finer details of how the TPM operates. Part 4 is rarely useful in isolation; it is primarily useful in combination with Parts 2 and 3.

11.6.3   2.0 Supporting specifications

To create a functional environment for using TPMs, you may need to go beyond the TPM itself. For example, manufacturers are expected to create credentials for a TPM's EK, and it's important that recipients are able to correctly interpret those credentials. Sharing expectations is especially critical for 2.0 TPMs, since primary keys such as the EK are regenerated when needed, and the manufacturer and the user need to have the same expectations of how to generate the key. The key template and credential definitions can be found in the *TCG EK Credential Profile for TPM Family 2.0* document, available at http://www.trustedcomputinggroup.org/resources/tcg_ek_credential_profile_for_tpm_family_20.

The new Registry of Reserved TPM 2.0 Handles and Localities sets out the reserved resource handles for certificates, TPM and manufacturer objects, and other resources that may be stored in the TPM. This covers all possible

```
TPM_RC TPM2_GetTime(
 GetTime_In *in, \\ IN: input parameter list
 GetTime_Out *out ) \\ OUT: output parameter list
 { TPM_RC   result;
   TPMS_ATTEST timeInfo;

 // Command Output
   // Filling in attest information
   // Common fields
 result = FillInAttestInfo(in->signHandle, &in->inScheme,
                          &in->qualifyingData, &timeInfo);

 if(result != TPM_RC_SUCCESS) {
     if(result == TPM_RC_KEY)
        return TPM_RC_KEY + RC_GetTime_signHandle;
     else
        return RcSafeAddToResult(result, RC_GetTime_inScheme); }

 // GetClock specific fields
 // Attestation type
 timeInfo.type = TPM_ST_ATTEST_TIME;

 // current clock in plain text
 timeInfo.attested.time.time.time = g_time;
 TimeFillInfo(&timeInfo.attested.time.time.clockInfo);

 // Firmware version in plain text
 timeInfo.attested.time.firmwareVersion = ((UINT64) gp.firmwareV1) << 32;
 timeInfo.attested.time.firmwareVersion += gp.firmwareV2;

// Sign attestation structure. A NULL signature will be returned if
// signHandle is TPM_RH_NULL. A TPM_RC_NV_UNAVAILABLE, TPM_RC_NV_RATE,
// TPM_RC_VALUE, TPM_RC_SCHEME or TPM_RC_ATTRIBUTES error may be returned at
// this point

 result = SignAttestInfo(in->signHandle,  &in->inScheme,
                         &timeInfo, &in->qualifyingData,
                         &out->timeInfo, &out->signature);
 if(result != TPM_RC_SUCCESS)
 return result;

 // orderly state should be cleared because of the reporting of clock info
 // if signing happens
 if(in->signHandle != TPM_RH_NULL)
   g_clearOrderly = TRUE;

 return TPM_RC_SUCCESS; }
```

Figure 11.6   *The C code defining the actions the TPM takes when running*
            TPM2_GetTime as defined in Part 3 of the TPM 2.0 specification.
            Notice that most of the interesting activity takes place in function
            calls: FillInAttestInfo, TimeFillInfo, and SignAttestInfo. You can get a
            general sense of the functions' intent just from the names, but to
            determine exactly what they're doing, you'll need to look up the
            functions in Part 4

platforms of TPM 2.0: in addition to the PC Client TPMs discussed in this book, the specification covers reserved handles used by virtual and mobile TPMs. `http://www.trustedcomputinggroup.org/resources/registry_ of_reserved_tpm_20_handles_and_localities`.

11.7   Platform specifications

The platform specifications define implementation and interface requirements for TPMs intended for different system architectures. These specifications are where you can find information about mandatory and optional commands, minimum resource requirements, and expected PCR contents. They also define the platform behaviour relative to the TPM when it comes to power, input and output, drivers, and the like. Most users will rarely make use of the platform specifications; I've included the most commonly needed information in this book. Implementers working at very low levels, such as BIOS authors, may find them very valuable.

11.7.1   1.2 Platform specifications

PC Client Specific TPM Interface Specification (TIS)
This document, available at `http://www.trustedcomputinggroup.org/ resources/pc_client_work_group_pc_client_specific_tpm_ interface_specification_tis`, defines the minimum resources TPC TPMs are required to provide, the mandatory and optional commands, the initial values for PCRs, and hardware-level interfaces to the TPM.

PC Client Specific Implementation Specification for Conventional BIOS
This document, available at `http://www.trustedcomputinggroup.org/ resources/pc_client_work_group_specific_implementation_ specification_for_conventional_bios`, contains everything BIOS implementers should need to know about interfacing with the TPM. For others, it is most valuable for detailed information about how BIOSes are expected to fill in PCRs.

Protection Profile PC Client-Specific TPM TPM Family 1.2
This document, available at `http://www.trustedcomputinggroup.org/ tpm-1-2-protection-profile/`, is primarily of interest if you're curious about TPMs' security properties and the threat models they were designed for. It is intended primarily for those certifying TPMs; the profile itself has been evaluated using the Common Methodology for IT Security Evaluation (CEM), Version 3.1, for conformance to the Common Criteria for IT Security Evaluation (CC), Version 3.1.

11.7.2   2.0 Platform specification

PC Client Platform TPM Profile (PTP) Specification
This document, available at `http://www.trustedcomputinggroup.org/` `resources/pc_client_platform_tpm_profile_ptp_specification`, provides the minimum requirements for a PC client TPM: internal storage size, required PCRs and their initial values, mandatory and optional commands, and other values that the main TPM specification does not define. It also defines hardware and software interfaces, and other information valuable to driver authors.

PC Client Protection Profile for TPM 2.0
This document, available at `http://www.trustedcomputinggroup.org/` `resources/pc_client_protection_profile_for_tpm_20`, sets out the security requirements for creating and evaluating a 2.0 TPM which conforms to the Common Criteria version 3.1 revision 4. It is primarily of interest to those who are concerned about certification for their TPMs.

11.7.3   Specifications applying to multiple TPM versions

PC Client Platform Physical Presence Interface
This document, available at `http://www.trustedcomputinggroup.org/` `resources/tcg_physical_presence_interface_specification`, is intended for those implementing OS and pre-OS interfaces with the TPM, and sets out how to securely allow software to indicate physical presence to a TPM. It uses the standard Advanced Configuration and Power Interface (ACPI).

D-RTM Architecture
While this document is not technically a TPM specification, it is of interest to some TPM users. It describes a number of details of how Dynamic Root of Trust implementations (see Section 9.1.3) should behave. It is available at `http://www.` `trustedcomputinggroup.org/resources/drtm_architecture_` `specification`.

11.8   Other useful resources

11.8.1   The `tpm-tools` package

The `tpm-tools` package, originally developed by IBM, provides a variety of command-line tools for working with 1.2 TPMs, and is available in most standard Linux distributions, including Ubuntu, Debian, and Red Hat. The selection of command-line tools is by no means comprehensive; the package was primarily intended to support use of the TPM for local password stores and encryption of user data. However, in addition to its `tpm_sealdata` and `tpm_unsealdata` functionality, the package also provides a tremendously useful set of TPM provisioning and testing utilities. These include `tpm_createek`, `tpm_getpubek`, `tpm_takeownership`, and `tpm_changeownerauth`. In combination, these command line tools give you everything you need to get started with the TPM on a Linux system. The package also includes the `tpm_clear` command, which is useful both for deprovisioning a machine no longer in use and for clearing out test data created while learning to use the TPM. Most of the other features are not tremendously helpful for the average user, but `tpm_version` and `tpm_selftest` can be handy when getting started to confirm that the TPM has been turned on and is available for use.

11.8.2 TPM manufacturers

Most TPM vendors have websites where you can find the hardware spec sheets for their TPMs. If you're trying to figure out what vendor made your TPM, the Vendor ID Registry available at `http://www.trustedcomputinggroup.org/resources/vendor_id_registry` contains an up-to-date list of vendors who have requested a Vendor ID and the values that will be returned by the GetCapability functions when the manufacturer is requested. (See Section 10.4 for how to retrieve this information, and the table as of September 2015.)

If a vendor provides certificates for its TPMs' root keys, their CA certificates should be available from the company. For example, Infineon's CAs for have downloadable credentials available under the 'Documents' section of their TPM product site, `http://www.infineon.com/cms/en/product/security-ic/trusted-computing/pc-tpm/channel.html?channel=db3a30433efacd9a013f10d3ded64daf`, along with information about their TPM product line.

11.8.3 TPM 2.0 simulators

While physical 2.0 TPMs are starting to become available, as of the end of 2015 they're still extremely rare. 2.0 TPMs have a number of very powerful features, as we've discussed, and enterprise security planners and researchers may find it useful to be able to start testing functionality for 2.0 TPMs even without a physical device. There are two convenient options, one from Microsoft and one from IBM, although they share code.

The Microsoft TPM 2.0 simulator is available as a Windows executable, downloadable at `http://research.microsoft.com/en-US/downloads/35116857-e544-4003-8e7b-584182dc6833/default.aspx`, or more conveniently from a link on `https://tpm2lib.codeplex.com/`.

IBM's software TPM 2.0 is available as source code at `http://sourceforge.net/projects/ibmswtpm2/`, and comes with instructions for compilation on several OSes including Windows and Linux.

11.8.3.1 Using TPM simulators in the real world

There are times when using a TPM simulator (often called a 'software TPM' in these contexts) is appropriate in the real world, though they are rare. It is *critically* important to remember that a software TPM does not provide *any* of the tamper resistance or secrecy guarantees that a hardware TPM does. Use cases tend to fall into two categories.

Enterprise-wide compatibility

When a large enterprise is seeking to roll out TPM-based authentication or attestation across its entire environment, it's not at all uncommon to discover that some subset of the machines can't use hardware TPMs. This could be because they don't have TPMs at all, as is the case with all Apple devices today, many consumer-grade laptops, and most servers which were not ordered with the TPM as an option. It could also be because their TPMs are non-functional, but the enterprise does not consider the risk from those machines to be high enough to justify not using the machines at all. In these cases, it is sometimes appropriate to use hardware TPM-based services on all platforms which support them, and roll out software TPMs on all other devices for compatibility. The devices with software TPMs are not gaining any particular security advantage, but the enterprise as a whole is improving their trust in the majority of machines. These use cases are often intended as a temporary measure, or for lower-trust applications; allowing a software TPM to authenticate a machine for access to a corporate wireless network, for example, but not for access to a high-sensitivity server.

Virtual TPMs

As cloud computing and virtualization become widespread, there is interest in many quarters in virtual TPMs to support these virtual machines. Being able to attest to a single VM's identity or software state would be highly valuable. Software TPMs are *not* the same as virtual TPMs, but they're an important first step; virtual TPMs are software TPMs with additional security features to provide assurance that the virtual TPM itself is trustworthy and its data is protected, rooted in an underlying hardware TPM. If you're interested in virtual TPMs, the TCG has a Virtualization Working Group that has spent the last several years developing a detailed architecture for creating trustworthy virtual TPMs.

11.8.4   Example open-source applications

11.8.4.1   Flicker

Flicker is a project out of CMU which provides a minimalist OS for using the RTM to perform limited, high-trust operations with 1.2 TPM verification. It is designed to allow user-created code to execute in the RTM's secure mode. Although a somewhat aged academic model, it is a working example of the same kind of techniques that trusted banking software or a corporate machine-health check might use to execute high-trust code while providing verification of both the code and the output. It is open source, with downloadable demonstration code and instructions for both Intel and AMD platforms. Note that it does not use the TSS; because it is designed to run at an extremely low level, it is calling the TPM directly.

`https://sourceforge.net/projects/flickertcb/`

11.8.4.2   TPM Quote Tools

The TPM Quote Tools package is designed to provide an easy-to-use implementation of the TPM quote feature, for applications where the goal is to confirm that the measurements present in the TPM's PCRs are the same as prior measurements. This open-source package provides a convenient example of working code using the 1.2 TSS, including error message handling, and is available at `http://tpmquotetools.sourceforge.net/`.

11.8.5 Useful trusted computing tools

11.8.5.1 Integrity measurement architecture

The IMA is a set of Linux kernel modules which provides a number of software integrity functions. It performs runtime measurements of files before reading or executing them, and stores the measurements in both an audit file and a TPM PCR for later reporting using TPM quotes. Policies can be used to determine what is measured. IMA can also be used on Android. More information can be found at `http://sourceforge.net/projects/linux-ima/`.

11.8.5.2 TrustedGRUB

GRUB is an open-source boot loader commonly used on Unix-like systems. There have been multiple projects modifying versions of GRUB to measure boot loader shell commands, kernels, kernel modules, and files loaded from disk into TPM PCRs for later use. This lets the SRTM chain of measurement (see Section 9.1.2) be extended up into the OS. TrustedGRUB is a modification of the GRUB boot loader, and is available at `http://sourceforge.net/projects/trustedgrub/`. TrustedGRUB2 modifies GRUB2, and is available at `https://github.com/Sirrix-AG/TrustedGRUB2`.

11.8.5.3 Trusted boot (tboot)

The tboot project provides open-source code designed to be run before the main OS. It uses the DRTM (see Section 9.1.3) to perform a measured and verified launch of the kernel or virtual machine manager (VMM). It can be found at `http://sourceforge.net/projects/tboot/`.

11.9 Commercial software

While there is commercial software on the market using TPMs, both 1.2 and 2.0, my rule of thumb with this book has been to not say anything that couldn't be backed up in experience or serious research. Unfortunately, the commercial marketplace moves quickly, and doesn't tend to provide comprehensive technical details on new products to people who aren't customers. There is information about a number of commercial software vendors in *A Practical Guide to TPM 2.0* (see Section 11.3.3), but as with most printed material it is unlikely to stay up to date for long relative to the marketplace. Those interested in TPM applications are advised to keep your eyes open and remember to always ask questions of your vendors; the security field is, sadly, full of as much snake oil as good software. I hope that, having read this book, you'll be well equipped to distinguish between good trusted computing products and those that represent a waste of money.

Chapter 12

Troubleshooting

This chapter is not a comprehensive list of everything that can possibly go wrong when using TPMs; they are complicated, finicky, and sometimes buggy devices. The problems and tips listed here are drawn from my personal experience; I hope that they will be of use to you when you (almost inevitably) run into a problem yourself.

Because these tips are drawn from personal experience, and I do not yet have any hands-on experience with 2.0 TPMs, there are few 2.0-specific troubleshooting tips here.

12.1 When all else fails

- Clear the TPM and activate it again. When you're getting started, you're likely to run into all kinds of errors, and some of them (especially those involving initial provisioning) are hard to correct. You can always start again.
  - Corollary to the above: Never encrypt the only copy of any data you care about to the TPM until you're sure you've got the software working.

12.2 There's no TPM in the BIOS menu

- Double-check to make sure it's not under any vendor-specific pseudonyms, for example, 'security chip'.
- Do you have a system where the TPM is on by default and the BIOS vendor does not provide a deactivation option? See if your OS has it on the list of devices.
- Are you sure your machine actually has a TPM? Many consumer-grade devices do not, and whether servers do or not depends on the manufacturer and configuration.
- If you're sure your machine has a TPM, but the OS can't find it and there's no BIOS option, you're in one of two scenarios. Either your TPM itself is quite thoroughly dead – though the BIOS might still register that there should be one – or you've found a machine where the firmware wasn't designed to use all of the hardware's capabilities.
  - If your TPM is damaged or defunct, you're effectively in the situation where your machine has no TPM. You may have to contact your manufacturer to see

if you can get a replacement motherboard – most commercial TPMs can't be usefully replaced.

– If your firmware for some reason doesn't support your hardware, check for updates. If you're in the very unusual circumstance of working with custom hardware which includes a TPM, you may, with luck, already have a BIOS/UEFI expert who can help remedy the problem.

12.3   Trouble getting any software working

- Check to see if your OS can actually detect your TPM. The exact location of the TPM device information varies based on system, but TPMs have drivers, and an OS with TPM drivers should be able to detect the device. If not, try going back to your BIOS and turning it on again.
- Check to make sure all of the necessary libraries and/or packages for your system are correctly installed and working.
- If you're using a TSS, check to make sure that the TSS daemon itself (`tcsd` in the case of TrouSerS) is actually up and running.
- TPMs have a self-test utility, which can be useful for determining whether you're capable of talking to your TPM at all, as well as whether your TPM is having fundamental problems. Note that the self-test will respond even if the TPM is disabled. While the exact details of the self-test return codes vary per manufacturer, some variation on zero (00, 00000000 00000000, etc.) indicates that the TPM has passed its internal test routine.

12.3.1   Linux-specific tips

- Check to see if you've got the right kernel modules running. Some versions may require you to separately load the `tpm_tis` module, although it is often loaded by default.
- If you're using Linux, see if you can install and run the `tpm-tools` utilities. These tools are very reliable. If they won't work, they may at least provide you with useful information about why they're failing, and if they do work, you'll have traced your problem to something in your own software or libraries.
- Some versions of Ubuntu have a bug where the new user (tss) that is used for the TrouSerS daemon won't be properly created until the machine reboots, causing configuration errors during installation of the TrouSerS package. Try rebooting and installing the package again.

12.4   TPM returning errors

- If you're receiving TPM errors, that's actually a very useful tool. Each TPM command has the list of the errors it returns in the specification, and the detailed description of the command you're trying to run should tell you quite a bit about why it might throw each error.

  – There are a few non-command-specific errors: if the TPM is deactivated or disabled or in failure mode, for example, the problem is with your TPM as a whole.

• If you can't tell what error you're getting, because it's just a string of meaningless bytes, your best hope is that you're using a library, such as TrouSerS, that includes a complete translation of TPM error codes. If you're using a 1.2 TPM, the `tpm_quote_tools` package has helpful functions for error reporting. If neither of those is true or will work at your abstraction level, you're going to be going back to the specification just to work out what the error is.

  – In 1.2 TPMs, you'll find the complete set of error codes in section 16 of the TPM Structures specification; in 2.0 TPMs, the response codes are listed in section 6.6 of the Structures specification. In each case, there is a very brief description of the sort of problem that will cause the error to be returned.

• If you're consistently having authorization issues, the problem may be as simple as the passwords you're using. This could be anything, from not correctly associating the authorization session containing the password with a given TSS object or TPM command, to problems with password encoding. And always double-check that you're typing the password correctly. It's amazing how frustrating a typo of the owner password during provisioning can be when you're debugging later software. If you're totally stuck, remember that you can always clear the TPM and start again.

  – If you look at the specification, you'll see that some 1.2 commands can produce odd-looking authorization errors in branches that say things like 'if tag=TPM_TAG_RQU_AUTH1_COMMAND'. Those tags have to do with what the TPM is expecting a given command to provide in terms of authorization sessions. These errors have little to do with whether a password is correct, and much more to do with whether or not the correct number and type of authorizations were presented at all.

12.5   TSS 1.2 code returning errors

• Some TSS error codes are really TPM error codes; in that case, see the previous section (12.4) to proceed. You can tell which layer produced an error by looking at bits 12–15 of the 32-bit error code. 0×0 means the error came from the TPM, while 0×3 means it was produced by the TSS service provider. 0×1 and 0×2 are rare, and indicate an error in the middle layers between the TPM and the TSS service provider. If you're using a library such as TrouSerS, which has a TPM error header file (e.g. `tpm_error.h`) you can save yourself a lot of lookup time, working out what error code you're actually looking at by searching that file.

• Bad parameter errors are very common, especially when getting started. They could result from the wrong type of data being provided, although that more commonly causes segfaults or internal software errors; but they more frequently occur when the data input to the function contains unexpected values. For example, providing a function that expects a symmetric cipher algorithm with an asymmetric algorithm will return a bad parameter error. Double-check the function definition you're using against the TSS specification. If the answer isn't obvious, go through each argument you're providing and make sure it actually contains what you think it does, and that the input is valid for the underlying TPM command.

- The most frustrating TSS-layer error code is, unfortunately, the uninformative 'Internal Error'. Tracing this one can be painful. You can try using your favorite debugger, or going through the source code. Many of these errors seem to occur owing to stack misalignment errors or memory problems. Because the TSS manages some but not all of its own memory for data structures, and has erratic expectations about data structure initialization, it's easy to make a very subtle mistake and end up in a state where your code is unexpectedly fragile. Double-check to make sure that you're freeing any TSS-allocated structures before reusing them, and that you're not allocating anything the TSS expects to allocate itself.

- If you're getting strangely inconsistent results – your code is working one minute, and then stops working when you change something completely unrelated later in the program, for example – you've probably got memory problems. Double-check to make sure that you're freeing any TSS-allocated structures before reusing them, and that you're not allocating anything the TSS expects to allocate itself.

12.6   Problems using TPM data structures

- Your TPM may have a different endianness (byte ordering) from that of the rest of your system. This can cause data to turn into garbled junk, if you're not expecting it. A good way to check is to find some 16- or 32-bit data whose expected value you know for sure, and try reversing the endianness to see if that resolves the problem.

- The TPM does not use padding in the data structures that it returns. Many compilers, however, do; for example, they may assume that all fields will start at an offset divisible by four. This can cause very strange and unpredictable problems if you try casting a TPM's byte array to a C representation of the corresponding data structure, especially since the early portions of the structure may look just fine. Try unmarshalling the data structure byte by byte into its expected components. If you need to do this, the Structures specifications will be your new best friend; on the bright side, they tend to be the clearest of the TPM specification documents.

Chapter 13

Conclusion and review

Over the course of this book, I've provided a basic introduction to TPMs, and how they can be used both directly and in a range of personal and enterprise contexts. I've discussed the TPM's primary functions at length: secure key storage, trusted cryptographic functionality, and reliable reporting of stored data. I've covered how TPMs need to be provisioned before use, and how establishing trust in a TPM can in some cases be a highly sensitive operation. I've discussed the different capabilities of different types of TPM keys, how to choose the correct key for an application, and how to set up appropriate access constraints. I've introduced many useful functions of the TPM, both well known and obscure, and provided guidance on how and when to use them. I've also shown how the TPM relates to the Roots of Trust for Measurement, the pros and cons of various measurement options, and how measurements can be used in the TPM.

13.1   What the TPM is good for

TPMs are most powerful when used for three purposes:

Machine Authentication: Identifying a computer to other systems, with a cryptographic identity bound to the hardware. Any operation that uses a TPM key can potentially be used for machine authentication, with either a signing or a decryption operation.

Data Protection: The TPM can store limited amounts of data in its own internal storage, and much larger amounts of data can be securely encrypted using TPM keys. It can also be used for rollback detection, using NVRAM or monotonic counters.

Attestation: A machine's software state can be proved to another party using measurements stored in the TPM's Platform Configuration Registers, and sent via a signed TPM Quote. Machine state as represented in PCRs can also be used to limit access to encrypted data or keys.

13.2   Common TPM use cases

TPMs can be useful in a wide range of scenarios. Some examples include:

- Enterprise machines can be reliably authenticated to VPNs, wireless networks, or corporate web servers.

- Password or key stores can be protected using the TPM's encryption, dictionary-attack protection, and hardware tamper resistance.
- Data can be securely distributed to trusted machines identified by TPM, allowing secrets or proprietary information to be safely updated without physical access.
- Data, including entire hard drives, can be encrypted to only be decryptable if the machine is running expected software, and also if they are on the correct machine and accessed by the correct password.
- Enterprise machines can prove they're running the approved corporate image before gaining access to the corporate intranet, or before being provided access to sensitive corporate data.
- Logs can be authenticated as having come from the correct machine; with good measurement support, the machine can be confirmed to have loaded the expected software.
- Routers can prevent unauthorized machines from connecting to a network.
- A high-security application can use a machine's secure mode to display sensitive user information and collect high-value data without risk of leaking that data to untrusted software, while using the TPM to prove to remote parties, such as banks or payroll departments, that the application ran correctly and that the user's input corresponded to the application's output.

13.3   The potential (and peril) of the future

Trusted computing technology is slowly but surely being adopted more widely. TPMs are ubiquitous in business-class computers, and OS integration is becoming more widespread. TPMs are being designed for applications well beyond personal computing: for mobile phones, for printers and other embedded devices, even for cars. With hardware-based trusted computing in a wide range of devices, many of today's security problems become more tractable. Enterprises can authenticate personal devices such as phones more reliably, and protect corporate data independently from personal data. Cars and embedded devices can have a protected place to verify manufacturer firmware upgrades. On the flip side, many of the features that are so powerful in an enterprise or home context for a PC TPM, where the system owner can choose what to protect, whom to provide with trackable identities, and what software states are acceptable, can become potentially problematic in contexts where the 'owner' is the car manufacturer or phone network provider. For trusted computing to remain a powerful force for security in the marketplace, it is important for vendors and manufacturers to keep user privacy and vendor flexibility in mind.

13.4   In conclusion

With trusted computing, we have the potential to dramatically improve the security of systems both small and large. Some day we may be able to realize the dream of systems which provide ongoing, meaningful measurements of their software state, dramatically raising the bar for malicious software attacks. As limited as our systems are today, however, trusted computing can still let us build systems that are more secure against a wide range of threats. TPMs by themselves will not solve every problem, but secure systems are built out of many small pieces, and TPMs provide powerful features as part of a larger security story.

TPMs and trusted computing aren't right for every application and every enterprise. Some may find them too difficult to use today, or may find the benefits not worth the cost of implementation. I hope that this book has provided you with the tools you need to decide whether TPMs and trusted computing are right for you; and if you've decided to use them, that I've provided you with what you need to get started using this underappreciated technology.

Appendix A

Basic cryptographic concepts

A.1 The limitations of this appendix

Cryptography is a deep and complicated subject, and this appendix is not intended to provide any kind of comprehensive grounding in the material. For those interested, there are some great resources out there where you can learn more. A few of note:

- If you're just looking for a slightly deeper layman's explanation, Wikipedia is a fine place to start.
- *Cryptography Engineering: Design Principles and Practical Applications* by Niels Ferguson, Tadayoshi Kohno and Bruce Schneier.
- *Introduction to Modern Cryptography* by Jonathan Katz and Yehuda Lindell.
- The *Handbook of Applied Cryptography* by Alfred J. Menezes, Paul C. van Oorschot and Scott A. Vanstone is a good choice for those with a strong mathematical background who want to understand the details of how cryptographic algorithms actually work. It can also be found online at `http://cacr.uwaterloo.ca/hac/`

A.2 Basic vocabulary

Sign A cryptographic technique for showing that a message is authentic and has not been modified or tampered with.

Encrypt A cryptographic technique for keeping data secret.

Authenticate To verify the identity of an entity, such as a person or machine.

Attest To make a claim about something; in this context, normally about machine state, document origination, or the accuracy of a particular report.

Secrecy A security property implying that unauthorized parties cannot read data.

Integrity A security property implying that unauthorized parties cannot modify data.

A.3 Symmetric cryptography

In symmetric cryptography, there is a single secret, which is used to both encrypt and decrypt data. The simplest form of symmetric cryptography is the one-time pad: a set of random bits which are combined with the data, perhaps using something as simple as XOR. Only someone who knows exactly which random bits were used (the pad) can retrieve the original data by reversing the operation. One-time pads are highly inconvenient for most purposes, because reusing them can make them vulnerable and they must be as long as the data they're being combined with. Modern symmetric algorithms use more complex functions to combine a secret key with input data of any size and produce encrypted data that only someone who knows the secret key can decrypt. The key must be distributed to all parties who should be able to either encrypt or decrypt, and it is critical to keep these keys secret to protect the data.

In order to allow the same, often small, secret key to be used to encrypt large files, **block ciphers** are used. A large file is broken up into blocks, each one of an appropriate size to be encrypted using the small symmetric key. There are many ways of combining these blocks; these are called **block cipher modes**.

In theory, there is no need to sign encrypted data with symmetric cryptography: only someone else with the key can verify that the key was used, by decrypting the data successfully. However, there are a number of attacks that can be performed by manipulating ciphertexts, so it is common to use an **HMAC**, which will be discussed in A.6.1. These also require knowledge of the original key to verify. Never use the same key for both operations.

1.2 TPMs do not provide symmetric encryption to users, because of old export regulations limiting the sale of devices capable of bulk encryption. 2.0 TPMs do provide symmetric encryption support; their standard symmetric algorithm is AES, and they provide a number of block cipher mode options, many of which take parameters. These are documented in detail in section 11.4.6.1 of the 2.0 Architecture specification.

A.4   Asymmetric (public key) cryptography

Asymmetric cryptography, also known as public key cryptography, is widely used in TPMs, as well as in day-to-day communications. In asymmetric cryptography, keys come in pairs: a public key and a private key. The public key is just that: public. There is no security risk from a public key's being known; in fact, it is critical for many applications that the public key be widespread. The private key, in contrast, is secret, and should be known only by the key owner. Anyone with the public key can encrypt data; only the person with the private key can decrypt it. Only the person with the private key can sign data; anyone with the public key can verify that signature. Asymmetric cryptography is thus tremendously powerful for providing cryptographic identities.

All public key cryptography relies on mathematical problems that are easy to calculate in one direction, but computationally infeasible – too slow to perform given known techniques and technology – to reverse. A good example of this is the problem of factoring large numbers, which is key to the security of RSA. Given two prime numbers, it is easy to multiply them; however, given a very large number, we do not know a way to factor it to its component primes in a reasonable span of time. Knowing the private key allows the secret-holder to retrieve the information quickly using the easy operation; someone without the secret must solve the vastly harder problem.

1.2 TPMs support only RSA. RSA keys come in different lengths, reflecting the sizes of the prime numbers used in their keys. While 1024-bit RSA keys are still in use, 2048-bit keys are recommended for strength.

2.0 TPMs are required to support both RSA and ECC, with options for additional algorithms in the future. ECC key sizes are much smaller than equivalent-security RSA keys; the minimum key size for ECC in a TPM is 256 bits. Elliptic curve implementations generally support some set of standard curves; the mandatory set for PC TPMs is NIST P-256 and BN P-256, although manufacturers may include additional curves.

A.5   Key derivation functions

Key derivation functions (KDFs) are exactly what the name implies: mathematical functions which take some input – usually a random seed – and produce cryptographic keys. Given the same input, a given KDF will produce the same output; this can be useful, since instead of storing an entire key, one can store the seed only. Even a tiny change in input should produce a different key. 2.0 TPMs contain several KDFs, so that the same primary seed value can be used to generate appropriate secrets for all of the cryptographic algorithms the TPM supports.

A.6   Hashes

Hashes are, at their simplest, one-way functions each intended to produce a small 'fingerprint' of data. It should be easy to input an arbitrary amount of data and produce a constant-length output, but difficult to go from the output to the original data. Equally important, hashes must be *collision-resistant*: different data should always produce different output, and it should be infeasible for anyone to find two pieces of data which produce the same output. Hashes are used to uniquely identify larger amounts of data succinctly. In TPMs, we see them used primarily in two ways: as input to PCR, and as the input to asymmetric signatures. In both cases, they allow arbitrary-length files to be effectively used as input in places where there are hard constraints on how long the input data can be.

Different hash algorithms produce data of different lengths. 1.2 TPMs use SHA-1 hashes, which are 20-byte long. While SHA-1 has not been broken, which for a hash algorithm would mean that an attacker could easily find collisions (cases where two different inputs produce the same output), there are attacks on SHA-1 that suggest it is weaker than originally believed, and it is being phased out. 2.0 TPMs support SHA-1, but use SHA-256 (a member of the SHA-2 family) for core functionality such as PCRs, and other algorithms may be supported. SHA-256 produces 32-byte output.

A.6.1   HMACs

Hash-based Message Authentication Codes, or HMACs, are used to prove the integrity of data while also providing authentication of the message. These algorithms combine a hash function, a secret key, and the message to be authenticated. The output is easy to calculate (and thus verify) for anyone who has the message and the secret key, but an attacker cannot work backwards from the HMAC to the key, nor can an attacker modify the data without making the HMAC invalid unless the hash function itself has been completely broken. 2.0 TPMs provide HMAC functionality to the user; both versions use them as part of their infrastructure for secure communications sessions.

A.7   Nonces

Nonces are random values used to avoid a number of replay attacks. Unlike keys, which often use random data as part of their security, nonces do not necessarily have to feature randomness of particularly high quality. They are intended to be single-use, and are only random in order to prevent an attacker from being able to predict the value in advance. We use nonces instead of timestamps because timestamps are easy to predict and easy to forge. If Alice receives a signed message from Bob containing a current timestamp, Alice can't tell if the message was actually just generated, or if Bob's clock had been set to a different value and an attacker had recorded the message, or if an attacker had tricked Bob into signing a message with that timestamp in it, thinking it was something else. If Alice sends Bob a random number – a nonce – and receives that random number back as part of a signed message, Alice knows that Bob must have responded since she generated the number, because an attacker couldn't have predicted the number to forge it.

Nonces are an essential part of many cryptographic protocols. In TPMs, they are used as part of the TPM's secure communications sessions with user software, and far more visibly as a component of Quotes (9.3.1). The TPM also uses a nonce-like feature called the *tpmProof* or *hierarchy proof*, where a random number is created by the TPM and used as part of certain encrypted structures or HMACs. When objects are provided to the TPM later, these proof values are used to verify that an object came from the same TPM, because an attacker could not have predicted them and forged the data structure.

A.8   Zero-knowledge proofs

Because the underlying mathematics behind the elliptic curve zero-knowledge proofs used by 2.0 TPMs is extremely complicated and require non-trivial background knowledge, this explanation will be even slighter than most in this appendix. Those interested in learning more should read the background material, and take a look at the description of the TPM-specific DAA algorithms described in *Trusted Computing Platforms* (see Section 11.3.3).

The purpose of a zero-knowledge proof is for the prover to demonstrate knowledge of a secret without revealing anything about the secret to the verifier. Zero-knowledge proofs are particularly useful in situations where the verifier is not trusted with even a pseudonym for the prover's identity, and thus should not know even a consistent public key. In the TPM context, we're primarily interested in zero-knowledge signatures, which can prove that a trusted party signed a particular piece of data, without revealing the identity of that trusted party.

Many zero-knowledge proofs are based on a challenge–response model where the verifier presents the prover with a challenge in which specific mathematical operations must be performed. The zero-knowledge proofs used by the TPM in 2.0's DAA algorithm (Section 9.3.4), however, do not. Instead, the TPM's zero-knowledge signature scheme requires a commitment to a specific random value using a private key, followed by a signature proving that the key used in the commitment and the random number used in the commitment were both also used in the signature. A verifier can perform certain algorithm-specific mathematical operations to prove that the random value and private key are the same in the commitment and the signature, without learning what either the random number or the key is. The TPM user can present a certificate that does not reveal the private key, but does prove that the private key in question is a member of a group trusted by a particular CA.

Appendix B
Command equivalence and requirements charts

These charts are intended to serve two quite unrelated purposes. The first is to allow someone who has a particular PC TPM to discover which commands will definitely be supported, which won't, and which may or may not be, depending on the manufacturer. The second is to provide a convenient reference for implementers using multiple TPM versions or programming abstraction levels.

The first chart is organized by TPM 1.2 commands. For each command, the chart indicates whether the command is required; the TSS 1.2 TSPI[1] functions, if any, that provide equivalent or overlapping functionality; and the TPM 2.0 commands which are the closest equivalents, if any are close at all. In some cases, where TPM 2.0 has introduced new but related functionality, I'm including it, so that those interested can look into the details and decide if it's useful to them.

The second chart is organized by TPM 2.0 commands. For each command, the chart indicates whether the command is required.

Note that many TPM 2.0 commands show up in the second chart but not the first; these are commands for which there is no real 1.2 equivalent.

B.1 Key

Although the command names are intuitive, the requirements notation is less so. The requirements column is labelled as 'R?' to save space.

M Command is mandatory for PC implementations of this specification
X Command must not be included in PC implementations of this specification; deprecated command from prior TPM version
O Command is optional, and may be included or not as the manufacturer prefers
O*n* Command is optional, but one of a set. If any command in the set is included, all commands in the set must be included. (So, if any O1 command is included, all O1 commands must be included by the manufacturer.) Sets are numbered for compatibility with specification tables; the numbers have no meaning, and are reused from chart to chart. Sets tend to provide multiple operations supporting a single feature.

Each chart is ordered according to its specification; the 1.2 chart in alphabetical order, and the 2.0 chart in groups according to functionality. The charts do not include the commands that are expected to be run only by low-level firmware; startup, shutdown, in it, and so forth.

---

[1]Lower-level TSS 1.2 functions have a much more direct correspondence to the hardware commands.

B.2 TPM 1.2 command equivalence and requirements

1.2 TPM Command	R?	1.2 TSS	2.0 TPM
TPM_ActivateIdentity	M	Tspi_TPM_ActivateIdentity	TPM2_ActivateCredential
TPM_AuthorizeMigrationKey	M	Tspi_TPM_AuthorizeMigrationTicket	–
TPM_CertifyKey	M	Tspi_Key_CertifyKey	TPM2_Certify
TPM_CertifyKey2	M	Tspi_Key_CertifyKey	TPM2_Certify
TPM_CertifySelfTest	X	Tspi_TPM_CertifySelfTest	–
TPM_ChangeAuth	M	Tspi_ChangeAuth	TPM2_ObjectChangeAuth
TPM_ChangeAuthAsymFinish	M	Tspi_ChangeAuthAsym	TPM2_ObjectChangeAuth
TPM_ChangeAuthAsymStart	M	Tspi_ChangeAuthAsym	TPM2_ObjectChangeAuth
TPM_ChangeAuthOwner	M	Tspi_ChangeAuth	TPM2_SetPrimaryPolicy
			TPM2_HierarchyChangeAuth
TPM_CMK_ApproveMA	M	Tspi_TPM_CMKApproveMA	–
TPM_CMK_ConvertMigration	M	Tspi_Key_CMK_ConvertMigration	–
TPM_CMK_CreateBlob	M	Tspi_Key_CMK_CreateBlob	–
TPM_CMK_CreateKey	M	Tspi_Key_CreateKey	TPM2_Create, with specialized duplication policy
TPM_CMK_CreateTicket	M	Tspi_TPM_CMKCreateTicket	–
TPM_CMK_SetRestrictions	M	Tspi_TPM_CMKSetRestrictions	–
TPM_ContinueSelfTest	M	–	TPM2_IncrementalSelfTest
TPM_ConvertMigrationBlob	M	Tspi_Key_ConvertMigrationBlob	TPM2_Rewrap
			TPM2_Import
TPM_CreateCounter	M	–	TPM2_NV_DefineSpace
TPM_CreateEndorsementKeyPair	M	Tspi_TPM_CreateEndorsementKey	TPM2_CreatePrimary
			TPM2_ChangeEPS
TPM_CreateMaintenanceArchive	O1	Tspi_TPM_CreateMaintenanceArchive	–
TPM_CreateMigrationBlob	M	Tspi_Key_CreateMigrationBlob	TPM2_Duplicate

	O3	Tspi_TPM_CreateRevocableEndorsementKey	TPM2_CreatePrimary
TPM_CreateRevocableEK			TPM2_ChangeEPS
TPM_CreateWrapKey	M	Tspi_Key_CreateKey[2]	TPM2_Create
TPM_DAA_Join	M	Tspi_DAA_JoinInit	TPM2_Commit
		Tspi_TPM_DAA_JoinCreateDaaPubKey	
		Tspi_TPM_JoinStoreCredential	
TPM_DAA_Sign	M	Tspi_TPM_DAA_Sign	TPM2_Commit
			TPM2_EC_Ephemeral
			Any signing operation
TPM_Delegate_CreateKeyDelegation	M	Tspi_TPM_Delegate_CreateDelegation	Policy commands
TPM_Delegate_CreateOwnerDelegation	M	Tspi_Delegate_CreateDelegation	Policy commands
TPM_Delegate_LoadOwnerDelegation	M	Tspi_TPM_Delegate_CacheOwnerDelegation	Policy commands
TPM_Delegate_Manage	M	Tspi_TPM_Delegate_AddFamily	Policy commands
		Tspi_TPM_Delegate_InvalidateFamily	
TPM_Delegate_ReadTable	M	Tspi_TPM_Delegate_ReadTables	—
TPM_Delegate_UpdateVerification	M	Tspi_TPM_Delegate_UpdateVerificationCount	—
TPM_Delegate_VerifyDelegation	M	Tspi_TPM_Delegate_VerifyDelegation	Policy commands
TPM_DirRead[3]	M	Tspi_TPM_DirRead	TPM2_NV_Read
TPM_DirWriteAuth[4]	M		TPM2_NV_Write
TPM_DisableForceClear	M	Tspi_TPM_SetStatus	TPM2_ClearControl
TPM_DisableOwnerClear	M	Tspi_TPM_SetStatus	TPM2_ClearControl
TPM_DisablePubekRead	M	Tspi_TPM_SetStatus	
TPM_DSAP	M	—	TPM2_StartAuthSession
TPM_EstablishTransport	M	—	TPM2_StartAuthSession
TPM_EvictKey	M	Tspi_Key_UnloadKey	TPM2_FlushContext
TPM_ExecuteTransport	M		TPM2_StartAuthSession
TPM_Extend	M	Tspi_TPM_PcrExtend	TPM2_PCR_Extend
			TPM2_PCR_Event
			TPM2_NV_Extend

(Continues)

1.2 TPM Command	R?	1.2 TSS	2.0 TPM
TPM_FieldUpgrade	O		TPM2_FieldUpgradeStart TPM2_FieldUpgradeData TPM2_FirmwareRead
TPM_FlushSpecific	M		TPM2_FlushContext
TPM_ForceClear	M	Tspi_ClearOwner	TPM2_Clear
TPM_GetAuditDigest	O2	Tspi_GetAuditDigest	TPM2_GetCommandAuditDigest TPM2_GetSessionAuditDigest
TPM_GetAuditDigestSigned	O2		TPM2_GetCommandAuditDigest TPM2_GetSessionAuditDigest
TPM_GetAuditEvent	X		—
TPM_GetAuditEventSigned	X		—
TPM_GetCapability	M	Tspi_TPM_GetStatus Tspi_TPM_GetCapability	TPM2_GetCapability TPM2_TestParms
TPM_GetCapabilityOwner	M		TPM2_GetCapability
TPM_GetCapabilitySigned[5]	X	Tspi_TPM_GetCapabiitySigned[6]	—
TPM_GetOrdinalAuditStatus	X		TPM2_GetCommandAuditDigest
TPM_GetPubKey	M	Tspi_Key_GetPubKey Tspi_TPM_Owner_GetSRKPubKey	TPM2_ReadPublic
TPM_GetRandom	M	Tspi_TPM_GetRandom	TPM2_GetRandom
TPM_GetTestResult	M	Tspi_TPM_GetTestResult	TPM2_GetTestResult
TPM_GetTick	M	Tspi_TPM_ReadCurrentTicks	TPM2_ReadClock
TPM_IncrementCounter	M	—	TPM2_NV_Increment
TPM_KeyControlOwner	M		TPM2_EvictControl
TPM_KillMaintenanceFeature	O1	Tspi_TPM_KillMaintenanceFeature Tspi_TPM_SetStatus	—
TPM_LoadAuthContext	O		TPM2_ContextLoad
TPM_LoadContext	M		TPM2_ContextLoad
TPM_LoadKey	M	Tspi_Key_LoadKey	TPM2_Load TPM2_LoadExternal

TPM_LoadKey2	M	Tspi_Key_LoadKey	TPM2_Load
			TPM2_LoadExternal
			TPM2_ContextLoad
TPM_LoadKeyContext	O		
TPM_LoadMaintenanceArchive	O1		—
TPM_LoadManuMaintPub	O1	Tspi_LoadMaintenancePubKey	—
TPM_MakeIdentity	M	Tspi_TPM_CollateIdentityRequest	TPM2_Create
			TPM2_CreatePrimary
TPM_MigrateKey	M		TPM2_Duplicate
TPM_NV_DefineSpace	M	Tspi_NV_DefineSpace	TPM2_DefineSpace
		Tspi_TPM_ReleaseSpace	TPM2_UndefineSpace
TPM_NV_ReadValue	M	Tspi_NV_ReadValue	TPM2_NV_Read
TPM_NV_ReadValueAuth	M		TPM2_NV_Read
TPM_NV_WriteValue	M	Tspi_NV_WriteSpace	TPM2_NV_Write
		Tspi_DirWrite	
TPM_NV_WriteValueAuth	M		TPM2_NV_Write
TPM_OIAP	M		TPM2_StartAuthSession
TPM_OSAP	M		TPM2_StartAuthSession
TPM_OwnerClear	M		TPM2_Clear
TPM_OwnerReadInternalPub	M		TPM2_ReadPublic
TPM_OwnerReadPubek	M	Tspi_TPM_GetPubEndorsementKey	TPM2_ReadPublic
TPM_OwnerSetDisable	M	Tspi_TPM_SetStatus	TPM2_HierarchyControl
TPM_PCR_Reset	M		TPM2_PCR_Reset
TPM_PcrRead	M	Tspi_TPM_PcrRead	TPM2_PCR_Read
		Tspi_TPM_GetEvents[7]	TPM2_NV_Read[8]
TPM_PhysicalDisable	M	Tspi_TPM_SetStatus	TPM2_PP_Commands
TPM_PhysicalEnable	M	Tspi_TPM_SetStatus	TPM2_PP_Commands
TPM_PhysicalSetDeactivated	M	Tspi_TPM_SetStatus	TPM2_PP_Commands
TPM_Quote	M	Tspi_TPM_Quote	TPM2_Quote
TPM_Quote2	M	Tspi_TPM_Quote2	TPM2_Quote

(Continues)

1.2 TPM Command	R?	1.2 TSS	2.0 TPM
TPM_ReadCounter	M	Tspi_TPM_ReadCurrentCounter	TPM2_NV_Read
TPM_ReadManuMaintPub	O1		–
TPM_ReadPubek	M		TPM2_ReadPublic
TPM_ReleaseCounter	M	–	TPM2_UndefineSpace
TPM_ReleaseCounterOwner	M	–	TPM2_UndefineSpace
TPM_ReleaseTransportSigned	M	–	–
TPM_Reset	M	Tspi_TPM_PcrReset	TPM2_FlushContext
TPM_ResetLockValue	M	Tspi_TPM_SetStatus	TPM2_DictionaryAttackLockReset
			TPM2_DictionaryAttackParameters
TPM_RevokeTrust	O3	Tspi_TPM_RevokeEndorsementKey	TPM2_ChangeEPS
TPM_SaveAuthContext	O		TPM2_ContextSave
TPM_SaveContext	M		TPM2_ContextSave
TPM_SaveKeyContext	O		TPM2_ContextSave
TPM_Seal	M	Tspi_Data_Seal	TPM2_Create
TPM_Sealx	O		TPM2_Create
TPM_SelfTestFull	M	Tspi_TPM_SelfTestFull	TPM2_SelfTest
TPM_SetCapability	M		TPM2_PP_Commands
			TPM2_DictionaryAttackParameters
			TPM2_SetAlgorithmSet
			TPM2_ClearControl
			TPM2_HierarchyControl
			TPM2_ClockSet
			TPM2_ClockRateAdjust

TPM command	M/O	Tspi function	TPM2 command
TPM_SetOperatorAuth	M	Tspi_TPM_SetOperatorAuth	—
TPM_SetOrdinalAuditStatus	O2		TPM2_SetCommandCodeAuditStatus
TPM_SetOwnerInstall	M		—
TPM_SetOwnerPointer	M		—
TPM_SetRedirection	O		
TPM_SetTempDeactivated	M	Tspi_TPM_SetStatus	TPM2_HierarchyControl
TPM_SHA1Complete	M		TPM2_SequenceComplete
TPM_SHA1CompleteExtend	M		TPM2_EventSequenceComplete
TPM_SHA1Start	M		TPM2_HashSequenceStart
			TPM2_HMAC_Start
TPM_SHA1Update	M		TPM2_SequenceUpdate
TPM_Sign	M	Tspi_Hash_Sign	TPM2_Sign
TPM_StirRandom	M	Tspi_TPM_StirRandom	TPM2_StirRandom
TPM_TakeOwnership	M	Tspi_TakeOwnership	TPM2_HierarchyChangeAuth[9]
TPM_Terminate_Handle	M		TPM2_FlushContext
TPM_TickStampBlob	M	Tspi_Hash_TickStampBlob	TPM2_GetTime
TPM_UnBind	M	Tspi_Data_Unbind	TPM2_RSA_Decrypt
TPM_Unseal	M	Tspi_Data_Unseal	TPM2_Unseal

[2] The confusingly named Tspi_Key_WrapKey is used to create a TPM-usable key blob out of an existing key.

[3] The DIR commands are an old and deprecated TPM 1.1 precursor to NV storage, and provide strictly fewer features.

[4] See B.1.

[5] Removed after the final TPM specification was released owing to a discovered vulnerability.

[6] Optional, for backwards compatibility with TPMs that shipped before the function was removed.

[7] The Tspi_TPM_GetEvents and Tspi_TPM_GetEventLog commands retrieve a complete log of all extend events that went through the TSS, providing a useful verification tool for PCR contents.

[8] For PCR-like NV indexes.

[9] After a clear, or before use, the non-platform authorizations are all the empty buffer.

B.3   TPM 2.0 command requirements

2.0 TPM Command	R?
TPM2_Startup	M
TPM2_Shutdown	M
Testing	
TPM2_IncrementalSelfTest	M
TPM2_SelfTest	M
TPM2_GetTestResult	M
Session Commands	
TPM2_StartAuthSession	M
TPM2_PolicyRestart	M
Object Commands	
TPM2_Create	M
TPM2_Load	M
TPM2_LoadExternal	M
TPM2_ReadPublic	M
TPM2_ActivateCredential	M
TPM2_MakeCredential	M
TPM2_Unseal	M
TPM2_ObjectChangeAuth	M
Duplicate Commands	
TPM2_Duplicate	M
TPM2_Rewrap	O
TPM2_Import	M
Asymmetric Primitives	
TPM2_RSA_Encrypt	M
TPM2_RSA_Decrypt	M
TPM2_ECDH_KeyGen	M
TPM2_ECDH_ZGen	M
TPM2_ECC_Parameters	M
TPM2_ZGen_2Phase	O
Symmetric Primitives	
TPM2_EncryptDecrypt	O
TPM2_Hash	M
TPM2_HMAC	O

(Continues)

2.0 TPM Command	R?
Random Number Generator	
TPM2_GetRandom	M
TPM2_StirRandom	M
Hash/HMAC/Event Sequences	
TPM2_HMAC_Start	M
TPM2_HashSequenceStart	M
TPM2_SequenceUpdate	M
TPM2_SequenceComplete	M
TPM2_EventSequenceComplete	M
Attestation Commands	
TPM2_Certify	M
TPM2_CertifyCreation	M
TPM2_Quote	M
TPM2_GetSessionAuditDigest	M
TPM2_GetCommandAuditDigest	O
TPM2_GetTime	O
Anonymous Attestation	
TPM2_Commit	M
TPM2_ECC_Ephemeral	O
Signature Verification	
TPM2_VerifySignature	M
TPM2_Sign	M
Command Audit	
TPM2_SetCommandCodeAuditStatus	O
Integrity Collection (PCR)	
TPM2_PCR_Extend	M
TPM2_PCR_Event	M
TPM2_PCR_Read	M
TPM2_PCR_Allocate	M
TPM2_PCR_SetAuthPolicy	O
TPM2_PCR_SetAuthValue	O
TPM2_PCR_Reset	M

(*Continues*)

2.0 TPM Command	R?
Enhanced Authorization (EA)	
TPM2_PolicySigned	M
TPM2_PolicySecret	M
TPM2_PolicyTicket	O
TPM2_PolicyOR	M
TPM2_PolicyPCR	M
TPM2_PolicyLocality	M
TPM2_PolicyNV	M
TPM2_PolicyCounterTimer	M
TPM2_PolicyCommandCode	M
TPM2_PolicyPhysicalPresence	O[10]
TPM2_PolicyCpHash	M
TPM2_PolicyNameHash	M
TPM2_PolicyDuplicationSelect	M
TPM2_PolicyAuthorize	M
TPM2_PolicyAuthValue	M
TPM2_PolicyPassword	M
TPM2_PolicyGetDigest	M
TPM2_PolicyNvWritten	M
Hierarchy Commands	
TPM2_CreatePrimary	M
TPM2_HierarchyControl	M
TPM2_SetPrimaryPolicy	M
TPM2_ChangePPS	O[11]
TPM2_ChangeEPS	O[12]
TPM2_Clear	M
TPM2_ClearControl	M
TPM2_HierarchyChangeAuth	M
Dictionary Attack Functions	
TPM2_DictionaryAttackLockReset	M
TPM2_DictionaryAttackParameters	M
Miscellaneous Management Functions	
TPM2_PP_Commands	O
TPM2_SetAlgorithmSet	O
Field Upgrade	
TPM2_FieldUpgradeStart	O1
TPM2_FieldUpgradeData	O1
TPM2_FirmwareRead	O1

(Continues)

2.0 TPM Command	R?
Context Management	
TPM2_ContextSave	M
TPM2_ContextLoad	M
TPM2_FlushContext	M
TPM2_EvictControl	M
Clocks and Timers	
TPM2_ReadClock	M
TPM2_ClockSet	M
TPM2_ClockRateAdjust	M
Capability Commands	
TPM2_GetCapability	M
TPM2_TestParms	M
Non-volatile Storage	
TPM2_NV_DefineSpace	M
TPM2_NV_UndefineSpace	M
TPM2_NV_UndefineSpaceSpecial	M
TPM2_NV_ReadPublic	M
TPM2_NV_Write	M
TPM2_NV_Increment	M
TPM2_NV_Extend	M
TPM2_NV_SetBits	M
TPM2_NV_WriteLock	M
TPM2_NV_GlobalWriteLock	O
TPM2_NV_Read	M
TPM2_NV_ReadLock	M
TPM2_NV_ChangeAuth	M
TPM2_NV_Certify	O

[10]Mandatory if TPM supports physical presence.

[11]Mandatory for FIPS.

[12]See footnote 11.

Appendix C

Complete code samples

Throughout most of the book, the code examples were presented as excerpts with explanations. Because it can sometimes be hard to work out how those excerpts come together, this appendix includes several complete programs. The 1.2 TSS examples are demonstration programs to show how several TPM functions work in combination. The 2.0 TSS examples are single-purpose utilities for production use that come with the IBM TSS 2.0 package, and are included with the kind permission of the author.

C.1   1.2 TSS code samples

C.1.1   Sealing and unsealing

This demonstration program includes:

- Basic TSS setup and cleanup
- Use of the SRK including its password
- Reading of current state of PCR values
- Creation of a storage key with PCR constraints
- Sealing of data
- Unsealing of data

```
#include <stdio.h>
#include <string.h>
#include <stdlib.h>
#include <sys/stat.h>
#include <sys/types.h>
#include <tss/tss_error.h>
#include <tss/platform.h>
#include <tss/tss_defines.h>
#include <tss/tss_typedef.h>
#include <tss/tss_structs.h>
#include <tss/tspi.h>
#include <trousers/trousers.h>
```

```
int debug(char msg[], int errorcode){
  printf("%s returned %08x, %s\n",
         msg, errorcode, (char*)Trspi_Error_String(errorcode));
  return 0;
}

int main(int argc, char **argv){
 TSS_HCONTEXT hContext;
  TSS_HTPM      hTPM;
  TSS_RESULT    result;


  TSS_HKEY hSRK;
  TSS_HKEY hStorageKey;
  TSS_HPOLICY hStoragePolicy, hSRKPolicy, hSealPolicy;


  result = Tspi_Context_Create(&hContext);
  result = Tspi_Context_Connect(hContext, NULL);
  result = Tspi_Context_GetTpmObject(hContext, &hTPM);

  result= Tspi_Context_LoadKeyByUUID(hContext, TSS_PS_TYPE_SYSTEM,
                                     (TSS_UUID) TSS_UUID_SRK, &hSRK);
  debug('''Loading' SRK'', result);

  result= Tspi_Context_CreateObject(hContext, TSS_OBJECT_TYPE_RSAKEY,
                                    TSS_KEY_SIZE_2048 |
                                    TSS_KEY_TYPE_STORAGE
                                    | TSS_KEY_AUTHORIZATION |
                                    TSS_KEY_NOT_MIGRATABLE,
                                    &hStorageKey);

 debug("Creating storage key object", result);

 // Setting PCR requirements for storage key.
 TSS_HPCRS hStoragePCRs;
 BYTE* tempPCRVal;
 UINT32 tempPCRLen;
 result = Tspi_Context_CreateObject(hContext, TSS_OBJECT_TYPE_PCRS, 0,
                                    &hStoragePCRs);
 debug("Creating PCR object for storage key", result);


 // Retrieving current values of DRTM PCRs (17--19)
 result = Tspi_TPM_PcrRead(hTPM, 17, &tempPCRLen, &tempPCRVal);
 debug("Retrieving value of PCR 17", result);
 result = Tspi_PcrComposite_SetPcrValue(hStoragePCRs, 17, tempPCRLen,
                                        tempPCRVal);
 debug("Setting value of PCR 17 in composite", result);
 /* Free memory for tempPCRVal, so allocation in next PcrRead won't
    cause problems. */
 Tspi_Context_FreeMemory(hContext, tempPCRVal);
```

```
result = Tspi_TPM_PcrRead(hTPM, 18, &tempPCRLen, &tempPCRVal);
debug("Retrieving value of PCR 18", result);
result = Tspi_PcrComposite_SetPcrValue(hStoragePCRs, 18, tempPCRLen,
                                       tempPCRVal);
debug("Setting value of PCR 18 in composite", result);
Tspi_Context_FreeMemory(hContext, tempPCRVal);

result = Tspi_TPM_PcrRead(hTPM, 19, &tempPCRLen, &tempPCRVal);
debug("Retrieving value of PCR 19", result);
result = Tspi_PcrComposite_SetPcrValue(hStoragePCRs, 19, tempPCRLen,
                                       tempPCRVal);
debug("Setting value of PCR 19 in composite", result);
Tspi_Context_FreeMemory(hContext, tempPCRVal);


// Creating key using PCR composite (current state of PCRs 17--19) as
   constraints
result = Tspi_Key_CreateKey(hStorageKey, hSRK, hStoragePCRs);
debug("Creating storage key", result);

// Set up SRK policy to allow key to be loaded
result= Tspi_Context_CreateObject(hContext, TSS_OBJECT_TYPE_POLICY,
                        TSS_POLICY_USAGE, &hSRKPolicy);
debug(''Creating SRK Use Policy'', result);

BYTE wks[] =TSS_WELL_KNOWN_SECRET;

result= Tspi_Policy_SetSecret(hSRKPolicy, TSS_SECRET_MODE_SHA1,
                              sizeof(wks), wks);
debug(''Setting SRK policy to use Well Known Secret'', result);

result= Tspi_Policy_AssignToObject(hSRKPolicy, hSRK);
debug("Assigning policy to SRK", result);

// Load storage key
result = Tspi_Key_LoadKey(hStorageKey, hSRK);
debug("Loading storage key", result);

// Create sealed object

TSS_HENCDATA hSealData;

result = Tspi_Context_CreateObject(hContext, TSS_OBJECT_TYPE_ENCDATA,
                              TSS_ENCDATA_SEAL, &hSealData);
debug("Creating sealed data object", result);

/* In a normal program, we'd usually get data to seal from a file or
 * the user, but for demonstration purposes we're using a simple
   string.
 */

BYTE* inData = "This is seal test data";
UINT32 inDataSize = sizeof("This is seal test data");
```

```c
/* Check to make sure data is not too large to seal, including
    padding.
 * Padding takes 103 bytes; data + padding has to be no larger
    than key.
 */
if (inDataSize > (2048 - 103)){
  printf("Error: data too large to seal.");
  return -1;
}


// Set policy for object to be sealed. Setting a policy with a
    secret is
// mandatory, and TSS_SECRET_MODE_NONE causes errors. As with SRK,
// using well-known secret.
result= Tspi_Context_CreateObject(hContext, TSS_OBJECT_TYPE_POLICY,
                    TSS_POLICY_USAGE, &hSealPolicy);
debug("Creating policy for sealed data", result);

result = Tspi_Policy_SetSecret(hSealPolicy, TSS_SECRET_MODE_PLAIN,
                    sizeof(wks), wks);
debug("Setting null secret policy for data", result);

result= Tspi_Policy_AssignToObject(hSealPolicy, hSealData);
debug("Assigning policy to sealed data object", result);

TSS_HPCRS hSealingPCRs = 0; // For now, not sealing to any PCR
                            // constraints.

result = Tspi_Data_Seal(hSealData, hStorageKey, inDataSize, inData,
                    hSealingPCRs);

debug("Sealing test data", result);

BYTE* outData;
UINT32 outDataSize;

result = Tspi_Data_Unseal(hSealData, hStorageKey, &outDataSize,
                    &outData);

debug("Unsealing test data", result);

printf("Result of unsealing: %s\n", outData);

Tspi_Context_Close(hTPM);

Tspi_Context_FreeMemory(hContext, NULL);

Tspi_Context_Close(hContext);

return 0;

}
```

C.1.2   Using NVRAM

This demonstration program includes:

- Basic TSS setup and cleanup
- Reading the NVRAM storage location for manufacturer Endorsement Credentials
- Taking actions as the TPM owner
- Creating a new NVRAM storage area
- Reading PCR values
- Writing to an NVRAM storage area
- Reading an NVRAM storage area

```c
#include <stdio.h>
#include <string.h>
#include <stdlib.h>
#include <sys/stat.h>
#include <sys/types.h>
#include <tss/tss_error.h>
#include <tss/platform.h>
#include <tss/tss_defines.h>
#include <tss/tss_typedef.h>
#include <tss/tss_structs.h>
#include <tss/tspi.h>
#include <trousers/trousers.h>


int debug(char msg[], int errorcode){
  printf("%s returned %08x, %s\n",
         msg, errorcode, (char*)Trspi_Error_String(errorcode));
  return 0;
}

int main(int argc, char **argv){
 TSS_HCONTEXT hContext;
  TSS_HTPM     hTPM;
  TSS_RESULT   result;


  result = Tspi_Context_Create(&hContext);
  debug("Creating Context", result);
  result = Tspi_Context_Connect(hContext, NULL);
  debug("Connecting context to default TPM", result);
  result = Tspi_Context_GetTpmObject(hContext, &hTPM);
  debug("Getting TPM object", result);


  TSS_HNVSTORE hEKCert;
  TSS_HNVSTORE hNVData;
  UINT32 EKDataLen = 1024; // Length will vary with manufacturer
  BYTE* EKCertData;
```

```
result = Tspi_Context_CreateObject(hContext, TSS_OBJECT_TYPE_NV, 0,
                                   &hEKCert);
debug("Creating EK Cert handle object", result);

/* Set to defined index for EK Cert 0x000F000 */
result = Tspi_SetAttribUint32(hEKCert, TSS_TSPATTRIB_NV_INDEX, 0,
                              TPM_NV_INDEX_EKCert);
debug("Setting NV Index value", result);

/* Read certificate out, if present. */
result = Tspi_NV_ReadValue(hEKCert, 0, &EKDataLen, &EKCertData);
debug("Reading NV contents for EK Cert", result);

/* Creating our own NV index to write to. Choosing index randomly
 * from non-reserved values. Because we're using the TSS, attempting
 * to create a new index over an existing one will fail until
 * Tspi_NV_ReleaseSpace is used, so checking for use in advance is
 * not mandatory. */
result = Tspi_Context_CreateObject(hContext, TSS_OBJECT_TYPE_NV, 0,
                                   &hNVData);
debug("Creating NV Data handle object", result);
result = Tspi_SetAttribUint32(hNVData, TSS_TSPATTRIB_NV_INDEX, 0,
                              0x0100000);
debug("Setting NV Index value", result);

/* Setting index to owner-only read and write, and writeall (must
 * completely be overwritten on each write) */
result = Tspi_SetAttribUint32(hNVData, TSS_TSPATTRIB_NV_PERMISSIONS,
                              0, TPM_NV_PER_WRITEALL |
                              TPM_NV_PER_OWNERWRITE |
                              TPM_NV_PER_OWNERREAD);
debug("Setting NV Permissions value", result);

result = Tspi_SetAttribUint32(hNVData, TSS_TSPATTRIB_NV_DATASIZE,
                              0, 20);
debug("Setting NV Data Size value", result);



/* Set up owner authorization, required to define NVRAM space */
TSS_HPOLICY hOwnerPolicy;
result= Tspi_GetPolicyObject(hTPM, TSS_POLICY_USAGE,
                             &hOwnerPolicy);
debug("Getting owner policy", result);

/* Setting owner secret explicitly. since popups aren't functional
 * on the demo system. */
char* pwd = "TPMDemo123";
result= Tspi_Policy_SetSecret(hOwnerPolicy, TSS_SECRET_MODE_PLAIN,
                              strlen(pwd), pwd);
debug("Setting owner secret", result);
```

```
/* Second and third arguments are optional TSS_HPCRS objects
   specifying
 * the PCR constraints associated with reading and writing
   respectively. */
result = Tspi_NV_DefineSpace(hNVData, 0, 0);
debug("Defining NV space", result);

UINT32 pcrLen;
BYTE* pcrVal;

/* Read a PCR to get a sample 20-byte value to write into NVRAM */
result =Tspi_TPM_PcrRead(hTPM, 1, &pcrLen, &pcrVal);
debug("Retrieving PCR data for NV input", result);
printf("PCR data: %20s\n", pcrVal);

/* Assigning correct authorization policy to NV object so that the
 * correct TPM command (for owner-authorized NV access) will be
 * used. Not doing so leads to authorization conflicts.
 */
result = Tspi_Policy_AssignToObject(hOwnerPolicy, hNVData);
debug("Assigning owner policy to NVData object", result);

/* The second value is the offset, which we can't use for writeall
   NV spaces even if we wanted to. */
result = Tspi_NV_WriteValue(hNVData, 0, pcrLen, pcrVal);
debug("Writing to NV Space", result);

/* The third argument is both input (expected length) and output
   (actual length) */
UINT32 dataLen = pcrLen;
BYTE* NVDataOut;
  result = Tspi_NV_ReadValue(hNVData, 0, &dataLen, &NVDataOut);
debug("Reading NV space for NVData", result);
printf("NV data: Len %d, %20s\n", dataLen, NVDataOut);

if (memcmp(NVDataOut, pcrVal, dataLen))
  printf("Write and read data do not match\n");
else
  printf("Write and read data match\n");


Tspi_Context_Close(hTPM);

Tspi_Context_FreeMemory(hContext, NULL);

Tspi_Context_Close(hContext);

return 0;

}
```

C.2   2.0 TSS code samples

C.2.1   Creating objects

```c
static void printUsage(void);
static void asymPublicTemplate(Create_In *in,
                               int type,
                               TPMI_ALG_PUBLIC algPublic,
                               TPMI_ECC_CURVE curveID,
                               TPMI_ALG_HASH nalg,
                               TPMI_ALG_HASH halg);
static void symmetricCipherTemplate(Create_In *in,
                                    TPMI_ALG_HASH nalg,
                                    int rev116);
static void keyedHashPublicTemplate(Create_In *in,
                                    TPMI_ALG_HASH nalg,
                                    TPMI_ALG_HASH halg);
static void blPublicTemplate(Create_In *in,
                             TPMI_ALG_HASH nalg);
/* object type */

#define TYPE_BL     1
#define TYPE_ST     2
#define TYPE_DEN    3
#define TYPE_DEO    4
#define TYPE_SI     5
#define TYPE_SIR    6
#define TYPE_GP     7
#define TYPE_DES    8
#define TYPE_KH     9

int verbose = FALSE;

int main(int argc, char *argv[])
{
    TPM_RC                   rc = 0;
    int                      i;    /* argc iterator */
    Create_In                in;
    Create_Out               out;
    TPMI_DH_OBJECT           parentHandle = 0;
    int                      keyType = 0;
    uint32_t                 keyTypeSpecified = 0;
    int                      rev116 = FALSE;
    TPMI_ALG_PUBLIC          algPublic = TPM_ALG_RSA;
    TPMI_ECC_CURVE           curveID = TPM_ECC_NONE;
    TPMI_ALG_HASH            halg = TPM_ALG_SHA256;
    TPMI_ALG_HASH            nalg = TPM_ALG_SHA256;
    const char               *policyFilename = NULL;
    const char               *publicKeyFilename = NULL;
    const char               *privateKeyFilename = NULL;
    const char               *dataFilename = NULL;
    const char               *keyPassword = NULL;
    const char               *parentPassword = NULL;
    TPMI_SH_AUTH_SESSION     sessionHandle0 = TPM_RS_PW;
    unsigned int             sessionAttributes0 = 0;
    TPMI_SH_AUTH_SESSION     sessionHandle1 = TPM_RH_NULL;
    unsigned int             sessionAttributes1 = 0;
    TPMI_SH_AUTH_SESSION     sessionHandle2 = TPM_RH_NULL;
    unsigned int             sessionAttributes2 = 0;
```

```
TSE_SetProperty(TPM_TRACE_LEVEL, "1");

/* command line argument defaults */
in.inPublic.t.publicArea.objectAttributes.val = 0;
in.inPublic.t.publicArea.objectAttributes.val |= TPMA_OBJECT_NODA;

for (i=1 ; (i<argc) && (rc == 0) ; i++) {
    if (strcmp(argv[i],"-hp") == 0) {
        i++;
        if (i < argc) {
            sscanf(argv[i],"%x", &parentHandle);
        }
        else {
            printf("Missing parameter for -hp\n");
            printUsage();
        }
    }
    else if (strcmp(argv[i], "-bl") == 0) {
        keyType = TYPE_BL;
        keyTypeSpecified++;
    }
    else if (strcmp(argv[i], "-den") == 0) {
        keyType = TYPE_DEN;
        keyTypeSpecified++;
    }
    else if (strcmp(argv[i], "-deo") == 0) {
        keyType = TYPE_DEO;
        keyTypeSpecified++;
    }
    else if (strcmp(argv[i], "-des") == 0) {
        keyType = TYPE_DES;
        keyTypeSpecified++;
    }
    else if (strcmp(argv[i], "-st") == 0) {
        keyType = TYPE_ST;
        keyTypeSpecified++;
    }
    else if (strcmp(argv[i], "-si") == 0) {
        keyType = TYPE_SI;
        keyTypeSpecified++;
    }
    else if (strcmp(argv[i], "-sir") == 0) {
        keyType = TYPE_SIR;
        keyTypeSpecified++;
    }
    else if (strcmp(argv[i], "-kh") == 0) {
        keyType = TYPE_KH;
        keyTypeSpecified++;
    }
    else if (strcmp(argv[i], "-gp") == 0) {
        keyType = TYPE_GP;
        keyTypeSpecified++;
    }
```

```c
else if (strcmp(argv[i], "-116") == 0) {
    rev116 = TRUE;
}
else if (strcmp(argv[i], "-rsa") == 0) {
    algPublic = TPM_ALG_RSA;
}
else if (strcmp(argv[i], "-ecc") == 0) {
    algPublic = TPM_ALG_ECC;
    i++;
    if (i < argc) {
        if (strcmp(argv[i],"bnp256") == 0) {
            curveID = TPM_ECC_BN_P256;
        }
        else if (strcmp(argv[i],"nistp256") == 0) {
            curveID = TPM_ECC_NIST_P256;
        }
        else if (strcmp(argv[i],"nistp384") == 0) {
            curveID = TPM_ECC_NIST_P384;
        }
        else {
            printf("Bad parameter for -ecc\n");
            printUsage();
        }
    }
    else {
        printf("-cv option needs a value\n");
        printUsage();
    }
}
else if (strcmp(argv[i], "-kt") == 0) {
    i++;
    if (i < argc) {
        switch (argv[i][0]) {
          case 'f':
            in.inPublic.t.publicArea.objectAttributes.val |=
              TPMA_OBJECT_FIXEDTPM;
            break;
          case 'p':
            in.inPublic.t.publicArea.objectAttributes.val |=
              TPMA_OBJECT_FIXEDPARENT;
            break;
          default:
            printf("Bad parameter for -kt\n");
            printUsage();
        }
    }
    else {
        printf("Missing parameter for -kt\n");
        printUsage();
    }
}
else if (strcmp(argv[i], "-da") == 0) {
    in.inPublic.t.publicArea.objectAttributes.val &=
      ~TPMA_OBJECT_NODA;
}
```

```
    else if (strcmp(argv[i],"-halg") == 0) {
        i++;
        if (i < argc) {
            if (strcmp(argv[i],"sha1") == 0) {
                halg = TPM_ALG_SHA1;
            }
            else if (strcmp(argv[i],"sha256") == 0) {
                halg = TPM_ALG_SHA256;
            }
            else if (strcmp(argv[i],"sha384") == 0) {
                halg = TPM_ALG_SHA384;
            }
            else {
                printf("Bad parameter for -halg\n");
                printUsage();
            }
        }
        else {
            printf("-halg option needs a value\n");
            printUsage();
        }
    }
    else if (strcmp(argv[i],"-nalg") == 0) {
        i++;
        if (i < argc) {
            if (strcmp(argv[i],"sha1") == 0) {
                nalg = TPM_ALG_SHA1;
            }
            else if (strcmp(argv[i],"sha256") == 0) {
                nalg = TPM_ALG_SHA256;
            }
            else if (strcmp(argv[i],"sha384") == 0) {
                nalg = TPM_ALG_SHA384;
            }
            else {
                printf("Bad parameter for -nalg\n");
                printUsage();
            }
        }
        else {
            printf("-nalg option needs a value\n");
            printUsage();
        }
    }
    else if (strcmp(argv[i],"-opu") == 0) {
        i++;
        if (i < argc) {
            publicKeyFilename = argv[i];
        }
        else {
            printf("-opu option needs a value\n");
            printUsage();
        }
    }
```

```
else if (strcmp(argv[i],"-opr") == 0) {
    i++;
    if (i < argc) {
        privateKeyFilename = argv[i];
    }
    else {
        printf("-opr option needs a value\n");
        printUsage();
    }
}
else if (strcmp(argv[i],"-pwdk") == 0) {
    i++;
    if (i < argc) {
        keyPassword = argv[i];
    }
    else {
        printf("-pwdk option needs a value\n");
        printUsage();
    }
}
else if (strcmp(argv[i],"-pwdp") == 0) {
    i++;
    if (i < argc) {
        parentPassword = argv[i];
    }
    else {
        printf("-pwdp option needs a value\n");
        printUsage();
    }
}
else if (strcmp(argv[i],"-pol") == 0) {
    i++;
    if (i < argc) {
        policyFilename = argv[i];
    }
    else {
        printf("-pol option needs a value\n");
        printUsage();
    }
}
else if (strcmp(argv[i],"-if") == 0) {
    i++;
    if (i < argc) {
        dataFilename = argv[i];
    }
    else {
        printf("-if option needs a value\n");
        printUsage();
    }
}
else if (strcmp(argv[i],"-se0") == 0) {
    i++;
    if (i < argc) {
        sscanf(argv[i],"%x", &sessionHandle0);
    }
```

```
        else {
            printf("Missing parameter for -se0\n");
            printUsage();
        }
        i++;
        if (i < argc) {
            sscanf(argv[i],"%x", &sessionAttributes0);
            if (sessionAttributes0 > 0xff) {
                printf("Out of range session attributes for -se0\n");
                printUsage();
            }
        }
        else {
            printf("Missing parameter for -se0\n");
            printUsage();
        }
    }
    else if (strcmp(argv[i],"-se1") == 0) {
        i++;
        if (i < argc) {
            sscanf(argv[i],"%x", &sessionHandle1);
        }
        else {
            printf("Missing parameter for -se1\n");
            printUsage();
        }
        i++;
        if (i < argc) {
            sscanf(argv[i],"%x", &sessionAttributes1);
            if (sessionAttributes1 > 0xff) {
                printf("Out of range session attributes for -se1\n");
                printUsage();
            }
        }
        else {
            printf("Missing parameter for -se1\n");
            printUsage();
        }
    }
    else if (strcmp(argv[i],"-se2") == 0) {
        i++;
        if (i < argc) {
            sscanf(argv[i],"%x", &sessionHandle2);
        }
        else {
            printf("Missing parameter for -se2\n");
            printUsage();
        }
        i++;
        if (i < argc) {
            sscanf(argv[i],"%x", &sessionAttributes2);
            if (sessionAttributes2 > 0xff) {
                printf("Out of range session attributes for
```

```
                              -se2\n");
                       printUsage();
                   }
               }
               else {
                   printf("Missing parameter for -se2\n");
                   printUsage();
               }
           }
           else if (strcmp(argv[i],"-h") == 0) {
               printUsage();
           }
           else if (strcmp(argv[i],"-v") == 0) {
               verbose = TRUE;
               TSE_SetProperty(TPM_TRACE_LEVEL, "2");
           }
           else {
               printf("\n%s is not a valid option\n", argv[i]);
               printUsage();
           }
       }
       if (parentHandle == 0) {
           printf("Missing handle parameter -ha\n");
           printUsage();
       }
       if (keyTypeSpecified != 1) {
           printf("Missing key attributes\n");
           printUsage();
       }
       switch (keyType) {
         case TYPE_BL:
           if (dataFilename == NULL) {
               printf("-bl needs -if (sealed data object needs data to
                   seal)\n");
               printUsage();
           }
           break;
         case TYPE_ST:
         case TYPE_DEN:
         case TYPE_DEO:
         case TYPE_SI:
         case TYPE_SIR:
         case TYPE_GP:
           if (dataFilename != NULL) {
               printf("asymmetric key cannot have -if (sensitive data)\n");
               printUsage();
           }
         case TYPE_DES:
         case TYPE_KH:
           /* inSensitive optional for symmetric keys */
           break;
       }
       if (rc == 0) {
           in.parentHandle = parentHandle;
       }
```

```
/* Table 134 - Definition of TPM2B_SENSITIVE_CREATE inSensitive */
if (rc == 0) {
    /* Table 133 - Definition of TPMS_SENSITIVE_CREATE Structure
       <IN>sensitive  */
    /* Table 75 - Definition of Types for TPM2B_AUTH userAuth */
    if (keyPassword == NULL) {
        in.inSensitive.t.sensitive.userAuth.t.size = 0;
    }
    else {
        rc = TPM2B_StringCopy(&in.inSensitive.t.sensitive.userAuth.b,
                              keyPassword, sizeof(TPMU_HA));
    }
}
if (rc == 0) {
    /* Table 132 - Definition of TPM2B_SENSITIVE_DATA Structure
       data */
    if (dataFilename != NULL) {
        rc = File_Read2B(&in.inSensitive.t.sensitive.data.b,
                         MAX_SYM_DATA,
                         dataFilename);
    }
    else {
        in.inSensitive.t.sensitive.data.t.size = 0;
    }
}
/* optional authorization policy */
if (policyFilename != NULL) {
    rc = File_Read2B(&in.inPublic.t.publicArea.authPolicy.b,
                     sizeof(TPMU_HA),
                     policyFilename);
}
else {
    in.inPublic.t.publicArea.authPolicy.t.size = 0;
      /* default empty policy */
}
/* TPM2B_PUBLIC */
if (rc == 0) {
    switch (keyType) {
      case TYPE_BL:
        blPublicTemplate(&in, nalg);
        break;
      case TYPE_ST:
      case TYPE_DEN:
      case TYPE_DEO:
      case TYPE_SI:
      case TYPE_SIR:
      case TYPE_GP:
        asymPublicTemplate(&in, keyType, algPublic, curveID,
          nalg, halg);
        break;
      case TYPE_DES:
        symmetricCipherTemplate(&in, nalg, rev116);
        break;
```

```
          case TYPE_KH:
            keyedHashPublicTemplate(&in, nalg, halg);
            break;
      }
  }
  if (rc == 0) {
      /* TPM2B_DATA outsideInfo */
      in.outsideInfo.t.size = 0;
      /* Table 102 - TPML_PCR_SELECTION creationPCR */
      in.creationPCR.count = 0;
  }
  /* call TSE to execute the command */
  if (rc == 0) {
      rc = TSE_Execute((RESPONSE_PARAMETERS *)&out,
                       (COMMAND_PARAMETERS *)&in,
                       NULL,
                       TPM_CC_Create,
                       sessionHandle0, parentPassword,
                       sessionAttributes0,
                       sessionHandle1, NULL, sessionAttributes1,
                       sessionHandle2, NULL, sessionAttributes2,
                       TPM_RH_NULL, NULL, 0);
  }
  /* save the private key */
  if ((rc == 0) && (privateKeyFilename != NULL)) {
      rc = File_WriteStructure(&out.outPrivate,
                              (MarshalFunction_t)
                              TSS_TPM2B_PRIVATE_Marshal,
                              privateKeyFilename);
  }
  /* save the public key */
  if ((rc == 0) && (publicKeyFilename != NULL)) {
      rc = File_WriteStructure(&out.outPublic,
                              (MarshalFunction_t)
                              TSS_TPM2B_PUBLIC_Marshal,
                              publicKeyFilename);
  }
  if (rc == 0) {
      if (verbose) printf("create: success\n");
  }
  else {
      const char *msg;
      const char *submsg;
      const char *num;
      printf("create: failed, rc %08x\n", rc);
      TSEResponseCode_toString(&msg, &submsg, &num, rc);
      printf("%s%s%s\n", msg, submsg, num);
      rc = EXIT_FAILURE;
  }
  return rc;
}

/* asymPublicTemplate() is a template for an ECC or RSA 2048 key.
```

```
    It can create these types:

    TYPE_ST:    RSA storage key
    TYPE_DEN:   RSA decryption key (not storage key, NULL scheme)
    TYPE_DEO:   RSA decryption key (not storage key, OAEP scheme)
    TYPE_SI:    RSA signing key (unrestricted)
    TYPE_SIR:   RSA signing key (restricted)
    TYPE_GP:    RSA general purpose key

    If restricted, it uses the RSASSA padding scheme
*/

static void asymPublicTemplate(Create_In *in,
                               int keyType,
                               TPMI_ALG_PUBLIC algPublic,
                               TPMI_ECC_CURVE curveID,
                               TPMI_ALG_HASH nalg,
                               TPMI_ALG_HASH halg)
{
    /* Table 185 - TPM2B_PUBLIC inPublic */
    /* Table 184 - TPMT_PUBLIC publicArea */
    in->inPublic.t.publicArea.type = algPublic; /* RSA or ECC */
    in->inPublic.t.publicArea.nameAlg = nalg;

    /* Table 32 - TPMA_OBJECT objectAttributes */
    in->inPublic.t.publicArea.objectAttributes.val |=
      TPMA_OBJECT_SENSITIVEDATAORIGIN;
    in->inPublic.t.publicArea.objectAttributes.val |=
      TPMA_OBJECT_USERWITHAUTH;
    in->inPublic.t.publicArea.objectAttributes.val &=
      ~TPMA_OBJECT_ADMINWITHPOLICY;

    switch (keyType) {
      case TYPE_DEN:
      case TYPE_DEO:
        in->inPublic.t.publicArea.objectAttributes.val &=
          ~TPMA_OBJECT_SIGN;
        in->inPublic.t.publicArea.objectAttributes.val |=
          TPMA_OBJECT_DECRYPT;
        in->inPublic.t.publicArea.objectAttributes.val &=
          ~TPMA_OBJECT_RESTRICTED;
        break;
      case TYPE_ST:
        in->inPublic.t.publicArea.objectAttributes.val &=
          ~TPMA_OBJECT_SIGN;
        in->inPublic.t.publicArea.objectAttributes.val |=
          TPMA_OBJECT_DECRYPT;
        in->inPublic.t.publicArea.objectAttributes.val |=
          TPMA_OBJECT_RESTRICTED;
        break;
      case TYPE_SI:
        in->inPublic.t.publicArea.objectAttributes.val |=
          TPMA_OBJECT_SIGN;
```

```
      in->inPublic.t.publicArea.objectAttributes.val &=
        ~TPMA_OBJECT_DECRYPT;
      in->inPublic.t.publicArea.objectAttributes.val &=
        ~TPMA_OBJECT_RESTRICTED;
      break;
  case TYPE_SIR:
    in->inPublic.t.publicArea.objectAttributes.val |=
      TPMA_OBJECT_SIGN;
    in->inPublic.t.publicArea.objectAttributes.val &=
      ~TPMA_OBJECT_DECRYPT;
    in->inPublic.t.publicArea.objectAttributes.val |=
      TPMA_OBJECT_RESTRICTED;
    break;
  case TYPE_GP:
    in->inPublic.t.publicArea.objectAttributes.val |=
      TPMA_OBJECT_SIGN;
    in->inPublic.t.publicArea.objectAttributes.val |=
      TPMA_OBJECT_DECRYPT;
    in->inPublic.t.publicArea.objectAttributes.val &=
      ~TPMA_OBJECT_RESTRICTED;
    break;
}

/* Table 72 -  TPM2B_DIGEST authPolicy */
/* policy set separately */

/* Table 182 - Definition of TPMU_PUBLIC_PARMS parameters */
if (algPublic == TPM_ALG_RSA) {
    /* Table 180 - Definition of {RSA} TPMS_RSA_PARMS
       rsaDetail */
    /* Table 129 - Definition of TPMT_SYM_DEF_OBJECT Structure
       symmetric */
    switch (keyType) {
      case TYPE_DEN:
      case TYPE_DEO:
      case TYPE_SI:
      case TYPE_SIR:
      case TYPE_GP:
        /* Non-storage keys must have TPM_ALG_NULL for the
           symmetric algorithm */
        in->inPublic.t.publicArea.parameters.rsaDetail.symmetric
          .algorithm = TPM_ALG_NULL;
        break;
      case TYPE_ST:
        in->inPublic.t.publicArea.parameters.rsaDetail.symmetric
          .algorithm = TPM_ALG_AES;
        /* Table 125 - TPMU_SYM_KEY_BITS keyBits */
        in->inPublic.t.publicArea.parameters.rsaDetail.symmetric
          .keyBits.aes = 128;
        /* Table 126 - TPMU_SYM_MODE mode */
        in->inPublic.t.publicArea.parameters.rsaDetail.symmetric
          .mode.aes = TPM_ALG_CBC;
        break;
    }
```

```
        /* Table 155 - Definition of {RSA} TPMT_RSA_SCHEME scheme */
        switch (keyType) {
          case TYPE_DEN:
          case TYPE_GP:
          case TYPE_ST:
          case TYPE_SI:
            in->inPublic.t.publicArea.parameters.rsaDetail.scheme.scheme
              = TPM_ALG_NULL;
            break;
          case TYPE_DEO:
            in->inPublic.t.publicArea.parameters.rsaDetail.scheme.scheme
              = TPM_ALG_OAEP;
            /* Table 152 - Definition of TPMU_ASYM_SCHEME details */
            /* Table 152 - Definition of TPMU_ASYM_SCHEME rsassa */
            /* Table 142 - Definition of {RSA} Types for RSA Signature
               Schemes */
            /* Table 135 - Definition of TPMS_SCHEME_HASH hashAlg */
            in->inPublic.t.publicArea.parameters.rsaDetail.scheme
              .details.oaep.hashAlg = halg;
            break;
          case TYPE_SIR:
            in->inPublic.t.publicArea.parameters.rsaDetail.scheme
              .scheme = TPM_ALG_RSASSA;
            /* Table 152 - Definition of TPMU_ASYM_SCHEME details */
            /* Table 152 - Definition of TPMU_ASYM_SCHEME rsassa */
            /* Table 142 - Definition of {RSA} Types for RSA Signature
               Schemes */
            /* Table 135 - Definition of TPMS_SCHEME_HASH hashAlg */
            in->inPublic.t.publicArea.parameters.rsaDetail.scheme
              .details.rsassa.hashAlg = halg;
            break;
        }

        /* Table 159 - Definition of {RSA} (TPM_KEY_BITS)
           TPMI_RSA_KEY_BITS Type keyBits */
        in->inPublic.t.publicArea.parameters.rsaDetail.keyBits = 2048;
        in->inPublic.t.publicArea.parameters.rsaDetail.exponent = 0;
        /* Table 177 - TPMU_PUBLIC_ID unique */
        /* Table 177 - Definition of TPMU_PUBLIC_ID */
        in->inPublic.t.publicArea.unique.rsa.t.size = 0;
    }
    else {          /* algPublic == TPM_ALG_ECC */
        /* Table 181 - Definition of {ECC} TPMS_ECC_PARMS Structure
           eccDetail */
        /* Table 129 - Definition of TPMT_SYM_DEF_OBJECT Structure
           symmetric */
        switch (keyType) {
          case TYPE_DEN:
          case TYPE_DEO:
          case TYPE_SI:
          case TYPE_SIR:
          case TYPE_GP:
            /* Non-storage keys must have TPM_ALG_NULL for the
               symmetric algorithm */
```

```
      in->inPublic.t.publicArea.parameters.eccDetail.symmetric
        .algorithm = TPM_ALG_NULL;
      break;
    case TYPE_ST:
      in->inPublic.t.publicArea.parameters.eccDetail.symmetric
        .algorithm = TPM_ALG_AES;
      /* Table 125 - TPMU_SYM_KEY_BITS keyBits */
      in->inPublic.t.publicArea.parameters.eccDetail.symmetric
        .keyBits.aes = 128;
      /* Table 126 - TPMU_SYM_MODE mode */
      in->inPublic.t.publicArea.parameters.eccDetail.symmetric
        .mode.aes = TPM_ALG_CBC;
      break;
}
/* Table 166 - Definition of (TPMT_SIG_SCHEME) {ECC}
   TPMT_ECC_SCHEME Structure scheme */
/* Table 164 - Definition of (TPM_ALG_ID) {ECC}
   TPMI_ALG_ECC_SCHEME Type scheme */
switch (keyType) {
  case TYPE_GP:
  case TYPE_SI:
    in->inPublic.t.publicArea.parameters.eccDetail.scheme
      .scheme = TPM_ALG_NULL;
    /* Table 165 - Definition of {ECC} (TPM_ECC_CURVE)
       TPMI_ECC_CURVE Type */
    /* Table 10 - Definition of (UINT16) {ECC} TPM_ECC_CURVE
       Constants <IN/OUT, S> curveID */
    in->inPublic.t.publicArea.parameters.eccDetail.curveID =
      curveID;
    /* Table 150 - Definition of TPMT_KDF_SCHEME Structure
       kdf */
    /* Table 64 - Definition of (TPM_ALG_ID) TPMI_ALG_KDF
       Type */
    in->inPublic.t.publicArea.parameters.eccDetail.kdf.
      scheme = TPM_ALG_NULL;
    break;
  case TYPE_SIR:
    in->inPublic.t.publicArea.parameters.eccDetail.scheme.
      scheme = TPM_ALG_ECDSA;
    /* Table 152 - Definition of TPMU_ASYM_SCHEME details */
    /* Table 143 - Definition of {ECC} Types for ECC Signature
       Schemes */
    in->inPublic.t.publicArea.parameters.eccDetail.scheme.
      details.ecdsa.hashAlg = halg;
    /* Table 165 - Definition of {ECC} (TPM_ECC_CURVE)
       TPMI_ECC_CURVE Type */
    /* Table 10 - Definition of (UINT16) {ECC} TPM_ECC_CURVE
       Constants <IN/OUT, S> curveID */
    in->inPublic.t.publicArea.parameters.eccDetail.curveID =
      curveID;
    /* Table 150 - Definition of TPMT_KDF_SCHEME Structure
       kdf */
    /* Table 64 - Definition of (TPM_ALG_ID) TPMI_ALG_KDF
       Type */
```

```
        in->inPublic.t.publicArea.parameters.eccDetail.kdf.scheme
          = TPM_ALG_NULL;
        /* Table 149 - Definition of TPMU_KDF_SCHEME Union
           <IN/OUT, S> */
        /* Table 148 - Definition of Types for KDF Schemes,
           hash-based key- or mask-generation functions */
        /* Table 135 - Definition of TPMS_SCHEME_HASH Structure
           hashAlg */
        in->inPublic.t.publicArea.parameters.eccDetail.kdf.details
          .mgf1.hashAlg = halg;
        break;
      case TYPE_DEN:
      case TYPE_DEO:
        /* FIXME keys other than signing are wrong, not implemented
           yet */
        in->inPublic.t.publicArea.parameters.rsaDetail.scheme.scheme
          = TPM_ALG_NULL;
        /* Table 152 - Definition of TPMU_ASYM_SCHEME details */
        break;
      case TYPE_ST:
        /* FIXME keys other than signing are wrong, not implemented
           yet */
        in->inPublic.t.publicArea.parameters.rsaDetail.scheme.scheme
          = TPM_ALG_NULL;
        break;
    }
    /* Table 177 - TPMU_PUBLIC_ID unique */
    /* Table 177 - Definition of TPMU_PUBLIC_ID */
    in->inPublic.t.publicArea.unique.ecc.x.t.size = 0;
    in->inPublic.t.publicArea.unique.ecc.y.t.size = 0;
  }
  return;
}


/* symmetricCipherTemplate() is a template for an AES 128 CBC key */

static void symmetricCipherTemplate(Create_In *in,
                                    TPMI_ALG_HASH nalg,
                                    int rev116)
{
    /* Table 185 - TPM2B_PUBLIC inPublic */
    /* Table 184 - TPMT_PUBLIC publicArea */
    {
        in->inPublic.t.publicArea.type = TPM_ALG_SYMCIPHER;
        in->inPublic.t.publicArea.nameAlg = nalg;
        /* Table 32 - TPMA_OBJECT objectAttributes */
        /* rev 116 used DECRYPT for both decrypt and encrypt.
After 116, encrypt required SIGN */
        if (!rev116) {
            in->inPublic.t.publicArea.objectAttributes.val |=
              TPMA_OBJECT_SIGN; /* actually encrypt */
        }
        in->inPublic.t.publicArea.objectAttributes.val |=
          TPMA_OBJECT_DECRYPT;
```

```
        in->inPublic.t.publicArea.objectAttributes.val &=
          ~TPMA_OBJECT_RESTRICTED;
        in->inPublic.t.publicArea.objectAttributes.val |=
          TPMA_OBJECT_SENSITIVEDATAORIGIN;
        in->inPublic.t.publicArea.objectAttributes.val |=
          TPMA_OBJECT_USERWITHAUTH;
        in->inPublic.t.publicArea.objectAttributes.val &=
          ~TPMA_OBJECT_ADMINWITHPOLICY;
        /* Table 72 -   TPM2B_DIGEST authPolicy */
        /* policy set separately */
        /* Table 182 - Definition of TPMU_PUBLIC_PARMS parameters */
        {
            /* Table 131 - Definition of TPMS_SYMCIPHER_PARMS
               symDetail */
            {
                /* Table 129 - Definition of TPMT_SYM_DEF_OBJECT sym */
                /* Table 62 - Definition of (TPM_ALG_ID) TPMI_ALG_SYM_
                   OBJECT Type */
                in->inPublic.t.publicArea.parameters.symDetail.sym
                  .algorithm = TPM_ALG_AES;
                /* Table 125 - Definition of TPMU_SYM_KEY_BITS Union */
                in->inPublic.t.publicArea.parameters.symDetail.sym
                  .keyBits.aes = 128;
                /* Table 126 - Definition of TPMU_SYM_MODE Union */
                in->inPublic.t.publicArea.parameters.symDetail.sym
                  .mode.aes = TPM_ALG_CBC;
            }
        }
        /* Table 177 - TPMU_PUBLIC_ID unique */
        /* Table 72 - Definition of TPM2B_DIGEST Structure */
        in->inPublic.t.publicArea.unique.sym.t.size = 0;
    }
    return;
}


/* keyedHashPublicTemplate() is a template for a HMAC key

   The name alg is SHA-256, but the key is not restricted */

static void keyedHashPublicTemplate(Create_In *in,
                                    TPMI_ALG_HASH nalg,
                                    TPMI_ALG_HASH halg)
{
    /* Table 185 - TPM2B_PUBLIC inPublic */
    /* Table 184 - TPMT_PUBLIC publicArea */
    {
        /* Table 176 - Definition of (TPM_ALG_ID) TPMI_ALG_PUBLIC Type */
        in->inPublic.t.publicArea.type = TPM_ALG_KEYEDHASH;
        /* Table 59 - Definition of (TPM_ALG_ID) TPMI_ALG_HASH Type */
        in->inPublic.t.publicArea.nameAlg = nalg;
        /* Table 32 - TPMA_OBJECT objectAttributes */
        in->inPublic.t.publicArea.objectAttributes.val |=
          TPMA_OBJECT_SIGN;
```

```
        in->inPublic.t.publicArea.objectAttributes.val &=
          ~TPMA_OBJECT_DECRYPT;
        in->inPublic.t.publicArea.objectAttributes.val &=
          ~TPMA_OBJECT_RESTRICTED;
        in->inPublic.t.publicArea.objectAttributes.val |=
          TPMA_OBJECT_SENSITIVEDATAORIGIN;
        in->inPublic.t.publicArea.objectAttributes.val |=
          TPMA_OBJECT_USERWITHAUTH;
        in->inPublic.t.publicArea.objectAttributes.val &=
          ~TPMA_OBJECT_ADMINWITHPOLICY;
        /* Table 72 -  TPM2B_DIGEST authPolicy */
        /* policy set separately */
        {
            /* Table 182 - Definition of TPMU_PUBLIC_PARMS Union
               <IN/OUT, S> */
            /* Table 178 - Definition of TPMS_KEYEDHASH_PARMS Structure */
            /* Table 141 - Definition of TPMT_KEYEDHASH_SCHEME Structure */
            /* Table 137 - Definition of (TPM_ALG_ID) TPMI_ALG_KEYEDHASH
               _SCHEME Type */
            in->inPublic.t.publicArea.parameters.keyedHashDetail.scheme
              .scheme = TPM_ALG_HMAC;
            /* Table 140 - Definition of TPMU_SCHEME_KEYEDHASH Union
               <IN/OUT, S> */
            /* Table 138 - Definition of Types for HMAC_SIG_SCHEME */
            /* Table 135 - Definition of TPMS_SCHEME_HASH Structure */
            in->inPublic.t.publicArea.parameters.keyedHashDetail.scheme
              .details.hmac.hashAlg = halg;
        }
        /* Table 177 - TPMU_PUBLIC_ID unique */
        /* Table 72 - Definition of TPM2B_DIGEST Structure */
        in->inPublic.t.publicArea.unique.sym.t.size = 0;
    }
}


/* blPublicTemplate() is a template for a sealed data blob.

*/


static void blPublicTemplate(Create_In *in,
                             TPMI_ALG_HASH nalg)
{
    /* Table 185 - TPM2B_PUBLIC inPublic */
    /* Table 184 - TPMT_PUBLIC publicArea */
    {
        /* Table 176 - Definition of (TPM_ALG_ID) TPMI_ALG_PUBLIC Type */
        in->inPublic.t.publicArea.type = TPM_ALG_KEYEDHASH;
        /* Table 59 - Definition of (TPM_ALG_ID) TPMI_ALG_HASH Type */
        in->inPublic.t.publicArea.nameAlg = nalg;
        /* Table 32 - TPMA_OBJECT objectAttributes */
        in->inPublic.t.publicArea.objectAttributes.val &=
          ~TPMA_OBJECT_SIGN;
        in->inPublic.t.publicArea.objectAttributes.val &=
          ~TPMA_OBJECT_DECRYPT;
```

```
        in->inPublic.t.publicArea.objectAttributes.val &=
          ~TPMA_OBJECT_RESTRICTED;
        in->inPublic.t.publicArea.objectAttributes.val &=
          ~TPMA_OBJECT_SENSITIVEDATAORIGIN;
        in->inPublic.t.publicArea.objectAttributes.val |=
          TPMA_OBJECT_USERWITHAUTH;
        in->inPublic.t.publicArea.objectAttributes.val &=
          ~TPMA_OBJECT_ADMINWITHPOLICY;
        /* Table 72 -  TPM2B_DIGEST authPolicy */
        /* policy set separately */
        {
            /* Table 182 - Definition of TPMU_PUBLIC_PARMS Union
               <IN/OUT, S> */
            /* Table 178 - Definition of TPMS_KEYEDHASH_PARMS
               Structure */
            /* Table 141 - Definition of TPMT_KEYEDHASH_SCHEME
               Structure */
            /* Table 137 - Definition of (TPM_ALG_ID) TPMI_ALG_
               KEYEDHASH_SCHEME Type */
            in->inPublic.t.publicArea.parameters.keyedHashDetail
              .scheme.scheme = TPM_ALG_NULL;
            /* Table 140 - Definition of TPMU_SCHEME_KEYEDHASH Union
               <IN/OUT, S> */
        }
    }
    /* Table 177 - TPMU_PUBLIC_ID unique */
    /* Table 72 - Definition of TPM2B_DIGEST Structure */
    in->inPublic.t.publicArea.unique.sym.t.size = 0;
}

static void printUsage(void)
{
    printf("\n");
    printf("create\n");
    printf("\n");
    printf("Runs TPM2_Create\n");
    printf("\n");
    printf("\t-hp parent handle\n");
    printf("\n");
    printf("\tAsymetric Key Algorithm\n");
    printf("\t\t-rsa (default)\n");
    printf("\t\t-ecc curve\n");
    printf("\t\t\tbnp256\n");
    printf("\t\t\tnistp256\n");
    printf("\t\t\tnistp384\n");
    printf("\n");
    printf("\tKey attributes\n");
    printf("\n");
    printf("\t\t-bl data blob for unseal\n");
    printf("\t\t\t-if data file name\n");
    printf("\t\t-den decryption, RSA, not storage, NULL scheme\n");
    printf("\t\t-deo decryption, RSA, not storage, OAEP scheme\n");
    printf("\t\t-des encryption/decryption, AES symmetric\n");
```

```
        printf("\t\t-st storage\n");
        printf("\t\t-si signing\n");
        printf("\t\t-sir restricted signing\n");
        printf("\t\t-kh keyed hash (hmac)\n");
        printf("\t\t-gp general purpose, not storage\n");
        printf("\n");
        printf("\t\t-kt (can be specified more than once)\n"
               "\t\t\tf fixedTPM \n"
               "\t\t\tp fixedParent \n");
        printf("\t\t[-da object subject to DA protection) (default no)]\n");
        printf("\t\t[-116 for TPM rev 116 compatibility]\n");
        printf("\n");
        printf("\t[-nalg name hash algorithm [sha1, sha256, sha384] (default
               sha256)]\n");
        printf("\t[-halg scheme hash algorithm [sha1, sha256, sha384]
               (default sha256)]\n");
        printf("\n");
        printf("\t[-pwdk password for key] (default empty)\n");
        printf("\t[-pwdp password for parent key] (default empty)\n");
        printf("\t[-pol policy file (default empty)]\n");
        printf("\n");
        printf("\t[-opu public key file name] (default do not save)\n");
        printf("\t[-opr private key file name] (default do not save)\n");
        printf("\n");
        printf("\t-se[0-2] session handle (default PWAP)\n");
        printf("\t\t01 continue\n");
        printf("\t\t20 command decrypt\n");
        printf("\t\t40 response encrypt\n");
        exit(1);
}
```

C.2.2   Retrieving the TPM's internal time

While the TPM2_GetTime function is not frequently used, especially compared to TPM2_Create, this is the function used to show how to read the TPM 2.0 specification (see Figures 11.4, 11.5, and 11.6), and is therefore included as an example of how the functions in the specification are used in practice.

```
/*******************************************************************************/
/*                                                                           */
/*                              GetTime                                      */
/*                          Written by Ken Goldman                           */
/*                   IBM Thomas J. Watson Research Center                    */
/*            $Id: gettime.c 348 2015-06-22 20:36:45Z kgoldman $             */
/*                                                                           */
/* (c) Copyright IBM Corporation 2015.                                       */
/*                                                                           */
/* All rights reserved.                                                      */
/*                                                                           */
/* Redistribution and use in source and binary forms, with or without       */
/* modification, are permitted provided that the following conditions are    */
/* met:                                                                      */
```

```
/*

 */

#include <stdio.h>
#include <stdlib.h>
#include <string.h>
#include <stdint.h>

#include "tse.h"
#include "tseutils.h"
#include "tseresponsecode.h"
#include "Unmarshal_fp.h"
#include "tssmarshal.h"
#include "tseprint.h"

static void printUsage(void);

int verbose = FALSE;

int main(int argc, char *argv[])
{
    TPM_RC                    rc = 0;
    int                       i;    /* argc iterator */
    GetTime_In                in;
    GetTime_Out               out;
    TPMI_DH_OBJECT            signHandle = 0;
    const char                *keyPassword = NULL;
    const char                *endorsementPassword = NULL;
    TPMI_ALG_HASH             halg = TPM_ALG_SHA256;
    const char                *signatureFilename = NULL;
```

```
const char                     *attestInfoFilename = NULL;
const char                     *qualifyingDataFilename = NULL;
TPMS_ATTEST                    tpmsAttest;
TPMI_SH_AUTH_SESSION           sessionHandle0 = TPM_RS_PW;
unsigned int                   sessionAttributes0 = 0;
TPMI_SH_AUTH_SESSION           sessionHandle1 = TPM_RS_PW;
unsigned int                   sessionAttributes1 = 0;
TPMI_SH_AUTH_SESSION           sessionHandle2 = TPM_RH_NULL;
unsigned int                   sessionAttributes2 = 0;


TSE_SetProperty(TPM_TRACE_LEVEL, "1");


/* command line argument defaults */

for (i=1 ; (i<argc) && (rc == 0) ; i++) {
    if (strcmp(argv[i],"-hk") == 0) {
        i++;
        if (i < argc) {
            sscanf(argv[i],"%x", &signHandle);
        }
        else {
            printf("Missing parameter for -hk\n");
            printUsage();
        }
    }
    else if (strcmp(argv[i],"-pwdk") == 0) {
        i++;
        if (i < argc) {
            keyPassword = argv[i];
        }
        else {
            printf("-pwdk option needs a value\n");
            printUsage();
        }
    }
    else if (strcmp(argv[i],"-pwde") == 0) {
        i++;
        if (i < argc) {
            endorsementPassword = argv[i];
        }
        else {
            printf("-pwde option needs a value\n");
            printUsage();
        }
    }
    else if (strcmp(argv[i],"-halg") == 0) {
        i++;
        if (i < argc) {
            if (strcmp(argv[i],"sha1") == 0) {
                halg = TPM_ALG_SHA1;
            }
            else if (strcmp(argv[i],"sha256") == 0) {
                halg = TPM_ALG_SHA256;
            }
```

```
            else if (strcmp(argv[i],"sha384") == 0) {
                halg = TPM_ALG_SHA384;
            }
            else {
                printf("Bad parameter for -halg\n");
                printUsage();
            }
        }
        else {
            printf("-halg option needs a value\n");
            printUsage();
        }
    }
    else if (strcmp(argv[i],"-os") == 0) {
        i++;
        if (i < argc) {
            signatureFilename = argv[i];
        }
        else {
            printf("-os option needs a value\n");
            printUsage();
        }
    }
    else if (strcmp(argv[i],"-oa") == 0) {
        i++;
        if (i < argc) {
            attestInfoFilename = argv[i];
        }
        else {
            printf("-oa option needs a value\n");
            printUsage();
        }
    }
    else if (strcmp(argv[i],"-qd") == 0) {
        i++;
        if (i < argc) {
            qualifyingDataFilename = argv[i];
        }
        else {
            printf("-qd option needs a value\n");
            printUsage();
        }
    }
    else if (strcmp(argv[i],"-se0") == 0) {
        i++;
        if (i < argc) {
            sscanf(argv[i],"%x", &sessionHandle0);
        }
        else {
            printf("Missing parameter for -se0\n");
            printUsage();
        }
        i++;
        if (i < argc) {
```

```
                sscanf(argv[i],"%x", &sessionAttributes0);
                if (sessionAttributes0 > 0xff) {
                    printf("Out of range session attributes for -se0\n");
                    printUsage();
                }
            }
            else {
                printf("Missing parameter for -se0\n");
                printUsage();
            }
        }
    else if (strcmp(argv[i],"-se1") == 0) {
        i++;
        if (i < argc) {
            sscanf(argv[i],"%x", &sessionHandle1);
        }
        else {
            printf("Missing parameter for -se1\n");
            printUsage();
        }
        i++;
        if (i < argc) {
            sscanf(argv[i],"%x", &sessionAttributes1);
            if (sessionAttributes1 > 0xff) {
                printf("Out of range session attributes for -se1\n");
                printUsage();
            }
        }
        else {
            printf("Missing parameter for -se1\n");
            printUsage();
        }
    }
    else if (strcmp(argv[i],"-se2") == 0) {
        i++;
        if (i < argc) {
            sscanf(argv[i],"%x", &sessionHandle2);
        }
        else {
            printf("Missing parameter for -se2\n");
            printUsage();
        }
        i++;
        if (i < argc) {
            sscanf(argv[i],"%x", &sessionAttributes2);
            if (sessionAttributes2 > 0xff) {
                printf("Out of range session attributes for -se2\n");
                printUsage();
            }
        }
        else {
            printf("Missing parameter for -se2\n");
            printUsage();
        }
    }
```

```
    else if (strcmp(argv[i],"-h") == 0) {
        printUsage();
    }
    else if (strcmp(argv[i],"-v") == 0) {
        verbose = TRUE;
        TSE_SetProperty(TPM_TRACE_LEVEL, "2");
    }
    else {
        printf("\n%s is not a valid option\n", argv[i]);
        printUsage();
    }
}
if (signHandle == 0) {
    printf("Missing sign handle parameter -hs\n");
    printUsage();
}
if (rc == 0) {
    /* handle of the privacy administrator */
    in.privacyAdminHandle = TPM_RH_ENDORSEMENT;
    /* Handle of key that will perform signing */
    in.signHandle = signHandle;
    /* Table 145 - Definition of TPMT_SIG_SCHEME Structure */
    in.inScheme.scheme = TPM_ALG_RSASSA;
    /* Table 144 - Definition of TPMU_SIG_SCHEME Union
        <IN/OUT, S> */
    /* Table 142 - Definition of {RSA} Types for RSA Signature
        Schemes */
    /* Table 135 - Definition of TPMS_SCHEME_HASH Structure */
    in.inScheme.details.rsassa.hashAlg = halg;
}
/* data supplied by the caller */
if (rc == 0) {
    if (qualifyingDataFilename != NULL) {
        rc = File_Read2B(&in.qualifyingData.b,
                        sizeof(TPMT_HA),
                        qualifyingDataFilename);
    }
    else {
        in.qualifyingData.t.size = 0;
    }
}
/* call TSE to execute the command */
if (rc == 0) {
    rc = TSE_Execute((RESPONSE_PARAMETERS *)&out,
                    (COMMAND_PARAMETERS *)&in,
                    NULL,
                    TPM_CC_GetTime,
                    sessionHandle0, endorsementPassword,
                    sessionAttributes0,
                    sessionHandle1, keyPassword, sessionAttributes1,
                    sessionHandle2, NULL, sessionAttributes2,
                    TPM_RH_NULL, NULL, 0);
}
```

```
if (rc == 0) {
    BYTE *tmpBuffer = out.timeInfo.t.attestationData;
    INT32 tmpSize = out.timeInfo.t.size;
    rc = TPMS_ATTEST_Unmarshal(&tpmsAttest, &tmpBuffer, &tmpSize);
    if (verbose) TPMS_ATTEST_Print(&tpmsAttest);
}
if (rc == 0) {
    BOOL match;
    match = TPM2B_Compare(&in.qualifyingData.b, &tpmsAttest
      .extraData.b);
    if (!match) {
        printf("quote: failed, extraData != qualifyingData\n");
        rc = EXIT_FAILURE;
    }
}
if ((rc == 0) && (signatureFilename != NULL)) {
    rc = File_WriteStructure(&out.signature,
                              (MarshalFunction_t)TSS_TPMT_SIGNATURE
                                _Marshal, signatureFilename);
}
if ((rc == 0) && (attestInfoFilename != NULL)) {
    rc = File_WriteBinaryFile(out.timeInfo.t.attestationData,
                                out.timeInfo.t.size,
                                attestInfoFilename);
}
if (rc == 0) {
    if (verbose) TPMT_SIGNATURE_Print(&out.signature);
    if (verbose) TPM2B_ATTEST_Print(&out.timeInfo);
    if (verbose) printf("gettime: success\n");
}
else {
    const char *msg;
    const char *submsg;
    const char *num;
    printf("gettime: failed, rc %08x\n", rc);
    TSEResponseCode_toString(&msg, &submsg, &num, rc);
    printf("%s%s%s\n", msg, submsg, num);
    rc = EXIT_FAILURE;
}
return rc;
}

static void printUsage(void)
{
    printf("\n");
    printf("gettime\n");
    printf("\n");
    printf("Runs TPM2_GetTime\n");
    printf("\n");
    printf("\t-hk signing key handle\n");
    printf("\t[-pwdk password for signing key (default empty)]\n");
    printf("\t[-pwde password for endorsement hierarchy (default
        empty)]\n");
```

```
        printf("\t[-halg [sha1, sha256, sha384] (default sha256)]\n");
        printf("\t[-qd qualifying data file name]\n");
        printf("\t[-os gettimeature file name (default none)]\n");
        printf("\t[-oa attestation output file name]\n");
        printf("\n");
        printf("\t-se[0-2] session handle / attributes (default PWAP)\n");
        printf("\t-se1 session handle / attributes (default PWAP)\n");
        printf("\t\t01 continue\n");
        exit(1);
}
```

Copyright Notices

Trusted Computing Group Specification Copyright Notice

IBM TSS 2.0 Source Code Copyright Notice

Index